SEVEN-HEADED
LUTHER

From Ioannis Cochlaeus: *Septiceps Lutherus*, 1529

SEVEN-HEADED LUTHER

———

*Essays in Commemoration
of a Quincentenary
1483–1983*

———

EDITED BY

PETER NEWMAN BROOKS

CLARENDON PRESS • OXFORD

1983

Oxford University Press, Walton Street, Oxford OX2 6DP
London Glasgow New York Toronto
Delhi Bombay Calcutta Madras Karachi
Kuala Lumpur Singapore Hong Kong Tokyo
Nairobi Dar es Salaam Cape Town
Melbourne Auckland
and associates in
Beirut Berlin Ibadan Mexico City Nicosia

Oxford is a trademark of Oxford University Press

Published in the United States
by Oxford University Press, New York

British Library Cataloguing in Publication Data
Seven-headed Luther.
1. Luther, Martin   2. Reformation—Germany
I. Brooks, Peter Newman
270.6'092'4   BR334.2
ISBN 0-19-826648-0

Set by Syarikat Seng Teik Sdn. Bhd., Kuala Lumpur.
Printed in Great Britain by
Hazell Watson and Viney Ltd., Aylesbury, Bucks

PREFACE

ALTHOUGH few would deny that the cartoonist's art developed considerably from the time of Hogarth's social satire to the present-day political sophistication of Gerald Scarfe, much the same approach is identifiable in the crude age of the Cranachs and their contemporaries. Cochlaeus may not have got the measure of Luther any more than aligned Protestant polemicists sought to grasp the nature of the papal hierarchy.[1] But if the range of 'heads' and headgear is anything to go by, at least the anonymous draughtsman who worked on *Septiceps Lutherus*—in common with rivals who fashioned the 'Seven-headed Papal Revelation'—was conscious of dealing with a colossus. Like music, visual imagery is capable of stirring the depths of man's fertile mind, and can prompt reaction to its range and impact. While this is particularly powerful in the case of profound choral compositions and great paintings, it remains true that even the daubed *graffito*, like a cheap joke, can be singularly provocative.

More than any other Renaissance scholar, the great Erasmus used fierce gusts of satirical humour to shake the late medieval Church to its very foundations with gales of laughter. For his part, the serious-minded Cochlaeus could not have written such *Colloquies*. Yet wit apart, humanist influence is clearly apparent in the skilful scheme contrived to condemn from his own mouth the heresiarch Cochlaeus held responsible for so great a crisis in Christendom. Luther as a monster symbolized the misfortunes that befell the papal Church, his seven 'heads' showing his sins in deadly, stark relief. The dreary debate of the text that followed, not to mention the lifetime of ceaseless argument Cochlaeus devoted to destroying the doctrine and blackening the character of Dr Martinus, have conditioned Reformation historiography ever since. Even as recently as November 1980, when that peripatetic Pope, John Paul II, visited the Federal German Republic, the Freiburg scholar Dr Remigius Bäumer chose to repeat many of the old judgements originating in the polemic of Cochlaeus much to the righteous indignation of Protestant leaders. If journalists seized on

---

[1] See, for example, 'The Seven-Headed Papal Revelation' (c.1530) reproduced at the end of this volume.

Bäumer's inaccuracies and basic indiscretion—rushing into print
with headlines like 'Ecumenism Clouded in Germany' and 'Luther
Again at Centre of Bonn Religious Dispute'—their reaction was
understandable. For it is certainly time that the poisoned teeth of
controversy were drawn in such matters. Indeed, if the Catholic
hierarchy genuinely sought *rapprochement*, it should not for
one moment have permitted the circulation of long-discredited
judgements of the kind Bäumer made in the *Short History of the
German Church* specially commissioned by a Catholic Bishops'
Conference for the people, particularly the young people, on
an important occasion.[2]

In a curious way, it is the frontispiece of *Septiceps Lutherus* that
has proved most enduring and effective. For when viewed without
the repetitive, tedious chapters of dreary dogmatism that follow in
the course of the tract, the cartoonist's work imparts, at the level
of laughter, brief flashes of real insight that span the centuries in a
way that period polemic does not. As the work of those already
converted, polemical writing serves rather to encourage or console
its author than to convince his adversary who has, after all, been
carefully conditioned against the medium. For it is certainly a
moot point for academic debate how far material of this kind managed to advance any particular cause. The pundits of modern
advertising in big business lay much store by the media for keeping
a product in the public eye. They also acknowledge the fact that
getting it there in the first place is a far greater feat. By 1529
Luther had certainly made his mark; and in preparing for the great
debate, Cochlaeus identified the threat posed for reigning Catholic
orthodoxy by the Wittenberg Reformer in his diverse roles. A
chronological scheme carefully relates the devastating impact of the
renegade religious to his biography by a series of slogans printed in
boxes above the seven 'heads'. Similarly, the headgear (or, in the
case of 'Barrabas', the lack of such headgear) notes and mocks the
status of the heretic at that stage of his disastrous ministry. Careful
draughtsmanship thus guides the eye along a bizarre rogues' gal-
lery of Aunt-Sally-type 'heads', at the same time bringing into

---

[2] Cf. B. Kötting (ed.), *Kleine deutsche Kirchengeschichte* (Herder, Freiburg/
Basel/Wien, 1980), esp. Section III, 'Das Zeitalter der Glaubensspaltung', where,
on pp. 64, 66, and 67, Dr Bäumer shows his dependence on Cochlaeus propaganda; and pp. 56, 57, 58, 59, 60, 62, and 68 where he forwards the kind of interpretation that, in the present state of Reformation Studies is at best 'old hat' and
at worst ill informed and misleading.

focus a well-worn copy of the Scripture. The book, Luther's *New Testament*, has a decorated binding, just like the belt taking in the monster's holed, rather than holy, habit. The decoration seems to be carefully tooled *Rosen*, but at this date these cannot be *Luther-Rosen*. That heraldic device contained an inset heart and cross, whereas the old family coat of arms shows two roses and a crossbow.³ This may therefore be a back-handed reference to the 'holy golden rose' consecrated by Leo X for Friedrich der Weise when the Pope sought to prevent Hapsburg succession to the Empire. It was a gesture that certainly gave the Elector, with his well-known love of relics, both delight and anxiety, for he was made to wait for delivery, the rose being lodged in a kind of safe-deposit box with the banking house of Fugger at Augsburg. Carl von Miltitz, assistant to Cardinal Cajetan, was to bestow the honour, but Friedrich suspected that he would first have to make a difficult concession. 'Miltitz', he noted, 'may refuse to give me the golden rose unless I banish the monk and pronounce him a heretic.'⁴

If the doctoral 'bonnet' and pseudo-monkish shroud speak for themselves, the third 'head' has recently been identified as that of a Turkish infidel complete with turban.⁵ Bearing in mind the parallel chronological scheme, this cannot be the case. Luther grew a beard during his period of involuntary exile in the Wartburg, and this is therefore Junker Georg (1521 to 1522), the Reformer as Godly Prince assuming the person of Friedrich, the baton depicted above his scissored nobleman's hat confirming the point at a time when the Elector was officially Marshal of the Empire. As befits the whole design, the central 'head' achieves prominence by providing an unpromising clerical countenance above a priest's crossed stole, the vestment set in the kind of 'Lilliputian' proportions intended to deride its sacred symbolism as the yoke of Christ. The visual link with the tattered Testament likewise serves to emphasize a preaching role that can afford mobsters any teaching they wish to hear. As the neckline descends, moreover, the wild imagery of a sectary, hornets humming in his hair, provides suitably extreme

³ Cf. Oskar Thulin, *Martin Luther sein Leben in Bildern und Zeitdokumenten* (München und Berlin, 1958), p. 113.
⁴ R. N. Bainton, *Here I Stand* (London, 1951), p. 104.
⁵ R. W. Scribner, *For the sake of simple folk: Popular propaganda for the German Reformation* (Cambridge, 1981), p. 233.

contrast with a libellous image of lawful authority in the form of 'Visitator', a prestigious personage intended rather like Oliver Cromwell in seventeenth-century England to be 'a good Constable set to keep the peace of the Parish'. The effectiveness of a good cartoon depended on accurate recognition of the various functions assigned by the artist; and in an engraving printed in 1493 by Koberger of Nürnberg for Hartmann Schedel's *Weltchronik* (well-known in Humanist circles) may be found Potiphar, wearing a helmet for use in the emerging bumbledom of Electoral Saxony (1528). It is headgear remarkably like that afforded Luther as Visitor by the cartoonist of the frontispiece.[6] Last but not least too, stands 'Barrabas', drawn as a Wild Man complete with spiked club effectively personifying the pillage and spoliation of Holy Church perpetrated by Luther's bid for Reformation.

A cartoon that makes such concentrated impact and affords at least as many messages as it displays 'heads', conjures from sixteenth-century controversy itself the kind of black art associated by some with Luther's heresy. With this in mind, a commemorative volume compiled five hundred years on from the Great Reformer's birth on 10 November 1483 can offer its readers with due modesty at least some reconstruction of the reasoning behind the prosecution charges mounted by Cochlaeus. It can also attribute Luther's mounting irascibility to the debilitating effect of severe attacks from kidney stone and vitamin deficiency, except that it is no part of the historian's task to offer excuses for doctrinal fixations in a thwarted idealist who was also a remarkable human being. Perfection in forgiveness has been counselled 'unto seventy-times seven'; and a mere seven essays explaining the 'heads' render scant justice to the achievement of Doctor Martin Luther. For that reason, other contributions printed here serve to supplement the reader's fare. Not that it is the editor's task to justify his choice of a team, but rather with them to stress that space, despite the generosity of the Delegates of the Oxford University Press in publishing the book as a specifically English celebration for *Lutherjahr*, precludes much in a discipline that, second only to the life and work of the Christ Himself, 'could not contain the books that should be written' (John 21: 25). In short, what follows is intended to provide for the widest possible readership some analysis of the ideal-

[6] I am grateful to Professor Gordon Rupp for this suggestion. Cf. Ph. Schmidt, *Die Illustration des Lutherbibel, 1522–1700* (Basel, 1962), p. 6.

ism and achievement of one who, by any standards, has to figure in the front rank of Europeans of all time—a veritable colossus who, however conservative his personal instincts and predilections, arguably brought down the curtain on his own medieval world.

PETER NEWMAN BROOKS

The Divinity School,
St John's Street,
Cambridge

The Editor wishes to record grateful thanks to his research students, Mr Roger Mills and Herr Gotthelf Wiedermann for help with the Index, as indeed to two Audreys for a fund of knowledge of Oxford House style.

P.N.B

CONTENTS

The Seven 'Heads'

Other Related Essays

ILLUSTRATIONS

ABBREVIATIONS

AC	*Augsburg Confession*
CR	*Corpus Reformatorum*
JTS	*Journal of Theological Studies*, Oxford
LCC	Library of Christian Classics
LW	*Luther's Works* (American edition, 55 vols., Concordia Publishing House, St Louis, and Fortress Press, Philadelphia)
SK	Johannis Cochlaeus, *Sieben Köpffe M. Luthers vom hochwirdigen Sacrament des Altars* (Leipzig, 1529), a German translation of:
SL	*Septiceps Lutherus, ubique sibi, suis scriptis, contrarius in visitationem Saxonicam per D.D. Joa. Cocleum editus* (Valentinus Schuman, Leipzig, 1529).
Smith	Preserved Smith, *Life and Letters of Martin Luther* (London, 1911)
WA	*kritische Gesamtausgabe der Werke D. Martin Luthers* (Weimar, 1883 ff. Given by volume, page, and line in [] after the quotation in the text to facilitate reference and lighten apparatus.
WA, Br	*kritische Gesamtausgabe, ... Briefwechsel* [Luther's correspondence in the Weimar edn., 1930 ff.]
WA, DB	*kritische Gesamtausgabe, ... Deutsche Bibel* [the *German Bible* in the Weimar edn.]
WA, TR	*kritische Gesamtausgabe, ... Tischreden* [the *Table Talk* in the Weimar edn., 1912 ff.]
ZKG	*Zeitschrift für Kirchengeschichte*, Gotha, 1876 ff.
ZTK	*Zeitschrift für Theologie und Kirche*, Freiburg i.B., 1891 ff.

I

DOCTOR

Doctor Martin Luther
Subjectivity and Doctrine in the
Lutheran Reformation

*

B. A. GERRISH

> I HAD to accept the office of doctor and swear a vow to my
> most beloved Holy Scriptures that I would preach and teach
> them faithfully and purely. While engaged in this kind of
> teaching, the papacy crossed my path and wanted to hinder
> me in it. How it has fared is obvious to all.[1]

AMONG the proceedings at the Diet of Worms (1521) was a ceremonial burning of Luther's books. An anonymous pamphleteer reports that on top of the bonfire was placed an effigy of the heretic
with the inscription in French, German, and Latin, 'This is Martin
Luther, the Doctor of the Gospel.' The high priests and the
Romanists, he goes on, objected: 'Write not, "A Doctor of
evangelical truth", but that he said, "I am a Doctor of evangelical
truth."'[2] The clear echoes of another story leave no doubt which
side the pamphleteer was on. But the justice of his comparison, to
say nothing of its propriety, may very well be doubted. Whether
Luther was, or only said he was, a teacher of the plain Gospel
truth has been a question for 'ecumenical theology', as it is now
termed, from his own times to the present day.

It was Philip Melanchthon, not Luther, who was given the nick-
name *praeceptor Germaniae*: teacher or schoolmaster of Germany.
Of course, he earned it. Whatever needs to be said about the effectiveness of Lutheran indoctrination and the understanding of human nature that sustained it, Melanchthon's impact on German
secondary and higher education was profound and lasting. If
Gerald Strauss is right, an Augustinian estimate of man caused the
Lutherans both to adopt a repressive pedagogy and to acquiesce in
its failure when opposed by a vigorous subculture of folk religion.
But he does not deny that significant educational measures were
taken by the Lutherans, who had better success in channelling the
religious energies of an intellectual élite; he reaches his conclusions
by uncovering the pedagogical principles *behind* the outward institutional and curricular changes. That the Reformations of the
sixteenth century do hold an important place in the history of

[1] *LW* 34, 103.
[2] Cf. R. H. Bainton, *Here I stand: A Life of Martin Luther* (Nashville, Tennes-
see, 1950), p. 191.

education is the 'familiar fact' with which Strauss begins.[3]
Melanchthon's place in this history is secure. The title *praeceptor
Germaniae* attests the unparalleled achievement of Luther's modest
colleague, who declined the title of doctor for himself. 'He was
the determining educational influence in Protestant Germany.'[4]

And yet, in another sense, it is Luther who has been the
praeceptor Germaniae, or at any rate of Germany's intellectual
élite. The instruction sought from him has less to do with the formal principles of education (though he did concern himself with
them, too), more with the potency of his ideas and of his personality. Again and again, eminent German thinkers—and not theologians only—have felt bound to come to terms with his intellectual
legacy, even if, as one may well suspect, their ideas have shaped
the image of Luther at least as much as Luther has inspired their
ideas. Indeed, theological differences within Lutheranism have
sometimes become debates on the question: Which party has the
real Luther?

To begin with, the Roman Church countered the Lutherans' reverence for their teacher by challenging both his credentials as a
doctor of the church and the soundness of his doctrine: Luther's
teaching, it was repeatedly alleged, was vitiated by his intense religious subjectivity. But the times have changed. One of the most
remarkable features of this ecumenical century has been a new willingness among Roman Catholic theologians to affirm that their
communion, too, may be instructed by Dr Martin Luther,
although the problem of his subjectivity has not quite been laid to
rest. In some ways, Roman Catholics may even be said to have a
keener ear for Luther's voice than their Protestant brethren, whose
faith was more radically transformed by the intellectual changes of
the eighteenth and nineteenth centuries.

Not all Protestant theologians have approved the course of modern Protestantism. Far from it! Some of them have perceived it as a
story of infidelity to the legacy of Luther; and some have been
convinced that even the Luther renaissance led by Karl Holl was
still tainted with the presuppositions of liberal Protestant thinking.
Here also, within Protestanism, the problem of religious subjec-

---

[3] Strauss, *Luther's House of Learning: Indoctrination of the Young in the German Reformation* (Baltimore, Maryland, 1978), esp. pp. 1–2, 106, 307.
[4] Robert Stupperich, *Melanchthon*, trans. Robert H. Fischer (Philadelphia,
1965), p. 151.

tivity has been in the middle of controversy, and it has ranged neo-
orthodox and liberals against each other. In the period between the
two World Wars, it was not uncommon for Roman Catholic
theologians to endorse the neo-orthodox case against liberal subjectivism, but they were naturally more inclined to see the link
between the Reformation and subjectivism as a necessary one—
and the Roman Church as the only secure haven of objectivity.

How has it come about that today Roman Catholics in Germany (and elsewhere) are more willing to hear Luther as a 'doctor
of evangelical truth'? And how did it come about that in the previous century there were German Protestants who may not have
heard Luther well enough? The first question, which comes close
to the centre of present-day relations between Roman Catholics
and Protestants, is all the more intriguing because an extensive,
fascinating, and still growing literature has sprung up in answer to
it. The second question is intriguing almost for the opposite
reason: though no less important, it needs a much closer scrutiny
than it has so far been given.

The title 'doctor' or 'teacher' probably comes nearer than any
other to the heart of Luther's self-understanding, and it was closely tied up, in his own mind, with the actual reception of his doctor's degree. Luther remarked that the Elector of Brandenburg's
son, on seeing the Cochlaeus cartoon, exclaimed: 'If Dr. Luther
has seven heads, he will be invincible, for so far they have not been
able to vanquish him though he has but one!' [*WA, TR* 2.382.12.]
Luther does not say so, but we can perhaps infer it for ourselves,
that the one authentic Luther head wears the doctor's bonnet—in
his own self-image and in the image others had of him. This, at
any rate, will be the place to begin (in Section I) the theme of subjectivity and doctrine in the Lutheran Reformation; how the theme
looks from the standpoint of present-day Roman Catholicism
(Section II), and how it looked to liberal Protestantism in the
nineteenth century (Section III), can then be explored in turn.

I

Shortly before entering the monastery in 1505, Luther had added
to his Erfurt bachelor's degree the master of arts from the same
university. Some four years later, on 9 March 1509, he received the
baccalaureate in Bible from Wittenberg, though an annotation in

the university record reports that he had not yet paid the customary fee. Luther himself later added the comment: 'And he's not
going to either. At the time he was a poor monk and had
nothing.'⁵ The next step was the *sententiarius* degree, which required the holder to lecture on the *Sentences* of Peter Lombard,
Books one and two. Luther prepared for the degree in Wittenberg,
but graduated at Erfurt (1509). And that, so far as he was concerned, was the end of his education; he had no ambition to become a candidate for the doctorate. But he was coerced into taking
yet another step up the academic ladder by Johann von Staupitz,
his superior in the Order of the Augustinian Eremites. Later, this
was to become a fact of some importance to Luther's self-
understanding.

The famous conversation with Staupitz, under the pear tree in
the garden of the Black Cloister, is one of the most memorable in-
cidents in Luther's entire career. When the news was broken to
him that he was to become a doctor of Holy Scripture, Luther replied with a list of fifteen excuses. None of them impressed his superior, who warned him not to be wiser than his elders. Finally,
Luther added that he was already worn out and did not have long
to live. (He was not yet thirty.) Staupitz replied cheerfully that
this would be fine, since the Lord God had many things to do in
heaven; if Luther died, he could become his adviser.

On 4 October 1512 Luther received the *licencia magistrandi*, or
permission to apply for the doctorate; and in the Castle Church
two weeks later, on 18 to 19 October, he engaged in the required
disputations, took his oath, and was invested with the doctor's in-
signia of Bible, cap, and ring. (His bonnet he later offered to place
on the head of anyone who could reconcile James and Paul.) The
Erfurters were miffed because he took the doctorate at Wittenberg.
Since he had never wanted to take the degree at all, he must have
found some irony in this consequence of his obedience. But
Staupitz's insistence changed the course of his life.

In later years, Luther sometimes styled himself 'doctor of theology', sometimes 'doctor of holy scripture'; frequently also, from
his profession rather than his rank, he used the titles 'lecturer' and

⁵ Quoted (in Latin) by Hermann Steinlein, 'Luthers Doktorat: Zum 400 jährigen
Jubiläum desselben (18./19. Oktober 1912)', *Neue kirchliche Zeitschrift* 23 (1912),
757–843, p. 767 n. 1. In the remainder of Section I, I have generally omitted documentation that can readily be found in Steinlein.

'professor'. But perhaps the most expressive of his chosen titles was 'sworn doctor of holy scripture'. In one respect the phrase has been found odd: his doctor's oath did not in fact include any express obligation to the Scriptures, whereas the bachelor's oath (for the *baccalaureus biblicus*) did. Still, a Bible was presented to the doctoral candidate, possibly with some appropriate words, and he was required to give an address in praise of Scripture both at his graduation and in his inaugural lecture. Hence it is not surprising that the new doctors were sometimes called 'masters of the sacred page' or 'teachers of holy scripture'.

According to Luther himself, the doctors in his day despised the Bible and always itched after something new [*LW* 34, 27]. For himself, however, the reception of the doctorate carried with it an inescapable demand to be a faithful teacher of the written word of God. The fact that he had not wished for the degree only heightened his sense of obligation: a responsibility had been laid upon him even against his will. Time and again, he identified his call to be a Reformer with the commission he received on that October day in the year 1512.

Naturally, Luther's opponents could always retort that his doctorate did not authorize him to teach heresy; as a doctor, he remained answerable to the Church. The licentiate oath before the Chancellor of Wittenberg University included an explicit pledge of obedience to the Roman Church, and the doctoral oath itself promised avoidance of strange doctrines condemned by the Church and offensive to devout ears. Be that as it may, Luther's self-understanding cannot be appreciated unless it is first recognized that in his own eyes he was a man under constraint. Indeed, he saw this constraint as an obligation laid upon him precisely by Pope and Emperor. But it was more than that: it came not only from a man-made ceremony, but from the Word of God itself. His calling as a sworn doctor of Holy Scripture made it impossible for him to keep silent even if Pope and Emperor subsequently opposed him.

I was forced and driven into this position in the first place, when I had to become Doctor of Holy Scripture against my will. Then, as a Doctor in a general free university, I began, at the command of pope and emperor, to do what such a doctor is sworn to do, expounding the Scriptures for all the world and teaching everybody. Once in this position, I have had to stay in it, and I cannot give it up or leave it yet with a good conscience, even though both pope and emperor were to put me under the ban for not doing so. For what I began as a Doctor, made and called at their command, I must truly confess to the end of my life. I cannot keep silent or cease to teach, though I would like to do so and am weary and unhappy because of the great and unendurable ingratitude of the people. [*LW* 13, 66.]

As Luther perceived the Reformation, then, it was an unforeseen by-product of his faithfulness to a sworn duty: it came about because the Pope, by whose authority the duty came to him in the first place, got in his way. No doubt, what he sincerely believed to be a matter of a doctor's duty and courage struck others as the wilfulness and arrogance of one paltry friar who presumed to defy the Catholic Church. Luther was clearly troubled by the contemptuous question: Could he alone be right, and all those who came before him fools and know-nothings? Or was he alone the darling of the Holy Spirit, and had God let his own people go wrong for so many years? Luther overcomes the taunt by weighing against it Christ and his Word [*LW* 36, 134, 43, 160]. And to this Word he was pledged by his doctorate to be faithful, come what may. As he put it in another memorable utterance, he would not trade his doctorate for all the world's riches; it was a remedy for loss of heart, the reassurance that he had not started a reformation as an interloper, without call or command [*LW* 40, 387–8]. It gave him the courage to tread on the lion and the adder, to trample the young lion and the serpent under his foot [*LW* 34, 103–4].

The strength Luther derived from his 'office' as a doctor of Holy Scripture has often been remarked upon in the secondary literature. Karl Holl, for instance, in his much-quoted lecture on Luther's judgements about himself, remarks: 'His consolation was always that he had planned nothing, but had instead been forced along his way while carrying out his office'.[6] A much more elaborate study of Luther's doctorate appeared in 1912, some years after Holl delivered his lecture but before its publication among his collected essays. The author, who signed himself 'Pfarrer Steinlein', timed his essay to coincide with the four-hundredth anniversary of Luther's graduation. Anyone who has since written on the subject will have found it difficult to add much to such a thorough investigation; it sets out to be an exhaustive analysis of all the pertinent

---

[6] Trans. by H. C. Erik Midelfort as Holl, 'Martin Luther on Luther', in *Interpreters of Luther: Essays in Honor of Wilhelm Pauck*, ed. Jaroslav Pelikan (Philadelphia, 1968), pp. 9–34; quotation on p. 16.

sources and yet, despite an occasional word of diffidence, manages to work the countless references into a smooth pattern.[7]

Naturally, Steinlein looks into the many passages in which Luther writes directly about the doctoral degree in general, the doctors of his day, and his own doctorate in particular. But he carries the search further: account is taken also of the way Luther styles himself in his public writings, and even how he introduces and signs himself in the myriad items of his correspondence (not yet available, in 1912, in the definitive Weimar Edition). The first impression, as Steinlein admits, is one of motley diversity. Even the obvious seems to be open to exceptions. We are told, for instance, that Luther tends, as we would expect, to drop his titles in letters to his friends. And yet one notes from Steinlein's own citations that Luther could style himself 'doctor' (apparently without intended humour) even in writing to his wife; and 'doctor', as the *Table Talk* abundantly shows, is how she in turn commonly addressed him.

Steinlein argues none the less that if the mass of material is set in . chronological order, a strikingly consistent picture meets the eye. What he calls Luther's *Doktoratsbewusstsein* (his 'doctor consciousness') rises and falls in tune with both his external circumstances as a Reformer and his corresponding attitude to the entire business of the academic community. Three main periods can be distinguished, if Steinlein's thesis is correct: the 'doctor consciousness' emerges (1517 to 1521), recedes (1521 until around the end of the 1520s), and emerges again (from the end of the 1520s to 1546).

The very first extant letter in which Luther signed himself 'doctor' was addressed to Archbishop Albert of Mainz on 31 October 1517; the second instance occurred the same year in a letter to the Elector Friedrich (*c.*11 November). Although the title did not appear again at the *end* of his letters (as part of his signature) until 1519, the impression is that from the first Luther undertook his Reformation on the strength of his doctoral office or calling. The explanation for the temporary disappearance of the title from Luther's signature, Steinlein suggests, is that soon after the beginning of the Reformation he took to styling himself *Eleutherius* ('the free'). And the first impression of the 1517 letters to Albert

---

[7] See p. 5 n. 1, above. The essay also appeared separately as an 87-page book (A. Deichert, Leipzig, 1912). I have seen only the journal printing, to which my page numbers refer.

and Friedrich is confirmed by express statements Luther made in 1518 *within* letters to his bishop, Jerome Scultetus (13 February), and Pope Leo X (*c.*30 May), by whose apostolic authority he claimed to hold his doctorate. Two years later, in a letter to George Spalatin (9 July 1520), he defended himself against the charge that ambition was what spurred him on. Anyone who wanted his 'offices' was welcome to them; but as long as he was not free from the duty of teaching, he would exercise his office freely. He was already burdened with enough sins and refused to add the unforgivable sin of dereliction of duty. In a similar vein, he assured Elector Friedrich der Weise the following year (25 January 1521) that he had written and taught because of his conscience, oath, and duty as a 'poor teacher of the holy scripture'.

The year 1521 marked the climax of academic attacks on Luther, when the University of Paris finally broke its silence and joined Louvain and Cologne in condemning him. Steinlein believes that the frequency and vehemence of Luther's utterances about 'the doctors' and 'the high schools' can be correlated with the pattern of these attacks upon him. More important, however, he shows that Luther's use of his own title diminishes in the second period, and that he occasionally speaks of his doctorate disparagingly and even seizes upon doctoral graduations at Wittenberg as occasions for expressing aversion to the folly of the entire academic establishment. What can account for this emphatic shift of attitude? The explanation, Steinlein plausibly argues, lies in the Edict of Worms, which placed Luther under the imperial ban.

Following closely upon the papal condemnation, the imperial ban stripped Luther of the office he had received by the hands of men; in response, he renounced his doctorate and took his stand on the title 'preacher', which he held by the grace of God alone. Evidently, it is the Apostle Paul of the Letter to the Galatians, Chapter one, who has now become the model, and Luther appeals expressly to verse eight: he will not have his doctrine judged even by an angel from heaven [*LW* 39, 247–9, 48, 390]. But remarkable though this change of attitude undoubtedly is, too much weight cannot be placed upon it, I think, as a clue to Luther's self-estimate; the renunciation of his doctorate was an impetuous reaction to the imperial ban, and it was not long before he had good reason to change his mind back again—that is, to revert to his former stress on his legitimate vocation.

The principal new factor in Luther's circumstances, which occasioned his second thoughts, was of course the growing menace of religious radicalism. Some of his best-known utterances about his doctoral office were in fact made as he looked back, from the conflict with unauthorized preachers, to his own early activity as a Reformer. And in the new situation he held that an appeal to the prompting of the Spirit is not a sufficient warrant for preaching and teaching in public: one also needs a legitimate call. It must have been particularly galling to Luther when his own colleague Andreas Bodenstein von Karlstadt joined the radicals, shed his doctor's degree, and refused to have part in any further doctoral graduations at Wittenberg University. (Karlstadt wanted the people to call him by no other title than 'brother Andreas'.) The conflict with 'enthusiasm', reinforced (as Steinlein points out) by the renewed conflict with Rome, accounts for Luther's reaffirmation of his doctoral office and calling. In 1535, in a letter to Justus Jonas (17 October), he can report that Katie is preparing a special feast to celebrate the twenty-third anniversary of his graduation.

To correlate Luther's 'doctor consciousness' with the changing circumstances of his career, as Steinlein has done, is a clear improvement on the procedure of culling utterances indiscriminately from all over his writings. One must note in particular the impact first of the Edict of Worms, then of the outbreak of radicalism, on his early sense of mission. Thus far we are taken by his own explicit statements. The further evidence Steinlein adduces—even calculating for each period the exact percentage of letters in which Luther signs himself 'doctor'—is striking, but precarious. Steinlein is puzzled, for example, to find that *within* the third period there is a temporary decrease, from 1534 to 1541, in the frequency with which Luther uses his doctor's title. Other interesting items of evidence he takes into account in the third period include the actual number of annual graduations (*Doktorpromotionen*) that appear in the university records and the letters of recommendation furnished for holders of the Wittenberg doctorate. All in all, Steinlein set in train a fascinating inquiry. Only a textual review as thorough as his could afford firm grounds for doubting or endorsing this side of his argument. But for the present purpose it is not necessary to attempt it. What I wish to carry over into my own argument is independent of any such approach.

It would be manifestly unfair to judge Luther's self-image by the claims he occasionally models on the first chapter of Galatians; that would place him too close to the radicals, whose pretensions he rejected. But there are problems also with his appeal to his legitimate vocation. Provoked by his adversaries, he proposed that he should be celebrated as 'a great doctor over all bishops, priests, and monks' [*LW* 23, 230], and perhaps one may detect—beneath the good fun—echoes of medieval debates on the relative authority of doctors and prelates (including the Pope)? But Luther could also boast of being 'a doctor over all doctors' [*LW* 35, 187]; and while that, too, is said partly in jest, his critics could well reverse his rhetorical question, 'Are they doctors? So am I' [*LW* 35, 186], and answer in the same spirit: 'Is he a doctor? So are we.'

II

Over the years, from his century onwards, Luther's sense of his doctoral vocation has constantly been echoed in the communion named after him. For the authors of the *Formula of Concord* (1577) he was '*Doctor* Luther, of blessed and holy memory', who on the basis of the Word of God had restored sound doctrine. The first editors of the Weimar Edition called their enterprise a critical edition of '*Doctor* Martin Luther's works'. A twentieth-century biography by W. J. Kooiman, identified its subject as 'Martin Luther, *doctor* of the holy scripture, reformer of the church'.[8] And so one might go on. What exactly his progeny have learned, or have believed themselves to have learned, from Dr Luther has varied astonishingly at different moments of Lutheran history; and a number of studies have attempted to trace, in whole or part, the story of his never-ending metamorphosis. One such study, by Ernst Walter Zeeden, is of particular interest for the present purpose; the work of an ecumenically-minded Roman Catholic, it goes a long way towards explaining how, in Roman Catholic eyes, Protestantism has become identified with religious subjectivism.

To begin with, as Zeeden shows, it was chiefly the Lutheran dogmaticians who interested themselves in Luther, and more in his doctrine than in his person. But by the eighteenth century Luther had become the object of a much broader party strife within Lutheranism, as pietists and rationalists alike claimed him for

---

[8] Translated from the Dutch by Bertram Lee Wolf, this appeared as W. J. Kooiman, *By Faith Alone: The Life of Martin Luther* (London, 1954).

themselves; and in the conflict of faith and philosophy he became at once a symbol of faith and a symbol of progress. It even became possible to view him apart from his doctrine, as a forerunner of intellectual freedom. In Lessing, for example, Zeeden finds 'the idea of a *formal* Lutheranism', which consists purely in the right to the same freedom that Luther himself exemplified.[9]

Zeeden's thesis is that attitudes to Luther were able to diverge along two distinct lines only because a certain ambiguity was already present in Luther himself: he stood at once for a new guiding principle, which was freedom of conscience, and a new form of belief, which was the doctrine of justification by faith alone. Protestant orthodoxy took the doctrine, pietism and rationalism only 'the primacy of personal religious experience and freedom from manmade codes'. Although the orthodox attitude may have been 'nearer to Luther than the whole body of modern research', Zeeden points out the irony in an appeal made to Luther instead of to Luther's own court of appeal, and in the refusal to grant his followers the freedom he had claimed for himself. But on the other side Luther's name was invoked only to support 'the right to form one's own idea of Christianity': religion became a private matter, and the world accordingly became secular. As Moehler argued, Protestants found themselves thanking Luther for freedom to believe the exact opposite of what Luther believed. Zeeden concludes that the history of Protestantism has disclosed the incompatibility of Luther's two original principles. 'Protestantism contains the seed of its own destruction.'[10]

A similar Roman Catholic critique of Luther and Protestantism appears in Joseph Lortz. His two-volume history is commonly viewed as a milestone along the road to a more eirenic historiography of the Reformation, but it nevertheless sharply reformulates some old charges. Lortz recognizes that Luther strove for objectivity, seeking it in the Christian congregation, the sacrament of the altar, the Word of God—ultimately, in Christ himself. Hence the severity of his attack on the fanatics, whose subjectivism made

---

[9] Zeeden, *The Legacy of Luther: Martin Luther and the Reformation in the Estimation of the German Lutherans From Luther's Death to the Beginning of the Age of Goethe*, trans. Ruth Mary Bethell (Westminster, Maryland, 1954), pp. xi–xiii, 139 (*my emphasis*). This is an abridged, somewhat free, and in places inaccurate version of Vol. i of the German work (1950).

[10] Ibid., pp. 8–9, 47, 207, 212. On Luther's two principles see also pp. 80, 86, 98, 209–10.

itself master over the Word. But Luther's objectivism was self-deception, since there cannot be religious objectivity without an infallible teaching authority; his illogicality is that he was a servant of the Word—according to his own very personal understanding. In the end, the crucial point is that he threw man back upon himself, alone before the Word; whatever objectivity he tried to preserve could only stand in tension with this subjectivism. The individual had won.[11]

By a longer and more circuitous route than was once the rule, Lortz revived a very old Roman Catholic image of Luther: the rebel whose vigorous individualism had its source in pride, and its consequences in a fragmented Church and a secular culture. His pride began with a deep need for utter independence—he had to be *Eleutherius*, 'the free'!—and ended with a repulsive arrogance and a colossal pugnaciousness. The primary token of this proud attitude was his rejection of what the Church had taught for one and a half millennia in favour of his private interpretation of Scripture. A procedure so essentially divisive can only end in a chaos of individual opinions, in uncertainty of what Christianity is, and in the unchristian life of modern culture.[12]

The question of Luther's temperament and its palpable defects may be set aside for the moment. Four comments of another order seem more appropriate in response to Zeeden and Lortz. First, instead of asserting that Luther wavers between two principles—whether freedom of conscience and the doctrine of justification (Zeeden), or subjectivism and objectivity (Lortz)—it would be closer to his intention to argue that he builds on a single principle, which is the strict correlation of subject and object.

In one sense, Luther did put a questionable stamp of religious subjectivity on the Lutheran version of Christian faith. This can readily be verified by noting how his experience of God is canonized in the Lutheran confessions. When Melanchthon asserts in his *Apology* that faith is conceived in terrors of conscience,[13] we are bound to ask: Surely not always? Luther proclaimed the good news that there is hope even for those who have drained the last

[11] Lortz, *The Reformation in Germany*, trans. Ronald Walls, 2 vols. (London, 1968), i, 443–51, ii, 340–1. On the identification of objectivity with the *magisterium* of the Roman Church see further i, 442, 456.

[12] Ibid., i, 471–7, 442–4, 455–8; ii, 340–1.

[13] *The Book of Concord: The Confessions of the Evangelical Lutheran Church*, trans. and ed. Theodore G. Tappert *et al.* (Philadelphia, 1959), p. 126.

drops of despair. Does it follow that there is no hope for those who have not? Still, the initial one-sidedness of the Lutheran Reformation was at this point something contingent and therefore itself reformable.

In another sense, however, forcefully presented in Luther's *Babylonish Captivity of the Church* (1520), the stamp of religious subjectivity is essential to Protestant understanding of the Gospel. Protestant grace comes as a word, a promise, a message—in fact, precisely as 'Gospel'. And the form of God's grace as spoken word determines the form of man's response as the hearing of faith. What is disclosed in the word is the character of God as gracious; the essence of faith is the perception of God in this, his true character and a corresponding trust or confidence in him. Faith in God is antecedent to love for God, because there can be no true love for God where his character is misconstrued. And faith is not so much a condition of salvation as what is meant by salvation: namely, the confidence of sons before God.

Once the word is identified as the primary, or even the sole, vehicle of grace [*LW* 27, 249], it no longer makes sense to describe the efficacy of the means of grace in terms of an *opus operatum*, or the corresponding subjectivity as the absence of impediment. A word is a means of communication: unheard, it is spoken in vain, loses its character as word; it attains its finality only as it awakens attention, discernment, and commitment. In short, Word and faith are correlatives [*LW* 36, 42, 67; cf. 3, 22]; in this sense, the objective and the subjective belong together.[14] He who believes, has. Neither is there anything 'uncatholic' in this principle. To put it in the old Augustinian formula, which Thomas and Calvin both liked to quote: the Word is efficacious 'not because it is spoken, but because it is believed'.[15]

Secondly, Luther's use of the Bible cannot be disposed of with the cliché 'private interpretation'; whatever its shortcomings, it marks an important stage in the evolution of biblical scholarship. Some of Luther's claims for his doctrine do make painful reading, even for many who sympathize with it. 'Whoever does not accept my teaching', he asserts, 'may not be saved—for it is God's and not mine.' [*LW* 39, 249.] But his assurance (or cocksureness) at

---

[14] Cf. Luther's *Large Catechism* (1529): 'These two belong together, faith and God' (*Book of Concord*, p. 365).

[15] Augustine, *In Joan.*, lxxx.3.

least took the form of a claim about the sense of Scripture ('I have the Scriptures on my side' [*LW* 32, 9]); he pointed to an external court of appeal. The intention was not to parade his own ego, but rather to insist that Christ alone was his master and everyone else a fellow pupil [*WA* 6, 587.1].

In other words, Luther has to be appraised as a figure in the history of hermeneutics. The final verdict on his achievement is bound to be mixed, since he refused to consider the interpretation of the Bible as a purely technical matter. Unquestionably, he thought of his doctorate as a qualification, not only a vocation, to interpret the Scriptures [*LW* 35, 186, 194]. But the interpreter's task, as he saw it, is not to 'play the master of the Word' but to listen to the Christ who speaks in the Scriptures: 'You must hear Him and not master Him or prescribe method, goal, or measure to Him.' [*LW* 23, 229–30.] The *doctor* of Holy Scripture is not the *master* of Holy Scripture. Luther assures us that he did not want the reputation of being more learned (*doctior*) than others; he wanted Scripture to be sovereign—interpreted neither by his own spirit nor by anyone else's, but understood by itself and by its own spirit [*WA* 7, 98.40]. The Scripture is *sui ipsius interpres*, its own interpreter [ibid., 97.23]. But it can surely be argued that to disclaim technical mastery of a text is in fact one important hermeneutic principle: the principle that one must always listen. Lortz, to be sure, denies that Luther was a good listener: 'This', he states, 'is the all-important fact: he who desires to surrender himself without reserve to God's word has never been a hearer in the full sense of the word. ... He did not listen to everything but chose what he wanted.'[16] The question is, however, whether this weakness of Luther's, if such it was, calls for a return to a teaching office, supernaturally preserved from error, or rather for moving on with the principles and practice of biblical scholarship, which is certainly fallible but can find the resources for correction and progress only within its own domain.

Luther insisted on confronting the ecclesiastical authorities on the same Scriptural grounds on which he stood against individual opponents. He raised above the doctors and councils, he said, not himself but Christ [*WA* 6, 581.14; cf. *LW* 32, 11]. And what he announced at the Diet of Worms was not that he trusted his own subjectivity, but that he was bound by the Scriptures, his consci-

16 Op.cit., i, 184, 456.

ence being captive to the Word of God [*LW* 32, 112]. Even the
Church authorities, therefore, could speak with him only as fellow
pupils of the Word; he denied them the right to silence him in any
other way than by refuting his understanding of Scripture. The
significance of Luther's Reformation for Protestant use of the Bible thus lies partly in his rejection of *false* objectivity. As Friedrich
Schleiermacher put it in a memorable phrase: the Reformation
established the basis for an 'eternal covenant between the living
Christian faith and completely free, independent scientific
inquiry'.[17]

Lortz, who did not trust doctrine to theologians, found biblical
scholars, too, incapable of rising above the babel of private interpretations, and he thought he saw the Protestant legacy in an
'arrogant biblical and dogmatic criticism, constantly revising its
position'.[18] But it is difficult to see how an unsound biblical
scholarship could be corrected by anything but a sounder biblical
scholarship. Whatever legitimate claims a Church may make in the
discipline of its own community of faith, in the work of biblical
scholarship its authority as such must be tacitly or expressly replaced
by the text, a method for interpreting it, and a community of
scholars. These days, the one community of biblical scholars includes both Protestants and Roman Catholics. Much the same
holds true of historical and theological scholarship, including
Luther research.

Thirdly, then, since the time when the major studies by Zeeden
and Lortz first appeared, transconfessional Luther research has
made immense strides. Lortz was ready to admit that Roman
Catholics could learn from Luther. But he continued to think of a
Protestant as a prodigal son whom 'the Church' would be glad to
forgive and welcome home: 'Those returning home', he wrote,
'lose nothing, but rather are enriched; they in turn enrich those to
whom they return, namely "in all that of positive value which they
have embraced and cherished with particular love".'[19] Luther was,
after all, a heretic, and something of the old ecclesiastical motto

[17] Friedrich D. E. Schleiermacher, *On the Glaubenslehre: Two Letters to Dr.
Lücke*, trans. James Duke and Francis Fiorenza, American Academy of Religion
Texts and Translations Series, No. 3 (Chico, California, 1981). p. 64.
[18] Op. cit., ii, 341; cf. i, 443, 455.
[19] Translated from Lortz's *Die Reformation: Thesen als Handreichung bei
ökumenischen Gesprächen* by Leonard Swidler, 'Catholic Reformation Scholarship
in Germany', *Journal of Ecumenical Studies* 2 (1965), 189–204, p. 201.

lingered on in Lortz's mind: *Oportet haereses esse*—there must be heresies if the Church is to clarify her teachings. Hence the most that Lortz and his school were able to do for Luther, as Otto Pesch wrote in 1966, was to excuse him. Announcing that Lortz's method of dealing with Luther had been superseded, Pesch maintained that Roman Catholic theology had learned to study Luther '*as a real possibility for its own theological thought and life*'.[20] Remarkably enough, Luther has become a 'doctor', it can be argued, even for German Catholicism. And parallel to this change of theological approach to Luther there has been a change of institutional attitude: among German Catholics, there is greater readiness today to think in terms of sister Churches rather than of 'the Church' and an obstinate rebel. It is certainly appropriate as a last comment on Zeeden and Lortz.[21]

Fourthly, only for a few years, at most, did Rome confront a solitary rebel. Luther, it must be admitted, continued to imagine himself the lonely prophet of Yahweh long after it had ceased to be true (if it ever was). The truth is that in a very short time his protest became a schism, and the Roman Church was faced by a Lutheran Church, which developed its own *magisterium*. The seeds of this new growth were already sown by Luther himself: in his treatise on *The Councils and the Church* (1539), for example, which contains one of his most defiant assertions of individual interpretation [*LW* 41, 119], there are the beginnings of a Protestant theory of Church authority. The individualism even of his belief in his doctorate must not be exaggerated; it should perhaps be appraised in relation to the new doctoral oath, instituted at Wittenberg in 1533, which not only bound the doctor to maintain the ecumenical creeds and the *Augsburg Confession* (1530), but also to preserve fellowship with other leaders of the Church:

I promise the eternal God ... that with God's help I shall faithfully serve the church in teaching the gospel without any corruptions and shall constantly defend the Apostles', Nicene, and Athanasian Creeds; and that I shall maintain accord with the doctrine comprised in the *Augsburg Confession*. ... And when difficult and intricate controversies arise, I shall

[20] Otto H. Pesch, 'Twenty Years of Catholic Luther Research', *Lutheran World* 13 (1966), 303–16, esp. pp. 307, 311, 316 (*emphasis Pesch's*).
[21] For a recent Roman Catholic perspective on relations with the Lutherans see Walter Kasper, 'What Would Catholic Recognition of the *Confessio Augustana* Mean?', in *The Role of the Augsburg Confession: Catholic and Lutheran Views*, ed. Joseph A. Burgess *et al.* (Philadelphia, 1980), pp. 123–9.

make no pronouncement on my own, but only after deliberation with some of the elders who teach churches holding the doctrine of the *Augsburg Confession*.[22]

In short, the ecumenical problem is totally misconceived if it is taken to be (still!) the problem: What shall 'the Church' do about Luther?

The debate over Dr Martin Luther's alleged corruption of doctrine with subjectivism has by no means been laid to rest; and will probably remain for a long time yet. The reason is obvious: because in Luther's theology there really is a new interest in the religious subject, and the problem is how to describe it fairly. The problem is particularly difficult for anyone who works with the kind of religious objectivity that Luther rejected. On the other hand, Protestants cannot assume that Roman Catholic research is getting better the less critical of Luther it becomes. Indeed, the tendency to be more positive toward him is by no means universal; in the same year in which Pesch's article was published, there appeared one of the most searching discussions yet of Luther's subjectivism. Its author, Paul Hacker, describes Luther's faith as 'reflexive faith': that is to say, by making salvation depend on believing that one is saved, Luther, according to Hacker, threw the religious subject back upon itself, precluding that self-abandonment to God in which true faith consists. I do not myself believe that this interpretation can do justice to the Christocentric character of Luther's *faith*, the heart of which is single-minded contemplation of Christ; the ego does not, in the act of faith, bend back upon itself. But Hacker seems to me correct when he discovers in Luther an early form of anthropocentric *theology*.[23]

In Luther's theological reflection the religious subject does turn back upon itself; it makes its believing the object of thought. By the very fact of singling out justification by faith as his 'chief article', Luther fostered a change of theological priorities and theological style in comparison with medieval Scholasticism. As he put it: 'The proper subject of theology is man guilty of sin and condemned, and God the Justifier and Saviour of man the sinner. Whatever is asked or discussed in theology outside this subject, is error

---

[22] Quoted in Latin by Steinlein, op. cit., pp. 762–3 n. 6.
[23] Hacker's study was translated into English as *The Ego in Faith: Martin Luther and the Origin of Anthropocentric Religion* (Chicago, 1970).

and poison.' [*LW* 12, 311.] Assertions about God and man in this theology are made strictly as answers to questions about sin and justification; the object of Christian teaching is the life of faith itself, viewed from the inside. And in this respect there is genuine continuity between the Reformation and liberal Protestantism. For Schleiermacher, the task of theology (or, more correctly, dogmatics) was to interrogate and describe the piety of the Christian. In this sense, the content of doctrine is precisely religious subjectivity.[24]

III

Luther started a Reformation, and Schleiermacher a new period in the history of Protestant thought. To inquire about the relationship between them seems natural enough. But less has been written on the subject than might be expected, and what *has* been written is in large part disappointing. Horst Stephan remarks on the absence even in the mature Schleiermacher of a 'warm, personal interest' in Luther, though he nevertheless concludes—on the slenderest of evidence—that Schleiermacher of course revered Luther as 'the highest authority next to the Bible'.[25] This, I suspect, is a statement only of what Stephan thought fitting in Germany's second most eminent theologian. Similarly, Heinrich Bornkamm finds Schleiermacher's few remarks about Luther 'wholly colourless'; like Stephan, he points out that Schleiermacher thought of history as the work of a 'common spirit' and was unwilling to attribute too much to any individual.[26]

Since the 'father of modern theology', as he is commonly called, was not a Lutheran, and often came under critical fire from the Lutherans, it is perhaps unreasonable to expect much warmth or colour in his remarks about Luther. Still, I would take with a grain of salt the profession he once made of allegiance to Zwingli's doctrine rather than Luther's. In any case, his own Reformed communion, he said, did not hesitate to join in the glorification of Luther' memory—even at the price of leaving their own Zwingli

---

[24] *On the Glaubenslehre*, pp. 49, 51, 58.

[25] H. Stephan, *Luther in den Wandlungen seiner Kirche*, 2nd edn. (Berlin, 1951), pp. 69–71.

[26] H. Bornkamm, *Luther im Spiegel der deutschen Geistesgeschichte*, 2nd edn. (Göttingen, 1970), pp. 78–9.

and Calvin in the shade more than they deserved. If one had to make a choice among the three Reformers, it would surely be Calvin whom one would have to single out as Schleiermacher's favourite. For now, however, the question is what light we can shed on subjectivity and doctrine in Dr Martin Luther.[27]

Schleiermacher conceived of dogmatics as an 'empirical' discipline, in the sense that its object of inquiry was to be the actual phenomena of religious experience. It was not to be a speculative theology of rational proofs, nor a biblical theology that would derive its propositions by exegesis: dogmatic propositions arise 'solely out of logically ordered reflection upon the immediate utterances of the religious self-consciousness', and Christian doctrines are 'accounts of the Christian religious affections set forth in speech'. Schleiermacher believed that he could claim Luther as his forerunner in this theological programme, because for Luther, too, theology arose as reflection on religious experience: his theology was the daughter of his religion, and not the other way around.[28]

Schleiermacher's belief that he was a legitimate son of the Reformation still lacks a fully satisfactory treatment. But the affinity of his theology with Luther's has not passed unnoticed. Georg Wobbermin, in particular, an almost forgotten captain of the liberal rearguard, protested vigorously against the neo-orthodox attacks on Schleiermacher's alleged subjectivism. He granted that the urgent task for Protestant theology in the 1930s was to ward off the peril of subjectivism; but he did not see this as a problem in Luther's theology, and he was convinced that Schleiermacher had directed Protestant theology back into Luther's path. The crucial point, he held, is the togetherness of God and faith: God reveals himself only to faith. But Luther's turn to the subjective, which it undoubtedly was, excluded both subjectivism and objectivism; it affirmed the strictly correlative character of faith and its object (that is, God himself). If we insist on pressing the question, Which is finally definitive, God or faith? Wobbermin's answer is: For

---

[27] For documentation and further discussion of the issues touched on all too briefly in this section see Gerrish, *Tradition and the Modern World: Reformed Theology in the Nineteenth Century* (Chicago, 1978), Ch. 1, and *The Old Protestantism and the New: Essays on the Reformation Heritage* (ibid., 1982), Chs. 11 and 12.

[28] Schleiermacher, *The Christian Faith*, trans. from the 2nd German edn., ed. H. R. Mackintosh and J. S. Stewart (Edinburgh, 1928), pp. 81, 76; *On the* GLAUBENSLEHRE, pp. 45, 40–1.

faith God (of course); but for theology the correlation itself—God and faith together.[29]

A more recent and more extensive study of Luther and liberal Protestantism was published in 1963 by Walther von Loewenich, whose earlier work on Luther's theology of the cross (1929) is a landmark in Reformation research. The influence of the dialectical theology (neo-orthodoxy) in his Luther book, von Loewenich admits, was unmistakable; but more than three decades later, the word is out that the end of liberalism may have been celebrated prematurely. In Luther's Scripture principle he finds a revolutionary factor that actually links liberalism with the Reformation. Unlike the medieval Church and the Council of Trent, Luther permitted Scripture to criticize tradition, not merely to support it; and he asserted the rights of a well-founded personal interpretation of Scripture against the traditional interpretation held by the Church. Von Loewenich writes accordingly of Luther's 'subjective approach', and he documents it from the famous remark that a simple layman, if he adduces Scripture, is more to be believed than Pope or council if they do not.[30]

Neither the expression 'subjective approach' nor the documentation in support of it seems quite to say what von Loewenich intends. He goes on to mention the right and duty of the *scholar* to understand Scripture in accordance with his best knowledge and conscience; and this, I have pointed out, is a different matter from an appeal to subjective conviction. It is, in fact, an appeal to objective standards. The establishment of scholarly criteria does have one thing in common with Reformation 'theonomy', which von Loewenich discovers in Luther's stand at Worms: neither can be attained except by way of *autonomy*, that is, by refusing heteronomous tutelage to a Church.[31] It is this common cause of Protestantism and free inquiry that lends plausibility to Schleiermacher's 'eternal covenant', established between faith and science by the Reformation. But von Loewenich comes closer to the point of continuity between Luther and Schleiermacher that I have chief-

---

[29] Wobbermin, 'Gibt es eine Linie Luther-Schleiermacher?', *Zeitschrift für Theologie und Kirche* 39 n.s. 12 (1931), 250–60. Wobbermin does not, as I did, argue from Luther's understanding of the Word, but from the passage in the *Large Catechism* (see p. 20 n. 1, above).

[30] W. von Loewenich, *Luther und der Neuprotestantismus* (Lutherverlag, Witten, 1963), pp. 5, 315–18.

[31] Ibid., pp. 319–22.

ly in mind when he turns from the 'subjective approach' (in his misleading sense) to what he calls a 'theology of experience'.

Put in modern terms, he stresses, the concern of a theology of experience is for the existential character of theological statements: they are not disinterested statements of objective knowledge, but statements in which the existence of the knower is at stake or on the line. In this sense, Luther's biblical theology was at the same time a theology of experience, and this is what justifies the liberal Protestant appeal to him.[32] I would myself wish only to add that, for Schleiermacher at least, theological (or dogmatic) statements are not strictly existential utterances, but *about* existential utterances.

The experiential starting-point has sometimes been held to represent the distinctive character of Lutheran, in contrast to Reformed (or Calvinistic), theology. The Danish Lutheran Hans Lassen Martensen wrote in his dogmatics: 'The Swiss Reformation started primarily from the formal principle, that of the authority of the Scriptures; whereas the Lutheran originated more especially in the material principle, in the depths of the Christian consciousness, in an experience of sin and redemption'.[33] The Calvinists have commonly replied that their concern, properly understood, is to correct the anthropocentrism of the Lutherans; and that while the experiential starting-point is indeed distinctively Lutheran, their own theocentric starting-point lies in the idea of God. An interesting consequence is that Alexander Schweizer, the historian of Reformed theology who proclaimed Schleiermacher the reviver of the Reformed school, felt obliged to admit that something of the 'empirical–historical–anthropological' approach of the Lutherans had rubbed off on his hero.[34] Be that as it may (it needs to be asked, I think, whether Schweizer took seriously enough the role of *pietas* in Calvin), the notion of a theology of experience does seem to forge a link between Luther and Schleiermacher—and so, a link with the existentialist theologians of our own day.

[32] Ibid., pp. 330, 332. However, I am not persuaded by von Loewenich's view that the problem of certainty underlies Schleiermacher's theology of experience.

[33] H. L. Martensen, *Christian Dogmatics: A Compendium of the Doctrines of Christianity*, trans. from the German edn. by William Urwick (Edinburgh, 1898), p. 49.

[34] Schweizer, *Die Glaubenslehre der evangelisch-reformierten Kirche dargestellt und an den Quellen belegt*, vol. i (Zurich, 1844), pp. 90–6.

Schleiermacher's keenest critic, Karl Barth, was well aware of the appeal the existentialist theologians made to Luther, and he said he did not doubt that out of the great Pandora's box of the Weimar Edition one could extract 'a theologically existentialist, and thus indirectly Schleiermacherian thread'. But he added: 'How many other threads one must then leave unconsidered or must even decisively cut off!'[35] The point is well taken. It invites the question of *material* continuity and discontinuity between Luther and Schleiermacher: To what extent did the liberal Protestant understand the actual *content* of Christian experience as the Reformer understood it? One of the most sensitive answers was given by Emanuel Hirsch, who showed how close Schleiermacher could come to Luther's faith in Christ, and yet how far from Luther is a faith that is no longer suspended over the abyss of despair but has become a safe possession.[36] But this is another question—and it would require us to ask not only where Schleiermacher may have been unfaithful to the Reformation, but also where his departure from it may rest on legitimate criticism. For now, our conclusion must be left at the formal level of the question: How did Luther and Schleiermacher, as teachers of Christian doctrine, go about their work, and what can be inferred for the theme of doctrine and subjectivity?

No more than Luther did Schleiermacher lose the religious object in subjectivism; like the Reformer, he held that the Christian God is not to be had as an object, but only in piety or believing. More than this, he also made religious subjectivity the actual referent of dogmatic statements, the content of 'doctrine'. In so doing, he believed himself to be a disciple of Dr Martin Luther. Schleiermacher, too, held that experience makes a theologian [*LW* 54, 7]. Indeed, he ventured to write on the title page of his dogmatics the Anselmian motto: 'He who has not experienced will not understand.' I am not myself persuaded that the work of the theologian calls unconditionally for commitment (empathy will do). But it does seem to me that, by focusing theological interest on the man

---

[35] Barth, 'Concluding Unscientific Postscript on Schleiermacher', trans. George Hunsinger, *Studies in Religion/Sciences Religieuses* 7 (1978), 117–35; quotations on p. 127.

[36] E. Hirsch, 'Fichtes, Schleiermachers und Hegels Verhältnis zur Reformation' (1930), repr. in Hirsch, *Lutherstudien*, vol. ii (Gütersloh, 1954), pp. 121–68; see esp. pp. 140–2, 156–7, 162–3. But whether Schleiermacher's faith was quite as serene as Hirsch assumes, really needs to be shown!

of faith, Luther's reformation nurtured a distinctively experiential style of Protestant theology, which points forward to the modern view of theology as disciplined reflection on the phenomenon of believing: that is, as an anthropocentric study of a theocentric phenomenon.

II

MARTINUS

'Heresy, Doctor Luther, Heresy!'
The Person and Work of Christ

*

NORMAN E. NAGEL

How can Luther's head be saved on a charge of heresy? For such a charge to stick as a capital offence, the heresy must diminish, distort, and divide (or deny) Christ. As the accused, Luther would himself certainly acknowledge the definition of the crime, noting as he does that 'All heresy strikes at this dear article of Jesus Christ.' [*WA* 50, 267.18.] Holy Scripture provides the primary documents of the case; but Luther's actions will also be set against the creeds and viewed in the light of tradition. His deposition will be from the time he was proceeding with his theological education; from the sermons he preached after the Diet of Worms, and before he had to face the enthusiasts; and from his academic achievement at the end of his career. As a rising scholar, a preacher, and professor, Luther cannot be accused of saying something only once; and in consequence, the plea of Athanasius that 'It is better to submit to the blame of repetition than to leave out anything that ought to be set down', seems singularly apt.[1] If Luther is to hang, there is thus evidence enough for it to be done a hundred times. Nor need the jury be unduly retained if the hearing of evidence is properly confined to the threefold charge under consideration.

The confession and proclamation of Christ does not stand still. In Jerusalem at Pentecost Peter proclaimed, 'Let all the house of Israel therefore know assuredly that God has made him both Lord and Christ, this Jesus whom you crucified.' The Book of Acts tells of the Word moving and growing. Men are mentioned as they carry the Word, or rather are carried by it. The Twelve of Israel are sealed and then surrender themselves to the service of the Word: 'My witnesses in Jerusalem, and in all Jordan and Samaria and to the end of the earth'. Paul is nudged into Europe and Greece, handing on 'the facts which had been reported to me: that Christ died for our sins, in accordance with the scriptures; that he was buried; that he was raised to life on the third day, according to the scriptures; and that he appeared to Cephas, and afterwards to the Twelve'. It happened; the verbs tell it, as also the Apostles' Creed.

'The word of the cross.' 'I decided to know nothing among you

---

[1] *De incarn.* 20 [*LCC* i, 74].

except Jesus Christ and him crucified.' 'A stumbling-block to Jews and folly to Greeks.' Jesus is confessed to be the Son of God when he hangs dead on the cross. What could be more repugnant to natural religion? Already in the New Testament there is a move to accommodate Jesus to the religious environment, an effort to take from Christ and give credit to man's religiosity, morality, and philosophy. The Apologists lay claim to the moral and philosophical superiority of Christianity. Ignatius proclaims that the antinomies by which things were sorted out among the Greeks have been overcome and joined by 'him who is above time, the Timeless, the Unseen, the One who became visible for our sakes, who was beyond touch and passion [ἀπαθής] yet who for our sakes became subject to suffering [παθητός] and endured everything for us'.[2]

He uses paradoxes born of Platonic dualism to extol the Incarnation, which is then the more wondrous the more opposite the divine and the human are considered to be. Terms of human limitation and weakness are negated to become the universal and infinite attributes of God, and man in turn the opposite of these, and the way of his salvation is then his way of attaining them. Jesus is the conjunction of the human and the divine and so he shows the way.

It is not fair to blame all this on Ignatius. He usually speaks simply in the ways of the New Testament. There is only one Jesus Christ. What he says and does, he says and does. What is said of him is said of him. There is no splitting into an earthly and a heavenly Jesus Christ, nor one down from above or up from below, nor for that matter a Jesus of history and a Christ of faith, for he lays no alien definition of God upon him. In Jesus he confesses 'the passion of my God', and 'the blood of God', anticipating, as Dr J. N. D. Kelly observes, the communication of attributes.[3] 'There is only one physician—of flesh yet spiritual, born yet unbegotten, God incarnate, true life in the midst of death, sprung from Mary as well as God, first subject to suffering then beyond it— Jesus Christ our Lord.'[4] This is close to the Gospels and is also what he would confess when he uses the antinomies; but with them the Incarnation is set toward becoming a hellenized problem.

---

[2] *Pol.* 3, 2 [*LCC* i, 188].
[3] *Rom.* 6: 3 [*LCC* i, 105]; *Ephes.* 1: 1 [*LCC* i, 88]. Cf. J. N. D. Kelly, *Early Christian Doctrines*, 2nd edn. (New York, 1960), p. 143.
[4] *Ephes.* 7: 2 [*LCC* i, 90].

Against the dualistic opposites must be set the statement of John
1: 11, 'he came to his own home [τὰ ἴδια], and his own people
[οἱ ἴδιοι] received him not.' The opposition does not lie here in
the antinomies but in 'sin, because they do not believe in me'.[5]

For the Greeks, and for Aristotle more than Plato, the non-
finite was no matter for rejoicing. Reality could only be grasped
by thinking and measuring and defining. These lay their necessities
also on the gods. A god subject to such necessity is most unlike
the living God who goes on in the Bible. Yet without this necessity God cannot be fitted into a system; scholastic theology is
impossible.

The infinite attributes which seem to honour God tend in fact
to do the reverse. Pannenberg, in correcting Harnack's sweeping
judgement on hellenization, applauds those who take up such
terms, work them for all they are worth and, breaking them open
from within, make them serviceable for Christian theology. He
sees unfinished business.[6]

The work [λειτουργία] of confessing and proclaiming Christ is
never finished. The problem here is how Luther advanced or im-
peded it. But first it is important to emphasize that Chalcedon itself did not finally settle the doctrine of the Person of Christ. It
was to be understood according to the *Tome* of Leo and the
teaching of Cyril. Leo, in the Western way (Tertullian), is strong
for the distinctness of the two natures, and even speaks of each
having its own activity (*agere*), to leave the way open for assigning
what is divine and what is human to the appropriate nature. Professor Henry Chadwick has pointed to something similar in the
Antiochene use of *hypostasis*.[7] Cyril, on the other hand, confesses

that the Word, in a manner indescribable and inconceivable, united personally [καθ' ὑπόστασιν] to himself flesh animated with a reasonable soul, and
thus became man, and was called the Son of Man. And this not by a mere
act of will or favour, nor by taking to himself a mere personal presentation [πρόσωπον, role]. The natures which were brought together to form
a genuine unity were different; but it was one Christ, and one Son, that
was produced out of these two natures. We do not mean that the difference of the natures is annihilated because of this union; but rather that the

[5] John 6: 9.
[6] W. Pannenberg, 'Die Aufnahme des philosophischen Gottesbegriffs-als dogma-
tisches Problem der frühchristlichen Theologie', *ZKG* lxx (1959), 15 f.
[7] 'Eucharist and Christology in the Nestorian Controversy', *JTS* i (1951), 52.

deity and the manhood, by their inexpressible and inexplicable concur-
rence into unity, have brought about for us the one Lord and Son, Jesus
Christ and Son. He was not first born an ordinary man of the holy Virgin
and then the Word came down and entered into him, but the union being
made in the womb itself, he is said to endure a fleshly birth making his
own the birth of his own flesh.[8]

If he endures such a birth and Mary is *Theotokos*, then the
Platonic principle that God cannot suffer has been somehow
breached. Cyril, however, does not follow this through. Yet for
him, as Elert observes,[9] God's apathy is not so much the supreme
principle to which what is said of the Incarnation must conform;
rather what Cyril says of the Incarnation presses hard upon this
principle, but yet does not break it. The cry of dereliction is not
Christ speaking in his own name but in the name of all nature. He
cries to the Father not for himself but for us. Yet it is the voice of
the divine *Logos* that cries. Nestorius heard only the voice of a
man. Cyril does not thus weaken Gethsemane. Nor is he captive
to *finitum non est capax infiniti* as the Antiochenes, nor its reverse,
nor to their *extra Calvinisticum*. 'The body of the Word with
which he sits with the Father, is not separated from the Word
himself, not as if two sons were sitting with him, but one by the
union with the flesh. We must not therefore, divide the one Lord
Jesus Christ with two sons.'[10] The cry of dereliction is the final
test whether the Platonic principle of divine apathy still holds its
grip on what may or may not be said of Jesus Christ. What Cyril
argues was already in Gregory of Nazianzus, and in the West, Augustine makes much the same point. Leo the Great states it was no
complaint but was spoken for our instruction.[11] Toward us rather
than toward God, when surely everything hangs on God.

But what if God is incapable of change, if he cannot be moved?
Then any change must be in man. Pannenberg notes the connection between God's apathy and his incapacity to change, and continues, 'God's incapacity to change can only lead to our having to
seek in man the transition toward any renewing of the relationship
between God and man. The fact that God became a man recedes

[8] *Ep.* 4. This was approved at Ephesus (431) and at Chalcedon (451).
[9] W. Elert, *Der Ausgang der Altkirchlichen Christologie* (Berlin, 1957), p. 89.
On apathy see Ben Drewery, 'Deification', in *Christian Spirituality, Essays in Honour of Gordon Rupp*, ed. Peter Brooks (London, 1975), p. 55.
[10] *Ep.* 4.   [11] *Serm.* 67, 7.

before the notion that God took to himself a human nature.'[12]
This is drawn into the scheme of growing likeness to God which is
then read off the ethical striving, obedience, and example of Jesus.
Pannenberg observes this from Origen and Paul of Samosata on
into the later Antiochene Christology, and Anselm. Here is matrix
for Pelagian notions.

Along this same line lies the source for the development of the doctrine of
gratia creata in the Scholasticism of the twelfth century, the so-called
'conversion argument'. That a man should move from being condemned
by God to one loved by God can only, because of God's incapacity to
change, be explained by a change on the part of man, and not by God's
turning with acceptance toward him.[13]

If God does not change, man must change himself or God must
change him. The change in man provides evidence for a favourable
judgement by God who remains unchanged.

An unchanging and apathetic God has great difficulty carrying
on in history. Spontaneity, contingency, action, his heart being
torn within him, generosity, his judgement, and dwelling in a
world from which have been deduced the rules for his nature and
behaviour, all these he had better be kept well above. If not, then
mankind is left with no necessary conclusions about him. Reason's
deductions from man and the world as to God will not hold.

The Creed of Caesarea proposed at Nicaea spoke of the *Logos*.
Nicaea declined the term. The Nicene Creed adds 'was crucified
for us under Pontius Pilate', 'was buried', and 'according to the
Scriptures'. Here is unfinished business. Nicaea confessed the
ὁμοουσιότης of the Son with the Father. This is so prior to the Incarnation, very God of very God; man and God in Jesus Christ,
Nicaea goes on to insist, have a history. This latter, Athanasius
holds, is bound to be mistaken 'by any one who has not properly
understood the genuine and true generation of the Son from the
Father'.[14] Athanasius speaks of crucified God.[15] 'Christ on the
cross was God.'[16] 'It was for this that he had the body.'[17]

It was owing that all should die—for which especial cause, indeed, he
came among us—to this intent, after the proofs of his Godhead from his

[12] Pannenberg, op. cit., p. 31; cf. p. 30, 'abbildliche Teilnahme'.
[13] Pannenberg, op. cit., p. 32.
[14] *c. Arian.* 1, 8.   [15] *ad Epict.* 10.
[16] *de incarn.* 19-20 [*LCC* iii, 73 f.].   [17] *de incarn.* 21 [*LCC* iii, 76].

works, he next offered up his sacrifice also on behalf of all, yielding his temple to death in the stead of all, in order firstly to make men quit and free of their old trespass, and further to show himself more powerful even than death, displaying his own body incorruptible as first fruits of the resurrection of all.[18]

Athanasius distinguishes between what the incarnate Logos does and says as man, and what he does and says as God. Yet all that he does is not done separately as if he did some things without his divinity and other things without his body. Everything happened together [συνημμένως]; it was only one who, paradoxically, is the Lord who did it all in his grace. Yet Athanasius stops short of the full paradox; he speaks here of body and not humanity.[19]

Of Christ the Nicene Creed confesses that the man born of Mary is truly God. He is not merely a likeness, similitude, symbol, sign, illustration, pointer, figure, or trope, but *est*. The phrase ὁμοούσιος τῷ πατρί has its counterpart in ὁμοούσιος καὶ ἡμῖν. This was confessed at Chalcedon. Ephesus approved Cyril's *anathemas*. Christ became the high priest and apostle of our confession as the Holy Scripture states. His flesh is life-giving because it is the very own flesh of the Word that can give life to all things. 'If anyone does not confess that the Word of God suffered in the flesh, and was crucified in the flesh, and tasted death in the flesh, and became first-born from the dead, and so as God is life and the one who makes alive, let him be anathema.'[20] Prestige wrote of Cyril,

He was probably never very fully understood, and, though his orthodox intentions were vindicated at Chalcedon, his actual line of approach was abandoned, and never renewed except by Monophysites. Chalcedon negatived Nestorianism, and negatived the Monophysite conclusions wrongly drawn from Cyril's premises. Negatively, it was a crowning mercy: it suppressed psychology, to the avoidance of untold heresy, though also to the complete postponement of positive Christological advance. Official Christology remained negative and abstract, and for that reason abstraction became a necessity of theological thought. The next stage necessarily came to consist in a refinement of the accepted abstractions in the cause of clearer and ever clearer statement. But this process did not and could not lead to clearer comprehension and insight into substantial truth and fact.[21]

---

[18] Ibid, 20 [*LCC* iii, 74]. [19] *ad Serap.* 4, 14.
[20] Second Council of Constantinople (553), *anathema* 12.
[21] G. L. Prestige, *God in Patristic Thought* (London, 1952), p. 280.

It is possible to continue to discuss the relationship between the
visible and the invisible, the mortal and the immortal, that which
passes away and that which does not pass away without ever coming down and making contact with Christology and John 1: 14.

The Gospels lead to Calvary. Did God suffer? Does Christ
show what God is like or the reverse? Ignatius spoke simply of the
suffering of my God, and similarly Melito of Sardis and Tatian.
For Irenaeus the incarnate Word of God hangs on the cross; the
impassible became passible. Tertullian against Marcion confesses
that God died; God was crucified. Combating Patripassionism in
Praxeas, Tertullian assigns the suffering to the human nature, and
Antioch is in sight with the twofold natures against which Cyril
emphasized the oneness of person [ἐκ δύο φύσεων, Chalcedon: ἐν
δύο φύσεσιν].

The unique [μονογενής] Word of God himself who was begotten of the
very substance of the Father, who is true God to true God, the Light of
Light, through whom all things came into being, both things in heaven
and things in earth, coming down for the sake of our salvation, and
humbling himself even to emptying, was made flesh and became man.
That is, taking flesh of the holy Virgin, and making it his own from the
womb, he underwent a birth like ours, and came forth a man of woman,
not throwing off what he was, but even though he became [man] by the
assumption of flesh and blood, yet still remaining what he was, that is,
God indeed in nature and truth. We do not say that the flesh was
changed into the nature of Godhead, nor that the ineffable nature of the
Word of God was transformed into the nature of flesh, for he is unchangeable and unalterable, always remaining the same according to the
Scriptures. But when seen as a babe and wrapped in swaddling clothes,
even when still in the bosom of the Virgin who bore him, he filled all
creation as God, and was enthroned with him who begot him. For the Divine cannot be numbered or measured, and does not admit of circumscrip-
tion . . . knowing only one Christ, the Word of God the Father with his
own flesh . . . though being by his own nature impassible, suffered in the
flesh for us, according to the Scriptures, and he was in the crucified flesh
impassibly making his own the sufferings of his own flesh. So by the grace
of God he tasted death for everyone, giving up his own body to it,
although by nature he was life, and was himself the resurrection.[22]

Cyril, first as an exegetical theologian and then as one embroiled in
controversy, does no better. Impassibility holds, and death is the

[22] *Ep.* 3.

little death of the body. The agony of Calvary, dying the death that is the hell of forsakenness of God, do not shatter through.

Our one and the same Lord Jesus Christ, the Word of God incarnate and made man, his were the miracles and the sufferings which he willingly endured in the flesh. If anyone does not confess that he who was crucified in the flesh, our Lord Jesus Christ, is true God and Lord of glory and one of the Holy Trinity, let him be anathema.[23]

And then there is the Athanasian Creed. Here the historical verbs do not carry the confession of the drama of salvation as in the Apostles' Creed.

But Luther grows impatient. The way the struggle went in the Early Church issued as it did. Some lines of developments continued and grew, some trickled on or remained static. Always the Scriptures were read in Church. There was Baptism and the Supper along with other things. The pressure of the antinomies made God more remote. Christ was ecclesiasticalized, juridified, and imperialized, a counterpart to the Emperor. In Leo's *Tome* it is divine power which effects most things. For Augustine the conflict of the attributes of justice and mercy is referred to the top fact about God, his power.[24]

In Erfurt Luther entered the more rigorous Augustinian monastery. He was troubled by God. It is God we cannot be certain of. In Klapper's phrase 'He suffered God.'; and for Holl, 'Luther denkt von Gott aus.' With Augustine's help he recognized the various ways of hedging as futile. There is no alternative but to submit to the judgement of God, a judgement on sinners that is inescapable. We cannot but take it. In Christ we see that judgement, the judgement that God works out upon us as in Christ, and therefore we may have hope if we humbly take that judgement conformably with Christ's taking it.

Luther's first major works were exegetical. From 1513 to 1515 he lectured on the Psalms. Augustine is everywhere. Following Augustine, he hears Christ in the Psalms, and most often not in his own person but as the voice of his body the Church. There is a good summary of much relevant Augustine in the *Epistle to Honoratus*.

---

[23] Philoxenus, *de trin. et incarn.*, *CSCO syr. ser.* II, 27.
[24] *Anathema* 3, and *anathema* 10 [*LCC* iii, 379].

These words [the cry of dereliction] Christ speaks in the person of his Body, which is the Church . . . These words the bridegroom speaks in the person of the bride, because, in a sense, he joined her to himself . . . If one flesh, then, they are properly one voice. What do you here ask, human infirmity, of the voice of the Word by whom all things were made? Hear, rather, the voice of the flesh . . . Here is the voice of the cure, by which you are made whole, that you may see God, whom he postponed as an object of sight, but he brought you a man to be seen, he offered him to be killed, he lent him to be imitated . . . Why, then, do we disdain to hear the voice of the body from the mouth of our head? The Church suffered in him when he suffered for the Church, just as he suffered in the Church when he suffered for the Church. For, just as we heard the voice of the Church suffering in Christ: 'O God, my God, look upon me, why hast thou forsaken me?' so we have also heard the voice of Christ suffering in the Church: 'Saul, Saul, why persecutest thou me?'[25]

It is a good sample of Augustine's sane approach to justification, salvation by way of the *corpus mysticum, Brautmystik, imitatio Christi*, Christ's sufferings located in his flesh, sufferings which seem to parallel those of his saints and so not unique. Their *proprium* is not evident. Paul also prayed and was not heard. We may note the antinomy of invisible and invisible. More often it is heavenly and earthly, eternal and temporal. By negation of the latter we come to the former. Old and New Testament are presented in conformity with this.

Thus the man Christ was not to be recommended to us by reason of earthly happiness, because by him the grace of the New Testament was to be revealed, which belongs to eternal not to temporal life. Hence, subjection, suffering, scourging, being spat upon, contempt, the cross, wounds, and death itself were to be his, as if he had been overcome and made prisoner by them, so that his faithful might learn what reward for their devotion they should ask and hope for from him whose sons they had become, and might not serve God for the purpose of seeking to gain temporal happiness as a great boon. God gives eternal goods only to the good. We changeable creatures then become sharers in the Word, to be changed for the better, but the unchangeable Word, in no wise changed for the worse, has become a sharer in our flesh by the medium of a rational soul.[26]

The soul being incorporeal provides the conjunction point with the incor-

---

[25] *Ep.* 140, 6. in St. Augustine, *Letters* 131–64, iii (1953), pp. 70f. *The Fathers of the Church*, Catholic University of America Press, Washington, Vol. xx.
[26] Op. cit., 5, 9 and 4.

poreal Word, and this ought to be easier to believe than a combination between an incorporeal and a corporeal.[27]

In the *Dictata* Luther proceeds exegetically and his hermeneutics centre more and more in Christ. Maurer notes that 'Luther's hermeneutics grow out of traditional Christology'.[28] Luther uses the traditional fourfold scheme of exegesis. The tropological sense becomes dominant by way of the allegorical. Often the same words are taken as those of Christ himself (*literaliter*), of Christ speaking for the Church, his body and members (*allegorice*), and of the believer (*tropologice*).

What of Calvary and the cry of dereliction? The cross in particular shows the saints the image to which they must be conformed [*WA* 3, 212.31]. The cross appears everywhere in Scripture [*WA* 3, 63.1]. It displays the judgement of God, the judgement with which we must identify and be worked through by God. Luther declined the customary ways of mastering and diminishing the cry of dereliction. Its terrifying impact is not lessened by recourse to seeing Christ as only the proxy of the Church, or to the scholastic division of natures and plurality of wills. Christ was made a curse for us, excommunicated, and anathematized [*WA* 3, 263.33; 211.16; 411.33]. He was cast off by God, judged, and damned. He suffered hell [*WA* 3, 136.26; 171.21].

Yet the cross does not so much mean what uniquely achieved for us there as to show us what we have to expect and accept. The tropological sense gives the application. We are to bear a similar judgement to that shown us in the cross.[29] The cry of dereliction signifies that whoever abandons and humbles himself before God is the more heard [*WA* 3, 171.2].

The cross is not the only example that shows God's hidden way of working, nor are the Scriptures the only place where it is depicted. It is taught by the whole creation [*WA* 3, 647.2]. As the saint flies toward God through diligent study of Scripture, so also by contemplation of the creation [*WA* 3, 397.4; 604.28]. God's works which are seen signify His works which are not seen. Every visible creature is a parable full of mystical instruction. Every crea-

[27] *Ep.* 141.
[28] W. Maurer, 'Luthers Lehre von der Kirche', *Lutherforschung Heute*, ed. V. Vajta (Lutherisches Verlagshaus, Berlin, 1958), p. 96.
[29] *WA* 3, 463.17. Cf. *WA* 4, 419.1., and R. Prenter, 'Der barmherzige Richter', *Acta Jutlandica*, xxxiii. 2.8., p. 117, 'als Beispiel vorgehalten wird'.

ture is a work of God which is to be heeded as a speech of God.
Yet they are only signs and not the substance; only God is that
[*WA* 3, 560.35; 239.40]. The creation of corporeal things is the beginning, figure, and shadow of redemption and spiritual things,
which are the goal of those things without which they are vain.
Therefore they are received as parables of spiritual things. The Incarnation of Christ is to be seen in everything, as also his passion
and resurrection [*WA* 3, 550.33; 533.38]. Created things are more
profoundly discerned when they are seen as God's marvellous
works, that is when they are seen to be full of his wisdom. The
mind is elevated from the works of God. The first step is that the
works of God are seen rather than God, the second that they are
recognized as *mirabilia*, while the third sees all, outside which
nothing remains. The first begins, the second progresses, and the
third perfects. Thus devotion and learning, understanding and disposition grow by steps [*WA* 3, 534.21]. This all sounds very upward, of process in man, Augustinian and Neo-Platonic. Man also
is spoken of in Neo-Platonic terms. His flesh belongs to a lower
order, his spirit to the higher. Our body is the back we turn to the
world, while the spirit is the face which always stretches and
hastens upward to God [*WA* 4, 175.14; cf. *WA* 83, 396.17].[30]

Christ is the goal and centre to whom all things look back and
point. Yet Christ as example of the works of God is coupled with
the saints; in both may be seen what God does and may do. When
Christ and the saints are spoken of as differing quantitatively
(*Abbild*), and their relation is seen as association and emulation, he
and his work are not unique. The way in which the cry of dereliction is heard may disclose development in this.

The cross as paradigm of divine judgement holds sway through
Luther's writing until the recognition begins to dawn that how it is
with us before God has its final ground not in a process which
God is working in man, but in 'God's turning with acceptance toward him', forgiving him and bestowing righteousness which is
only gift, complete and saving, because of Christ. Righteousness is
not then what is demanded and effected as a progressive process in
man, upon completion of which man is cleansed and righteous

[30] Cf. L. Pinomaa, 'Die profectio bei Luther', *Gedenkschrift für D. Werner Elert*, ed. F. Hübner (Lutherisches Verlagshaus, Berlin, 1955), p. 121, 'das Streben zur Heiligung noch deutlich im Rahmen des Neuplatonismus'.

enough for God whose unchangeableness is thus still intact.

'God's turning with acceptance toward him' came to Luther from the cross when the cross was Christ's alone, uniquely his, and what he did and suffered there has given us complete and sure salvation.

In his subsequent lectures on Galatians, Romans, Hebrews, and the second course on Psalms, we may observe Luther intensifying this basically Augustinian way of salvation. The tropological *corpus mysticum* way has its high-water mark in his *Sermon on the Blessed Sacrament* (1519). During the time that Luther began lecturing on the Psalms again he issued the invitation to debate indulgences. Those for whom he was pastor were wanting to escape the punishments which show that God is indeed working them through his judgement.

There is no echo of the *Ninety-Five Theses* in the lecture hall. But we do hear the cry of dereliction more shatteringly than ever before. When lecturing on Psalm 22 Luther says of Christ that he, not just his humanity, was forsaken, as a sinner is in every way forsaken. This that happened in Christ is the truth, and these words may not be explained away or emptied of meaning. He was made to be sin for us. Christ suffered this sin, *qualis persona, talia et opera*. To be forsaken of God is to be away from life and salvation in the far land of death and hell. Luther confesses that he is prostrated by these words and cannot come near to understanding them. Those before us, and above all Augustine, have understood these words to refer not to the head but to the members. Luther seeks to understand them also of the head. What the Fathers have put together is uncertain and full of contradictions [*WA* 5, 601.21; 605.39; cf. *WA* 2, 604.8; 606.39; 607.23; and 608.31].

When Luther was lecturing on the Epistle to the Hebrews (1517 to 1518), he was confronted by the blood of Christ [*WA* 9, 14.57; 207.26; cf. *LCC* xvi, 171]. This is a most untropological item. Not any blood avails, but only Christ's. He shed his blood for the forgiveness of sins. Christ is he 'whom God set forth to be a propitiation through faith in his blood'. When the shedding of Christ's blood is regarded as in this *scholium*, the cross is uniquely coming into its own. The death that means forgiveness is Christ's, and not man's dying in conformity with that death. As long as the cross is the pattern of the way man must suffer for his sins in conformity with Christ, *iustitia* remains retributive and of the Law. Such righteousness is not altered by being mystically transposed to humbled man. A similar *iustitia* is suggested by the place which remains for *poena*.

The forgiveness of sins wrought by the shedding of Christ's blood does not fit into this old pattern. There is a similar intractability in the fact that Christ bore our sins as the great High Priest. This appears in the *scholium* on Hebrews 5: 1 [*WA* 57³, 165.15; *LCC* xvi, 102]. Aaron is fulfilled in Christ who suffered vicariously, not for his own sins but for the sins of the world. Moses (i.e. *per legem*) exposed sins; Aaron (i.e. *gratiam*) bore them for others. Christ does both, but more the work of Aaron, and this above all on the cross. His blood cries for forgiveness and mercy.

Where the Scriptures refer to God's testament they are to be understood as stating that God one day will die and dispose of an inheritance. Hebrews 9: 16 is quoted and this is seen fulfilled in Christ [*WA* 57³, 193.18. *LCC* xvi, 144]. At Hebrews 9: 17 the gloss declares that a testament is confirmed and made effective by the death of the testator; at Hebrews 9:18 that the old testament was also God's testament though not confirmed by his own death. Animals were ordained to be killed in his place. Their death he took as his own [*WA* 57³, 51.12. *LCC* xvi, 176 f.]. In the *scholium* on Hebrews 9:17 the crucial significance of Christ's death is set forth [*WA* 57³, 211.16]. God had promised to die for he had made the testament. God cannot die. He therefore had to become man to fulfil what he had promised. The Incarnation and death of Christ were implicit in the testament which bequeathes forgiveness of sins and everlasting life.

Here what is asserted of Christ can only relate to him. Who he is and what he does are all together in his being born, living, doing, suffering, dying, rising, and saving. The verbs tell the story, not categories or definitions of human construction, and the story is all of one piece, so that the Incarnation, which has more often suffered being drawn into philosophical patterns and categories, is not one way of salvation and Calvary another, nor Easter, nor Ascension. No one of these may be played off against any other. His achieving salvation for man is whole and complete. What he did and what he suffered go together, as do his person and his work. God's involvement shows scant respect for those definitions of God which put him opposite us, most God by negation of terms of the human condition.

B. Lohse has observed that in the debate about indulgences the terms *exemplum* and also *exemplar* give way before the image of God,[31] and they were themselves an advance on the imitation of Christ, for Augustine had led Luther to acknowledge the monergism of God. This monergism in Augustine was ultimately an exercise of his power. What resolution there is in Augustine of the confrontation of God's attributes of justice and mercy is by reference to his almighty power. For Luther it comes to be the cross, and then from the cross the attributes receive their content, and so also the image of God.

The next range of evidence will be from Luther's sermons preached after Worms and before his controversy with the enthusiasts. There is nothing sly or surreptitious about Luther, but rather than gather *in flagrante delictos* from all over the place we shall weigh the evidence of his barefaced preaching at this particular time. In the lectures he weaves forward and back; in the pulpit he stands and proclaims. As a called pastor and preacher he acknowledges the weight and the glory of proclaiming the news of how it is with us before God *propter Christum*. Christmas evokes some of his most vivid and happy preaching. Here we may note the coherence of Christ's birth, life, and work, what he did and what he suffered, and of his person and work. What Luther said of the Lord's Supper, 'Let the sacrament remain whole' [*WA* 30¹, 55, 19], may also be said of Christ, and of his salvation. Bethlehem, Calvary, Easter, the forgiveness of sins, and eternal life are the vital happening whole, within which he speaks of pre-existence, virgin birth, communication of attributes, and the Logos, all within the proclamation of it having been done 'for you', without which saying all the right formulas is of no avail. 'To know Christ is to know why he came, and from that comes our joy.' [*WA* 10³, 123.29.] It is a joy that deepens with the narrative:

Here, travelling by foot across the land in the middle of winter, is the mother of God carrying such a load in her body . . . The birth itself is even more pitiful . . . This woman no one had pity on. I imagine she herself had not expected the birth so soon, otherwise she would perhaps have stayed

---

[31] B. Lohse, 'Luthers Christologie im Ablass-streit', *Lutherjahrbuch*, xxvii (1960), p. 57.

in Nazareth . . . It happened with her as with other women . . . she is his true and natural mother, and he her natural and true son. Grace does not break nature in pieces or thwart it or its works, but betters it, sustains and helps it on. What singular honour is here given to nature and her work. It is impossible to draw Christ more deeply into our nature and flesh. The more deeply we know Christ to be submerged in our nature, by that the more sure is what our faith holds . . . Christ is born for you and his birth is yours; it happened for your good. That is what the Gospel teaches, Christ was born for our sakes, for our sakes everything that he did and suffered, just as the angel says here, 'I proclaim to you a great joy' . . . There you see how he has loved us and done all his work for us, and so we also do in our turn, not for him, for he has no need of it, but for our neighbour . . . It is by way of faith that he is ours, and by way of his love that we are his. He loves, that is what we believe . . . [*WA* 10¹, 63–74.]

And again:

Let us stay close to the Gospel that says what we need to know of his childhood, as Luke here writes, 'He grew and became strong in spirit and filled with wisdom,' and then also that he was obedient to his parents. What more should he write? It was not yet time for him to do miracles. It went with him and his being brought up as with any other child. Some children are more gifted than others . . . We should have a straightforward faith that believes only what has basis in Scripture . . . They [the sophists] think of the soul as if it were a wineskin which gets filled up and nothing more can go in . . . If I cannot understand what Luke says, that Christ increased in spirit and wisdom, I will yet receive his word as God's word and so honour and believe it. It is true even though I could never figure out how it could be true . . . Before God's wisdom human foolishness is too slight a thing to be able to impose on it measurement and definition . . . Christ was not always uniformly sweet and gentle; at times he was wrathful and outraged . . . We should therefore take what Luke says of Christ's humanity with utter straightforward simplicity. His divinity was housed in his humanity and used it as he chose. Even though he was at all times full of Spirit and grace, the Spirit did not always move him in the same way. Rather he quickened him now to this and now to that according to however things were. Similarly if we accept that the Spirit was in him from the beginning of his conception, yet in the way in which his body grew and his reason developed in the natural way as in other men, so also the Spirit settled in him more and more, and moved him the longer the more. These are not figments of which Luke speaks. [*WA* 10¹, 445.12–447.19.]

Luther has fun telling of Jesus fetching for his mother water and beer and the meat. He lugs timber and sweeps up the shavings. Luther is here preaching vocation and the Lord's obedience under the Law. In his being there, and in the fact of his love, Jesus is truly God. For only God could love us so, be human, weak, obedient, and suffer so much. This is the opposite of the way sophists and natural religion think of God. The attributes of God which are negations of our creatureliness imply regret that we are human. Salvation is then dehumanizing deification. What is wrong with us is not that we are human, but that we are sinners.

As little as it lies within anyone's power whether he is born and receives his natural being, so little does it lie in his power to be without this sin or to get free of it. He who made us is he alone who can do away with it. Therefore he gives us first the Law by which a man is brought to recognize that such is his sin and need of grace. Then he gives man the Gospel and helps him. [WA 10¹, 509.11.]

Accordingly:

To know Christ aright is to know him as the one who died for me and took upon himself my sin . . . There Christ is God and has put himself in my death, in my sin, and so gives me his loving favour. There I recognise how he befriends me and the utter love of the Father too much for any heart. Thus I lay hold of God where he is most weak, and think, 'Yes, this is God, this is his will and his good pleasure, what there Christ has done for me . . .' Therefore God is to be known alone in Christ. [WA 10¹, 2,277, 18–297, 3.]

In fact:

What should be God's work and word they see as subject to their pleasure and judgement. They would judge God in all his works and refuse to be judged by him, as if it were their option to say what God is or is not . . . Just take a look and see in Scripture whether he does not abominate such utter arrogance, whether he would not rather be with men and women who are known to be sinners than with these pretty saints . . . They are godmakers and godmasters; what seems so to them should be God and what is his . . . He dwelt among us men on earth just like any other man though he was indeed God. He became a citizen of Nazareth and Capernaum and carried on like any other man . . . No one could have recognized him for God . . . The unbelievers who had eyes only for worldly glory missed this divine glory . . . He who is despised before the world for God's sake is glorious before God . . . Reason says what is God's honour and what is God's dishonour, and the reverse. [WA 10, 240. 9–246. 17.]

There is a remarkable passage (Cranmer found it so) in *That These Words of Christ* . . . (1527): 'Our God, however, has his honour in this that for our sakes he gives himself down to the utmost depth, into flesh and bread, into our mouth, heart and bosom, and more, for our sakes he suffers himself to be dishonourably treated both upon the cross and altar.'[32]

On John 1: 5 Luther rejects the speculations of the dualism of higher and lower. 'This comes from the Platonists having drawn St. Augustine into this way of thinking . . . After that, Augustine pulled us all along with him.' [*WA* 10¹, 210.14.]

There is enough Christology in the sermons of 1522 to see Luther through. He had no need to make up any for defending the Lord's Supper and the Personal Union against the enthusiasts. More striking and telling statements may be found scattered throughout his works and be more familiar; the evidence presented here is not from big events or controversy, but observed while he was simply going about his everyday business, and so it may perhaps weigh more against him. Now, the doctor deals with his students and colleagues in disputation exercises.

Recurrent resource for proclaiming the one Jesus Christ, truly man and truly God, wholly Saviour and Lord, are the ecumenical creeds. Luther's most deliberate weighing of their use is in the *Disputation on the Divinity and Humanity of Christ* (1540). The Disputation on John 1 : 14 (1539), will also be drawn on. Here, near the end of his career, the Reformer is fulfilling his calling as doctor, teaching students the catholic faith, the calling that even through the darkest days held him to his task. He works and lives within that faith and is not engaged in the apologetic task as was more often the case with the early Fathers. While equations back and forth may be hazardous, there is something antiphonal as faith, across the centuries, speaks to faith in the vitality of that, of him, who is there alive and enlivening—even in school exercises.

The data of the faith are simply given; everything follows and nothing may be set above or before such data. Divine initiative and freedom may not be infringed. The living God cannot tolerate any *a priori*; if there is to be definition only he can give it. This he has

---

[32] *WA* 23, 157.30. cf. *LW* 37, 72. This was noted by our editor in the *Commonplaces* of Thomas Cranmer, *see* Peter Brooks, *Thomas Cranmer's Doctrine of the Eucharist* (London, 1965), p. 25.

done in his and Mary's son. This is without necessity and analogy. He did it; it happened, there it is.

The Christology of Luther may be presented as so soteriological, so 'for you', that salvation may slip back into being too much a process effected in man—hence the Ritschlian and Existentialist popularity of the young Luther. Bonhoeffer asserts that the person of Jesus Christ is his work.[33] For Luther, on the other hand, his person is the unshakeable ground of the salvation he achieved— *qualis persona, talia opera*. It is not necessary to establish a metaphysics or ontology so that what Luther confesses may stand. His *est* at Marburg does not stand or fall with some ontology. What Christ says he gives us to eat. At Marburg Luther would have no 'mathematics'. Wernle, incidentally, sees Zwingli's idea of God as the product of Neo-Platonic dialectic; Zwingli sees Luther as unwilling to have any Christ in whom the divinity did not suffer.[34]

For Luther could certainly make use of the ecumenical formulations of Christology, so that no *significat*, or *fit*, will do. Now from the *Sixty-Four Theses* of 28 February 1539:

1. The catholic faith is this that we confess the one Lord Christ to be true God and man.
2. From this truth of his twofold being and the unity of the person there follows what is called the communication of attributes.
3. It is true to say this man created the world, and this God suffered, died and was buried, and so on.
15. It is right to teach that in this matter it is the usage of Scripture [*usus loquendi*] that rules, as this is also maintained by the orthodox Fathers.
17. Hence in this matter one must beware of etymology, analogy, consequence, and suggesting similar instances.
20. It is certainly the case that all words when used of Christ, take on a new meaning in the thing they describe. [*WA* 39^2, 93 f.]

They must all be understood from him. When Christ supplies the content of the words, and that does not fit some notions of ours, then too bad for our notions. We are completely at his

---

[33] D. Bonhoeffer, *Gesammelte Schriften*, ed. E. Bethge (Munich, 1960), ii, 176 f. Cf. Maurice Wiles, *The Making of Christian Doctrine* (Cambridge, 1967), p. 97. cf. pp. 99 f.

[34] *WA* 30^3, 139.29. Wernle is quoted by G. Locher, *Die Theologie Huldrych Zwinglis im Lichte seiner Christologie* (Zürich, 1952), p. 44.

mercy. He is the one who is Saviour and Lord. No etymology or analogy may work diminution, division, or separation of his person or his work, and so utterly unique also and 'once for all' the cry of dereliction [*WA* 39², 113.1].

In using the classical terms of Christology, Luther appears rather rough and ready. He does not begin with a definition of such terms and then subordinate Christ to them, but rather the reverse. *Homoousios* does not engage him with its philosophical presuppositions. It is an impenetrable defence against Arius' denial of Christ as truly God. 'They were at the heart of it with Christ *homoousios* with the Father. Christ has one and the same godhead with the Father, one and the same power. Then there was no more trick, escape, way round or feinting possible.' [*WA* 50, 571.23. *LW* 41.82.] That it is not in Scripture deters Luther no more than it did Athanasius. Its content is afforded by Scripture.

We observed in the ancient Church the incubus of a philosophical notion of God, who was more surely God the more unlike and opposite to man he was. The Greek antinomies of temporal and eternal, of finite and infinite, of changeable and unchangeable, suffering and apathy, were resistant to more than their native content. Even Cyril of Alexandria could not break the hold of apathy in the definition of God, although this was clearly broken at Constantinople in 553. That it was broken shows the power of the witness of the Gospels and the liturgy; but the way natural religion thinks about God and with God serving as upstairs counterpart to his vice-regent the Emperor, God was distanced to a remoteness of power and infinite attributes.

When Luther came to know God gracious and near in Christ, he cried God is not far but near, so near he could not be nearer [*WA* 23, 147. 24. *LW* 37, 66]. The Occamists insisted on the infinite difference [*praedicatio disparata, nulla proportio est finiti ad infinitum*]. The infinite gulf is indicated by the assertion that a man might more readily become a donkey for they are both created. Augustine saw affinity with God in man's rational soul. The soul being incorporeal provides the conjunction point with the incorporeal Word, and this ought to be easier to believe than a combination between an incorporeal and a corporeal.

Between those mutually exclusives finite and infinite, Thomas made differentiation in the notion of *proportio*. Biel asserts here a proportion of perfection and a suppositional dependence, and so the

Word is said to be man but in a way which does not contradict the principle *nulla proportio est finiti ad infinitum*. In turn, this does not allow the personing of the human nature; and so there is little actual communication of attributes. The distinction between substance and accidents is applied to *Deus est homo*, and this is found to be an accidental statement. Luther observed that this would permit of a transubstantiation.[35]

It is not possible to predicate the same of God and man. *Ergo etc.* Response: This is a philosophical argument. There is no proportion of creature and Creator, of finite and infinite. However, we do not so much make here a proportion as a unity of finite and infinite. If Aristotle were to hear the above argument, it would never make him into a Christian because he does not himself concede the aforesaid proportion because it is the same proportion of finite and infinite. [*WA* 39², 112.13.]

When Aristotle and Luther are comrades against the Occamists, then passing fair indeed is the damsel Dialectica, *divinitus data* [*WA* 39², 24.20; cf. *WA*, *Br* 9, 444.35]. The Occamist Christology that he opposes he sees as Eutychian and Docetic. Theirs is a Christ of glory like the Messiah of Glory, 'der Juden glauben'. He finds equivocation in the use of *homo*. That Peter is a man and Christ is a man are not univocal for them, and in *Deus est homo*, the term undergoes such qualification that in the end only the formal idea remains. 'All equivocation is the mother of errors.' They claim to unite philosophy and theology, but in matters of the faith they have to resort to equivocation.[36]

Does Luther do this with his Thesis 20 above? Schwartz comments as follows:

All predicates of creaturely being receive in Christ a new meaning. The creaturely being they refer to maintains in Christ its identity ... Words such as man, humanity, suffered and so on, become new words when they are spoken of Christ. They refer to the same thing as when not used of Christ, but now in a way that is new and different.[37]

In short, Schwartz makes much the same point as Pannenberg. The theologian does not simply set aside the distinctions of phil-

[35] See Reinhard Schwartz, 'Gott ist Mensch. Zur Lehre von der Person Christi bei den Ockhamisten und bei Luther', *ZTK* lxiii (1966), 325 f.
[36] *WA* 39², 36; 16. 24; 23. 13; 28. 28. Cf. Schwartz, p. 341.
[37] Op. cit., p. 334.

osophy; he pushes them further. If they break, they break. For
Luther, the gulf between God and man is, when he looks away
from Christ, even deeper than it is for the philosophers.[38] When
they get knotted up with terms he finds it helpful to point out that
it is the sentence which carries the meaning.[39] This he does with
the help of Aristotle. Aristotle speaks within the order of things
that he does, and this is not respected by the Occamists with their
resort to God's absolute power.

God's absolute power Luther has come to see more shatteringly
than they. They have somehow managed to fit it into their system.
Luther sees it in the dread and terror of the *Deus nudus*, the fearful
Majesty that can wipe us out, and before which we cannot stand.
In Christ the word God has a new meaning. 'The Son is the per-
fect image of God.' [*WA* 39², 23.33.]

The gulf between Creator and creature is joined in Christ, and
this can never be denied. That he is God may not be separated
from his being man, and one dare not speak of his being man apart
from his being God. Luther pushes further than the prepositions,
Cyril's ἐκ and Chalcedon's ἐν, to an *est*.

Christ according to his humanity is a creature and Christ according to his
divinity is God; they are so utterly conjoined that one person is two
natures.' [*WA* 39², 120.8.]

The human nature is not to be spoken of with the divinity excluded
from it. The humanity is not a person but a nature. The two natures are
distinct . . . That person who created in the beginning was made man. This
remains the same person. So very close are the humanity and divinity conjoined in Christ, as soul and body in man, that it is not possible to speak
concerning the natures as if they were divided from each other . . . I confess two natures, but they cannot be separated. This makes a unity greater
and more sure than the conjunction of soul and body. These are separated, but that conjunction never, for there are united in one person the
immortal divine nature and the mortal human nature. That is Christ, the
impassible son of God. God and man is crucified under Pontius Pilate.

Objection: What is immortal cannot become mortal. God is immortal.
Therefore he cannot become mortal.

Response: In philosophy that is true. [*WA* 39², 107.29, 101.4–102.8.]

---

[38] Ibid, p. 343.
[39] Cf. J. Barr, *The Semantics of Biblical Language* (Oxford, 1961), pp. 249 f.;
and Gordon Rupp, *The Righteousness of God* (London, 1953), pp. 81–101, esp.
novum et mirum vocabulum, p. 101.

The form of the syllogism may be the same in philosophy and theology, but the conclusions do not have equal standing. In philosophy man is *persona subsistens*, in theology the term used of Christ includes also his divinity. The words used by philosophy take on then a new meaning [WA 39², 22.7 and 34]. In every profession dialectic is a seeker of truth, but in theology a handmaid and servant [WA 39², 24.24 and 36]. Philosophy can never arrive at the Gospel; it operates in the realm of the Law. Philosophy and theology have diverse subject matter, *diversa, non contraria* [WA 39², 13.12.; cf. WA 39², 26.4 and 29.33]. Philosophy would lay necessity on God and so rob him of his freedom [WA 39², 9.9].

With such statements as the foregoing and the consequent communications of attributes Luther pushes the Personal Union so that there is no more 'trick, escape, way round or feinting possible'. This last was said to extol the ὁμοούσιος, and in opposition to the Nestorians. His defence against the Eutychian tendencies of the Occamists has already been noted. The traditional phrases 'according to his human nature' and 'according to his divine nature' Luther uses so that the distinction of the natures is not lost; but his usage of them has come free of the dualism which sees divine and human, heavenly and earthly, infinite and finite, impassible and passible, as opposites unreconcilable. They are if you look at God separately, and if you look at man separately, but in Christ this separation is gone. In Christ they have a new meaning; the old meaning applies only to them when separated. In speaking of him we may not speak of the divinity separated from the humanity, or of the humanity separated from the divinity. By such separation our Saviour and salvation are undone. *Extra Christum non est Deus alius*. For this reason Luther recoiled from Oecolampadius' suggestion at Marburg that he raise his thought up to the heavenly Christ. 'He neither knows nor worships any other God than him who became man. He would have no other apart from him, for there is no other who can save. Hence he could not bear that the humanity be treated as so little worth and cast aside' [WA 30³, 132. 23]. Words from a Christmas sermon of 1527 make the point:

He has power to cast us into hell and yet he took soul and body like ours... If he were against us he would not have clothed himself in our flesh... Here God is not to be feared but loved, and that love brings the joy of which the angel speaks... Satan, on the other hand, brings home to me the Majesty and my sin, and terrifies me so that I despair... But the

angel does not declare that he is in heaven... 'You shall find...' He
points out that he has come to us and put on our flesh and blood... Our
joy is not that we ascend and put on his nature as is the case when the
Mass is made a boastful decking of ourselves in divinity. Do not be driven
to distraction by the Majesty, but remain down here and listen, 'Unto you
a Saviour'. He does not come with horses but in a stable... Reason and
will would ascend and seek above, but if you would have joy, bend yourself down to this place. There you will find that boy given for you who is
your Creator lying in a manger. I will stay with that boy as he sucks, is
washed, and dies... There is no joy but in this boy. Take him away and
you face the Majesty which terrifies... I know of no God but this one in
the manger... Do not let yourself be turned away from this humanity...
What wonderful words (Col. 2. 9)! He is not only a man and a servant,
but that person lying in the manger is both man and God essentially, not
separated one from the other but as born of a virgin. If you separate them,
joy is gone. O Thou boy, lying in the manger, thou art truly God who
hast created me, and thou wilt not be wrathful with me because thou com-
est to me in this loving way—more loving cannot be imagined. If you
would truly love, let him be this way in your heart.

If you regard the boy according to the flesh, he means nothing to you; but
much, if this little Jesus is God and Saviour, acknowledged not according
to the flesh but in the flesh... Therefore, so that you do not scorn the
boy, give heed to the words of the boy that he is Lord and Saviour.[40]

Because people usually think of a creature as separate from the
Creator, which is not the case in Christ, Luther exhorts his students to use a certain caution, and he is not the first teacher who
'recks not his own rede'. There should be understanding, however,
as for Augustine when he is rather carried away and exclaims, 'Is
this not a wondrous mystery! He who is the Creator wished to be
a creature.' Luther says the holy Father is not to be condemned
because he was driven to speak that way by just too much joy [*WA*
39², 105.7].

Luther rests his case in 1528 with his *Large Confession* when he
thought he was like to die and 'appear before the judgement seat of
our Lord Jesus Christ'.

This man became true God, as one eternal, indivisible person, of God and
man, so that Mary the holy Virgin is real, true mother not only of the
man Christ, as the Nestorians teach, but also of the Son of God, as Luke

says [1.35], 'The child to be born of you will be called the Son of God',
i.e. my Lord and the Lord of all, Jesus Christ, the only, true Son by
nature of God and of Mary, true God and true man.

All men along with him [Adam] are born, live, and die altogether in sin,
and would necessarily be guilty of eternal death if Jesus Christ had not
come to our aid and taken upon himself this guilt and sin as an innocent
lamb, paid for us as a faithful, merciful Mediator, Saviour, and the only
Priest and Bishop of our souls.[41]

Before he died his pastor asked him whether he died trusting
only in Christ, and his last word was a firm 'yes'. The last words he
wrote, 'We are beggars; that is true' are important, for beggars live
only by what is given them, that is by faith *alone*. Faith's content
Luther never brought to more strong and simple expression than
in the explanation of the Second Article of the *Small Catechism*.

I believe that Jesus Christ, true God, begotten of the Father from eternity, and also true man, born of the Virgin Mary, is my Lord, who has re-
deemed me, a lost and condemned creature, purchased and won me from
all sins, from death, and from the power of the devil, not with gold or silver, but with his holy, precious blood and with his innocent suffering and
death, that I may be his own, and live under him in his kingdom, and serve
him in everlasting righteousness, innocence, and blessedness, even as he is
risen from the dead, lives and reigns to all eternity. This is most certainly
true.

[41] WA 26, 501.29–35; 502.26–34. LW 37, 362.

III

LUTHERUS

Luther and the Princes

*

MARTIN SCHWARZ LAUSTEN

LUTHER's view of princely rule must be considered against the background of his teaching on the two kingdoms through which God guides the world and rules his people.[1] This conception was not an original idea, for Luther built on an existing tradition; and the notion of the two kingdoms is to be found both in the New Testament, and in Augustine. It is true that in the Middle Age a dualist picture of the world prevailed, but the two 'arms' do fight one another, and are two forces within Christendom—the *societas Christiana*. The concept is thus one of power-sharing between *regnum* and *sacerdotium*; and Luther's innovation his understanding of the theological significance of the teaching of the two 'realms'. In particular, it must be emphasized that the Reformer does not produce a political or social doctrine. He concerns himself solely with the theological issue, as was his custom. His grasp of the problem is thus firmly connected with that counterweight in his theology—justification by faith. Just as a Christian can, at one and the same time be both righteous and a sinner, so too he belongs to both the sacred and secular realms. The two most important sources outlining Luther's ideas are his *Von weltlicher Obrigkeit, wie weit man ihr Gehorsam schuldig sei* (1523), and *Ob Kriegsleute auch in seligem Stande sein können* (1526) [*WA* 11, 230–80 and *WA* 19, 623–62]. The former is a classic published principally because the Saxon authorities had proscribed Luther's translation of the New Testament into German, even demanding that he surrender the edition. Then too, Luther had a sharp exchange of views with one of Germany's leading lawyers on the matter.

Luther wished to define the nature of authority, especially its limits, and asked fundamental questions about the relationship of Christianity to the secular power. He posed the problem by contrasting the ethics of non-violence preached in the Sermon on the Mount (Matt. 5: 39), with the necessity of secular power. In the

[1] A wide, representative range of the innumerable papers on this theme are collected in *Luther und die Obrigkeit*, ed. G. Wolf, *Wege der Forschung lxxxv (Darmstadt, 1972)*, and *Reich Gottes und Welt: Die Lehre Luthers von den zwei Reichen*, ed. H-H. Schrey, ibid., cvii (Darmstadt, 1969). Both contain detailed bibliographies.

first part of his book, Luther stated that authority was created by God to keep good order, peace, and to subdue evil persons. The Reformer rejected the medieval solution that the Sermon on the Mount failed to lay down unconditional commandments, but indicated instead 'directions' for the 'perfect', the commandments being thus applied to the 'imperfect'. In marked contrast, Luther made a sharp distinction between the kingdom of God and the kingdom of this world. Those who truly believe in Christ live in the kingdom of God and need neither the secular arm, nor secular laws. After all, the Holy Spirit lives in their heart, enlightens them, and keeps them from personal wrong-doing. He gives them love for all men, and makes them joyful and willing to accept any wrong done to them—even death at any hand. For if a man is willing to do only what is right, and simply to accept wrong, then there is neither strife, nor division, nor tribunal, nor judgement, nor punishment, nor law, nor sword. It is therefore unthinkable that the secular arm and the secular law can find work among Christians [WA 11, 250]. Why then must the Christian submit to lawful authority? It has to be because of love for his neighbour, and his readiness to protect that neighbour against wrong. But apart from this, a Christian should also be ready to co-operate positively in society. He can thus take on any work with a clear conscience, just as long as he has the necessary ability:

Therefore if you notice that an executioner, a courtier, a judge, a master, or a prince is needed, you must then offer yourself for such positions if you feel you are qualified. Otherwise the power of the state, which we cannot do without, will be respected less, and weaken or completely dissolve. There is certainly no doubt that the world cannot work without it. [WA 11, 255.]

Precisely because the power of the State is a servant of God, it exists for all to use. In fact, none in the service of the State is nearer to serving God than the Christian. It should therefore be understood that the sword is as important in the State as marriage, farming, or any other calling of God. Accordingly he who has reason to use power to punish evil in the service of the State also serves God. For his own sake, a Christian will gladly accept wrong done to him, but uses the sword in love for the sake of his neighbour. It is Luther's solution to the problem of combining the secular power with the commandments of the Sermon on the Mount. All those who are not Christians belong to the kingdom of this world—and this includes the vast majority of men since 'Christians are few and far between.' [*WA* 11, 251.] Directly corresponding to these two kingdoms, God has devised two rules, the spiritual and the secular. In the spiritual kingdom, Christ rules by the Holy Spirit alone, to make men righteous, and to save them in the eyes of God. And the secular rule seeks to control non-Christians so that, by evil deeds, they cannot cheat the pious and create chaos in life. Here laws, threats, and punishments are necessary, just as wild beasts have to be chained. But it is crucial to distinguish between the two rules.

At this point Luther makes reference to a twofold misunderstanding of lawful authority. The Catholic bishops, for example, should seek to rule the soul with the Word of God alone. They should proclaim the Word, but instead they observe secular rule and

. . . have become secular princes who rule with laws which are only concerned with life and property. They have turned everything upside down . . . Moreover it is impossible to find real faith and honesty among them, for they behave worse than robbers and highwaymen. Their secular rule has sunk to the same low ebb as that of bureaucratic tyrants; and that is why God has deranged their minds, so that they work back to front and want to rule spiritually over souls just as the others exercise secular rule. [*WA* 11, 265.]

This is Luther's argument in the second part of his work where he is particularly concerned with the limits of power and legal authority. Here too he established the purely secular task of such authority—namely to keep peace and order, to safeguard God's creation against evil and destruction, and to create peace necessary for men to lead their lives and enable the Gospel to be proclaimed. But authority of this kind should not be the responsibility of the Church as was the case in the Middle Age: it is the direct responsibility of God. In short, for Luther, the State is not completely secular as authority is established by God. Similarly, the spiritual sphere should steer clear of purely secular authority, as a rough, brutal world cannot be ruled by the Gospel and by love. For in the spiritual realm, faith, the Word, love, and forgiveness govern. Belief is a free and personal matter, and there is no room for force.

Table to show the main points of this relationship

	The Spiritual Realm	The Secular Realm
The Ruler:	God	God
How ruled?	By Word and Spirit. With neither force nor compulsion. *Hörreich.*	By sword, law, force, and punishment. *Tatreich.*
The aim:	The recreation of the relationship with God broken by sin in man. Forgiveness, faith & new life.	To sustain human society and prevent anarchy and chaos.
Its Concept of Justice:	The righteousness (*justitia*) of Christ is given to man who thus stands in the presence of God (*coram Deo*).	Social justice must prevail, if necessary by force. This is possible if all pursue their vocation before one another (*coram Hominibus*).
Who is included?	Only those to whom God gives faith through the Word.	All without exception. Here there is no equality as different offices are held in society.

Unity between the realms is achieved by the fact that both were created by God to be expressions of his dominion over mankind. The divine will to love works in both realms, albeit in different ways. Both realms coexist, and the Christian belongs to both. He must carry out the will of God, and is constantly confronted with new decisions of conscience. It is a situation that naturally prompts a whole series of questions, some of which demand analysis. What, for example, are the consequences for the individual of his duty to obey the secular authority?

In general a Christian must be subordinate to authority, and if it is evil and unjust, he must accept the fact and suffer accordingly. Self-sufficiency is an act of unbelief because it shows a lack of trust in God to maintain the order which he has himself created in the world. Nevertheless there is a limit to the duty of obedience, and the point Luther addresses here relates to his conviction that the secular authority can have no power over souls. It cannot force faith because belief is a matter of free will. In fact, faith is the work of God through the Holy Spirit, and a matter for the individual conscience. If an authority thus really tries to force men to adhere to certain beliefs, it will involve both lies and trickery [*WA* 11, 264]. In practice this means that if a prince demands loyalty to the Pope from his subjects, requires them to believe papal doctrine, and dispose of certain books, then this subjects must reply that Satan has no right to a position next to God!

It is my duty to obey you [the secular power] with life and property. Command me as far as your authority extends on earth, and I will obey. But if you command me in matters of faith, and order me to dispose of my books, then I will not obey because you have now gone too far and become a tyrant issuing demands in areas where you have neither right nor authority. [*WA* 11, 267.]

If the prince therefore punishes his subject for passive refusal to obey, the subject must needs accept the fact and suffer.

Both in his own day and later, Luther was criticized in some quarters for cringing and grovelling before his rulers. In actual fact, the Reformer's over-all view of secular authority set out in this work, and in a number of other tracts, gives a completely different and realistic picture.

You must be aware that, since the creation of the world, an astute prince has been a rare being, and a pious and just ruler even rarer. Usually they are the greatest idiots and the worst scoundrels on earth. One must therefore always expect the worst from them, and not hope for anything particularly good, above all in spiritual matters concerned with the soul's salvation. [*WA* 11, 267–8.]

Luther made similar remarks in a tract the following year, calling upon the city authorities to improve the educational system since the princes had neglected such affairs: 'The rulers and master should do this, but they are too busy going on sleigh rides, attending drinking parties and masquerades, and burdened with the great, important matters of cellar, kitchen and bedroom!' [*WA* 15, 45.]

Then too, how should heretical preaching be treated? Certainly not by the use of violence in the manner of the Catholic Church, for heresy is a spiritual matter. As such it should be dealt with by the Church, and not secular rulers, for 'heresy is a spiritual matter which can in no way be defeated with weapons, burnt with fire or drowned with water.' The Reformer is clear that 'God's Word alone can do it', because that Word 'enlightens the heart, and in consequence all kinds of heresy disappears of its own accord.' [*WA* 11, 268–9.] It should, however, be noted that Luther was later to have difficulties of his own putting such theory into practice.

In the third section of the book, Luther considers the question of princely use of secular power, and it is important to note that he avoids suggesting how rulers should conduct affairs of state. For Luther is a theologian, not a constitutional theorist, economist, or politician, and as such he only wants to guide the 'hearts' of the princes and help them to live as Christians. The Reformer nevertheless shows a healthy scepticism because, although he does not deem it impossible for a prince to be a Christian, he finds it exceptional and notes that 'a prince is a rare bird in heaven.' [*WA* 11, 273.] How, for example, can a prince go dancing, hunting, or racing without causing his people suffering? [*WA* 11, 274.] In short, for Luther, a godly prince should show a good example in four principal respects. First, he should serve God with sincere trust and persevere in prayer; secondly, he should consider his subjects in love and Christian service; thirdly, he should value his advisers and magnates with independent judgement and understanding; and lastly, he should deal with evil-doers firmly and without hesitation.

It is intriguing to note that, in these suggestions, Luther commends common sense and love to the prince. He does not simply quote Scripture at him. A specific point later to become the subject of much debate was the mention Luther made of the prince's attitude to war. Can a prince lead his people to war? and are his subjects obliged to follow him in such a violent recourse? Briefly, Luther's attitude observed three basic conditions. First of all, war against the head of State, the emperor, or king, is forbidden, because force may not be used against lawful authority. Recourse to suffering is the only way out. Yet secondly, a war between equals is permitted if an offer of peace has been refused. In the third place, if a subject's own prince is clearly in the wrong, any command to take part in war should go unheeded because no man should act unjustly [*WA* 11, 276–8].

In the tract, *Ob Kriegsleute auch in seligem Stande sein können* (1527), Luther treats such topics, likewise distinguishing between three kinds of war. First, in the case of a war between two evenly-matched states, the power taking the initiative is in the wrong. In other words, a war of defence is possible, but no war can be embarked upon if the prince is in the wrong. Luther adduces Acts 5: 29 as relevant, urging obedience to God rather than to man. Secondly, a state can conduct a war against its subjects if they are in rebellion. But thirdly, no subject may involve himself in a war against those in authority, for this is rebellion and cannot be allowed when God has himself permitted the authority to rule. Indeed, a prince can only be removed in a single instance—namely when he is of unsound mind 'for in that case you can no longer consider him a human being, for he has lost his sense.' [*WA* 19, 634.] Luther imagines his reader may object and argue that a tyrannical prince can behave with such cruelty that he can be declared insane. Are subjects therefore bound to accept all the evil such a tyrant can inflict on their wives, children, life, and property? In his answer, Luther is adamant that authority should not be resisted because it comes from God. Subjects must not act as judges, for God himself has his own way of punishing the tyrant, for example, through violent death, or by means of a rebellion brought against him by non-Christians—in such a case themselves used as divine instruments. Offering an example of an unjust revolt against a prince, Luther cites the Danish rebellion against Christian II. It is an illustration that will receive further comment in due course. War must serve to ensure law and order. So it is rightly God who acts, not the people. The brutal and bloody craft of the soldier Luther thus deems to be an 'office' or 'station' in life in the same way as, for example, the estate of marriage or the role of a judge. At the end of the tract, too, he touches on a series of problems facing the soldier. It is, for example, the task of the fighting man to refuse obedience if he is convinced that his prince is conducting an unjust war. The job of a soldier should in any case only be accepted because God commands it, and not undertaken for any personal gain. That is why the fighting man should pray to God immediately before battle commences, and act throughout as a Christian. For he can then join battle with a clear conscience.

As has now been shown, Luther's views on the two realms have an important relationship to stewardship in the Church; and naturally enough it is also linked to his definition of the nature of the Church. The Reformer's idea of the Church cut the clergy down to size. For wherever the Gospel is proclaimed and the sacraments duly administered, wherever Christ is in communion with his people in Word or sacrament, and wherever the faithful are called to commune with him—there is the Church as the body of Christ. This Church is invisible; its belief is invisible; but it expresses itself in outward forms, and this is also a visible Church. The specific Catholic view of the official structure, in which the Church cannot function without a properly ordained priest, is thus rejected. All Christians belong to the ranks of the 'clergy', but for the sake of order and reason, a congregation delegates the task of proclaiming the Gospel and administering the sacraments to the person most fitted for the task; and this minister is the servant of his congregation.

For whoever has been baptized can already commend himself as a consecrate priest, bishop or pope, even if not everyone is well suited to hold such office ... That is why the position of the priest in Christendom can only be an official one. While he is in office, he is the leader; but when he is out of office, he is a peasant or a citizen like everyone else. So the truth is that a priest is no longer a priest when dismissed ... likewise those we call clergy or priests, bishops or popes today are not set apart from other Christians, nor do they have a greater value except for their stewardship of the Word of God, and the sacraments, according to their duty and vocation. [*WA* 6, 408–9.]

But who then should rule the Church since the clergy has lost its privilege and power and is merely the servant of the congregation? Who should choose and install priests and bishops? How should a man ensure that the tidings of reformation are spread? The abolition of canon law ended the idea of the Church as a legal institution, and deprived it of an effective means of restraint. But how in future should the Church defend its rights and economic possessions? By what authority can Church organization be determined and laid down in territories owning the Reformation?

At first, Luther put all his hopes in the power inherent in the proclamation of the Word. No force would be necessary, and the congregation—a voluntary union of believers—would sort out practical problems for themselves. The practical organization of Church affairs Luther felt, on the whole, to be of no great importance. He certainly did not think that uniformity was necessary. But these ideas had to be revised. The ability of the congregation, for example, soon proved to be completely inadequate; and even the proclamation of the Gospel itself did not bear the fruit Luther imagined. In fact, it rapidly became necessary to keep a close eye on congregations, pastors and Church property. The behaviour of the radicals (Luther's 'fanatics') made this essential, just as the rising of 1525, when the peasants pleaded the Gospel and 'Christian freedom' in a political and social protest, embarrassed the cause and proved fatal for the Reformer. The peasants revolted against authority and confounded the two realms. They wanted to be their own judges, and after warning both princes and peasants in vain, Luther sided with authority. It certainly seems that he called upon princes to use completely harsh and unrestrained methods to defeat the peasants:

. . . stab, beat, slay now whoever you can! If you die in the process, happy are you! A more blessed death can never be, for you die in obedience of God's Word and commandments, Romans xiii., and in the service of love to save your neighbour from the chains of hell and the devil. So I ask you all to avoid the peasants as you would the devil himself! [WA 18, 361.]

Among the many consequences of the Peasants' Revolt, an unbridgeable gap between Luther and the radicals became clear to all. But it was equally important that the Reformation ceased to be a popular movement. The peasants felt Luther had let them down; and Luther lost his own trust in the ability of the common man— *Herr Omnes* as he henceforth called him. Likewise, the Reformer now stressed even more strongly than before the duty of obedience to secular authority, urging that 'the donkey must be beaten, and the mob ruled by force'. And again, 'God knew this, and that is why he did not hand authority a fox's tail, but a sword to hold.' [WA 18, 394.]

But it should also be emphasized that Luther's critical view of the princes in no way diminished. Quite the contrary in fact, for he already knew the Christian prince to be a rare animal, and the war had unmistakably shown him that among the ranks of the princes there were

. . . wild, uncontrollable, insane tyrants who, even after battle, cannot have enough blood-letting, and who throughout life have not the least concern for Christ . . . Such bloodhounds do not care if they kill the guilty or the innocent, or whether it pleases God or the devil . . . these scoundrels are pigs . . . [WA 18, 400.]

Nevertheless, princes must be honoured and obeyed, because of the office to which God has raised them.

In the matter of Church government, Luther had to surrender the voluntary principle, and appealed for help to the local prince. Already, several years earlier, in company with other baptized Christians, he had called on the princes to reform the Church when the bishops had failed to do so. His argument at the time was that secular authority had a duty to protect subjects against the evil, exploitation, and harm which useless bishops had done to their souls. [*WA* 6, 409.] But now he proposed that the godly prince of Scripture was in duty bound to create conditions favourable to the Church. For, he reasoned, the Church needed the backing of authority if it was to spread the true Gospel of Christ, to create uniformity of worship, and defend itself against those who would usurp its estates and property. The point Luther made is important, for in this instance he urged the prince to help as a Christian brother. In short, Luther by no means held it to be part of the princely duty to exercise authority over the Church. But whenever the Church finds itself in a state of distress, the prince's help is necessary, although that should not be understood to mean that the secular power should therefore involve itself in matters pertaining to spiritual rule. Luther expressed this clearly to his own magistrate, the Prince Elector of Saxony, when he agreed to such co-operation: 'For although, Most Honourable Elector, you have not been commanded to practise spiritual rule, as the secular authority you nevertheless have a duty to make sure that dissension, riot, and rebellion does not break out among your subjects.' [*WA* 26, 195.]

In Electoral Saxony, an inquiry was thus begun. The members of the commission—Melanchthon, a professor of law, and two members of the Council—had to investigate the salaries of the clergy, inquire into moral conduct, and assess the teaching of biblical doctrine to the congregations, as well as consider matrimonial affairs. They were given instruction from the prince as the secular authority, and were dispatched as his officials. In such a way the movement against the *Landesherrliche Kirchenregiment* was first started. The princes were given an inch, but soon took a yard; for it cannot seriously be in doubt that the widespread establishment of the *Obrigkeitskirche* was far from Luther's thoughts. A large share of the responsibility for such development thus rests with

Melanchthon who, as a humanist, held it to be the duty of a prince to care for the salvation of the souls of his subjects. Indeed, for Melanchthon, *cura religionis* was the primary task of authority.[2]

Some insight into Luther's role as an advisor to the princes is of interest. It will come as no surprise that, because of the special authority he enjoyed, Luther found himself overwhelmed with letters from princes, magistrates, institutions, and private individuals. Indeed, much of his time was involved in correspondence—far too much, as he was already complaining by 1516. After the Diet of Worms (1521), his correspondence grew to enormous proportions, and when in 1529 a friend complained that the Reformer took a long time to reply to his letter, he was told not to express surprise as his correspondent was daily so inundated with letters, requests, complaints, and petitions for prayer that they lay everywhere in his home, on tables, benches, stools, desks, and windowsills! And on another occasion, Luther wrote that he could have filled an entire house with the letters he had received [*WA, TR* 3, No. 3472].

The Weimar edition contains fourteen volumes of Luther's correspondence, and includes almost 3,700 items of which there are about 2,650 letters and reports from the Reformer's own pen. Much has also been lost, especially letters sent to Luther who was never particularly careful about their safe keeping. About half of the correspondence extant to 1530 was addressed to close friends; and about a third was sent to secular authorities. But in the period after 1530, there is a marked shift of emphasis, almost half the letters going to secular authorities. The most frequent recipients were naturally Luther's rulers, the Princes of Saxony. To Friedrich der Weise (Elector from 1486 to 1525), there were 32 letters; to Johann (Elector, 1525 to 1532), 114 letters; and to Johann Friedrich (Elector, 1532 to 1546), 165 letters.[3] Other princes who regularly received letters from Luther included Duke Albrecht of Prussia, Count Georg of Brandenburg–Ansbach, Duke Philip of Hesse, Joachim II, Elector of Brandenburg, and the Princes of Anhalt. Among foreign correspondents mention can be made of the Danish King, Christian III. A great many letters also found

---

[2] J. Heckel, *Lex caritatis. Eine juristische Untersuchung über das Recht in der Theologie Martin Luthers* (Martin Heckel, Köln and Wien, 1973).

[3] Karl Trüdinger, *Luthers Briefe und Gutachten an weltliche Obrigkeiten zur Durchführung der Reformation*, Reformationsgesch. Studien u. Texte (Münster, 1975), iii, 5.

their way to city authorities—there are, for example, 132 letters and reports for 54 different cities. The range of subject-matter in the letters is naturally very wide. There are pleas beseeching Luther to ask secular authorities for economic aid, or for help with local administration; there are reports of pastoral appointments and matrimonial matters; and there are opinions on Reformation achievements and university affairs. In his book on Luther's letters to secular authorities, Karl Trüdinger concludes that Luther generally had reservations about entering into any detailed correspondence.[4] His letters were first and foremost replies, and strange to relate he did not use them as propaganda to further the cause of the Reformation. He kept to the issue his correspondent raised with him (in marked contrast to Calvin in similar circumstances), and he did not feel his advice had any wider application. Thus Luther by no means gave dogmatic directions, but rather discussed specific circumstances with the result that his answers only had validity for a single situation.

For the present purpose, Luther's role as a kind of political advisor to the princes is of particular interest. It is a subject with which Professor Kurt Aland concerned himself in *Luther als Staatsbürger* (1960). Later, in 1977, Dr Erich Wolgast published a careful analysis of the same subject.[5] But what right did Luther have to express his thoughts and opinions on political matters to the princes? First and foremost, it should be stressed that any Church matter in Reformation Germany was *ipso facto* a political matter, and vice versa. Religion and politics was closely intertwined both directly and indirectly. Nevertheless, it should be more widely appreciated that Luther never saw himself as a political figure *per se* when asked for an opinion by one of the princes. Rather did he assume that he was approached in his pastoral capacity, and his replies always evidence the inspiration that results from much soul-searching. It was certainly the conscience of the prince he sought to advise. Yet did not this action of the Reformer conflict with his doctrine of the two kingdoms? The answer must be in the negative, because in

[4] Ibid., 13.
[5] E. Wolgast, *Die Wittenberger Theologie und die Politik der evangelischen Stände. Studien zu Luthers Gutachten in politischen Fragen*, Bd. XLVII, Quellen u. Forschungen z. Reformationsgesch. (Gütersloh, 1977). Cf. Martin Schwarz Lausten, *Religion og politik. Studier i Christian III's forhold til det tyske rige i tiden, 1544–1559*, mit deutscher Zusammenfassung (København, 1977), p. 11.

Luther's view God commanded the authorities to make sure that peace and order prevailed. Accordingly any attempts at disturbance must be seen as rebellion against the divine order, and any conflict set in a theological context. Luther derived his duty to express a theological opinion in such matters from the *Letter* of Paul the Apostle to Timothy (I Tim. 2: 1 f.). After all, it was the preacher's task to proclaim the Word of God, and to see that the Lord's commandments were obeyed. To do this he must admonish and comfort, and show how the Christian message of love can survive in the secular realm. Luther was not quite sure of his ground here, and on one celebrated occasion wrote as much in a terse aside to Elector Johann: 'It is not for me to be concerned with the affairs of secular government . . .'.[6]

Luther naturally had most contact with his local rulers, the Prince Electors of Saxony. Friedrich der Weise was Elector until 1525, and throughout his life behaved in a distant, formal, and non-committal way towards the Reformation in his territories. Despite such an attitude, however, he used his political position to bring Luther under safe-conduct for interrogation before the Diet of Worms in 1521. This was against normal practice, and when Luther came under the Imperial Ban, his Elector refused to hand him over to the authorities for punishment. Friedrich even ignored appeals from the Emperor himself. Electoral pride in his new University of Wittenberg, where the Reformer was such a strength to his faculty, naturally played its part; but at the same time, for political reasons, Friedrich consciously desisted from showing Luther and the Reformation any partiality. Yet if he remained neutral in the formal sense, he nevertheless benefited and helped to forward that Reformation by his very inactivity! It was an attitude that, on the whole, Luther respected. The two men never exchanged a single word, and probably only saw one another at the Diet of Worms in 1521; all the same their relationship was in no way indifferent in nature but quite the contrary. Friedrich thus asked Luther to write *Adventspostille*; presented his personal friends with Luther's tracts; and received a letter of sympathy from Luther when he fell ill in 1519. For his part, too, Luther had only praise for the Elector. Nevertheless it is interesting to note that on several occasions

---

[6] 'Ich sol und will nicht mich des weltlichen Regiments annemen', cf. *WA, Br* 6, 122.

Luther acted directly contrary to the hesitant politics of his prince.[7] For example, after his condemnation by the Diet, Luther was removed to a place of safety in the Wartburg palace. His prince was secretly behind this, but while Luther was there, the events in Wittenberg took a serious turn. In their zeal for reform, radical elements created much confusion, unrest, and the danger of riot. Called on by the congregation, Luther decided to return to restore peace, and intimated as much to his prince. Friedrich, however, already under considerable political pressure because of the Reformation, could not allow any such compromise of his formal lack of commitment in religious matters. His hostile cousin, the confirmed Catholic Duke Georg, had succeeded both in preventing the abolition of the monasteries and in prohibiting the previously promoted reform of the Mass. As an outlaw, Luther would thus place himself in personal jeopardy by returning to Wittenberg, and many would hold Friedrich responsible. With military confrontation with the Emperor likewise a possibility, the Elector thus asked Luther to abandon the idea, but at the same time sought the Reformer's advice, a fundamental lack of assurance prompting him to avoid any act against the will of God. Yet he stressed the terrible political consequences of Luther's return, particularly underlining the harm it could have on the whole population of Ernestine Saxony. In his famous reply of 5 March 1522— 'eine der herrlichsten, die er geschrieben hat' (Heinrich Born- kamm)—Luther wrote with all the self-confidence complete trust in God gave him. He was convinced that his course was the will of God, and that in consequence, Friedrich's political doubts should give way.

As far as my course is concerned, my gracious lord, I will answer as follows. Your serene highness knows, or if you do not, then hear now, that the Gospel has come to me not from people, but from heaven alone, through our Lord Jesus Christ . . . I therefore go to Wittenberg with greater security than a prince can. I do not seek protection from your highness—indeed, I believe I can protect you better than you can protect me . . . for a sword can neither rule, nor should it rule to help this cause. For this one God alone must solve, without any human anxiety or exertion. Therefore he who is the strongest believer will receive most protection; and as I

[7] Heinrich Bornkamm, *Luther und sein Landesherr Kurfürst Friedrich*, Schriften d. Vereins f. Reformationsgesch. Nr. 188 (Gütersloh, 1975), pp. 33–8.

assume your royal highness is still a rather weak believer, I can in no circumstances consider you to be the man to protect or save me. [*WA, Br 2,* 455.]

Luther saw the work of the Devil behind the unrest at Wittenberg, as indeed behind the work of Duke Georg. He therefore had to return, and as he felt unable to accede to Friedrich's request, he exonerated his prince from all responsibility should he be caught and made to suffer. It is interesting to study Luther's attitude to the secular authority in such a concrete case. He knew he owed obedience to the prince, mentioning it himself and expressing a deep sense of loyalty to his ruler. All the same, however, the Reformer remained convinced that his duty to show obedience had been overruled by a more important commandment that he obey God rather than man. 'Gott zwingt und ruft.' [*WA, Br 2,* 460–1.] And Luther firmly believed his action to be in accordance with the will of God. Then too, Friedrich had asked how he should behave if the Emperor arrested Luther or demanded his surrender. Luther declared that Friedrich, as a Saxon Prince, was subordinate to the Emperor—he actually referred to the Imperial constitution!—so that the prince should show obedience to the Emperor. In short, the Reformer clearly denied Friedrich the right to resist if the Emperor chose to arrest and execute Luther. He did so because the Emperor, as the highest secular authority, was installed directly by God. To resist him thus amounted to defiance of God himself, for God could, if he wished, easily intervene with the Emperor direct. Luther did, however, qualify his case, adding that Friedrich was only obliged to render a certain measure of obedience, as if, for example, he were to open the gates to the Imperial envoys and afford them safe conduct when they came to seize Luther. For 'then your royal highness has shown sufficient obedience'. Luther was clearly of the opinion that the prince need not feel obliged to arrest him on his own account, but he did not expand the point. He merely promised to render further advice should it become necessary. As for the prince's political problems, Luther argued from a religious base and referred to his conviction that God would intervene on his side. He also concluded a letter on this subject to the prince with these words: 'If your Grace could believe, then you would see the glory of God; but because you do not yet believe, you have seen nothing yet. God be loved and praised for ever. Amen.' [*WA, Br 2,* 457.]

Political developments after the meetings of the Diet at Speyer (1526) allowed the Lutheran Reformation scope to spread in German territories but this advance was halted by a majority decision at the next Diet in 1529. The evangelical princes made their celebrated 'protest' on both legal and religious grounds, but the situation worsened and, expecting to be attacked by the Catholic opposition, they were obliged seriously to consider joint defence proposals. Once more, questions both of the right to oppose the Emperor, and the right to resort to arms for the sake of belief and conscience, became live issues. Landgrave Philip of Hesse in particular worked hard actively to forward the Protestant cause, and planned a great coalition against the Emperor in which Zwingli and his followers were to participate. Luther and the Wittenberg theologians were naturally involved in such deliberations at a critical stage for the whole evangelical movement. As soon as he heard of the plans, in fact, Luther went uninvited to his prince, the Elector Johann, and attempted to dissuade him from such a course. He believed it would be an expression of distrust in God; just as it would be wrong to enter into a political coalition with those who, through their heretical doctrines of the eucharist, showed themselves to be enemies of God and his Word. But Luther also offered political counsel as, so he held, the evangelical cause was in no real danger for the time being. A fundamental part of Luther's argument, moreover, was his strong opposition to Landgrave Philip's activist policy. The Reformer clung to such fundamental perception for some time, urging that, even if the Emperor were to attack the evangelicals with military force, it would be wrong to take up arms against him. For was not Charles V the highest secular authority set over evangelical subjects so that God might yet intervene and alter the Emperor's view?[8]

During and after the Diet of Augsburg (1530), however, Luther changed his view. The evangelical politicians were unwilling to accept these negotiations, and the princes' lawyers were now of the opinion that the duty of obedience to the Emperor had, in certain circumstances, to be qualified, even, at times like these, abolished! For any attack by the Emperor on evangelicals holding Lutheran beliefs would be unjust and without legal basis. The Emperor was not competent to judge matters of faith; and the

[8] *WA, Br* 5, 20.

princes were not merely Imperial subjects, but also authorities in their own right and as such responsible for the salvation of their subjects' souls. They were thus entirely correct in their resort to arms. In other words, Luther had thought the whole problem through again and changed his mind! Until now, he had been of the opinion that it was merely a matter concerned with conscience and religion; but now he capitulated to the politicians, convinced as he was that it was right in the circumstances to offer resistance to the Emperor. But he was also clear that the question of the right to resistance should be left to the lawyers and politicians. In 1531, the League of Schmalkalden was formed as a Protestant military and political alliance founded in the Lutheran doctrines of the *Confessio Augustana*. Its leaders were Landgrave Philip of Hesse, and the Elector Johann of Saxony. The movement soon became important and politically powerful, not least because foreign princes— among them those of England, France, and Denmark—negotiated association. However, the League was the result of more than merely religiously motivated politics, and must be seen as part of the opposition of the German princes to. Imperial power as a whole.[9]

Prominent among foreign monarchs, King Henry VIII of England was a most bitter foe of Martin Luther. The two had a strange relationship, but one that is of value to the Reformation scholar because of the way it illustrates links between religion and politics in Luther's attitude to princely power, his view of the place of the Church in society, and his understanding of the relation between faith and politics. The incident likewise shows how the princes could use Luther to further their political ambitions.[10] Luther's works were beginning to be read seriously in England from about 1520–1521. In Cambridge's so-called 'Little Germany' a new group led by Robert Barnes was deeply concerned with the new divinity, and already by May 1521, Thomas, Cardinal Wolsey had directed the public burning of the Wittenberg Reformer's

---

[9] Heinz Scheible, *Das Widerstandsrecht als Problem der deutschen Protestanten 1523–1546*, Texte zur Kirchen- und Theologiegeschichte 10 (Gütersloh, 1969); and Ekkehart Fabian, *Die Entstehung des Schmalkaldischen Bundes und seiner Verfassung 1529–1531/33* (Tübingen, 1962).

[10] Cf. G. R. Elton, *Reform and Reformation: England 1509–1558* (London, 1977); J. J. Scarisbrick, *Henry VIII* (London, 1968); and Erwin Doernberg, *Henry VIII and Luther: An Account of their Personal Relations* (Stanford, 1961).

writings. Such action made England one of the first countries to
try to eradicate the Lutheran heresy so dramatically, Henry VIII
in person taking much interest in developments. In April 1521, the
King's Secretary had seen Henry read Luther's *De captivitate
babylonica*, the Reformer's sharpest attack on the Catholic doctrines of the sacraments up to that date. The king admitted he was
busy writing a refutation of the work, and this was actually
published shortly afterwards under the title *Assertio septem sac-
ramentorum adversus Martinum Lutherum* (1521). At first there
was some debate about the authorship of the book, but a convincing case has now been made that it was in fact written by the king,
although revised by Thomas More. Henry VIII attacks Luther for
being an immoral heretic whose erroneous teachings must stem
from the fact that he has fallen away from God. The king is convinced that Luther will very soon deny the presence of Christ's
body and blood in the sacrament of the altar, as too that he will
dismiss baptism completely. The book caused a sensation, and few
members of royal houses showed such loyalty to the Pope in this
period as Henry did in writing the work. A publishing success,
moreover, the *Assertio* had already appeared in two German editions by the following year. And it was entirely characteristic that
Duke Georg of Albertine Saxony, another bitter enemy of Martin
Luther, ordered one such edition and dedicated it to the Duchess
Barbara. As the translator Hieronymus Emser wrote in the foreword, 'Nobody has protected our holy faith, the mass, indulgences and all other sacraments so powerfully, or defended them in
such magisterial terms against Luther, as the King of England
....'.[11] The Pope rewarded the king at once with the title *Defensor
Fidei*, his action greatly gratifying Henry.

The *Assertio* itself naturally brought a sharp reaction from
Luther, his answer *Contra Henricum Regem Angliae* (1522) being
unusually harsh in tone and completely lacking in respect for a
royal opponent. Luther, for example, did not shrink from referring
to 'Henry, by God's disgrace, King of England', the tract likewise
containing many attacks of a personal nature on the monarch. In
particular, the title the Pope had bestowed on Henry came in for
frequent attack from the Reformer. 'The papist Church, which
forsakes God and denies Christ, has to have such a protector! But

[11] Doernberg, op.cit., p. 26.

the Christian Church does not care about the scorn and blasphemy
it suffers when a human being is made its protector. Rather will it
sing [Ps. 118: 9.]: "It is better to trust in the Lord than to have
confidence in princes." [WA 10², 228.] As Luther states in his introduction, the King, like many others, has not grasped the difference between the authority of the Word and mere tradition in the
Catholic Church. The Reformer certainly denies that he has
changed his own viewpoint over the years, and goes on to explain
his faith and practice and to show that the teaching of Rome on
papal power, the Mass, and purgatory actually contradicts Scripture. He then accuses Henry VIII of being a swollen-headed fool
and a stupid liar whose use of language is more poisonous than
that of any prostitute. Of the rules of debate, the English king has
not the slightest idea; and his book is so stupid it might well have
been written by an enemy using the royal name just to bring him
annoyance! It was no wonder that, albeit in times accustomed to
vicious polemic, the opinion was widely held that Luther had gone
too far. Even the Reformer felt some anxiety, although he had no
regrets about a matter far too important to be toned down. At the
end of the book he thus delivered himself of an *apologia* that gave
nothing away.

... if my severity and violence towards the king offends any man, let
him hear this in reply: ... my book deals with wild, senseless monsters
who have despised whatever I argue, and my writing was conducted in
calm and moderate tones. ... I have certainly abstained from the poisonous slanders and lies that abound in the *Assertio*.

Henry VIII did not pursue the controversy further himself. Instead, he tried to persuade the German princes to put a stop to
the Lutheran movement, and instructed John Fisher, Bishop of
Rochester, and Thomas More to refute Luther's theology.

The affair had a sequel well described in words of Dr Erwin
Doernberg:

Some time during the year 1525, [the] exiled king [Christian II of
Denmark] wrote a letter either to the Elector Frederick or to Spalatinus—
he knew Luther and his circle personally, having lived at Wittenberg for a
time during the beginning of his exile—to pass to the Lutherans the information that Henry VIII of England had come to be 'inclined towards
the Gospel'. He suggested that Luther should approach the English King
with an apology which would be received most graciously. Now, Spalati-

nus had been among those of Luther's friends who had taken a critical view of Luther's rude reply to Henry VIII's book. It was he who told the news to Luther. The latter was quite sceptical of Henry's alleged change of convictions, but Spalatinus managed to persuade him to write out a sketch for a conciliatory letter.[12]

It was a great surprise, for in a humble, even submissive, tone Luther told Henry (1 September 1525) that he was ready publicly to retract, and to apologize for his book. He rejoiced that the Tudor king was inclined to the Gospel, and much regretted that, in the past, evil advisors had made Henry write against him. The Reformer then warned the English king of such poisonous and hypocritical counsellors, and hoped that Henry could fall in with the evangelical Lutheran princes who were convinced of the truth of the Gospel. Luther's letter was a fatal mistake. He had been misadvised; Christian II's report was false; and Henry VIII quick to take advantage of such ready-made propaganda! His royal prestige had received a considerable boost, and he made sure that the sharp dismissive reply he wrote by return was published alongside Luther's letter. Translation and publication in German followed and polemical war raged. In *A Copy of the Letters wherein the most redoubted and mighty Prince our souerayne lorde kynge Henry the eighth ... made answere vnto a certayne letter of Martyn Luther* (1528), Henry rejected the main point of Luther's theology in the theory of justification. He also attacked Luther's reforms, defended Thomas, Cardinal Wolsey, and portrayed the Reformer as a sensual heretic damning him out of hand for entering the married state: '... ye beyng a Frere haue taken a Nonne & not onely vyolate her ... but also which mouche worse it haue openly maried her & by that menes openly abused her in synne.'

The renewed conflict between Henry VIII and Luther had dire consequences for the 'new religion' and its supporters in England, although a tenuous link between Henry VIII and Luther was at least resumed. Because, for instance, the English King sought a 'divorce' from Queen Katherine of Aragon which the Pope was unwilling to grant for political and personal reasons, Henry was glad to have Luther's views on the matter! The Reformer sent his opinion in a most lengthy letter addressed to Robert Barnes as an

[12] Doernberg, op.cit., pp. 49–50.

intermediary. In this communication of 5 September 1531, Luther took strong exception to the idea of 'divorce' as that would contravene the Law of Moses. Indeed, the Reformer used the opportunity of discussing the implications of the problem for Christians, hoping that his letter would prevent the English king and queen from falling into 'that godless and illegal divorce which will only serve to give them a guilty conscience for evermore'. Badly bruised by the recent brawl, moreover, Luther was naturally sceptical of the royal reaction. 'It may well be possible', he wrote, 'that hatred of my name will lead to a rejection of my verdict, however sound my judgement in the matter.'

At the time, Henry VIII was actively engaged in forging links with the German Protestant princes, whose defensive alliance—the League of Schmalkalden—had by this time become an important political factor in Europe. Luther again became involved, and gave it as his view that, should Henry now join the evangelical cause, 'provided that his Royal Majesty is truly earnest', it would greatly harm the Catholics. Although remaining somewhat sceptical, the Reformer was thus overjoyed to sense God's intervention. Rumours of the execution of Bishop Fisher and Sir Thomas More certainly shocked the Germans, but negotiations between them and Henry continued, and in January 1533 an English delegation arrived in Wittenberg to meet Luther and other members of the theological faculty, having already had political discussions with some of the German princes.

A serious problem was posed by Henry's lack of commitment to the cause. Was it possible to make a military and political alliance without his making some kind of assurance to the Lutherans? For several months such theological issues were discussed between the two parties in Wittenberg, but without any agreement. For it was Luther's firm conviction that political factors had to yield before religious considerations. If Henry VIII did not wish to accept the faith, there should be no political alliance. The Wittenberg negotiations accordingly broke down. But a Lutheran delegation to London was no more successful, and with the publication of the *Six Articles* by Henry VIII in 1539, theological agreement was out of the question. For his part, too, Luther was clear that he had seen through Henry VIII. That he certainly condemned the King severely is apparent from an extract from the *Tischreden* where the Reformer is on record as thanking God

... for having delivered us from this exasperating King of England who, though he eagerly sought a treaty with our princes, was not‧himself acceptable. No doubt God's special counsel prevented it, for [the king] has always been inconsistent and uncertain. He wants to be the head of the Church in England, immediately under Christ ...

The following year too, Luther seriously warned the Elector, Johann Friedrich, against having anything to do with Henry, for 'the King is a tempter, and means nothing sincerely ... Gold and money make him so frivolous that he thinks he is worthy of adoration, and indeed that God cannot manage without him.'

Luther developed a special and very close relationship with Christian II and Christian III of Denmark.[13] Christian II, who shocked Europe by permitting, in defiance of an amnesty, the execution of about eighty people, some of them clergy, in the so-called 'Stockholm bloodbath' of 1520, concerned himself a great deal with contemporary thought. In February, 1520, he thus prohibited the publication of the papal bull against Luther; and during a conversation with the great Erasmus that same year apparently expressed most positive and warm views of the Wittenberg Reformer. Some plans for law reform clearly show Christian II's humanitarian tendencies, a sympathy also revealed in his endeavours to improve academic standards in the University of Copenhagen. The King summoned learned men, among them Karlstadt, from Wittenberg; and when Karlstadt returned to Saxony after only a few weeks, the rumour spread that Melanchthon, and perhaps even Luther himself, were to come to Denmark. Yet despite such concerns, it seems likely that Christian II merely showed the interest of a typical humanist towards the Scriptures; for after his expulsion from Denmark, the various visits he made to Wittenberg were largely concerned with attempts to raise money and troops for the reconquest of his former kingdom. For example, he also turned in his misfortune to the Emperor Charles V (the brother of his Queen, Elizabeth), to the Elector Friedrich der Weise (an uncle on his mother's side), to the English king, and to the Protestant princes. When in Wittenberg in 1523, he stayed at the house of Lucas Cranach, and on one occasion gave a gold ring to a servant girl. That girl was Katherine von Bora, later to be Luther's wife!

[13] Cf. E. H. Dunkley, *The Reformation in Denmark* (London, 1948); Georg Schwaiger, *Die Reformation in den nordischen Ländern* (München, 1962); and P. G. Lindhardt, *Den Danske Kirkes Historie* (København, 1965), iii, 105–433.

Christian was certainly much taken with Luther's preaching, a letter he wrote at this time bearing the heading from 'the Holy City of Wittenberg'. Whilst in Wittenberg, the exiled monarch engaged two men to translate the New Testament into Danish. Their work— a rushed job of poor linguistic merit—was completed about the beginning of September 1524, and various sections were dispatched in secret to Denmark without delay. The *Preface* suggests that the translation was to serve as political propaganda for the royal exile, and in consequence the Danish Parliament banned both written and spoken Lutheran heresy. Characteristically, Luther himself took a personal interest in the case of the exiled king and his queen. He had in any case already heard of Christian II's positive attitude, and he now concerned himself actively with Danish affairs. He thus wrote both a draft and, on 6 November 1525, the actual letter sent by Christian II to the Elector Friedrich, begging that prince to provide Christian with economic and political support, albeit in vain.

Queen Elizabeth, who felt a touching devotion and love for her husband superbly shown in their letters, shared Christian's Lutheran sympathies. She took communion after the manner of Luther, and in March 1524, also heard Luther preach. It was probably on this occasion that Justus Jonas saw the unfortunate Queen depart from the city 'crying loudly'. After a short illness, Elizabeth died (January 1526) aged only twenty-five years. Her death proved a severe blow to the already distressed Christian, who now had to accept separation from his three children who were taken into the bosom of the Imperial family for a Catholic upbringing. In a very moving letter to Luther, Christian recounted the last hours and death of his Queen, and mentioned that, despite subjection to much pressure, she would not profess to Catholicism on her deathbed but took her Eucharist 'nach rechter christlicher Weise'. Christian himself returned to the Catholic fold in 1531, after receiving Imperial aid in an attempt to regain his kingdom. This proved a signal failure, and he was arrested to be imprisoned in Denmark for twenty-seven years, only gaining release in 1559 shortly before he died. Luther did not forget him, and sent the incarcerated monarch a touching letter of much comfort. He also tried to persuade Frederick I to release Christian, but in vain. Luther likewise mentioned Christian II several times as an example of the way God treats regents who 'go too far' in the exercise of their sovereignty. He blamed the improper life Christian had led, but of particular interest is the fact that the Reformer used Christian's expulsion from Denmark as an illustration of unjust rebellion by subjects against lawful authority. The affair was discussed in *Ob Krigsleute auch in seligem Stande sein können* (1526). Luther could not have known the dubious reputation of Christian II's reign, nor did he seek to defend the king. Quite the contrary in fact—yet even if Christian had behaved unjustly, that did not justify his condemnation and expulsion by the Danes for it was God who had placed him in a position of supreme authority. In Luther's view, God would one day rebuke the Danes severely for their misdeeds, and charge them as rebels 'who steal from me, interfere with my office, and who, as criminals, have stolen the power of divine punishment'. The Reformer thus held them 'guilty of *laesae maiestatis divinae*, which means you have offended and contravened divine majesty'.[14]

Nevertheless, Luther was once again to become closely involved with a King of Denmark. Exactly ten years later, Christian III ascended the throne of Denmark and Norway; and after a bloody civil war, dramatically introduced Luther's Reformation by imprisoning all Catholic bishops, seizing their estates, and unjustly holding them solely responsible for the civil strife. A convinced Lutheran, the new king conveyed the fact to Luther, and the Reformer's positive reaction and assurances are of great interest.

I have with joy received your Royal Majesty's letter, and it has pleased me greatly that your Majesty has rid himself of [*ausgerottet thaben*] the bishops, for they cannot stop persecuting God's Word and cause much disturbance in the secular realm [*weltlich regiment*]. I am also willing to help, if I can, to explain this in the best possible way. [*WA, Br* 7, 602.]

Strong links were thus established between the Danish King and Wittenberg. Before he sent the ordinances of the Church for Luther's approval, Christian III promulgated them as law in 1537, and in the *Preface* names the Reformer as the man 'through whom God in his gentleness and compassion has of late sent again the holy and pure Gospel of Christ'. The faith of Wittenberg certainly made an important impact on both the inner and outer life of the Danish Church. If Luther and Melanchthon together repre-

[14] Martin Schwarz Lausten, *Biskop Niels Palladius. Et bidrag til den danske kirkes historie, 1550–1560* (København, 1968), pp. 148 f.

sented theological authority, the King exercised practical supremacy over the Church. Christian III was certainly well disposed towards the Church, although Denmark remained in a poor economic state during the first few years of his reign. Christian himself was sincere and devout, a *Beterfürst* and keen student of Scripture and theology, particularly the works of Luther which received his daily attention. A considerable correspondence, much of it with the Wittenberg Reformers Luther, Melanchthon, Bugenhagen, and Jonas, highlights such interests and shows the royal admiration for these celebrated divines. The King sent food-parcels and other gifts for them and their wives, from 1545 affording them an annual pension of 50 gulden (*Gnabengeltt*), continuing his support to Luther's widow after 1546. In retun, they frequently sent books, news, advice, and suggestions in patronage matters to Christian III. In his foreign policy towards the German Empire, however, Christian of Denmark acted with the customary pragmatism of the politician whose religious commitment regularly yielded before pressing issues of dynastic interest and national security.

In a letter of 14 January 1546, Martin Luther informed Christian III that he now 'daily walked on the edge of the grave'. In his reply, the Danish king prayed that God 'will allow you to live in health and strength for many more years to come for the benefit and advancement of the Christian Church and our true religion'. In the chancellery copybook, however, a poignant note has been added in a contemporary hand: '*Nota.* This last letter, the good and pious Luther never did read in this world.' [*WA*, *Br* 11, 260 and 264.]

IV

ECCLESIASTES

A. Doctor Martin Luther
Churchman
A Theologian's Viewpoint

*

ROBERT H. FISCHER

MARTIN LUTHER's Christian faith was a churchly faith through and through. This has not always been apparent either to his adversaries or to his admirers, but that his faith was intensely and stalwartly personal is abundantly clear. Friend, foe, and agnostic were stirred to the heart, just as they can be today, both by his trumpet-call, 'A Christian is a free lord over all, subject to no one'; and by his courageous stand at Worms where, before the assembled might of Empire and Church, he declared it to be 'neither safe nor right to go against conscience'. Yet to the dismay of some and the delight of others, this personal faith may appear to imply that the individual has become the arbiter of truth, and that the Church is superfluous—or at best a voluntary association of the religiously congenial.

Luther however by no means intended such inferences. His trumpet-call was a flourish of two notes. The first—'A Christian is a free lord'—announces Christian faith; and the second, in harmony, heralds Christian love: 'A Christian is a dutiful servant of everyone, subject to all.' Together these notes form and constitute a paradox of Christian life, the 'faith active in love'.[1] The Christian life is a life in community. The real point of Luther's stand at Worms, moreover, was not that Luther stood on his conscience, but upon what his conscience stood: 'My conscience is captive to the Word of God, and . . . it is neither safe nor right to go against conscience.'[2]

Luther's faith thus is no unbridled spiritual individualism. He intends his freedom to be altogether dependent on the Holy Spirit. It is to be based in the Word of God, and active in love for the neighbour. Its mother, its homeland, its workshop, its base-camp is the Christian Church, as Luther taught generations of catechumens through the Third Article of the Creed:

I believe that by my own reason or strength I cannot believe in Jesus Christ, my Lord, or come to him. But the Holy Spirit has called me through the Gospel, enlightened me with his gifts, and sanctified and pre-

---

[1] Cf. 1 Cor. 9: 19, and Rom. 13: 8 [*WA* 7, 49].

[2] *Luther at the Diet of Worms, WA* 7, 838.

served me in true faith, just as he calls, gathers, enlightens, and sanctifies the whole Christian Church on earth and preseves it in union with Jesus Christ in the one true faith. In this Christian Church he daily and abundantly forgives all my sins, and the sins of all believers, and on the last day he will raise me and all the dead and will grant eternal life to me and to all who believe in Christ. This is most certainly true.[3]

Luther's adversaries, naturally, found his intention anything but churchly. In the words of John Eck, he was 'an enemy of the Church within the Church'. The Edict of Worms (1521), which declared Luther an outlaw of the Christian Empire, called him 'a madman plotting the manifest destruction of the holy Church'; he 'would destroy obedience and authority of every kind'; and accordingly, 'the said Martin Luther shall hereafter be esteemed by each and all of us as a limb cut off from the Church of God, an obstinate schismatic and manifest heretic.'

John Cochlaeus, to be sure, labelled the central figure of *The Seven-Headed Luther* 'Ecclesiast', but behind the caption lay in tense irony. Luther had been stripped of his ecclesiastical titles and functions by papal excommunication. Nevertheless, as the Reformer insisted, if he was really proclaiming the Gospel of Christ, such a ban could in no way expel him from the Church of Christ, and he thus proceeded with his colleagues to tackle the enormous task of rebuilding Church life on an evangelical basis. During his seclusion at the Wartburg Castle Luther had already begun to address his colleagues as 'ecclesiast' and 'evangelist'. These titles he claimed for himself in his salvo *Against the Spiritual Estate of the Pope and the Bishops Falsely So Called* (1522), to which Jerome Emser wrote a counterblast *Against the Ecclesiast Falsely So Called, Really the Arch-Heretic*. For Luther's arrogance Cochlaeus felt only antipathy. As he subsequently explained when introducing 'the seven heads' of Luther, 'ecclesiast' meant the preacher who told the common people only what they wanted to hear, the preacher from whose thirty-six sermons Luther's adversary had culled five hundred errors.

Indeed, more than irony was in Cochlaeus's mind. *Seven-Headed Luther* was intended to demonstrate that the would-be Reformer had lapsed by stages from questionable to bad to worse, until with the Saxon Visitations beginning in 1528 he started

---

[3] *Small Catechism*, II. 6.

clumsily to steer his new Church into more orderly channels. According to Cochlaeus, Luther's deliberate, overt radicalism thus began with his assuming the role of 'churchman'. By trying to form his own Church, he had effectively cut himself off not only from the true universal Church, but also from himself, for the seven 'heads' were hopelessly at variance with one another. By contrasting the communions Cochlaeus would make his readers' choice crystal-clear: over against Luther's Church, splintered, self-contradictory, and ever-changing, there stood the true Church, united and fixed in its teaching; in contrast to Luther's Church, so recently aborted in a corner of Germany, there stood the true Church, universal in space and time.

This was about as far as John Cochlaeus went in grasping Luther's churchmanship; and many thoughtful persons from that day to the present, have been persuaded that at least the main lines of Cochlaeus's sketch are accurate—namely, that Luther is a radically subjectivistic, confused, and confusing churchman.

How shall we accord Luther a fresh hearing, to inquire what sort of churchman he really was? Several options lie at hand. One is a systematic analysis of 'Luther's conception of the Church'. To my knowledge, the most perceptive example of this genre is Wilhelm Pauck's essay with just that title.[4] A second approach is found in an unusually stimulating little book by Jaroslav Pelikan, *Spirit versus Structure*.[5] Starting from Luther's criticism of the basic institutions of medieval Christendom in the *Babylonian Captivity of the Church* (1520), the author then examines how Luther subsequently had to address each of these structures again, to reform or replace them, in his campaign for the evangelical renewal of the Church.

In this essay, however, I propose to follow another sampling method: to explore a cross-section of Luther's career, and inquire how Luther's concern for the Church of Jesus Christ manifested itself—both theologically and practically—during the most critical period of the shaping of the evangelical Reformation.

At the imperial Diet of Augsburg, 1530, the fledgeling Lutheran movement faced the supreme challenge to its right—or power—to exist. Here not just the opinions of theologians nor the religious

[4] In *Heritage of the Reformation*, Glencoe, Illinois: The Free Press of Glencoe, rev. edn., 1961 (OUP paperback, 1968).
[5] J. Pelikan, *Spirit versus Structure* (London, 1968).

preferences of individuals were at stake, but the destinies of several states and free cities which had committed themselves to evangelical Christianity. The Reformation, in the sense of public changes in religious practice and ecclesiastical administration, had been going on for nearly a decade, in defiance of the Edict of Worms. The Roman Catholic majority of princes would have liked to suppress it. Churchmen like John Eck and the papal legate Lorenzo Campeggio solemnly urged this—by persuasion if possible, by force if necessary. But suppression did not prove possible.

At the zenith of his power, the Emperor Charles V determined to come to Germany to settle the religious dissension. His summons proposed 'to give a charitable hearing to every man's opinions' and 'to reconcile them to a unity in Christian truth', and thus 'to see to it that one single, true religion may be accepted and held by us all, and that we all live in one common Church, just as we all live and battle under the one Christ . . .'.[6] Did Charles intend to come to Augsburg as the unpartisan judge between two antagonistic parties, or as the protector of the established Catholic order? The evangelical princes and statesmen hoped the former. At all events they were determined to plead that they were entitled to legal recognition as Catholic Christians. But how should they establish their claim? And what should they do if it were rejected? It was a dangerous and uncharted terrain which a handful of evangelical rulers and cities, together with their legal and theological advisers, were committed to cross.

As an outlaw, Luther could not be with them at Augsburg. Elector Johann, therefore, stationed him at Coburg, his southernmost stronghold, 250 kilometers from Augsburg—some three or four days' distance by courier. There Luther remained for nearly six months, while 'his cause' (as Melanchthon put it) was being decided. He chafed and fretted, but he did not pass the time pacing the floor in helpless trepidation. Indeed, it was Luther who 'in quietness and in trust' managed to strengthen the hearts of both the statesmen and the theologians at the Diet. Meanwhile, in spite of recurring illness and grief over his father's death, the Reformer turned the months he spent at Coburg into one of the most productive periods of his entire literary career.

---

[6] *The Augsburg Confession*, ed. M. Reu (Wartburg Press, Chicago, 1930), 71*. Cf. *Augsburg Confession* [hereafter: *AC*], Preface §§ 2–4, 10–11.

The situation was critical. The sources available are abundant and varied, and in this testing time, indicate the kind of *ecclesiast* Luther proved himself to be.[7]

Three kinds of inquiry into Luther the churchman suggest themselves from his Coburg writings. In the first place, several intimate expressions of his personal character and Christian faith prompt the question: how churchly was his own spirituality? Secondly, Luther's past experience and present challenge required him to rethink the essentials of his Christian faith. What role did the Church play in his theology? Thirdly, his reflection and counsel were solicited on all kinds of practical churchly questions under deliberation at Augsburg. What influence did he wield, during this crisis period, in the shaping of evangelical church life?

Early in July, 1530, the Reformer penned to his good friend Lazarus Spengler, syndic of Nuremberg, an extemporaneous interpretation of his personal seal, 'the Luther rose'. Luther was still exultant that a few days earlier Christ had been so beautifully proclaimed 'by his staunch confessors'. However, as he well knew, the weeks ahead would be fraught with uncertainty over how to deal with the next moves of the Catholic authorities. Luther described his seal as 'a symbol of my theology'. It is as if this letter gave him an occasion to get his Christian bearings anew.

[7] A general survey of Luther's Coburg-period writings may be helpful. The majority are accessible in English in the American Edition of *Luther's Works*, a few others in Reu, op.cit.

(a) 7 treatises in 'applied theology', averaging about 40 pages each in English translation: *Exhortation to the Clergy* (written in May); *Disavowal of Purgatory* and *A Sermon on Keeping Children in School* (July); *The Keys* (August); *On Translating* (September); *Admonition concerning the Sacrament* and *Warning to His Dear Germans* (the latter published in 1531) were begun at the Coburg.

(b) 5 exegetical commentaries: a brief one on Ezekiel 38–9; and 4 important and lengthy expositions of Psalms: 118, 117, 1–25, and (begun at the Coburg) 111.

(c) Nearly 125 letters were written from the Coburg, about 75 of them directed to Melanchthon and other theologian colleagues in Augsburg, or to Elector John and other princes and jurists. Accompanying some of these letters were important memoranda on questions under negotiation at the Diet. Amounting to a tract, too, is the open *Letter to the Cardinal Archbishop of Mainz* dated 6 July.

Rounding out this collection of sources on Luther at Coburg are several letters by Luther's secretary, Veit Dietrich; a large number of letters from Melanchthon; the Elector; and others to Luther and Dietrich, and various official documents of the evangelical party. Unmentioned here are several other minor writings of Luther, a few sermons, and a vast amount of work on his translation of the Old Testament prophets.

There is first to be a cross, black and placed in a heart, which should have its natural red colour, so that I may remind myself that faith in the Crucified saves us. For if one believes from the heart, one is justified ... This heart is to be in the midst of a white rose, to symbolise that faith gives joy, comfort, and peace; in a word, it places one into a white joyful rose, for this faith does not give peace and joy as the world gives, and therefore, the rose is to be white and not red ... The rose is to be in a sky-blue field, symbolising that this joy in the Spirit and in faith is a beginning of the heavenly joy to come; it is already a part of that joy and is already grasped by hope, even though not yet manifest. And around this field is a golden ring symbolising that in heaven this blessedness lasts forever and has no end, and that it is precious beyond all joy and all possessions, just as gold is the most precious of metals [*WA, Br* 5, 445]

Throughout his life Luther loved to return to the essentials of the Gospel both for his witness to others and for his own inner renewal. On the walls of his living quarters at the Coburg Castle, a well-attested tradition recounts, he wrote the words and the plainsong notes of Psalm 118: 17, 'I shall not die but live, and recount the works of the Lord.' [Cf. *WA, Br* 5, 636 and 638n.]

Above all, however, Luther's biblical studies and letters of encouragement to colleagues at Augsburg make the Coburg period an unexcelled vantage point for observing his faith under fire.

Luther loved the Psalter as 'the Bible in miniature' and as an experience of 'the communion of saints'. [*WA Deutsche Bibel* 10.1, 98, 102] Of Psalm 118 he wrote, 'This is my own beloved psalm. Although the entire Psalter and all of holy Scripture are dear to me as my only comfort and source of life, I fell in love with this psalm especially.' [*WA* 31^1, 66.] Its poetic power and spiritual profundity enthralled him. In the tempestuous month of June 1530 the Reformer settled down to write his own *Exposition of Psalm 118*, 'the beautiful *Confitemini*' [*WA* 31.1, 65–182], finishing it just about the time his colleagues were presenting their confession in Augsburg. It is a sermonic exposition—not an academic study for scholars and clergy but a search for the psalmist's message which he could apply helpfully to all contemporary Christians. It certainly bears an intensely personal stamp, but in what sense is it also churchly?

The first nine verses of the psalm explore God's blessings and the believers' response. 'It is good to give thanks to the Lord, for his love endures for ever.' (verse 1.) Luther refers this thought to

God's providence for all mankind through nature and the common life. 'House of Israel' (v. 2) he takes to mean the civil government and peace, without which society could not exist. 'House of Aaron' (v. 3) is 'the spiritual government', the leadership of the Church. God's love endures, even though all three groups—the people at large, the civil rulers, and the rulers of the Church—commonly ignore or abuse God's gifts.

But it is the fourth group, 'those who fear the Lord' (v. 4)—'the elect children of God, and all the saints on earth, the genuine Christians'—for whom this psalm was specially written. Its membership is gathered from the other three groups. One still finds faithful, God-fearing bishops and ministers, princes, aldermen and judges, artisans and farmers, servants and maids, no matter how few they may be. God's gracious help for this little flock never fails. But that help is hidden from 'the world'; Christians must suffer all kinds of calamity from the other three groups, from the devil, and from their own flesh [87–92].

Faith, cross-bearing, prayer, joy, comfort, and courage are the terms, in which Luther describes this blessing which God showers upon the small band of true Christians (vv. 5–9).

Let everyone become a falcon and soar above distress ... God does not send him this distress to destroy him ... He wants to drive him to pray, to implore, to fight, to exercise his faith, ... to accustom himself to do battle even with the devil and with sin, and by the grace of God to be victorious ... Trouble and distress constrain us and keep us within the Christian Church. Crosses and troubles, therefore, are as necessary for us as life itself. [*WA* 31¹, 95.]

Confident prayers thus brings joy surging through me, for 'God plants comfort within my heart', and rescues me from my enemies. Accordingly, the psalmist warns the faithful to put their trust not in humans, even Emperors, but in God.

David then parades a full range of examples: first, his own experience (vv. 10–14); next, 'the common example of all the saints' (vv. 15–21); and finally, Christ, the head of the Church (vv. 22–7). David breaks into a song. 'Faith cannot do otherwise; it always confesses what it believes.' (Rom. 10: 10.) God 'helps us overcome and hold the field, while our persecutors go down in disgrace.' [*WA* 31¹, 135 and 137.]

The saints of the Old and New Testaments—'a unanimous

chorus'—provide another mighty encouragement. 'It must comfort and strengthen my heart when I see that St. Paul and the apostles had the same Word, God, faith, and cross as I do.' [138.] Under the triumphant motto, 'I shall not die but live', Luther launches into an eloquent exposition of the Christian's battle against his or her *Anfechtungen* [146–157]. These are the powerful assaults upon our spirit which threaten to engulf us in despair, whether they come from enemies without or from conscience within. When we cast off all reliance on our own strength and place our trust in the Lord alone, however, our sins are forgiven and death is vanquished. 'Isn't this an amazing help? The dying live; the suffering rejoice; the fallen rise; the disgraced are honoured.' [*WA* 31¹, 152.]

This is no private relationship with God; it is the experience of Christian fellowship, the communion of saints, according to the Third Article of the Creed, for Christ's little flock is the true holy Christian Church.

Since we are baptized and believe in Christ, we are holy and righteous in Christ and with Christ. He has taken our sin from us and has graced, clothed, and adorned us with his holiness. Thus the whole Christian Church is holy, not by itself or by its own work but in Christ and through Christ's holiness. [*WA* 31¹, 167.]

But there is holiness in anticipation and hope: faith knows that Christ has begun to remake the faithful in holiness and will complete his work.

In thanksgiving to the Lord, therefore, the Christian enters 'the gates of righteousness', that is, 'the parish or bishopric where the ministry of the Church is publicly exercised—preaching, praising God, thanksgiving, singing, baptizing, distributing and receiving the sacrament [of the Altar], admonishing, comforting, praying, and whatever else pertains to salvation.' [*WA* 31¹, 162.] 'Hypocrites, scoundrels, and sinners' can enter the temple physically, but only true believers—the righteous and holy—truly enter the gate of the Lord; only they truly belong to the holy Christian Church.

Finally (vv. 22 ff.), the psalmist presents Christ the Cornerstone and head of the holy Church as an example. If Christ was rejected on earth, we must not be amazed that it is still difficult for the world to acknowledge him as Lord. Indeed, states Luther, 'I consider myself a Christian, but I know full well how hard it was, and still is, to grasp and hold this Cornerstone. People may call me a

Lutheran, but they misjudge me; or at best I am a poor and weak Lutheran. May God strengthen me!' [*WA* 31¹, 174]. 'Yet, when the glad day dawns which the Lord has made, that is, when I do respond in faith, my life is filled with joy: Hosanna!' [175 ff.] What Luther preached in the commentary, he had ample need to practise during difficult months when the fate of the whole evangelical movement was in the balance. But he met the challenge with remarkable consistency.

On the way to Augsburg the Saxon Elector's entourage stopped over at Coburg, arriving on Good Friday, 15 April. Preaching to the group on the six following days, Luther began with a *Sermon on Cross and Suffering* [*WA* 32, 28–39]. He reminded the Saxons that Christians must be crucified with Christ; 'each person must bear a part of the holy cross.' 'If I want to be a Christian, I must also wear the colours of the court; . . . suffering there must be.' But if suffering comes because we witness to Christ, one should say: 'So let it be, in God's name. I shall let him take care of it and fight it out . . .'. Christ will transform suffering to advantage.

The Elector's party proceeded to Augsburg; and Luther remained behind. Throughout the ensuing half-year he poured out a flood of magnificent letters of encouragement to his colleagues; the richest of which were written between 27 and 30 June, and one on 5 August. These Coburg letters deliver the same message already encountered. Faith under fire becomes joyful courage, for it confidently commends to God both the cause of the Gospel and a man's own fate. Chiding Melanchthon for his anxiety, Luther confesses his own faith:

Christ knows whether it comes from stupidity or the Spirit, but I for my part am not very much troubled about our cause. Indeed, I am more hopeful than I expected to be. God, who is able to raise the dead, is also able to uphold his cause when it is falling, or to raise it up again when it has fallen, or to move it forward when it is standing still. If we are not worthy instruments to accomplish his purpose, he will find others. If we are not strengthened by his promises, where in all the world are the people to whom these promises apply? [*WA*, *Br* 5, 400 (27 June).]

To a colleague he wrote: 'Admonish Philip not to overdo that "sacrifice of a contrite spirit", or he may have nothing left for further sacrificing! . . . Sacrifice is pleasing to God, but not destruction; God does not want souls to be destroyed.' Melanchthon recounted a verbal exchange that he had had with Cardinal Lang of Salzburg; Luther observed to Veit Dietrich that Philip should have retorted: 'If your Emperor will not tolerate public turmoil, our Emperor will not tolerate blasphemy. You trust your Emperor, and we will trust ours; let us see which one holds the field!' [*WA, Br* 5, 420.]

The letter Dietrich wrote to Melanchthon on 30 June affords the most intimate glimpse of all into Luther's indomitable spirit under fire:

The remarkable constancy, cheerfulness, faith, and hope of the man in these bitter times I cannot sufficiently admire. These he nourishes by diligent meditation on the Word of God. Not a day passes that he does not devote at least three hours, indeed the very hours most suitable for study, to prayer. Once I happened to hear him praying. Good heavens, what spirit, what faith dwelt in those words! With such reverence he utters his petitions, knowing that he is speaking with God; with such hope and faith, knowing that he is conversing with a father and friend. 'I know', he said, 'that you are our God and Father. I am sure, therefore, that you will destroy the persecutors of your children; if not, the danger is yours as well as ours. This affairs is altogether yours; we have been forced to become involved in it; defend us, then! etc.' These are virtually the very words which I heard him pray with a clear voice as I stood some distance away. My heart, too, burned with extraordinary intensity when he spoke with God so intimately, so gravely, so reverently, and when between prayers he recited the promises of the psalms in such a way that he appeared certain that everything would turn out just as he asked. [*WA, Br* 5, 420.]

Impressive though Luther's boldness and courage may be, they do not, of course, prove that he was right, for such qualities can also characterize the fanatical, opinionated, and domineering. When addressing the princes at Worms in 1521, Charles V only repeated a standard Catholic refrain when he charged, 'According to his opinion all Christendom has always been in error.' Indeed, a recurring *Anfechtung* throughout Luther's career was the question, 'Are you alone wise? What if you are mistaken, and are leading many people into error and damnation?' [*WA* 8, 483.]

Luther was aware of the risk. But that which—according to his conviction—removed his religious obduracy from the realm of subjectivism is best expressed in a word from his great *Galatians Commentary* of 1531 to 1535: 'Our theology is certain, because it places us outside ourselves, so that we depend not on our powers, our conscience, our feelings, our person, our works, but on that which is outside us, namely, on God's promise and truthfulness which cannot deceive.' [WA 40^1, 589.]

One can discern three major features in this battle against subjectivism, all of them prominent in Luther's piety during his months at Coburg. First and foremost, it is the Gospel itself which invalidates all human boastfulness before God and creates in its stead the faith which liberates, transforms, and sustains.

The second closely related feature concerns the role of the Church. Faith in Christ, this creation and gift of the Holy Spirit, is mediated through God's own people. It is a community faith, not a private possession. Two Coburg treatises exalt the role of corporate worship in nourishing and supporting Christian faith. *Admonition concerning the Sacrament of the Body and Blood of our Lord* [WA 30, 2, 595–626] rhapsodically expounds the character of Eucharistic worship. If worship is an intensely personal 'remembrance of Christ', it is also true that its normal setting is 'the house of God, ... among the multitude keeping festival' [Psalm 42: 5]. The first great benefit of receiving the Eucharist is that you 'praise God, thank Christ, honour his suffering, benefit your neighbour, help promote and preserve the Sacrament and the Gospel as well as the Christian Church ...'. The second great benefit, 'given to us personally', is not only the strengthening of our faith and love toward Christ, but also the renewal of our love of our neighbour, the equipping of our heart to do all good works and to resist the Devil. Luther proclaims the same message in his *Exposition of Psalm 111* [WA 31^1, 393–426], which treats the psalm as pointing toward the Christian passover, the Eucharist.

Luther's third curb against subjectivism is a very human corollary of the God-given Gospel and Church: his singular lack of personal ambition. For all his stubbornness in insisting that the Gospel must be given free course in Christian society, Luther consistently committed the outcome of the whole affairs to God's hands, and clearly regarded himself as dispensable.

From the Coburg, through popular tracts and inimitable letters of counsel, Luther helped to shape the presentation of the evangelical party's ecclesiastical position at Augsburg. Three main aspects of the Reformer's eccelsiology gain prominence in these writings:

first, the idea of the Church; secondly, the nature of authority or power in the Church; and thirdly, the role afforded the ordained ministry. From careful focus on Luther's writings in their own context, the historian can gain a lively and realistic impression of his churchmanship. At the same time, too, he can grasp the connection the Reformer made between what theologians have come to term his 'constructive' and 'applied' theology.

The principal areas of the faith 'which must be dealt with in the true Christian Church', wrote Luther, 'have in large part become utterly meaningless'. Among thirty-two topics he listed were these: 'What the Church is. What the keys are. What a bishop is . . . What the office of preaching is' [*WA* 30², 345 f.].

This charge appeared in an *Exhortation to the Clergy assembled at Augsburg*, Luther's first major tract written from Coburg Castle (May 1530). If his aim was to impress bishops that thoroughgoing reform was desperately needed and the Evangelicals had made the right start, his approach was scarcely that of friendly persuasion. On the contrary, he brusquely seized the offensive, and did so in a most truculent manner. For Luther knew well enough that 'diplomacy' was the name of the game in progress at Augsburg, and genuinely appreciated much 'gentle stepping' from Melanchthon, and Chancellor Brueck's judicious influence in the writing of the *Confession*. In the battle to win over public opinion, therefore, he determined to fight with fire. As a Reformer, he was well aware that Cardinal Campeggio and other Roman theologians were urging through diplomatic channels the extirpation of Protestantism, if needs be by sword and stake. He also knew that John Eck's *Four Hundred and Four Articles* (the ablest example of more than a dozen versions of 'that favourite and futile form' of controversial weapon, the catalogue of heresies) were circulating in Augsburg, and effectively tarring all Protestant dissenters with the same brush. To Eck, moreover, Luther was the prime instigator of all such heresy.

Yet no amount of polemical fervour can be allowed to obscure the substantive issues. Statesmen and theologians, both Romanist and Evangelical, realized that the very nature of the Christian Church was at risk. By and large, the Romanists did not want the matter debated, as ever maintaining that their identification of the Church established by law and custom, had been fixed long ago. Dissenters must therefore be tried in that light. For the Romanists

had no intention of admitting their doctrine and hierarchical system to be in need of reform, and simply demanded the restoration
of episcopal jurisdiction.

By contrast, the Evangelicals were contending that the Roman
conception of the Church was itself a large part of the problem. A
decade earlier Luther had accused the Romanists of entrenching
themselves behind 'three walls' which prevented real reform [*WA*
6, 406]; and he now challenged the bishops in his *Exhortation* on
much the same grounds.

You allege that nothing should be changed or renewed without the consent of the Church. Who, then, is the Church? Are you? Then show the
seals and credentials, or prove it otherwise with deeds and fruits. Why are
not we also the Church, since we are baptized as well as you; since we
teach, preach, have the sacraments, believe, pray, love, hope, and suffer
more than you? ... You should not keep repeating to us, 'Church,
Church, Church.' You should rather demonstrate to us that you are the
Church. That is the crux of the matter. [*WA* 30^2, 321.]

Again, as he wrote (29 June 1530) to his colleague Melanchthon:
'If Christ is not with us, where is he then in the whole world, I
earnestly wish to know? If we are not the Church, or a part of the
Church, where is the Church?' [*WA, Br* 5, 407.]

In short, behind this peppery partisanship lay Luther's continuing conflict with Rome, a conflict that had originated many
years before. When the Reformer first challenged Roman theology
and practice in ministering the grace of God, the authorities had
simply sought to silence him by forbidding criticism of the
Church. In his *Dialogue* (1518), Sylvester Prierias, the Curia's
house theologian, had thus laid down 'four foundations':

1. The universal Church *essentially* is the gathering of all believers in
Christ for divine worship. The universal Church *virtually* [that is, in regard to its power] is the Roman Church, the head of all the Churches, and
the supreme pontiff. The Roman Church *representatively* is the college of
cardinals, but *virtually* it is the supreme pontiff, who is the head of the
Church, although in another sense than Christ.

And the argument continued:

2. As the universal Church cannot err in determining matters of faith or
morals, so neither can a true council err, nor the Roman Church, nor the
supreme pontiff. 3. He who does not place his trust in the teaching of the
Roman Church and the Roman pontiff as the infallible rule of faith, from

which even holy Scripture derives its strength and authority, is a heretic. Likewise, 4. ... He who holds wrong opinions in regard to the teaching and acts of the Church concerning things pertaining to faith and morals is a heretic. Corollary: In regard to indulgences, he who says that the Roman Church cannot do that which it in fact does, is a heretic.[8]

Luther inevitably asked himself: if I am teaching the Gospel according to Holy Scripture, can this be the Church when it simply tries to silence me? What, indeed, is the Church?

In all three areas of ecclesiology, Luther's thought had matured, especially in the years 1518 to 1521, as he had met the attacks of Eck, Alveld, Murner, Emser, and Catharinus (not to mention others whom he did not bother to answer). In 1523 he had sketched the basic rights and powers of a Christian community, addressed the Evangelicals' problem of providing themselves with an ordained ministry, and composed an evangelical order of the Mass. With the Saxon Visitations, beginning in 1528, an evangelical programme of ecclesiastical supervision had been initiated.

Luther's ecclesiology had thus developed considerably a decade before the showdown at Augsburg, as may readily be discerned by a glance at his popular treatise *Against the Papacy at Rome* (June 1520).[9] The Church in its essence as the body of Christ is a spiritual community, distinguished but not separated from the institutional, juridical Church. The true Church, the community of believing hearts, is born of the Word of the Gospel, and has spiritual unity in its life in Christ. It is not bound to Rome nor to any other earthly place, but exists wherever the Gospel is found. The true Church, however, is not an abstraction—'a Platonic city'; at the very least, it is as real and as recognizable as are believing persons. Re-examining the traditional scriptural supports of papalism (Matthew 16: 18 f. and John 20 and 21), Luther argued that the Church has indeed received a unique authority (*de iure divino*) from Christ, but this divine authority is solely the power of the

---

[8] Cf. Erlanger Ausgabe, *op. var. arg.* 1, 346 f.

[9] *WA* 6, 285–324; most of the following thoughts are to be found on pages 287, 292–301, 309 ff. Luther's hearing before Cajetan (1518), and the Leipzig Debate (1519), had been whetstones for sharpening his technical theological ideas. See also *Luther's Explanation of His Thirteenth Proposition on the Power of the Pope* (1519), *WA* 2, 183–240, esp. 187, 190 f, 194; *Answer to the Superspiritual Book by Goat Emser* (1521), *WA* 7, 621–88, esp. 683; *Reply to Ambrose Catharinus* (1521), *WA* 7, 705–78, esp. 719–21, 742.

keys: not a power to rule the earth but a power to serve—the power to administer the Gospel, loosing or binding sins. It was, moreover, a power given to the whole Church, not to St. Peter individually, and still less to certain of his successors. The special power of the papacy, therefore, is of human right, subject to the Church, and alterable. In conclusion, wrote Luther,

I fight for only two things: First, I will not tolerate it that humans establish new articles of faith and judge . . . as heretics, schismatics, and unbelievers all other Christians in the whole world only because they are not under the pope. . . . Secondly, I shall accept whatever the pope establishes and does, on condition that I judge it first on the basis of holy Scriptures. [*WA* 6, 322.]

The phrase, 'On condition that I judge it first', does not mean an autocratic pretension on Luther's part; for according to the Reformer's conviction *every Christian* has the power and responsibility to test on the basis of Scripture what he hears in the Church [*WA* 11, 408 ff.; 12, 187 ff. (1523)].

All these Lutheran ideas, so easily misunderstood in the abstract, were put to the crucial test at Augsburg in 1530, both in the drafting of the *Confession* and in the weeks of delicate negotiations which followed. Recent studies enable us to understand the actual course of events at Augsburg with much greater clarity than was possible in the past, and it is important to examine the intentions and expectations of the Lutheran party there.

The principal issue that had to be resolved at the Diet was in fact straightforward, namely how was Church life to be publicly ordered in the Empire? It was thus the second, far more lengthy part of the *Confession* (Articles 22–8) which set in focus the primary religious agenda at Augsburg, to deal with the correction of 'abuses', like withholding the cup from the laity, prohibition of clerical marriage, and abuses concerning the Mass. The Evangelicals claimed that their reforms in Church order and practice had been undertaken only 'on the basis of the Holy Scriptures' and by virtue of the responsibility of governments to protect their people and maintain public order. In particular, they insisted that 'the Gospel be left free' to them. It was a slogan that not only recurred frequently in Luther's writings from the Coburg, but one that had also been expressed in preparatory documents like the *Torgau*

Articles. The Evangelicals were thus demanding the right to coexist within the Empire; and certainly did not expect to convert the Catholics to their position. The significance of this slogan was made clear in Article 28 of the *Confession* (especially in sections 69–77) which confronted the Catholic demand for restoration of episcopal jurisdiction. The Evangelicals here offered explicit conditions for compliance: first the bishops should cease prohibiting, on pain of sin, such practices as communion in both kinds and clerical marriage; and secondly they should cease making priestly ordination contingent upon a prescribed oath that the candidate 'will not teach the pure [i.e. evangelical!] doctrine of the Gospel'.

The dissension between the two religious parties at the Diet was brought into clear focus by the *Augsburg Confession* (25 June) and the *Pontifical Confutation* (3 August), official documents that when set side by side show at a glance the current shape of the controversy over the Church. Thus whereas the *Confessio Augustana* (5) affirmed that the Holy Spirit produces saving faith through the ministry of teaching the Gospel and administering the sacraments, the *Confutation* (rightly recognizing that in this article the Evangelicals meant to emphasize the Church's activity of administering the means of grace, rather than the clerical office) simply approved the article, to add only a notation warning against the evangelical assertion of *sola fide*.

Again, Articles 7 and 8 stressed of the *Confession* the perpetuity of one Church defined as a community of believers or saints; they stated that its unity did not depend on uniformity of practices; and declared that the ministry of the means of grace was effectual in spite of ungodliness still found among laity and clergy in the Church.. The *Confutation* criticized the Evangelicals' definition for its implication that all Church members were pure saints. It also agreed that diversity in ecclesiastical rites did not destroy Church unity, but only if that principle of diversity was applied to 'special', not 'universal' rites.

Augsburg Article 14 likewise asserted that a proper call is necessary for the exercise of public ministry. The *Confutation* agreed, but added that canonical ordination must be observed. In Article 15, the Evangelicals affirmed that they retained traditional liturgical and other usages, as long as these contributed to peace and order and were not regarded as means to merit salvation. The *Confu-*

tation responded that the universal rites of the Church must be restored, and rejected the evangelical view that rites have no propitia-
tory and satisfactory value.

Finally, Article 28 of the *Confession* brought the entire religious
controversy to a head: how is the one Christian Church to be
administered? It is a lengthy article that binds the whole *Confession* together; it constitutes the key to the correction of abuses,
and addresses that problem on the basis of the Gospel of justification by faith expounded in the 'doctrinal articles'. Three questions
are faced. First, what is the power of bishops? [Sections 1–29] By
divine right it is simply the power of the keys, namely 'a power or
command of God to preach the Gospel, to remit and retain sins,
and to administer the sacraments'. This is an authority limited to
the handling of the Gospel; the power of the keys grants no coercive authority on earth. The divine power of the clergy must therefore be kept clearly separate from all civil authority, which retains
the power of coercion. Secondly, what power, then, do bishops
have to issue statutes for liturgical worship and for other aspects of
the Church's life such as marriage cases, tithes, foods and holy
days, and ranks of clergy? [Sections 30–68]. Only a human right,
which means that 'bishops or pastors' regulate these matters
according to their best wisdom, in the light of the Gospel [i.e.
must not presume to be a means of meriting grace, nor to be
necessary for salvation], and they must 'preserve the teaching of
Christian liberty' [i.e. must not 'burden consciences with bondage']. And thirdly (a subject already discussed), on what conditions can the Evangelicals restore the jurisdiction of the bishops?
[Sections 69–77.]

To this exposition, the *Confutation* replied briefly but firmly.
'Ecclesiastical power in spiritual things has been founded upon divine right' and granted to the bishops and clergy. All current 'im-
munities, privileges, dignities, and prerogatives' must therefore be
preserved. It is quite clearly a very different conception of 'spiritual' power from that held by the Evangelicals. In short:

Bishops have the power not only to administer God's Word and the sacraments, but also to rule and discipline and guide, in order that their subjects may be finally and eternally blessed. But where there is the power to
rule, there must also be the power to judge, determine, distinguish, and
regulate what is good and expedient for the attainment of eternal blessedness. [Cf. Article 26.]

According to the *Confutation*, this power did not conflict with true Christian liberty, and it was finally stressed that the Catholic authorities were themselves committed to the reform of genuine abuse. The Confutators sensed that the Evangelicals would not recognize the validity of any judgement which constricted their freedom to proclaim the Gospel as they understood it; and in consequence the Evangelicals' 'offer' took from the bishop their long-established responsibility to determine the nature of the true Gospel and to condemn erring doctrine.[10] To this proposal the bishops could not consent.

What, then, was Luther's influence as 'Ecclesiastes' on the drama unfolding at Augsburg?

It is certainly curious that he made no direct theological contribution to the final revision of the *Confession*. Of his eighteen letters written from Coburg to friends at the Diet between April and the presentation of the *Augustana* on 25 June, most are filled with small talk or personal news and views, some are cheerfully whimsical, a few inspirational, but only three can be construed as offering any theological or practical counsel at all. To Elector Johann, the Reformer expressed approval of an early draft of the irenical *Confession*, and advised obedience if the Emperor forbade evangelical preaching in the city (15 May). Again, eloquently commending the Elector's protection which 'allows God's Word to have free course' in Saxony, Luther encouraged him to remain steadfast and patient (20 May). To Philip of Hesse, not yet fully committed to co-operation with the Saxons, he vigorously recommended avoidance of the Zwinglians (20 May). But that was all, however much it remains important to stress that Luther's theological influence had already been firmly built into the *Augsburg Confession* from the start.

In striking contrast to this comparative reticence stands Luther's enormous output in treatises and letters during the following weeks. When he received the news and a copy of the *Confession* from Augsburg on 29 June, his first response was to send a packet of encouraging letters to his colleagues by return. He likewise

[10] E. Iserloh, hrsg., *Confessio Augustana und Confutatio: Internationalies Symposion der Gesellschaft zur Herausgabe des Corpus Catholicorum in Augsburg, 3.–7. Sept. 1979*, Reformationsgeschichtliche Studien und Texte 118 (Aschendorff, Münster, 1980), p. 481.

voiced his elation to other friends in words borrowed from Psalm
119: 46 and Matthew 10: 32. The former text, 'I spoke of your
testimony before kings, and I was not put to shame', became the
motto printed on the title-page of all authorized editions of the
Confession. Meanwhile, in June and July, Luther's anger at the
'abominations' of the papacy blazed up again into a raging new
offensive. In an ironically-titled tract, *Disavowal of Purgatory*
[*WA* 30^2, 367–90], written in July, he did not withdraw the
evangelical offer of conditions for reconciliation, but he clearly
held no hope any longer that the Catholics would give it a hearing.
Even his *Open Letter to the Cardinal Archbishop of Mainz* [*WA*
30^2, 397–412] (dated 6 July), urging Albert to use his influence to
promote peace, aimed only at mutual tolerance; for Luther did
not expect agreement over the doctrine of the Gospel.

The immediate situation at Augsburg, however, set the Reformer and his colleagues intently to work on the doctrine of the
Church, its authority, and ministry. Diplomatic manoeuvres were
beginning, and a commission of Catholic theologians was preparing
a reply to the *Confession*. The evangelical party had to formulate
guidelines for its response. In the very letter which reported on the
presentation of the *Augustana*, Melanchthon sent an urgent request for Luther to ponder 'what we are willing to concede to
them' [*WA, Br* 5, 397 (26 June)].

Philip directly posed the question in a letter of 14 July [*WA, Br*
5, 475–7]: Who has the right to issue or alter statutes regarding
Church practice, and what obedience is owed to these laws?
Canon law had said: the bishops have this authority *jure divino*,
and the people must obey divinely instituted authority. Melanchthon was clear in his conviction that, apart from the divine right
and duty to administer the Gospel through the power of the Word
alone, bishops have authority in the Church only *jure humano* [cf.
AC 28, 29 ff.]. But a further question perplexed him: if bishops
issue ecclesiastical statutes (Melanchthon called them *traditiones*)—
e.g. laws for feasts and fasts—which are 'in agreement with
faith', are not even the Evangelicals bound in conscience to obey
them? Melanchthon's tentative conclusion was that 'bishops may
rule *jure humano*.'

Thus began a debate which occupied several letters until mid-
August. Luther's first contribution to it, the letter of 21 July, has
been called 'the clearest and most carefully formulated expression

of his "two kingdoms" doctrine', and 'the foundation of an evangelical church law' [Maurer i, 247].[11] Before writing that letter Luther sketched out forty disputation theses, which were soon published under the title *Propositions . . . against the Whole Synagogue of Satan and All the Gates of Hell* [WA 30², 420–4 (–427)]. Theses 1–8 declare that *ecclesia dei* has no authority to devise articles of faith and divine moral laws, for these are sufficiently instituted by the Holy Scriptures. In 'approving' articles of faith and morals or 'approving' the Scriptures themselves, the Church acts not as their superior but as their inferior; 'it acknowledges and affirms them as a servant confirms the seal of his lord' (Thesis 7). That is to say, when the lord issues an official pronouncement, the servant simply confirms by the seal that the document is authentic. Theses 9–18 state that '*ecclesia dei* does have the authority to institute ceremonies', e.g. feasts and fasts, but under definite limitations: first, these statutes must not be contrary to Scriptural directives on faith and morals, nor oppressive to Christian consciences. Moreover, the Church has this power to issue ordinances 'not for others but only for itself'. It becomes clear from Thesis 15 that, in this context, *ecclesia* means an ordered Christian community, *whether local, regional, or world-wide*: 'The Church is the number or gathering [*collectio*] of baptized and believing persons under one pastor, whether of one city or of the whole province or of the whole world.' In Thesis 16 Luther clarifies the relation of a pastor and his *ecclesia*: 'This pastor or prelate [in the contemporary German version: *pfarher oder Bisschoff*] has no power to issue regulations (*for he is not the Church*), except with the *consent of his Church.*' Thesis 17 continues: 'The pastor may urge and persuade the Church to consent . . . to lay down regulations for a time, and again to alter or omit them.'

Luther amplified these thoughts in a fragmentary disputation or memorandum *On the Power to Propose Laws in the Church* [WA 30², 681–90], written apparently in August. In it he sketched out his arguments in rebuttal of the Roman Catholic conception of the Church and its authority. Noteworthy here is his question: 'Who then is certain where the Gospel is?' It finally comes to this, replies

---

[11] W. Maurer, *Historischer Kommentar zur Confessio Augustana*, 2 Bde. (Gütersloh, 1976–8), p. 24. This essay is much indebted to the masterly work of Dr Maurer.

Luther, that

He will be certain about the Gospel, who has within himself the testimony of the Holy Spirit *that this is the Gospel*, as we read in Acts ii [v.v. 37–41]. He who believes [the Gospel] then believes the person who proclaims it, and he who does not believe it does not believe him. The believer becomes certain, the unbeliever remains uncertain; but the Lord gathers the believers into one body, that it may become the Church. [688.]

In this light, as often in the past,[12] Luther interprets the warmly debated dictum of Augustine, 'I would not believe the Gospel unless the authority of the catholic Church moved me': it is through the proclamation and experience of the Church that the Gospel came to Augustine; but that testimony did not make the Church superior to the Gospel.

These memoranda shed light on Luther's concern that the Church shall be administered in accordance with the Gospel of Jesus Christ. First, the Church does not control the Word of God; the Word creates the Church and remains 'its superior and its judicial authority'.

Secondly, *Ecclesia* here means the visible Church, whether small or large in size (according to Luther's usage, *Gemeinde*, a German term which Luther preferred to *Kirche*, did not necessarily mean a local congregation). Thirdly, Luther was aware that the visible Church needs an order. For the Church to be administered in accordance with the Gospel does not mean that the Church issues no laws; it simply means that the Gospel defines the character, the spirit, and the limitations of Church law and its exercise. Finally, Church order involves a form of supervision. The Lutherans had already declared that 'pastor' and 'bishop' are essentially identical—indeed, that 'the pope has no more power in the use of the keys than any pastor.'[13] But for 'a Church' to be 'under one pastor' does not mean that, even in matters of Church practice, that pastor rules the ecclesiastical community autocratically; rather does he issue regulations with the consent of the community, for 'the pastor or bishop is not the Church.' On this condition not only an episcopal system but even a reformed papacy would be acceptable.

It is against this background that Luther's important letter of 21

---

[12] *WA* 6, 561 (1520); 10.2. 89 f. (1522); 26, 575–7 (1528).

[13] *AC* 28, 30. 53. Cf. Melanchthon's revision of the *Torgau Articles*, May 1530, in *Bekenntnisschriften der ev.-luth. Kirche*, 6 Aufl. (Göttingen, 1970), p. 124.

July to Melanchthon [*WA, Br* 5, 492–5] can be understood. Its specific question was this: what power do bishops have to issue statutes for Church practice? Behind Luther's reply stands his guiding principle that the Church is to be ordered in accordance with the Gospel—without a claim to coercive power: 'In the world, kings lord it over their subjects. ... Not so with you.' [Luke 22: 25 f.]

Consequently, Luther insists, the two *administrationes* (types of order or government), namely, the ecclesiastical and the political or civil, must be kept 'distinct and unmixed'. The Reformer refers to the concrete case of the Bishop of Würzburg who by law is also duke of Franconia. His jurisdictions overlap; for some subjects he is both duke and bishop, whereas for others he is merely the former or the latter. 'As bishop', argues Luther,

a bishop has no authority to impose on his Church any statute ['tradition'] or ceremony, except *with the express or silent consent of the Church*. For the Church is free and lordly [*libera et domina*], and bishops ought not lord it over [*dominari*] the faith[14] of the Churches, nor burden nor oppress them against their will. The bishops are simply servants [*ministri*] and stewards, not lords of the Church. If the Church has agreed, however, as *one body with the bishop*, they may impose on themselves whatever they wish, as long as faith is not violated, and again, they may overlook the statutes for sufficient reason. [492.]

However, 'as a prince, a bishop may impose even less on the Church, for this would mean completely to mix these two powers.' That is, if the bishop uses coercive power (which belongs to a prince) to enforce ecclesiastical statutes, it must be resisted even to death if necessary. 'I am speaking', says Luther, 'of the Church as Church, which is *distinct from the political commonwealth.*' A prince-bishop as prince may exact obedience from his subjects for proper laws, but then 'they obey not as the Church but as citizens.' For example, if the Emperor were to order all his subjects to fast, 'even those who comprise the Church would obey him, since according to the flesh the Church is under the Emperor, but the Church here does not obey as Church.' Hence, neither by ecclesiastical nor by 'profane' law does a bishop have 'the power to impose anything on the Church,' except with the consent of the people [492 f.]. In other words, the Church is the realm of spiritual

---

[14] Cf. 2 Cor. 1: 24, also 1 Pet. 5: 3 and Luke 22: 25.

freedom, not of human lordship. Legitimate statutes for Church practice are those which the faithful are willing freely to obey 'for the sake of love and peace'.

Wilhelm Maurer has remarked how conservative and yet how revolutionary this ecclesiological thought of Luther was [i, 247]. On the one hand, the Reformer still clung to the tradition of 'a Christian society' (*corpus christianum*) with its stratified social order; yet on the other hand, Luther was groping towards a new vision of ordering society which must destroy the whole concept of the prince-bishop. In Maurer's own judgement:

The centuries-old unity between the office of an imperial prince and that of a bishop would inevitably break apart if a bishop functioned in an evangelical way. It was clear that the existing episcopal office in Germany could not be carried over intact into the new situation, as it happened in England and Scandinavia. [Ibid.]

Luther was also groping towards a Church order which could carry out the real task of the Church as the people of God in the world and could effectively curb the autocratic power of the clergy. He was making a start in the direction of checks-and-balances in the administration of the Church, and insisting that even in respect of 'human statutes' the Church 'as Church' must operate by persuasion, not coercion. Above all, the Reformer was attempting to base his entire ecclesiology directly on the Gospel of Jesus Christ—in short, on the reality of justification by grace alone through faith alone.

Throughout July and the succeeding months, Luther continued to carry his thought to the public. In August he completed both his polemical treatise, *The Keys*, and his pastoral *Exposition of Psalm 117*. In the former [WA 30², 465–507], he launched a slashing attack on Roman hierarchical claims. Once again the Reformer repeated that 'the keys' were simply the application—without coercion—of the Gospel of the forgiveness and retention of sins; they did not convey power to make laws or to rule. He particularly assailed the idea that whatever the hierarchy decreed or did was *eo ipso* 'spiritual' and thus beyond the criticism of the laity.

The *Exposition of Psalm 117* [WA 31¹, 223–57] paints a winsome picture of Christ's kingdom. The commentary has four main points: First, that it was God's mission to gather one flock from the ends of the earth, through the means of grace. 'Wherever one finds the Gospel, baptism, and the sacrament [of the Altar], there is his Church, and in that place there are certainly living saints. There people praise him and he rules over them.' [232.] Secondly, this kingdom of Christ is a spiritual kingdom, ruled not by laws as in a civil state but in the spirit of the Gospel. The two types of rule must not be confused. 'What have the popes and bishops made of the Gospel and the Christian Church but a purely "spiritual", yes, even a worldly dominion? And what else are all the new sectarians . . . trying to do but turn the Gospel into outward holiness or a new monasticism . . .?' [242.] Ecclesiastical and civil government there must be, of course, but people are not made Christians or saved thereby. Indeed, 'the substance of Christianity [*ein Christlich wesen*] is a much higher thing and altogether different from all civil *and spiritual* [i.e. ecclesiastical] codes and laws . . .' [241]. The Gospel thus stands above the ecclesiastical administration; Christ's rule in the Christian community is not identical with rule by the organized Church's leadership. Church-sanctioned laws are invalid if independent religious worth is ascribed to them. Thirdly, Christ's kingdom of grace is hidden under the cross, but faith clings to it and remains victorious; and fourthly, the Christian's life is one of thanks, and praise, and service. This is true worship, the true priestly office. The core of this biblical doctrine is salvation by God's sheer grace in Christ; by this teaching the Church stands or falls. [254f.]

Meanwhile in a sheaf of popular tracts during these summer months, Luther addressed several aspects of practical life in German society. *A Sermon on Keeping Children in School* (written in July) [*WA* 30², 517–88], treating the vital importance of education for the welfare of society and Church, was directed toward citizens and parents, while *Psalm cxvii* was beamed to the nobles and princes, and *Psalm cxi* and *Admonition concerning the Sacrament* (both begun in September) to the sacramental community. The *Open Letter on Translating* (September) [*WA* 30², 632–46] set another landmark in Luther's campaign to let the Scriptures speak directly to all people. Here, in short, are to be found a series of sketches of a Christian society not dominated by papal bishops, but ordered instead by 'the Christian conscience guided by love'.[15]

---

[15] Maurer, op.cit., i, 241.

Observers may judge variously the real significance of Luther's declaration in this letter (29 June) to Melanchthon: 'As I have always written, I am ready to yield all things to them [our opponents] provided only that the Gospel is permitted to remain free with us. What is contrary to the Gospel, however, I cannot yield.' [*WA, Br* 5, 407.] No doubt Martin Luther was in any case sincere in disclaiming any thought that *he* should control the Church; only the Gospel should rule in it. His *Exhortation to the Clergy* had proposed to the Roman bishops: Leave us free to preach the Gospel, and you may retain the office with its honours [*WA* 30², 342]. In an *Opinion* [*Judicium*] of late August, commenting on the floundering negotiations at Augsburg, he wrote, 'We do not desire to be bishops or cardinals, but only good Christians ...' [*WA, Br* 5, 595].

It would be irresponsible, of course, to judge Luther simply on the basis of his intentions and hopes while overlooking both his limitations and the complexities of the historical situation. He was not only astigmatic about Roman Catholicism; he vastly underestimated its religious strength. He dismissed the Zwinglians and the newly emerging Protestantism of the Left Wing from his sympathetic concern. The pamphleteer's boast of the achievements of his Reformation was subjected to sharp qualification or denial by some sincere Christians. Despite his vision of administering the Church in accordance with the Gospel and of securing 'the express or tacit consent' of the people for Church statues, he was unable to prevent his movement from developing into a clergy-dominated, authoritarian State-Church system, from which Lutheranism only belatedly began to work free.

At the same time, it would also be irresponsible to overlook the very real, if mixed, results of his practical churchmanship during the crisis of 1530, and of the pioneering ideas which he set loose in European Christendom. It was a time when a world was being lifted off its hinges. As Europeans groped to determine in what directions that world should turn, Luther was one major influence upon their decision-making. But other influences were also at work. The conflict at Augsburg was excruciating, especially for conscientious Christians. At all events, the vision which summoned Luther to his struggling, persistent efforts to renew the Church still gleams before all ecumenically minded Christians today. For how can the Gospel be given free course among God's children, without our pretensions of supporting it by coercive power? Luther's passionate conviction remains challenging: wherever the Gospel is freely proclaimed, 'the form of the Church' is truly, recognizably present.

IV

ECCLESIASTES

B. Luther *Ecclesiast.*
An Historian's Angle

*

LEWIS W. SPITZ

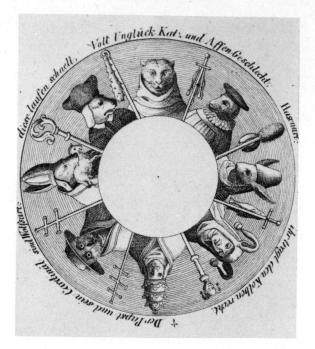

1. The woodcut is an anonymous German satire of the sixteenth century in the Albertina, Vienna. Formerly catalogued as Albertina D. I, Bd. 15, fol. 97, it is currently being given a new inventory number. I wish to thank Professor Christiane Andersson of the Art History department of Columbia University for drawing this woodcut to my attention and Dr Fritz Koreny of the Graphische Sammlung, Albertina, for supplying the identification. A later version and poem printed in 1620 was reprinted by Scheible in 1850 under the title 'Römische-katholisches wunderseltsames Glückrad, auch wahre Abcontrafactur des anti-christlichen Bapstthums'. The poem begins:

> Der Bapst
> Dreh um disz Rädlein, lieber Christ,
> Allhier siehst du den Antichrist,
> Der steht im Anfang oben an,
> Wie bei Marco thut klärlich Stahn,
> Dieser ist des Verderbens Kind,
> Voll Laster, Mord, Geitz, Schand und Sünd,
> Der römisch Bapst, Oelgötz zu Rom,
> Steht hier samt Kreuz und dreifach Kron.

J. Scheible, ed., *Die fliegenden Blätter des XVI. und XVII. Jahrhunderts, in sogenannten Einblatt-Drucken mit Kupferstichen und Holzschnitten; zunächst aus dem Gebiete der politischen und religiösen Caricatur. Aus den Schätzen der Ulmer Stadtbibliothek Wort und Bildgetreu* (Stuttgart: Verlag J. Scheible, 1850), p. 56.

The famous woodcut of *The Seven Heads of Martin Luther* which graced the title-page of Cochlaeus's notorious blast against Luther in 1529 was but one example of that device.[1] An anonymous volvelle of the sixteenth century, now in the Albertina, Vienna, arranged eight clerical heads on a pin-wheel, so that, as it turned, the body of the Antichrist received successive heads, the head of the Pope bearing the triple tiara, an owl decked out in a cardinal's cap, a bishop-wolf with a lamb in its jaws, a Jesuit dog in black costume, a flagellating cat Capuchin, an idolatrous fox-like priest, a Carthusian rabbit, and a foolish nun.[2] Later the *septiceps* device was turned against the Calvinists with a 1619 seven-headed Calvinist spirit depicting him as a friendly human, humble as a lamb, sly as a fox, insatiable as a wolf, bloodthirsty as a leopard, fiery as a dragon, and in every activity like the very Devil.[3] Propagandists of that polemical age were clearly fascinated by the beast who rose up out of the sea 'having seven heads and ten horns, and upon his horns ten crowns, and upon his heads the name of blasphemy'.[4]

Polemicists were fond of describing Luther's theology as chaotic, replete with self-contradictions. The Edict of Worms had already denounced Luther's teaching as a 'stinking slough' of ancient heresies. Cochlaeus argued that Luther constantly contradicted himself and was of different minds about doctrine, for in his unhistoric way Cochlaeus did not take Luther's personal development into account and accordingly cited the early against the mature Luther. Against Henry VIII Luther replied that if it is self-contradiction to cite earlier false opinions against one who has finally seen the truth, then St. Paul's confession in Philippians 3: 7 f. and St. Augustine's *Retractions* make them, too, self-contradictory, to say nothing of Henry VIII himself, who once drank nurse's milk but now enjoyed his wine. Luther saw the doctrine of justification through faith by grace *alone* as the organizational principle and the *theologia crucis* as the key to his theology.[5]

---

[1] Anonymous, yet arguably the work of Brosamer?
[2] See opposite page.   [3] Op. cit., p. 209.   [4] Rev. 13: 1.
[5] Hans Preusz. *Martin Luther der Prophet* (Gütersloh, 1933), pp. 165–7.

For Luther's was a theology with unity, coherence, and special emphasis.

The central head of the seven was 'Luther the ecclesiast'; and quite rightly so, for it was Luther the Churchman, not Luther the humanist, the liberator, the national hero, nor the other roles he played, that characterized his most important contribution to history. For it was his vocation to reform the Church as prophet and priest that moved Luther to action as *ecclesiast*. Despite the fact that Erasmus was more scholar than martyr, more author than priest, more humanist than theologian, he had a very well-thought-out ideal of what a churchman should be like and how he should preach. His last major work was *Ecclesiastes sive de ratione concionandi* in which, as explained in the dedicatory epistle, he both showed the dignity of the office and the virtues which a preacher should possess, as well as how he ought to preach and about what he should preach. This work may, in fact, serve as a mirror to view the full image of Erasmus himself as a reforming churchman. [*LW* 39, 244 and 247] With Luther, the historian is less fortunate, for there is not a single treatise which either spells out all the concerns of the ministry or which reflects Luther's image of himself as an ecclesiast. It is therefore necessary to draw on his many writings, especially those on Church and ministry, comprising three whole volumes in the American edition of the Reformer's works.

Luther was quite self-consciously an 'ecclesiast'. He signed both treatises and letters as 'Ecclesiast of God's grace' or 'Ecclesiast of Wittenberg'. Not only did he find comfort in the title *doctor in biblia* and adopt the humanist moniker 'Eleutherios', the liberator, but he also used the title 'ecclesiast' to denote his role as preacher and priest. In the treatise *Against the Spiritual Estate of the Pope and the Bishops Falsely So Called*, 1522, he began:

Martin Luther, ecclesiastic in Wittenberg by the grace of God ... Although I might be regarded as a fool by you, dear lords, because of the haughty title I call myself, an ecclesiastic by the grace of God, you should know that I am not at all surprised by this ...

This was a decidedly ironic thrust, since by the bull of excommunication, *Exsurge, Domine* (1520) and the Edict of Worms (1521) Luther had been stripped of all ecclesiastical titles. His enemy Jerome Emser, 'goat of Leipzig', Secretary to Duke Georg, and court chaplain, responded with a pamphlet entitled *Against the Ecclesiastic, Falsely So Called, and True Arch-heretic Martin Luther*. But Luther continued to use the title 'Ecclesiast' in many subsequent writings, was addressed as such by others, and even so entitled on medallions and sculptures.[6] Since he preached the Gospel, Luther asserted, he could even call himself an 'unworthy evangelist, an apostle, a prophet.' Little did he know that some day in a funeral sermon Bugenhagen would declare him to be 'that angel of God of which the Apocalypse speaks in Chapter 14 flying in mid-heaven with an eternal gospel to proclaim to those who dwell on earth.'

Luther levelled a devastating criticism against the hierarchical structure of the Church, the claims of the Pope to the headship of the Church, the appropriation by the clergy, secular and regular, of a higher state of spirituality than that of the mere laity, the schism between higher and lower clergy, the forbidding of appeals to a council (*Execrabilis*), and other ecclesiastical developments. From the Wartburg he wrote to Melanchthon (12 May 1521):

Sitting here all day, I picture to myself the state of the church and I see fulfilled the word of Psalm 89 [47]: 'Hast thou made all the sons of men in vain?' God, what a horrible picture of God's wrath is that detestable kingdom of the Roman Antichrist. . . . O kingdom of the pope, worthy of the end and dregs of the ages: God have mercy upon us: [*LW* 48, 215]

Criticism of medieval Church structures grew out of his maturing evangelical theology and personal experience rather than as an offshoot of late medieval conciliarism. He did not from the beginning intend to lead a reform of the Church, but was forced into it by the pressure of public events arising from the indulgences controversy.

Luther thought of the Church not in terms of the clerical hierarchy above and the laity below, nor as an externally-structured institution, nor as a passive association of men, but as the kingdom in which the immanent God works through the Gospel, redeeming and converting mankind. 'For this reason', he explained, 'the Church is and is called the kingdom of God, because in it God alone rules, commands, speaks, acts, and is glorified'. [*WA* 8, 656.] Luther sought to restore the apostolic understanding of the

---

[6] H. Preusz, op. cit., 101 n. 1.

Church as the communion of saints (*communio sanctorum, die Gemeinde der Gläubigen*):

The creed clearly indicates what the Church is, a communion of saints, that is, a company, or assembly, of such people as are Christians and holy, which is called Christian, holy company or church. But the word church [*Kirche*] is too un-German for us now and does not give the sense or thought one must get from the article. [*WA* 50, 624.]

The spiritual kingdom is a realm of listening [*audire*] to the Word of God in which those who hear trust in the promises of God and the benefits of Christ [*promissa dei et beneficia Christi*].

As early as his commentary on Lombard's Sentences in 1509, Luther stressed the Word as the operative force in building the Church. Later he repeatedly declared: 'Where you hear this Word or see it preached, believed, confessed, and acted upon, do not doubt that there most certainly is and must be the true, holy, universal church, a holy Christian people'. [*WA* 50, 629.] The true Church of believers is hidden from human eyes, for the Lord knows those that are his [*WA* 6, 301]. 'For the church, which is called the new heaven and the new earth is invisible but is intelligible through faith', he explained [*WA* 4, 189]. The Church is not invisible in the Platonic sense but in the sense of being abscondite or hidden from human eyes. There is no Church outside individuals like Peter, John, Amsdorf, and such believers, and yet in the Church there is neither Greek nor Jew but Christ alone [*WA* 7, 683]. Moreover, Luther held that there was but one holy catholic or universal Christian Church on earth [the *una sancta*] and not a variety of Churches reflected in the denominations. His treatise *Von den Consiliis und Kirchen* (1539) is properly translated *On the Councils and the Church* and not as 'and the churches', as has often been done [cf. *LW* 41, 8]. In this work Luther consistently pointed to the one, ecumenical, Christian Church made up of all believers and not represented by the Pope and Church councils. In 1520 he declared:

I believe that there is on earth, through the whole wide world, no more than one holy, common, Christian Church, which is nothing else than the congregation, or assembly of the saints, i.e., the pious, believing men on earth, which is gathered, preserved, and ruled by the Holy Ghost, and daily increased by means of the sacraments and the Word of God. [*WA* 7, 219.]

Despite the radical nature of this reformed conception of the Church, Luther believed it to be perfectly comprehensible even for the simplest Christian. 'Thank God', he once exclaimed, 'a child of seven knows what the church is, namely, the holy believers and the lambs who hear their Shepherd's voice'.[7] His Catholic opponent Cajetan, who confronted him at Augsburg, took up the issue of what constituted the Church, for he saw the question as central to the issue of authority and the definition of all other doctrines.

The presence of the true visible Church is known through three signs [*notae*], the preaching of the Word and the administration of the dominical sacraments, baptism and the Lord's Supper. The sacraments are also carriers of the Gospel promise of God's grace and forgiveness. His parole read: the Word comes to the element and makes of it a sacrament [*WA* 50, 631]. Since the Word must be preached and the sacraments administered, a ministry is needed. The *ecclesiast*, the minister, thus relates to the Christian congregation in a new way in Luther's theology. His concept of 'the priesthood of all believers' had radical implications for clerical priesthood and ministry. In 1520 he began to spell out the implications of the believers' priesthood for the *ecclesiast*:

If they [the clergy] were forced to admit that as many of us as have been baptized are all equally priests, as we truly are, and that only the ministry was committed to them, but with our consent, they would soon know that they have no right to rule over us except insofar as we freely agree to it. [*WA* 6, 564]

The Christian congregation has the responsibility for Church government, power over the preaching office, including the administration of the sacraments, the orders of worship, ordination, and the office of the keys. It may and should depose false prophets who are opposed to the Gospel and call a new evangelical pastor, as he argued in his treatise *That a Christian Assembly or Congregation Has the Right and Power to Judge All Teaching, to Call All Teachers, Install and Depose Them, the Basis and Grounds Taken from Holy Scripture* (1523). His ideal was that the true Church order in the world belonged to the Christian people themselves, not to the people who just happened to be members of the

---

[7] *Die Bekennknisschiften der evangelisch-lutherischen Kirche*, 7th edn. (Göttingen, 1976), 459, 20–2.

community or of historical Christendom, but to the Christian believers who had been apprehended by the Word of God.[8] In 1526
Luther gave the fullest expression to his concept of the Church as a
congregation of true believers who voluntarily assemble with
Christ among them in his *German Mass and Order of Worship*.

Given this revision of doctrine, the role of the *ecclesiast* or
minister underwent basic change. No longer was the priest a mem-
ber of a clerical hierarchy which dispensed grace to the laity by the
administration of the sacraments including the penitential system,
but a pastor or minister who shared with his congregation the
priesthood of all believers. In striving to emulate the New-
Testament pattern of Church government, Luther frequently referred to the local minister as a bishop or *episcopus* who oversees
the congregation. The minister has a different office or *Amt* which
is bestowed upon him by the congregation through the call and
ordination, not a different station, estate, or *Stand* from that of lay
Christians. The minister derives his authority from the congregation and he is to serve as preacher of the Word, and administer the
sacraments for and on behalf of the congregation. Thus he sought
to bridge the gap that had developed through the medieval period
between clergy and laity. Luther used the word *Amt* for both
secular offices such as the public work of princes and for the 'spiritual public work of ministers'. If they have been baptized, the
princes and preachers alike belong to the 'spiritual estate'. 'A
pastor exercises the office of the keys, baptizes, preaches, administers
the sacrament, and performs other functions not for his own sake
but for the sake of the congregation', he explained. 'For he is a
servant of the whole congregation, to whom the keys have been
given, even though he himself is a knave; For if he does it in place
of the congregation, the Church does it. If the Church does it,
God does it'. [*WA* 10^3, 215–216.]

The congregation should thus decide upon its own order of service, and Luther objected to imposing one congregation's order of
service on others. The model adopted at Wittenberg, for example,
should not be mandatory for other congregations. If such a model
was adopted by other congregations, it should be done voluntarily
and not under any pressure from a council or group of congregations, for the Church should be a realm of love in the spiritual

---

[8] W. Pauck, *The Heritage of the Reformation* (London, 1968), pp. 48–9.

sphere and should not be ruled by legalism or force [*WA* 10², 140–5]. The minister should be what the word *Amt* implies, a vassal, a servant, a *servus servorum dei et populi*.

Luther's own understanding of himself as an *ecclesiast* and his personal role as a preacher reflected and concretized his theological understanding of Church and ministry. He was, after all, the great Reformer of the Church at large. Professionally he was an exegete who twice weekly during his thirty-three years as a theologian entered the lecture hall and expounded his understanding of the Scriptures, armed with biblical texts on his lectern, annotations on one side and collations on the other. So professorial was he that on 9 October 1531, while lecturing on Galatians, he had to confess *Ego oblitus sum* ['Help me, class, for "I have forgotten" exactly where I was!'] Gordon Rupp, the leading English Luther Scholar, has given us a vivid and impressive picture of the Wittenberg Reformer and his lectures from the pen of one of his students.[9]

Martin Luther was not a scholar in the modern technical sense of excelling in scholarship, winning points in a one-upmanship profession. But he was a great scholar in using the latest and best tools whether linguistic or textual for rendering more precise and authentic his Scriptural interpretation and understanding. He was a productive scholar and an author of consequence. Often, as when he wrote his *Address to the Christian Nobility*, the printers snatched the pages from his hands as he wrote them before he had completed the work. 'I deliver as soon as I conceive!' he exclaimed. He contrasted the scholar who writes with just three fingers but whose whole body, soul, and spirit is engaged in an exhausting enterprise, with the peasant who physically follows the plough and oxen around the field, and the knight whose work consists of sitting in a suit of armour letting one leg dangle down each side of a horse. His 450 books and treatises and sixty-thousand pages bear witness to his prolific output. To a student who asked why he stayed in the 'ivory tower' and did not enter the front line of the parish, he gave the professorial reply that he was sending his books forth into all the world. In the *Table Talk* he pronounced that 'every great book is an action just as every great action is a book!' 'We continue to be disciples', he wrote in his commentary on Psalm 101, 'of those speechless masters which we call books'.

[9] E. G. Rupp, *Luther's Progress to the Diet of Worms* (New York, 1964), p. 44.

'Learning, wisdom and writers must rule the world', he said in his *Table Talk*. He would have agreed with Emerson who called scholars 'the eyes and the heart of the world'. He was a great scholar in the modesty with which he approached his awesome subject. 'Theology', he wrote, 'is infinite wisdom which can never be learned. [*WA* 40³, 63]

In history Luther emerged as the great Reformer of the Church. He never spoke of his movement as the reformation of the Church, but reserved the word 'reformation' for the more modest though, knowing universities, perhaps more difficult enterprise of the reformation of the university. He is thought of in those heroic moments as the stand at Worms or the anguish at Coburg. 'We have become the spectacle of the world!' he exclaimed in 1521. The Reformation as a movement has been the subject of a scholarly examination almost without parallel, for one historian has asserted that more has been written about Luther than about any other person in the history of the world with the exception of Christ. A student who examined Lord Acton's notes on which his unannotated essays on the Reformation were based reported that he had read over twenty thousand volumes. Luther's professorial career on the one hand, and the dramatic events of the Reformation on the other, have obfuscated the simple fact that all he did as professor and reformer he did as an *ecclesiast*, a minister of the Church. Over two thousand of his sermons are still extant. When he preached he was exegetical, just as when he lectured exegetically, he preached. Over two thousand five hundred and eighty letters are still extant, and most of them are concerned not with personal matters but with the care of souls, the cause of the Gospel, and the rebuilding of the Church.

In 1515 the city council of Wittenberg called Luther to serve as regular assistant pastor in the *Stadtkirche* or City Church. When the main pastor, Johannes Bugenhagen, left on various reforming missions to Denmark, Bremen, and elsewhere, Luther served as interim pastor and undertook a heavy preaching schedule. On his return to Wittenberg from the Wartburg (1522), he undertook to preach an entire week beginning with *Invocavit* Sunday. When the Saxon delegation stayed in Coburg in 1530 *en route* for the Diet of Augsburg, Luther preached no less than seven times in St. Moriz church between 16 April and 21 April. He was above all a preacher of the Gospel and a *minister verbi divini*.

When in Article seven of the *Augsburg Confession* Melanchthon defined the Church as 'the congregation of the saints in which the Gospel is rightly preached and the sacraments are rightly administered', he was in perfect harmony with the man who waited restlessly in the Feste Coburg and wrote on the wall of his room in that castle: 'I shall not die, but live, and declare the works of the Lord'. [Ps. 118: 17.]

Luther once called the Church a speech-house [*Mundhaus*] rather than a pen-house. These statements are characteristic of his assessment of the preaching office: 'The Gospel ministry [*evangelizandi officium*] is the greatest of all; it is apostolic; it is the office that lays the foundation of the other offices'. [*WA* 12, 191.] 'On the man who is ordained to the ministry the highest office in Christendom is conferred'. [*WA* 11, 415.] 'Next to the preaching office God speaks with us. In prayer I speak with God'. [*WA* 34¹, 395.] 'The preaching office is the office of the Holy Spirit. Even though men do the preaching, baptizing, forgiving of sins, it is the Holy Spirit who preaches and teaches. It is his work and office'. [*WA* 28, 479.] 'A Christian preacher is a minister of God who is set apart, yes, he is an angel of God, a very bishop sent by God, a saviour of many people, a king and prince in the kingdom of Christ and among the people of God, a teacher, a light of the world. There is nothing more precious or nobler on earth and in this life than a true, faithful parson [*Pfarrer*] or preacher'. [*WA* 30², 533.]

The Reformers most frequently referred to the minister as 'preacher' [*Prediger* or *Praedikant*]. They also spoke of the minister as a pastor or shepherd, but this term did not come into general use until the eighteenth century under the influence of Pietism. The German Reformers likewise retained the medieval term *Pfarrer* or parson, which was derived from the word *parochus*, or parson, and *parochia*, the parish. The common folks usually called the minister the 'preacher', although they retained the word 'priest' [*Pfaff*] and other Catholic terms.[10] Even before Luther's advent, there had been in the fifteenth and early sixteenth century a widespread revival of reform-minded preaching. Preacherships were endowed alongside the regular parochial priests, especially in the South West and in Switzerland, much like the Puritan lectureships

---

[10] W. Pauck, op. cit., 101–43.

a century later. But for Protestantism, preaching and the sermon were central to worship.

Luther's own preaching was plain and expository. Anything but a *rusticus*, as he called himself in deference to Erasmus in the treatise *On the Bondage of the Will*, he was a learned scholar and a sophisticated theologian. Nevertheless, in his sermons he made no display of his erudition but spoke to the hearts of plain folk in the congregation. In a clear tenor voice he spoke on the basis of the text, usually using the standard pericopes. With his highest academic degree, *doctor in biblia*, 1512, he received the right and duty to preach. Nearly all of his extant sermons do not come from his pen but from the notes of students and colleagues. They all bear witness to his conviction that the sermon, the *verbum evangelii vocale*, as the spoken Word of God was the key instrument by which the Holy Spirit worked faith in the heart of the hearer and moved him to greater holiness of life. 'When the Word of God goes forth', he wrote, 'it proceeds with power!' [*WA* 56, 422.] Luther learned much from the classical and humanist rhetorical and pedagogical tradition, specifically from Quintilian, but he adopted no single methodology. The goal of homiletics was *doctrina et exhortatio Evangelii Christi*!

Idiosyncratic or personal intrusions were marks of the non-evangelical preacher. It is remarkable that in the most tense crises of his life, when the storms of the Reformation were raging and his enemies were threatening his destruction, he did not turn his sermons into *ad hominem* or self-serving pleading, but to glorify the God of grace, whom he had found in Christ the Saviour. The hearer for Luther was a neighbour in need. But Luther often felt dissatisfied with his own preaching. 'Often when I have come down from the pulpit', he confessed, 'I have spat upon myself: Phew on you, how have you preached? Certainly you delivered the message well, but you did not follow the outline'. [*WA, TR* 4, 446–7, No 4719.] Luther confided that he was frequently troubled in his sleep by the dream that he had to preach but did not have an outline [*WA, TR* 3, 357–8, No 3494].

The full range of Luther's concern as preacher–teacher can best be seen in his catechisms in which he taught children and laymen rather than theological students or candidates for the ministry. It is possible to develop a picture of Luther's Wittenberg congregation as reflected in his sermons in the City Church. To these parishion-

ers who knew him so well he made allusions to personal experiences during his monastic period, his struggle for a right relation
to God, his conversion to the evangelical understanding of theology, and his Reformation battles. He always did so, however,
to make a point about works-righteousness and the Gospel, the
hierarchical Church, and the new congregation of faith. He was
much more intimate in revealing his personal feelings and much
more personal in his admonitions and encouragement than in sermons preached to other congregations far distant from home. He
knew that preaching was a wearing, wearying, and often thankless
task, yet it was his calling and he held to it. As he wrote:

I often complain, and the old Adam in me often drives me to give up
preaching. But still, that is my task. I have God's command and know
that it is right. But they cast so many stones into my garden and so much
salt into my soup, that I am compelled to complain . . . But if I should become king or emperor today, I would not quit preaching . . . When I
preach and lecture, I know that I have preached a sermon for God and
have lectured to his glory.[11]

Luther the *ecclesiast* served his congregation, his university, and
evangelicals throughout the Church as a sensitive and perceptive
Seelsorger or curator, a caretaker of souls. He was critical of the
fear-inducing and legalistic penitential system of late medieval
Catholicism. He retained the confessional as a useful form of pastoral contact and care, and he developed an 'evangelical ethos' of
ministerial counselling. His personal approach as *ecclesiast* to the
spiritual and personal problems of others is reflected in his own
letters of spiritual counsel. He offers comfort for the sick and
dying, consolation for the bereaved, cheer for the anxious and
melancholy, instructions to the perplexed and dying, admonitions
to steadfastness and courage, counsel in questions of sex and marriage, suggestions for problems facing preachers, exhortations to
rulers, and many other pastoral matters. The four thousand two
hundred and eleven letters in the eleven volumes of the Weimar
edition of his works reveal Luther the *ecclesiast* at work. Most
touching for academics in this context is Luther's social concern
for students, their financial and their personal problems. His concern for students extended well beyond their religious and intellec-

[11] Quoted in Harold J. Grimm, *Martin Luther as a Preacher* (Columbus, Ohio,
1929), p. 121.

tual problems to embrace their social affairs as well. His interest in them lasted through the years, far beyond their promotion to degrees, for he looked after their professional deployment, their social well-being, their career prospects, and continued to intervene on their behalf with city and princely authorities years later. 'Let them call us doctors and masters if they please', he declared, 'but youth is the seed and the fount of the church'. [*WA, TR* 5, 239. No 5557.]

Luther's biographers have consistently focused their attention on the heroic early years, and allowed their narrative to ebb away during the last three lustra of his life. Luther as *ecclesiast* becomes increasingly important, however, during the decade and a half following the Diet of Augsburg of 1530. His correspondence with city councils and territorial chancellors was largely concerned with the introduction of reformation into new areas and with the organization of the Evangelical Churches. So great was his prestige that the general pattern was for councils or chancellors to consult him on how they should proceed. In contrast to Calvin, he did not introduce a new Church order juridical in nature, but rather his contribution was a *ius liturgicum*, orders of worship, of baptism, of ordination, and marriage. His authority as 'the reformer' gave him the power of moral suasion. He was constantly consulted about the organization of reformed Churches throughout the empire and well beyond to the North, East, and North-East especially. His colleague Bugenhagen composed the Church orders for Braunschweig, Hamburg, Lübeck, Pomerania, and Schleswig-Holstein. Luther once joked about their roles on the occasion of the visit of the papal nuncio Vergerio in Wittenberg in 1535. He and Bugenhagen rode in front in a gala state-coach and Luther laughed: 'There go the German pope and his Cardinal Pomeranus'.[12] Luther was the sovereign ideological expert and Bugenhagen the curial administrator who looked after practical arrangements.

Contrary to some scholarly opinion, Luther did not alter his views regarding the ideal form of Church government after 1526. In the Saxon visitation documents of 1527 to 1528, he understood the role of the authorities as that of Christians in authority, not as a Christian authority, gifted with the means and power to effect reforms for the community Church. He never before nor after the

---

[12] Bugenhagen came from Pomerania.

mid-1520s resolved the tension between a congregation of true believers and a *Volkskirche*, a community or people's Church, which
would at least promote good public morals, even if it was not a
congregation composed of true believers in Christ. Luther's emphases were determined by the situation in which he found himself,
for against the papal hierarchy, he stressed the 'priesthood of all
believers', and against the enthusiasts or *Schwärmer*, he emphasized the importance of called and ordained ministers of the Word.
But he held to both views consistently and simultaneously over the
years, for he believed the special and common ministries to be not
merely compatible, but mutually interdependent.

The special role played by the Christians in authority in the
Saxon Church and elsewhere, he viewed as a temporary measure
until the people were ready to take over leadership. The governments
and their representatives acting as visitors or as members of the
consistory which administered the external support of the Church
were in his mind merely *Nothischöfe,* emergency bishops. Luther
was not even opposed in principle to episcopacy as a way of ordering the Church; but the bishops would serve *de iure humano* and
not *de iure divino*. Early on he even dreamt of episcopacy in Germany under the headship of the Archbishop of Mainz [*WA*, 6, 429
ff.]. Later on he wrote, on 20 May 1539, to Prince Georg of
Anhalt: 'I do not desire the ruin but the reformation of episcopacy'. [*WA, Br* 8, 432] He wrote 'directives for the consecration of
a truly Christian bishop' [*WA* 33, 219 f]. Elector Johann Friedrich
of Saxony asked Luther to write a defence of his ordination of
Nikolaus von Amsdorf as Bishop of Naumburg-Zeitz on 20 January 1542. And Luther explained that:

The matter depends on whether the congregation and the bishop agree,
that is, whether the congregation wishes to be taught by the bishop and
the bishop is willing to teach the congregation. This settles the matter.
The laying on of hands blesses, ratifies, and bears witness to this agreement, as a notary public and witnesses testify to a secular matter and as a
pastor in blessing groom and bride ratifies their marriage and testifies that
they have previously taken each other and have publicized this fact. [*WA*
53, 257.]

The Scandinavian churches were not out of line, then, with
Luther's willingness to accommodate external forms of Church
government forced upon the Evangelicals by circumstances so long

as the principle of the priesthood of all believers and ministerial
and episcopal authority as derived from the congregation and not
bestowed by a clerical hierarchy was preserved. In a treatise of
1523, Luther laid down the principle that it is the call from the
congregation, and not the authority of the bishop who ordains
him, that makes a minister's office valid. 'No bishop is to install
anyone', he wrote, 'without the choice, will, and call of the congregation, but he is to confirm him who has been chosen and
called by the congregation. If he does not do this, the person is
nonetheless to be considered confirmed by the call of the congregation'. [*WA* 11, 414.]

History may have played tricks on Luther, as Dame Veronica
Wedgwood once observed, because territorial churches developed
into juridical structures, the state dominating the Church in Germany down to 1918. A remnant of that dependence remains with
the state still collecting the *Kirchensteuer* or tax money for the
Church.[13] The developments within Lutheranism during the
second half of the sixteenth century in theology, the confessions,
and ecclesiastical developments for the most part reflected Luther's
own understanding of the concepts of Church and state, and the
nature of their interrelationship as developed in the Reformer's
'two-kingdoms,' theory. A comparison of the views of Martin
Chemnitz (1522–1586), the great Lutheran dogmatician, with
those of Luther bears out their theoretical and theological consan-
guinity. A popular adage ran: 'If Martin [Chemnitz] had not come
along, Martin [Luther] would hardly have survived.' Chemnitz
was one of the fathers of the *Formula of Concord* (1577), that final
symbol of the Lutheran confessional era, which remained basically
true to Luther's teaching in the area of Church and State.

Luther the *ecclesiast* undertook to live a life of service which
corresponded to the requirements of his theology, to his conception of the Church and of the ministry. 'My office', he wrote, 'and
that of every preacher and minister, does not consist in any sort of
lordship but in serving all of you, so that you learn to know God,
become baptized, have the true Word of God, and finally are
saved.' [*WA* 47, 368.] The *ecclesiast* must bear the burdens of the
preacher, of the caretaker of souls, of the minister and the organizer of the Churches. Though he often longed to lay down those

[13] See E. G. Rupp, *The Righteousness of God* (London, 1953), pp. 310–28.

bųrdens, Luther was unable to do so until his dying day. He often wrote of the all but frightening burdens of the ministry:

If I wanted to write about the burdens of a minister as I know and have experienced them, I would frighten all away from the office. For a good minister, must hazard everything, so that nothing is dearer to him than Christ and eternal life and that, after he has lost this life and everything, Christ may say: Come to Me, son. I hope He will speak this way to me, too, on that Day, for here He speaks very unkindly to me. I am burdened with the entire world, with the emperor and the pope. [*WA, TR* 1, 197–8. No 453.]

Two days before his death Luther included these words in his farewell note to the world: 'Let no one who has not guided the congregations with the prophets for one hundred years believe that he has tasted Holy Writ thoroughly.'[14] As an *ecclesiast* Luther was a pivotal personality, a man of universal appeal and of lasting historical importance.

Luther did not take Cochlaeus very seriously as an antagonist and announced that he would not respond to his books, for to ignore those books would make Cochlaeus even more furious. He considered Cochlaeus a man of inflated *ego*. He compared him to a fly on top of a wagonload of hay. When the wagon was pulled in and the hay unloaded, the fly said, 'Oh, the devil! how much dust one fly can stir up!' Luther chuckled that Cochlaeus was like a flea that fell off a camel and said to the camel: 'Oh, I think you must feel what a great burden you have been carrying!' When he saw the woodcut of the seven-headed Luther adorning Cochlaeus', or *Kochlöffel's* (cooking spoon) *Septiceps Lutherus*, Luther was very much amused and remarked: 'Everything about the seven heads pleases me well, but it is a sin and a shame that seven heads cannot bring forth or be worthy of a neck.'[15]

[14] Quoted in H. Bornkamm, *Luther's World of Thought* (St. Louis, 1958), p. 291.
[15] *WA, TR* 2, 381–2, No 2258b.

V

SUERMERUS

Luther's Own Fanatics

*

MARK U. EDWARDS, JR.

FOR Catholic John Cochlaeus, the fanatic with bees in his bonnet was but one voice in the discordant dialogue among the seven 'heads' of Martin Luther. The discord itself proved to Cochlaeus' satisfaction that Luther could not be of the true Church or possess the Holy Spirit, for he was a spirit of unity not of discord. Cochlaeus certainly recognized that Luther had his own buzzing fanatics, against whom the Reformer made the same indictment— namely that their disunity disclosed their satanic spirit. 'Thus he speaks against his own fanatics', Cochlaeus wrote. 'The devil is the father of all disunity. But God is not a god of disunity. And all Christians are of one mind.' For as he urged upon his reader, 'Keep this in mind as you peruse this book, and you shall amply realize which is the true Church ruled by the Holy Spirit.'[1]

For once Cochlaeus had a point. Luther did blast his Evangelical opponents—his 'fanatics'—for their alleged lack of unity; and that there was in fact no unity is hardly surprising when it is considered that Luther lumped together under the category of 'fanatics' such diverse opponents as Andreas Bodenstein von Karlstadt, the Zwickau Prophets, the rebellious peasants, Ulrich Zwingli, Johannes Oecolampadius, Martin Bucer, and Thomas Müntzer. The only actual connection binding all these opponents was Luther's view that they were all 'false brethren', minions of Satan, bent on subverting the Reformation from within. This essay will examine the way in which Luther acquired his own fanatics, and his striking view of their unity in discord.

I

In 1522 Luther was summoned home from the Wartburg by members of his Wittenberg congregation to grapple with a reform

---

[1] John Cochlaeus, S[ieben] K[öpffe Martini Luthers vom hochwirdigen Sacrament des Altars] (Valentinus Schumann, Leipzig, 1529), Ai verso. This is a German translation by Cochlaeus of 6 of the 45 articles of his *Septiceps Lutherus, unique sibi, suis scriptis, contrarius in visitationem saxonicam per D. D. Joa. Cocleum editus* (Valentinus Schumann, Leipzig, 1529). The charge of self-contradiction recurs frequently in the polemic of Cochlaeus.

movement that some felt had got out of hand. On leaving the castle, he wrote an ironic letter to his prince, the Elector Friedrich der Weise, congratulating him as an avid collector of relics on the acquisition of a 'new relic'. Disturbances always accompany God's Word, Luther explained; and if Satan attacks from without, he also attacks within [*WA, Br* 2, 448–9]. *En route* to Wittenberg, he wrote again. This time he explained that his first letter was intended to reassure the Elector about the 'untoward movement introduced by our friends in Wittenberg to the great detriment of the Gospel', which he feared would be a great burden to his prince. He was particularly distressed that such disturbances would be blamed on him, and even worse, impugn the good name of the Gospel [*WA, Br* 2, 454].

The 'untoward movement' in question began when, on 29 September 1521, the young humanist Philip Melanchthon, with several of his students, took communion in both kinds. A few days later, the Augustinian Gabriel Zwilling preached an impassioned sermon against the Mass, and shortly afterwards the Order discontinued celebrations. Presiding at a disputation, Luther's faculty colleague Andreas Bodenstein von Karlstadt also questioned the Mass; and Melanchthon advocated its reform without regard for objections from those of tender conscience.

The pace soon quickened, and during November the Augustinians left their Wittenberg cloister. On 3 December a mob interrupted Mass in the Parish Church; and the following morning a manifesto was nailed to the door of the Franciscan Church threatening its seizure by the people. On 12 December, Karlstadt, Melanchthon, and other reforming members of a commission charged with investigating the Augustinians' recent actions, submitted a majority report which strongly advocated the reform of the Mass. At much the same time, too, the Wittenberg citizenry submitted six articles to the *Rat* and demanded free preaching, the abolition of various practices related to the Mass, communion in both kinds, and the abolition of taverns and brothels.

On Christmas Eve, bands of students and townsfolk roamed the streets harrassing those faithful to 'the old religion'. The next day, Karlstadt entered the parish Church of All Saints without the customary vestments, preached a sermon urging the congregation to communicate even if they had not been to confession, and then administered communion in both kinds. He omitted all references

to sacrifice; spoke the words of institution in German; and eliminated the elevation of the consecrated host. The day after Christmas
too, with a group of notables drawn from both town and gown
(including Melanchthon and Justus Jonas), Karlstadt visited the
neighbouring village of Sagrena to announce his betrothal to the
young daughter of a poor nobleman. Their marriage took place in
mid-January.

Meanwhile there were other problems. Late in December, three
men who were to be called the 'Zwickau Prophets', arrived in Wittenberg. These men—Nicholas Storch and Thomas Drechsel, both
weavers, and Marcus Stubner, an alumnus of Wittenberg and ac-
quaintance of Melanchthon—claimed that they had been called of
God, and that their teaching came from the Spirit rather than from
Scripture. Their visit caused Melanchthon and the Elector some
considerable anxiety, but no action was taken.

During the month of January, the reforms spread throughout
the surrounding towns and villages as 'evangelical masses' were
celebrated and priests were married. The General Chapter of the
German Augustinians met in Wittenberg and issued two documents supporting and justifying their exodus from the Wittenberg
cloister. Then too, on 10 or 11 January, the Augustinian brethren
led by Zwilling demolished all the altars in their convent except
one, and likewise removed religious paintings from the walls and
burned them. The movement reached its climax on 24 January
when, in the Wittenberg Ordinance, the reforms of the previous
months were codified. The mayor then announced to the Elector
that the University and the City Council were united in their
decisions.

This last step proved too much for Frederick who feared political repercussions if it seemed that he sanctioned any ordinance that
changed ecclesiastical practice. For some months he had allowed
Wittenbergers to dispute, write, and preach about innovations, but
not to introduce them in practice as if he was waiting for general
agreement. But now the Elector refused to accept the Ordinance,
not only in its original form, but also in the compromised revision
worked out in mid-February. It was a stand that faced the citizen
body with a dilemma: either they must undo their reforms, or they
would defy their prince. Subsequent events indicate that the
majority were unwilling to take the second option, although Karlstadt may well have been an exception to the general rule. As

several of his later treatises indicate, he firmly held that it was sinful to neglect many of the reforms set out in the Ordinance, and also believed that lenience to those of tender conscience often disguised a sinful unwillingness to institute reforms demanded by the Gospel.

For his part, Luther had without doubt encouraged and supported many of the reforms set out in the Wittenberg Ordinance. In public treatise and private letters he had inspired and endorsed clerical marriage [WA, Br 2, 4231], the exodus of religious from convents and monasteries [WA 8, 323–5, 573–669; WA, Br 2, 379, 404–5, 415], and changes in the practice of the Mass [WA, Br 2, 372–3; WA 8, 411–76]. In early December 1521, after a short and secret visit to Wittenberg, he had announced to Spalatin his approval of events taking place there—despite the fact that students and townsfolk had recently occupied the parish Church and disrupted the Mass and threatened to do the same to the Franciscan Church [WA, Br 2, 409–10]. Moreover, Luther's friends in Wittenberg, who were certainly his primary source of information on events there, were apparently agreed on the reforms of mid-February despite some disturbances accompanying their implementation.

Perhaps the first hints of disquiet on Luther's part appear in his letter of 17 February to the Elector's Chaplain-Secretary, George Spalatin, in which he reports hearing rumours about more significant goings-on in Wittenberg than those that prompted his brief December visit. He informed Spalatin that he was considering another trip, although not because of the Zwickau Prophets. Such laymen were dismissed at this time as unimportant [WA, Br 2, 443].

There was no clear word from Luther between 17 January and about 22 February, 1522, when he wrote to inform the Elector that he was returning to Wittenberg, and congratulated him on the 'new relic'. The Elector tried to dissuade Luther, but to no avail [WA, Br 2, 449–53]. On 6 March Luther thus arrived in Wittenberg; and three days later, tonsured and robed once again as an Augustinian, Dr Martinus mounted the pulpit of the Parish Church to begin the famous *Invocavit* sermons and thus reestablish his control over the progress of the Reformation [WA 10^3, 1–64].

Why did Luther return to Wittenberg? Perhaps partly because

he now feared that the movement there was directed not only against clergy of the old faith, but also against secular authority. In his *Admonition against Insurrection and Rebellion* (December 1521), he had warned that mob action and rebellion never brought about necessary advance so that insurrection was never right, no matter how just the cause it sought to promote. Satan, he argued, was trying to stir up rebellion through supporters of the Gospel in order to bring their teaching into disrepute [*WA* 8, 680–3]. It should also be recalled that Luther felt strongly that reforms in ecclesiastical practice should never be made matters of conscience, or carried through precipitately without due regard for the sensibilities of those sincere Christians who were slow to understand and accept the changes. This was the central message of the *Invocavit* sermons [*WA* 10³, 1–64].

Taking these convictions of the Reformer together with the events in Wittenberg, it seems reasonable to argue that Luther returned to forestall a confrontation between the Elector and the Wittenbergers caused, on one side, by the Elector's fears that the Ordinance would lead him into conflict with the imperial government, and on the other by the insistence of some citizens (at least Karlstadt) that certain ecclesiastical reforms were matters of conscience and must be carried through immediately, whatever the consequences. For Luther, defiance of the Elector on these issues was theologically unwarranted; and to make matters worse, such defiance lent credence to the charge that the Reformation movement led inexorably to rebellion and violence.

Within days of his return to Wittenberg, Luther singled out Karlstadt and Zwilling as the authors of the disturbances [*WA*, *Br* 2, 478]. He also held Karlstadt responsible for the Wittenberg Ordinance despite the fact that the City Council and the University had apparently agreed upon the reforms in January, and the representatives of the University, including Melanchthon, Jonas, and Nicholas von Amsdorf, had stoutly defended them in mid-February [*WA*, *Br* 2, 491]. Not without justice, Karlstadt later complained that he had been left 'holding the bag' [*WA* 15, 337].

Luther's subsequent attack on Karlstadt and Zwilling suggests that he felt it necessary to make the issue of responsibility clear-cut. Believing that his own reputation and, more important, the reputation of the Reformation movement to be at stake, he went out of his way to disavow those allegedly responsible as unequivocally and convincingly as possible. The disavowal took the form of *ad hominem* attack on grounds Luther himself felt to be theologically sound, and which his supporters likewise found credible. Drawing on Scriptural accounts and episodes in the long history of heresy, the Reformer thus warned that Satan had once again sent false prophets to confound the true Church. Although such prophets appeared to follow the Gospel, they were in fact 'Judases'; and Luther laid all responsibility for their excesses on the satanic spirit which he claimed motivated each one of them.

In order that the false prophet could be recognized for what he was, Luther defined the salient characteristics of the true prophet and apostle in a letter to Melanchthon early in January 1522. Relying on the Bible for his authority, he told Melanchthon that a true prophet must be called through men, or at least attested to by signs, and must also have experienced spiritual distress and the divine birth, death, and hell [*WA, Br* 2, 424–5]. When he wrote this, Luther intended such criteria to be applied to the Zwickau Prophets. But they could as well be applied to Karlstadt and Zwilling since, as far as Luther was concerned, they too confessed to no spiritual distress, temptations, and doubts of the kind true prophets, apostles, and even he himself had experienced. Furthermore, they all lacked the proper calling. Karlstadt may thus have been called to preach in the Castle Church, but he had done most of his inflammatory preaching in Luther's pulpit in the Parish Church where, technically at least, he did not belong. Zwilling had not been called to public preaching in Wittenberg or elsewhere. The Zwickau Prophets had the least justification for their preaching of any, for they were mere laymen who claimed their authority solely from a divine call, and yet were unable to produce any signs other than those Satan himself could produce, namely violence and unrest [*WA, Br* 2, 424]. The failure of Karlstadt, Zwilling, and the Zwickau Prophets to meet these tests identified them to Luther's satisfaction as false prophets and Satan's minions.

Further evidence of the satanic motivation of such men, Luther believed, was their insistence that people were guilty of a sin if certain Old Testament commandments and New Testament examples were not followed to the letter. Such insistence imposed the secular kingdom upon the spiritual and reshackled consciences with laws and regulations from which Christ had freed them. Karlstadt, for example, had clearly argued for the enforcement of the Old

Testament commandment against the worship of idols, and had applied it to images in Church.[2] He had also argued that the example of the first institution of the Lord's Supper made it mandatory that communion in both kinds be taken by the communicants, preferably in their own hands and without prior confession and absolution.[3]

Luther accused Karlstadt of expending all his efforts on ceremonies and external matters while neglecting true Christian doctrine—namely faith and love. In all this, Luther saw Satan attempting to ruin the Gospel by making non-essential issues a burden to consciences. He also alleged that Karlstadt wished to become the community's teacher and set up his ordinances among the people on his own authority [WA, Br 2, 491]. If Luther still harboured any doubts that Karlstadt believed ceremonies to be a matter of conscience, they were removed when he read Karlstadt's latest manuscript, which was passed to the printers in April 1522. The treatise was ostensibly directed against the Catholic theologian Ochsenfart, but in its more heady passages it could equally well have applied to Luther. For example, Karlstadt wrote that if a pastor who was celebrating the Lord's Supper failed to turn towards the congregation and speak the words of institution to them, he made the people commit a deadly sin; and he also stressed that it was a greater sin to have images on the altar than to commit adultery and robbery, since the worship of images was against the first commandment.[4] Open conflict between the two Faculty professors was only avoided when the University censorship committee forbade the publication of Karlstadt's manuscript.

Karlstadt and the Zwickau Prophets demonstrated for Luther another important characteristic of the false prophet: they stubbornly resisted a fraternal admonition, and wished to have their teaching and claims accepted without question [WA, Br 2, 427, 448–9, 460, 471, 478, 491, 493]. Karlstadt would not admit that he had erred despite several conversations with Luther [WA, Br 2, 471, 509]; and the Zwickau Prophets were even more obdurate in the face of a 'fraternal admonition'. Gabriel Zwilling was the only one

---

[2] See Karlstadt's *Von abtuhung der Bylder, Und das keyn Betdler unther den Christen seyn soll*, ed. Hans Lietzmann (Bonn, 1911).

[3] Hermann Barge, *Andreas Bodenstein von Karlstadt* (Leipzig, 1905; Nieuwkoop, 1968), vol. i, 290, 359–60.

[4] Barge, op.cit., ii, 563–5.

of Luther's colleagues who acknowledged that he had erred and had pressed the matter too far [*WA, Br* 2, 472, 478].

In short, all demonstrated to Luther's satisfaction the traditional view that false prophets and heretics were vain men who sought the applause of the mob. Karlstadt's sensational public sermons, and the Zwickau Prophets' activities among the artisan classes, revealed to Luther's conservative eyes an interest more in rabble-rousing than in God's Word. Within weeks of his return, too, Luther had regained complete control of the Wittenberg movement for reform. He had easily overcome his first evangelical opponents, and in so doing had set the pattern he was to follow in the decades ahead. He saw Satan's spirit at work in an opposition attempting to accomplish through guile what could not have been brought about through force; and he identified many of this spirit's distinguishing characteristics. In the years ahead, the actual behaviour and beliefs of his evangelical opponents—his 'fanatics'—tended to disappear behind this vision of the false prophet and minion of Satan.

II

In the summer of 1523, isolated and in disrepute at the University, Karlstadt finally left Wittenberg for the Thuringian countryside to settle down in the vicarage at Orlamunde, much of the delight of the City Council and congregation. He had not, however, given up all interest in the wider world, and continued to turn out tracts on various theological subjects. Unable to get any of his more controversial works past the censors at Wittenberg, he turned first to presses in Strassburg, ahd later in Jena.[5] Early in 1524 Luther tried unsuccessfully to put a stop to these publishing activities, or at least to bring them under some kind of control [*WA, Br* 3, 233].

To add to Luther's distrust of Karlstadt, rumours began reaching Wittenberg about the removal of images from the Orlamunde Church, about changes in the celebration of the Lord's Supper, and even about the abolition of infant baptism [*WA, Br* 3, 231, 255 n.3]. By March 1524, Luther was characterizing these reforms as 'monstrosities', and both he and the University felt it

---

[5] See Erich Hertzsch, ed., *Karlstadts Schriften aus den Jahren* 1523–25 (2 vols., Halle, 1956–7).

necessary to recall Karlstadt from Orlamunde, 'to which he was not called', to Wittenberg, where he had the responsibility to teach and preach [WA, Br 3, 254, 256].

Karlstadt wisely heeded the university summons. After some negotiations, he agreed to resign the Orlamunde vicarage and return to his academic duties in Wittenberg. When packing up in Orlamunde, however, he apparently had second thoughts, and with his congregation sought delay but to no avail. A formal summons was thus issued for Karlstadt's return, and this he ignored.[6]

In March of the same year, the followers of Thomas Müntzer burned a chapel outside the gates of Allstedt. Müntzer had been pastor in Zwickau from 1519 to 1521, having been recommended for the position by Luther.[7] His beliefs had, however, gradually diverged from those of Luther, and his increasingly radical preaching and association with the Zwickau Prophets had involved him in such controversy in Zwickau that he had been forced to leave (April 1521). After a largely successful visit to Prague, where he had attempted to rally support for his spiritualistic and chiliastic vision of the Gospel, Müntzer had taken up residence in the Thuringian town of Allstedt.

After the burning of the chapel, Duke Johann of Ernestine Saxony, as Lord of Allstedt, insisted that the culprits be punished. But the Allstedt Council and Müntzer successfully resisted the implementation of this order. In a letter to Duke Johann's son, Johann Friedrich, Luther labelled Müntzer the 'Satan at Allstedt', complaining that he was using the freedom and safety secured through the triumph of the Gospel to spread his poison. Luther saw Müntzer's unwillingness to give account of his teachings before Wittenberg University or to risk persecution outside Ernestine Saxony as a sure sign that Müntzer was a false prophet [WA, Br 3, 307–8].

On the basis of such rumours about Karlstadt and Müntzer, Duke Johann Friedrich thought it wise for Luther to visit some of the cities in the principality to check on local Church conditions. The Duke himself, with his father Duke Johann, visited

[6] Barge, op.cit., ii, 106–12.
[7] The literature on Thomas Müntzer is considerable, but for a recent survey see Siegfried Bräuer, 'Müntzerforschung von 1965 bis 1975', Luther-Jahrbuch 44 (1977), 127–41, and 45 (1978), 102–39.

Allstedt; and on 1 July, Müntzer preached his extraordinary 'Princes' Sermon' to the two noble visitors. He urged the princes to place their swords at the disposal of a militant, spiritualized Christianity; threatened dire consequences if they failed to do so; and openly attacked Luther. In the sermon, Müntzer based his arguments less on Scripture than on his dreams and visions.[8]

Some time in July, Luther responded with a warning letter to the princes concerning the 'rebellious spirit'. Satan always opposed the Gospel first with force and then, when that failed, attacked it with false brethren and false teaching. This was what he did when the Gospel first came into the world; and now he was doing the same in Luther's own day. For Catholic authorities originally used force to attack the Gospel; and then the false spirits attempted to subvert it from within. The Bible meant nothing to these false spirits—they were only interested in their proud boast of direct discourse with God. Yet the satanic spirit intended to go further and resort to violence in support of its undertaking. Luther admonished the princes, and reminded them of their duty to anticipate the intentions of these spirits and forestall incipient rebellion [*WA* 15, 210–19].

On 1 August, Müntzer and a number of Allstedt officials were cited to appear at Weimar, seat of the Elector. There Müntzer was apparently ordered to quit the Electoral territories. A few days later he was to be found in the nearby Imperial city of Muhlhausen, where his radical convictions were better appreciated.

While on the visitation suggested by Duke Johann Friedrich, Luther had a skirmish with Karlstadt in the town of Jena. Among the charges and counter-charges the two men hurled at each other, was a complaint from Karlstadt that Luther had unfairly linked him with the 'murderous and rebellious spirit at Allstedt'. Luther retorted that he had not named Karlstadt in his attacks, but added that if the shoe fit, he would have to wear it' [*WA* 15, 366 f.]. Two days later, Luther and Karlstadt had another collision, this time in Orlamunde itself. Neither Karlstadt and the Orlamunders on one side, nor Luther and his travelling party on the other showed much respect to their opponents in this meeting. Rather did each side provoke the other in a way that confirmed judgements already

[8] Gunther Franz, ed., *Thomas Müntzer: Schriften und Briefe* (Gütersloh, 1968), pp. 242–63.

held. Convinced that Luther had condemned them and Karlstadt without a hearing, the Orlamunders had sent him, two weeks before they met, an impolite, censorious letter [WA 15, 343]; and in return, they received a visit from an angry, offended man unwilling to hear their views. It is certainly clear that Luther believed the Orlamunders to be violent fanatics, and went to them for the express purpose of confrontation. They should learn the error of their ways, and any discussion of the issues at stake was thus out of the question. No wonder then that Luther's demeanour prompted hot 'fanatical' replies and curses, born perhaps of frustration in communication.

Back in Wittenberg, Luther shared his unfavourable impressions of Karlstadt with the young Duke Johann Friedrich [WA, Br 3, 353]. For his part, Karlstadt complained in a letter to the Duke that Luther had unfairly characterized his teachings and conduct.[9] Luther naturally disagreed, and made the most of his opportunities to renew complaints about Karlstadt [WA, Br 3, 346. Cf. 343 and 353]. On 18 September, the Duke and his father ordered Karlstadt to leave Electoral Saxony, and he did so by the end of the month.

News of the conflict between Luther and Karlstadt soon spread beyond the borders of Electoral Saxony, for in the autumn of 1524, several of Karlstadt's attacks on Luther were published. Of particular note was the attack on Luther's belief in the real presence of Christ's body and blood in the bread and wine of the Lord's Supper. This rift in the Evangelical ranks, together with the questions raised by Karlstadt's treatises, led the preachers of Strassburg (a city visited by Karlstadt in October) to write to Luther and obtain his opinion [WA, Br 3, 381–7]. The Reformer's response began with his warning that the true Gospel would always be attacked, persecuted, and tested 'from both sides', for 'Christ finds not only Caiaphas among his enemies, but also Judas among his friends.' He advised the Strassburgers to hold to the single question: what made a man a Christian? All else was of minor importance, and merely external. 'Beware of the false prophet', he warned them, 'for no good will come from him' [WA 15, 392–7].

Luther also published a considered reply to Karlstadt's treatises.

---

[9] Hertzsch, *Karlstadts Schriften*, ii, 53–4.

If the first part of the tract *Against the Heavenly Prophets* thus dealt with a miscellany of issues raised by Karlstadt, the second part afforded Karlstadt's arguments about the presence of the body and blood of Christ in the elements of the Lord's Supper exclusive treatment [*WA* 18, 62–125]. It was, in short, a treatise in which Luther took deadly aim at Karlstadt and his opinions. Yet from the outset it was clear that the Reformer had more than Karlstadt in his sights, for standing behind Karlstadt he saw Satan, prince of this world! As Luther thus attacked Karlstadt, he intended to beat down Satan as well, and to thwart his plan to overthrow the Gospel; and it was this metaphysical dimension of the struggle that influenced all Luther's arguments and characterizations, and enabled him to view the controversy solely in shades of black and white.

Against the Heavenly Prophets was thus directed at all fanatics and false prophets, and not just against Karlstadt. If much of the treatise nevertheless dealt directly with Karlstadt, it was actually Karlstadt's spirit (in Luther's opinion, the same spirit that motivated Müntzer, the Zwickau prophets, and other 'heavenly prophets') that bore the brunt of Luther's attack. Karlstadt thus found himself indicted not merely for what he was alleged to have done, but also for what, given the opportunity, his spirit was capable of doing. It was a 'tactic' that entailed among other things Luther's charge that Karlstadt was impelled by the 'Allstedt spirit', that is, by the same 'rebellious, murderous, seditious' spirit that drove Thomas Müntzer; and the whole treatise was liberally sprinkled with *ad hominem* attacks and ridicule. Lying against his own conscience, Karlstadt had been driven to such hypocrisy by the Devil, who wished to discredit Luther by lumping him with the papists so that he could destroy everything God had accomplished in the Reformation. Along with such ridicule, Luther also made a number of telling theological points against Karlstadt's position on such issues as images and the real presence in the Lord's Supper. Even so, the treatise did not decide the issue, for in the wings awaited formidable opponents with arguments altogether more coherent.

III

Before these opponents took the stage, there was the brief but

bloody intermezzo of the Peasants' War.[10] In the spring of 1525,
peasant unrest in Southern Germany spread northwards into Thur-
ingia. In Southern Germany there appeared that most widely
circulated manifesto, the *Twelve Articles*, which called for religious, social, and economic reform and buttressed its demands
with citations from Scripture.[11] As eager to correct what he held to
be misunderstanding of the Gospel as he was to disclaim responsibility for the unrest, Luther penned his *Admonition to Peace* in
reply [*WA* 18, 291–334]. In the first section, addressed to the
princes and rulers, the Reformer blamed the unrest on their
persecution of the Gospel and behaviour towards their subjects.
He certainly saw the justice of some of the *Twelve Articles*, and informed the princes that, for the sake of peace, they should
accommodate the peasants. Addressing the peasants in the second
section, Luther stressed that their rebellion violated the Gospel,
not to mention both Christian and natural law. By quoting the
Gospel to justify secular demands, the peasants thus blasphemed
the name of Christ. For the Gospel taught obedience to secular
authorities and expected the faithful to suffer injustice. Recourse
to the sword thus betrayed a lack of faith in God. Finally, in the
third section, Luther advised both rulers and peasants that he
found nothing Christian to commend either side. Accordingly, if
they came to blows, they must take full responsibility and by no
means blame either Luther or the Gospel. In fact, the *Admonition*
barely eased the situation and unrest spread. When visiting the
Thuringian countryside, Luther personally experienced heckling
and disturbances, and even felt his life threatened [*WA, Tr* 5, No.
6429]. The turn of events now swung the Reformer over to the
side of the princes. In May, he thus wrote the uncompromising
tract, *Against the Robbing and Murdering Hordes of Peasants* [*WA*
18, 357–61]—a treatise first published in one volume with the
Admonition to Peace under the title *Admonition to Peace and also
Against the Robbing and Murdering Hordes of the Other Peasants.*

---

[10] The recent literature on the Peasants' War is so numerous that the specialist
has to make considerable efforts to keep up with it. The best book to emerge from
the 1975 anniversary is Peter Blickle, *Die Revolution von 1525* (Munich/Vienna,
1975). For a useful survey see Tom Scott, 'The Peasants' War: A Historiographical
Review', *The Historical Journal* 22 (1979), 693–720, 953–74.

[11] See Hubert Kirchner, *Luther and the Peasants' War*, trans. D. Jodock (Philadelphia, 1972), 8–10, for discussion of Luther's sources.

It was Luther's intention to direct the *Admonition* to the 'good' peasants, and *Against the Robbing* ... to the 'bad' peasants, but printers quickly split the two treatises with the result that the harsher tract rapidly found a wide circulation of its own.[12]

Since Luther had concluded that the peasants were doing the Devil's work, and particularly the work of that 'archdevil' Thomas Müntzer, he felt it to be his responsibility both to show the peasants their error and to advise the rulers how to proceed. The peasants had violated their oaths of obedience to their rulers, oaths confirmed by Christ and St. Paul. They were thus in open rebellion, and cloaked their service to the Devil under the name of the Gospel. To the rulers, the Reformer offered sanguine advice. He would not fault even an enemy of the Gospel if he smote the peasants without prior judicial process. Christian rulers, however, should take their case to God in prayer and then offer the peasants terms. If their offer was refused, the rulers should at once have recourse to the sword, for justice was on their side. All who could should thus smite, slay, and stab, secretly or publicly; for nothing was more poisonous, harmful, or devilish than a rebel. The end of the world was imminent. There was not a devil left in hell—all had gone into the peasants! The uprising was thus brutally suppressed by the princes. Müntzer was captured, interrogated under torture, and executed; and soon afterwards several of his writings were published with Luther's own commentary [WA 18, 367–74]. This explained that God had made an example of Müntzer to warn and to terrify all those who promote rebellion. For Müntzer's fate showed that it was not God but the Devil that had spoken through him.

Although the revolt was over, the question of Luther's role in it remained a matter for controversy, and Catholics held him and the Reformation responsible for the unrest. If they dwelt on the hypocritical nature of the Reformer's attacks on the peasants, even his friends and supporters were offended by the hysterical violence of *Against the Robbing and Murdering Hordes of Peasants* [cf. *WA, Br* 3, 510–11, 515–16, 517–18]. In consequence, Luther felt the need to justify his earlier work, but his treatise or *Open Letter on*

---

[12] See Kurt Aland, '"Auch wider die reuberischen und mörderischen rotten der anderen bawren", Eine Anmerkung zu Luthers Haltung im Bauernkrieg', *Theologische Literaturzeitung* 74 (1949), 299–303.

the *Harsh Book Against the Peasants* proved as much an attack on his critics as a defence of his book. The peasants, he argued, had received their just deserts; and to sympathize with such rebels was itself to rebel. Nevertheless, he in no way accepted responsibility for the excesses of the princes who must answer for themselves [*WA* 18, 384–401].

As matters turned out, Luther was not the only theologian of the new faith who felt obliged to justify his conduct during the uprising. Caught in the middle of the disturbances, and harried by both peasants and princes, Karlstadt was thought by some to be an accomplice of the peasants. By mid-June 1525, he found himself forced to turn to Luther for haven and assistance in clearing his name. Accordingly, either on his own initiative or at Luther's suggestion, Karlstadt wrote his *Apology . . . for the False Reputation of Insurrection which is unjustly attributed to him*, a piece which Luther then published with his own generous, if uncompromising, foreword. Although he still disagreed with Karlstadt's teachings [*WA* 18, 436–45], Luther secretly took him with his family into his own home and there undertook to effect a reconciliation between his former colleague and the Elector. The price of reconciliation proved high, for Karlstadt was forced to retract in writing his earlier teaching on the Lord's Supper [*WA* 18, 453–66]. In fact, Karlstadt's published statement did not recant such teaching, and merely argued that he had never claimed their certainty so that his readers ought to check them against Scripture. For Luther, however, even such a qualified admission demonstrated the error of Karlstadt's teachings, and as he pointed out in his foreword, the Holy Spirit granted certainty. In short, since Karlstadt, Zwingli, and others of their persuasion presumed to venture opinions on the matter of the Lord's Supper, they lacked the true Spirit and taught only human fancy.

For Luther the events surrounding the uprising confirmed his judgement on the 'rebellious spirit'. As he saw it, that spirit had driven Müntzer into rebellion and earned him a violent death at the hands of the authorities. Indeed, as Luther had anticipated, it had prompted the war itself and led to Karlstadt's contempt for authority, and his attack on the Lord's Supper. Caught up in the Peasants' War, Karlstadt had been forced to seek refuge in Luther's own house and beg forgiveness and assistance. With the advantage of hindsight, Luther was thus strongly of the opinion that Satan himself was behind all his so-called 'evangelical' opponents.

IV

In the autumn of 1524, Luther informed correspondents that Ulrich Zwingli and Leo Jud of Zurich were following Karlstadt's teachings on the Lord's Supper; and early in 1525 another correspondent was advised that Karlstadt had also converted Johannes Oecolampadius, Konrad Pellican, other Baselers, Otto Brunfels, and other Strassburgers [*WA*, Br 3, 373, 397]. So from the outset of the controversy with Zwingli and Oecolampadius, Luther believed that such simply followed Karlstadt when they denied Christ's body and blood to be physically present in the Lord's Supper. This belief shaped much of the controversy that followed, for it led Luther to attribute the same satanic spirit to these new opponents that he had previously attributed to Karlstadt, Müntzer, and the Zwickau Prophets. His opponents, naturally enough, did not appreciate the fact, and complained repeatedly in the exchanges that followed.

It was hardly surprising that Luther concluded that Zwingli and Oecolampadius simply followed Karlstadt, although their beliefs had actually been reached independently and often rested on different reasoning. The crucial test Luther used to identify Karlstadt's 'error' was a denial of the real presence of Christ's body and blood in the bread and wine of the Lord's Supper. Zwingli and Oecolampadius passed this test.[13] In a well-circulated letter to Matthew Alber of Reutlingen (November 1524), and in his *Commentary on True and False Religion* (March 1525), Zwingli, while faulting some of his exegesis, nevertheless praised Karlstadt for his recognition that physical presence could not be understood from the words of institution.[14] He continued the argument in his *Rearguard or Supplement concerning the Eucharist*, and several other treatises. For his part, Oecolampadius had addressed his *Genuine Exposition of the Words of the Lord, 'This is My Body'*, according

---

[13] The definitive study of these controversies is Walther Köhler, *Zwingli und Luther. Ihr Streit über das Abendmahl nach seinen politischen und religiösen Beziehungen* 2 vols. (Leipzig, 1924; Gütersloh, 1953). Cf. i, 178–84.

[14] *CR* 90, 335–54, and 628–912.

to the Most Ancient Authors to some of the Lutheran preachers in
Upper Germany.[15]

Although they advanced slightly different arguments to support
their positions, Zwingli and Oecolampadius were thus in substantial agreement in their denial of Christ's physical presence in the
elements of the Lord's Supper. They specifically denied that
Christ's body and blood were, or even could be literally and physically, present in the elements, either through the transformation
of the substance (as opposed to the accidents) of the bread and
wine, or by 'co-existence' in and under the bread and wine. They
argued that the words of Christ at the Last Supper must be taken
tropologically, symbolically, metaphorically, or as a metonymy,
the words 'This is my body' meaning 'This represents my body'
or 'This is the sign of my body.' And they acknowledged a real
spiritual presence, holding that Christ was truly present through
and in the faith of the participants in the Supper. Hence they
could even speak of a spiritual eating by faith, which was faith in
Christ's act of redemption. But this presence was not tied to the
elements, and depended on, and was mediated by, the faith of the
communicants.

Underlying this tropological interpretation, especially in Zwingli's mind, was a very different understanding from Luther's concept of what the biblical idea of spirit and flesh entailed. For
Zwingli it sharply distinguished man's soul from his body, and
Christ's divinity from his humanity. If man's soul was a spiritual
entity, it must have spirit as its object of trust and love, and could
only be nourished by spiritual food. While insisting that he was
not unduly separating Christ's divinity from his humanity, Zwingli
argued that only Christ's divinity could save man's soul. Accordingly, if the Lord's Supper provided any special nourishment for
the soul (a view Zwingli adopted only late in the great debate), the
single source from which it could derive was Christ's spiritual presence. As physical matter, Christ's body could in no way nourish
the soul.

Zwingli believed that he had found sure confirmation of this in
the sixth chapter of St. John's Gospel, where Christ announced

---

[15] For a detailed exposition of these treatises, as well as a picture of the situation
prior to the outbreak of the dispute between Luther and the two men, see Köhler,
op.cit., i, 61–282.

that 'the spirit alone gives life; the flesh is of no avail' [John 6: 63]. The passage proved to his satisfaction that Christ's physical presence in the elements would be of no avail even if it were there. It was an absurdity, he concluded, and a backsliding into the papal error of transubstantiation, to maintain that there was a bodily presence. Of course Zwingli could, and did, adduce other arguments to buttress his position, arguments concerning the nature of a physical body, the fact that Christ in his body sat at the right hand of God, and among others Christ's statement that he would no longer be in the world.[16]

For his part, Luther was convinced that the words of institution were to be understood literally. Accordingly, he challenged his opponents to prove that they must be understood figuratively, not that they could be, or might be, but that they must be figurative. As Luther interpreted the controversy, therefore, his opponents' two basic arguments were that Christ's ascension into heaven, there to sit at the right hand of God, removed him physically from the world and that John 6: 63 made his physical presence unnecessary. Luther attacked the first argument by attacking reason, for reason cannot prove or disprove any matter of faith. God's right hand thus refers not to some physical location in heaven, but to God's almighty power which at one and the same time was nowhere and yet everywhere [*WA* 23, 133]. It followed that presence to Luther was not circumscribed or local, but an essential presence that created and preserved all things; and he argued for a special presence in the Lord's Supper, as God was present to find his presence through the Word. It was in short one thing for God to be present; but another matter altogether for him to be present for the individual. Yet there he was when he added his Word and bound himself, saying 'Here you are to find me.' [*WA* 23, 151.]

As for the argument from John's Gospel (6: 63: 'The flesh is of no avail'), Luther insisted that this could not apply to Christ's flesh without a simultaneous denial of the Incarnation. His opponents, he contended, had misconstrued the words 'spirit' and 'flesh' as used in Scripture. There are spiritual and fleshly acts, but not spiritual and fleshly things:

---

[16] See Köhler, op.cit., i, 462–562; and Erich Seeberg, 'Der Gegensatz zwischen Zwingli, Schwenckfeld, und Luther', in *Reinhold Seeberg Festschrift* (Leipzig, 1929), 43–80.

Thus, all that our body does outwardly and corporeally, if God's Word is added to it and it is done through faith, is and may be called spiritual. Nothing can be so corporeal, fleshly, or outward, but it becomes spiritual when it is done in the Word and in faith. 'Spiritual' is nothing else than what is done in us and by us through the Spirit and faith, whether the object with which we are dealing is corporeal or spiritual. Thus, there is Spirit in the use, not in the object, be it seeing, hearing, speaking, touching, begetting, bearing, eating, drinking, or whatever it may be. [*WA* 23, 189.]

By such an understanding of 'spirit' and 'flesh', Luther turned his opponents' argument upside down:

Our fanatics, however, are dizzy in the head. They think there can be nothing spiritual where there is anything corporeal and allege that flesh is of no avail. Actually the opposite is true, that the Spirit cannot be with us except in corporeal things such as the Word, water, and Christ's body and in his saints on earth. [*WA* 23, 193.]

The sacrament was a visible embodiment of God's promise of salvation through Christ, so that to question Christ's words was to deny his promise. If, by reasoned argument the real presence could be rejected as absurd, then even the Incarnation could be denied, since it was far more 'absurd' than the real presence in the Supper. For Luther the essence of the Gospel (God's promise of justification through faith in Christ's sacrifice) was at issue in this dispute, and the Reformer could no more accept his opponents' position than he could deny the doctrine of justification by faith *alone*.

The dispute between Luther and his supporters, and Zwingli, Oecolampadius, Bucer, and other Swiss and South Germans (for Karlstadt was quickly relegated to the status of a minor participant), raged for several years. It was a particularly acerbic controversy because of Luther's charge that all his opponents, possessed by the spirit of Satan, were bent on destroying the true Church. With a stroke then, he lumped together such disparate spirits as Karlstadt, the Zwickau Prophets, Müntzer, Zwingli, Oecolampadius, and even Bucer. The unitary categorization of his opponents that resulted became part of an elaborate system, and was extremely difficult for his opponents to invalidate or attack. Because, as Luther asserted, they were ruled by the satanic spirit, he pressed home his attack more against this spirit than against the men it possessed, and attributed to them not only what they were alleged to have done but what, because of the satanic spirit, they were capable of doing. When his opponents objected to a classification that made them all of one mind, and pointed to the differences that existed among them, Luther replied that such differences were only on the surface. He was in short clear that the satanic spirit was a spirit of discord, and convinced that because his opponents disagreed among themselves, they were *ipso facto* possessed by Satan.

Those who resisted his admonitions and arguments, Luther singled out as demonstrating satanic perversity, obduracy, and vanity; whilst those who requested concord, or expressed willingness to be instructed if in error, the Reformer held to be uncertain. For him, such doubt was proof of the absence of the Holy Spirit, who above all bestowed certainty of faith. Moreover, those who appeared to yield to any of his arguments, or to abandon a previous position (even a position adopted by only some of their number), Luther held had tacitly admitted their error. Weakness in these particulars falsified belief as a whole, for the Holy Spirit did not allow true believers to err in a single article of faith. In short, to lack the Holy Spirit was to be enslaved to Satan, just as all avowals of Christian belief were a sham, and evidence to the contrary to be dismissed as deception and works-righteousness.

Such was the state of affairs in 1529, at the close of the second Diet of Speyer, which had revoked the recess of the first Diet of Speyer, an assembly that had been so favourable to the Evangelical cause. War now threatened, and Landgraf Philip of Hesse concluded a secret alliance with Electoral Saxony, Nuremberg, Strassburg, and Ulm. He nursed plans for a wider alliance that included the Swiss Evangelicals, but religious divisions made such an alliance unacceptable to the Lutheran theologians and princes. First, the Landgraf realized that the religious differences among the Evangelicals must be reconciled, and to this end Philip, in the autumn of 1529, brought Luther, Melanchthon, Zwingli, Oecolampadius, and Bucer together at his Marburg castle. To everyone's surprise, the leading theologians there agreed, at least on the surface, to fourteen out of fifteen articles. The only point of disagreement was the article on the Lord's Supper, and even here there was movement. All parties, including Zwingli, now agreed on a spiritual partaking of the true body and blood of Jesus Christ, and the only remaining disagreement was whether the true body and blood were bodily present in the bread and wine. Before taking leave of one another too, all parties undertook to refrain from further public controversy.[17] While this was a definite improvement on the former state of affairs, it nevertheless left Landgraf Philip's plans for a wider Evangelical alliance unfulfilled. For his part, moreover, Luther continued to hold such disagreement on the bodily presence as evidence that his adversaries, albeit unwittingly, served the Devil.

v

At the Diet of Augsburg (1530), the Lutherans offered their *Confession* just as Zwingli and Oecolampadius submitted their own formularies, and Bucer the *Confessio Tetrapolitana* for several South German cities. Divisions in the Evangelical ranks were thus painfully obvious, and with the danger of Catholic attack seemingly very great, the need for concord and alliance presented itself more than ever before. In an attempt to resolve the situation, the political lead was taken by Landgraf Philip, the role of leading theologian falling to Martin Bucer.[18]

In a sense, Philip's proved the easier task, and by February 1531, he had formed the League of Schmalkalden. Soon afterwards, Strassburg, with other Upper German cities, joined the League on the basis of the *Tetrapolitana*, and an 'understanding' was reached between Bucer and Luther. But their acceptance rested on very insecure foundations, for although Luther felt hopeful of eventual agreement with Bucer and the Strassburgers, he still believed Zwingli and Oecolampadius to be unrepentant and firmly stuck in satanic error. Zwingli's death and the defeat of the Zurich forces at the second battle of Kappel (1531) was shortly fol-

[17] On the Marburg Colloquy see Walther Köhler, *Das Marburger Religionsgespräch 1529: Versuch eine Rekonstruktion* (Leipzig, 1929). Hermann Sasse, *This is My Body: Luther's Contention for the Real Presence in the Sacrament of the Altar* (rev. edn. (Adelaide, 1977), pp. 180–220, reconstructs the Colloquy in English. For the texts, see WA 30³, 110–71. See also Köhler, *Zwingli und Luther*, ii, 66–163.

[18] On the negotiations leading to the Wittenberg Concord see Köhler, *Zwingli und Luther*, ii, 181–455; Ernst Bizer, *Studien zur Geschichte des Abendmahlsstreits im 16. Jahrhundert* (Gütersloh, 1940; Darmstadt, 1962); Hastings Eells, *Martin Bucer* (New Haven, 1931); and G. W. Locher, *Die Zwinglische Reformation* (KG, 1979).

lowed by that of Oecolampadius—a grievous double-blow that deprived Strassburg and its allies of Swiss support and dramatically increased the demand for more substantial agreement with the Lutherans. Whether they liked it or not, Bucer and the other Upper Germans had to fall in with the convictions of the obdurate Saxon Reformer and his Elector.

The next few years saw repeated meetings and negotiations, the seemingly indefatigable and eirenically-minded Bucer being almost permanently in the saddle visiting the Upper German cities in search of an understanding with the Lutherans on the Supper. By now both sides agreed that in the Supper Christ was 'truly' present to believers. But when Bucer tried to argue that the remaining issues in dispute were largely verbal, Luther disagreed. In fact, the theological sticking-point was now whether Christ could be 'truly' present to unbelievers. Luther was clear that he was, and insisted that the real presence depended not on the faith of the participants, but solely on the promise of God. Bucer and the Upper Germans could not agree, however, and would have preferred to ignore the whole issue. Gradually, even painfully, Bucer nevertheless brought the two sides together; and the problem of reception by 'unbelievers' was finally solved by a distinction between the 'unworthy' who received the body and blood to their damnation, and the 'godless' who received mere bread and wine.

It was thus in the Wittenberg Concord (1536) that Bucer and other German representatives finally joined with the Lutherans. Most of the concessions had been made by the Upper Germans, although Luther had himself shown a greater measure of flexibility than hitherto. Obliged to recant their previous errors, the Upper Germans had to agree that in future they would teach the same as the Lutherans. Whether their concession was the result of political necessity, or a sincere acceptance of Luther's position, their action effectively vindicated Luther's uncompromising stance during the long dispute and likewise confirmed the Reformer's judgement about the uncertainty, and falsity, of his opponents' beliefs. Because of a frank recognition of genuine differences between his own position and Zwingli's, Luther never accepted Bucer's contention that the dispute had been merely a matter of words. Rather was it a quarrel between the true and false Church, and with the Wittenberg Concord the Reformer felt that victory had gone to the true Church.

For the rest of his life, Luther continued sporadically to lash out at 'fanatics'. In the late 1530s, for example, he had a fundamental disagreement over the issue of law and Gospel with Agricola; and in the 1540s he published his last major attack against the Zwinglians.[19] But by this time, the Reformer had firmly set ideas about 'fanatics', and his views of their unity in disunity were not to be shaken.

It was thus fateful for the course of Luther's controversies with other Evangelicals that his first opponents were men like Karlstadt, the Zwickau Prophets, and Müntzer. For the Reformer, each of these men possessed many of the characteristics of false prophets: they lacked a proper call; they boasted of special revelations; and they confused worldly and divine kingdoms. They were legalistic, involved themselves in mob action, were vain, and resisted fraternal admonition. Luther had built up his stereotype of the false prophet from Scriptural accounts and encounters with such men. He found it confirmed in Orlamünde and in the Peasants' War, and tended to find the same characteristics in other Evangelical opponents, and so ignore, misunderstand, or rationalize characteristics and actions inconsistent with the stereotype.

In short, Luther acted by sharply rebuking Evangelical opponents and refusing them fellowship—treatment that provoked the very 'hot, fanatical replies' his stereotype led him to expect. If the approach was decidedly unfair, it was also remarkably effective and where reasoned argument often failed to convince, impassioned invective could carry the day. Serious and sincere theological differences certainly divided Luther from his 'fanatics', and they from each other; for any unity among the fanatics derived solely from Luther's theological world-view.

[19] See my *Luther and the False Brethren* (Stanford, 1975), chaps. 7 and 8.

VI

VISITATOR

Luther as Visitor

*

PETER NEWMAN BROOKS

IN origin, visitation procedures sought to take the pulse of the
Church and determine its state of health by carrying out regular
check-ups in diocese and parish. Deriving authority from conciliar
decrees and papal pronouncements, medieval ordinaries perfected
elaborate inquiries which, granted the sanction of canon law, were
part of a recognized jurisdictional process. The bishop or his representative thus held legal sway for himself and his superiors, carefully collating the findings of visitation as a written record laid
down for posterity. But if medieval Rome symbolized measured
lawful authority in the localities by such means, the advent of the
Reformation with. its Gospel priorities had considerable reservations to make about a Church so firmly under the law. Once
Luther and his supporters therefore began fundamentally to question papal and episcopal jurisdiction—in effect opposing Gospel to
legal procedures—traditional routines, for so long taken for
granted, came under threat.

   Not that Luther relished the task of visitation, or took any kind
of precipitate action in the matter. For he only came to it with the
responsible reluctance of one obliged to react to his prince when,
prompted by growing lawlessness among his subjects, the Elector
himself sought the Reformer's guidance. If the Peasants' Revolt
delayed any immediate response, it also ensured ultimate action
from the authorities. This came in 1528, when Luther was invited
to contribute a *Preface* to *Instructions* written by his colleague
Melanchthon for those chosen to scrutinize the economic, social,
and religious affairs of parishes owning the sway of the Ernestine
Saxon Elector. Couched in language of convincing brevity, his introduction stressed the precedent, both patriarchal and apostolic,
that enabled the Reformer to commend the role. Luther's sense of
history likewise prompted his approval of those 'holy bishops'
who diligently applied papal laws derived from 'holy synods', before compelling the Reformer's denunciation of the sickening
abuse that corrupted a system that had after all, as he claimed,
been observed by Christ himself [WA 26, 195.17].

   Despite such confident assertions, Luther's *Preface* affords the
historian that saddest of all impressions—a glimpse of the idealist

who is fast losing confidence in his own cause. For the Luther who had been so outspoken in his condemnation of a whole range of papal decrees, was of course immensely vulnerable when obliged to defend his Reformation by reviving precisely the visitation procedures his own pastoral sense had recently derided; and that he was conscious of caricature comes as no surprise.

But the devil, using venomous, worthless scandalmongers, leaves no godly work without stain or caricature. He has already prompted our foes to ridicule and condemn us, some even boasting that we have regretted our teaching and are withdrawing and recanting. ... For this reason I have decided to publish everything prepared by the visitors and shown to our gracious Lord after my own careful review ... so that all may appreciate that we are not attempting to conceal or cover anything up, but gladly and genuinely bring it into the open and permit it. Although we cannot set out strict injunctions as if we were publishing a new set of papal decrees, and seek rather to give an account or record to witness to our confession of faith, yet we hope that all devout and peace-loving pastors, who find true joy in the Gospel, and take pleasure in being of one mind with us, will act as St Paul teaches in Phil. ii [2: 'Fulfil ye my joy, that ye be likeminded, having the same love, being of one accord, of one mind.'], and will give heed to our prince ... [*WA* 26, 199–200].

Cochlaeus naturally made much capital out of Luther's latest dilemma, and not only ridiculed the new-fangled visitatorial role in *Septiceps*, but with careful chronological reference to the Saxon scrutiny in his *Commentaria de actis et scriptis Martini Lutheri* (1549), also ensured for the whole episode an enduring place in posterity. Despite the fact that Melanchthon wrote the [*Contents of the*] *Instructions* to afford four chosen Visitors a basis of inquiry, Cochlaeus's *Septiceps* thus consistently held Luther responsible for his downright usurpation of the place of the hierarchy. In the *Commentary*, however, he came clean—although in acknowledging the predominant part played by Melanchthon, his respect for the humanist in Master Philip prompted the assessment 'more moderate and meaningful' compared with the acerbic aside 'more verbose and insolent', the *en passant* judgement he handed down for Luther.[1]

The sudden impact of stinging side-swipes from such an adversary inevitably concealed the halting, faltering approach Luther

---

[1] J. Cochlaeus, *Commentaria de actis et scriptis Martini Lutheri* ... facsimile reprint Farnborough, 1968), p. 180.

had to take in reverting to the traditional procedures of visitation. For this original idealism was such that, apart from holding justification by *only* faith as the *sine qua non* of preaching and teaching, the Reformer cherished a principle of voluntarism and pondered well his every move. Regimentation of any kind he felt to be foreign to the freedom of a Christian man, and no doubt because he realized that only the most sensitive inquiry can discern spiritual health, set his face firmly against the re-establishment of a legalism that at its best could only have checked the outward conformity and externals of the new religion. As a liturgical reformer, Luther thus respected the hallowed diversity of local rites and 'used neither authority nor pressure' [WA 12, 205.12] to bring them into line. In this introduction to the Wittenberg *Formula Missae et Communionis* (1523), he thus refused 'to prejudice others against adopting and using a different order' [WA 12, 206.10–11]; and it was only later that experience brought home the undoubted fact that few colleagues in the pastoral ministry possessed his own massive range of talent.

If voluntarism thus initially dictated the Reformer's over-all pastoral approach, a point readily appreciated from the *ad hominem* reference of much of his writing, Cochlaeus could never admit the validity of Luther's distinction between the old papal compulsions and his plea that the people 'subject themselves in a spirit of love . . . and with us peacefully accept these visitors until such time as the Holy Spirit of God brings to pass something better, through them or through us' [WA 26, 200.18f.].

Although they had secured approval from the Prince Elector himself, Cochlaeus naturally had reservations about both noble and scholar visitors. John of Plaunitz and Erasmus of Haubitz were competent as courtiers, just as Jerome Schurff and Philip Melanchthon were capable academics—but none possessed the priestly qualifications that alone could make them credible as visitors in the tradition of the Western Church. Luther, Cochlaeus was clear, had no authority to recommend such appointments. To do so was to sanction an altogether new departure not only from canon and imperial law, but also from custom and natural law. The Wittenberg Reformer had in short presumed to set himself up as Pope of Saxony—and it is not difficult to interpret the headgear the *Septiceps* bestowed on *Visitator* as symbolizing the barren crudity of a tiara bereft of the three crowns of genuine papal dominion.[2] No wonder that, at the end of the chapter (II: *De Quatuor Visitatoribus*), Cochlaeus made his first, but by no means his last, reference in the tract to Matthew 22: 21: 'Render therefore unto Caesar the things which are Caesar's; and unto God the things which are God's.' [*S L*, B, verso.]

In actual fact, Luther attempted to obey such Scriptural counsel to the letter. Accordingly, when the world of learning simplifies and reduces his complex teaching to near-Erastian terms, it might more often recall that the Professor of Old Testament at Wittenberg University very much took to heart some wise words of the psalmist [Ps. 146: 3.]

He does not say: 'Do not obey princes', rather 'Do not put trust in princes', for trust belongs solely to God. You should not exchange gold for dung. Dung has its use, but is of no value if it is deceitfully exchanged for gold. For you see that this Psalm only deals with faith, trust, certainty, and confidence—all of them qualities too sublime to be applied to princes ... [*WA* 19, 579.20–5]

As a polemicist, Cochlaeus found Luther's dilemma in the matter of lawful authority contemptible, and he deplored doctrines that, by subjecting Holy Church to the whims of the temporal overlord, clearly sold the pass. The Reformer whose protest overturned legitimate papal and priestly authority in the Church, Cochlaeus thus vilified as a wrecker. His conservative outlook was quick to recognize the problem of *auctoritas* as a central issue in the movement for Reformation; and in both *Septiceps* and the *Commentaria* he set considerable store by Luther's defeat in the celebrated Leipzig debate with Eck (4 to 14 July 1519).[3] In terms of Luther's reputation the implication was devastating, for Cochlaeus held that once the renegade religious had cut himself off from the Papal Church, the sheer impracticality of the venture made the whole bid for reform absurd. When plans for the 1528 Visitation thus became common knowledge, the derision of Cochlaeus knew no bounds; and the technique adopted in the first twenty-four chapters of *Septiceps* where confusion reigned in destructive debate between the various 'heads', proved remarkably effective. As prime mover of the inquiry into faith and Church order in Saxony,

---

[2] *S[epticeps] L[utherus]*, ..., ed. Ioannis Cochlaeus (Valentinus Schumann, Lypsiae, 1529), ii, verso.

[3] *S L*, K., recto; *Commentaria*, pp. 13 f.

Visitator attracted a large number of well-aimed brickbats. But despite the sound and fury of such sixteenth-century controversy, for the historian the odd ray of light can at times dispel the otherwise dreary devastation of a bitter encounter.

In the first place, Luther's use of the prince's mandate to authorize visitation was not new. Rather did it take to a logical conclusion the great argument of 1520 which allowed the prince to reform the Church when the bishops had signally failed in their duty. Cochlaeus condemned Luther's *Appeal* to the Christian nobility, and the summary set out at the end of almost every chapter of *Septiceps* thus served to remind the Elector of Saxony that approaches to reformation could only increase discord [*S L*, A. iii, recto]. His plea was for territorial princes to leave religious affairs to those qualified by ordination to deal with them. Anything less would bring Germany further contempt and spiritual disaster [*S L*, D. ii, verso]. Princes and counsellors who gave heed to the 'Martinians' should certainly beware, for such sectaries wrote not only against Popes and councils, constitutions, and canon-law decretals, but against all lawful authority and man-made traditions [*S L*, F. ii, recto]. Conscious that fear of sedition united princes and all secular powers in common cause, Cochlaeus did not scruple, in a chapter on 'War against the Turk' (xlii), to liken Luther to both Turk and Tartars. For him indeed, the Reformer was just as bad as both for spreading sedition through his preaching and writing.

The Church had stood on the Petrine foundation for fifteen centuries and a mere fifteen-year-old protest could have no meaning at all. With the dangers of Christian liberty apparent to lawful authority therefore, only a disordered and deranged Luther could fail to see that God and Caesar—not to mention the Council Cochlaeus longed to call—were all against him. A Pope of Saxony and Teutonic Priscus who thus arrogated to himself both princely and episcopal power was in fact a complete 'cuckoo'. The seven 'heads' thus belonged to one and the same hopelessly mixed-up individual who was all the time brawling and squabbling with himself [*S L*, O. iii, verso]. Accordingly, in a peroration to the Prince of Saxony, Cochlaeus made loud his own protest. Judgement of Luther he would leave to the apostolic see; but he tactfully allowed the Elector to decide what matters might profitably go before a General Council of the Church!

That such generalized assessments from Cochlaeus misrepresented the relationship Luther conceived for the Saxon Prince when adapting and reinterpreting visitation procedures to the Reformation cause is, of course, an understatement. For in *Septiceps*, Cochlaeus edited Luther to his own advantage, much as clever interview techniques used by present-day media can distort and misrepresent the opinions of the unwary, often to their manifest surprise and invariable discomfort. Luther may thus always have been deferential to his prince (as to secular authority in general); but constantly aware of his responsibilities as a Reformer facing pastoral problems, he rarely shrank from independent action, especially when circumstances he interpreted as the will of God in ministry seemed to him to dictate such a course. In 1522, for example, when his presence was demanded to quell radical elements that threatened to turn the ordered Reformation achieved in his university town into chaos, Luther left involuntary exile in the Wartburg Castle, and in so doing returned to Wittenberg against the express wish of the Prince Elector, Friedrich der Weise.

Then too, in the case of the 1528 Visitation itself, the Reformer was clear that the kind of inquiries Melanchthon had framed in the *Instructions* by no means afforded spiritual rights to secular power. He sought not a rigid separation of powers, but a balanced dualism that, carefully based on Scriptural principles and historical precedent, could achieve the necessary *modus vivendi* to meet the emergency situations and day-to-day encounters of on-going Reformation. Likening such co-operation to the effort of separating grain from chaff on the threshing floor, Luther's *Preface* did not 'neglect to seek the backing of our gracious Lord'. For although the Reformer is clear that 'his serene Highness the Elector is not obliged to teach and reign over spiritual matters, as temporal sovereign he is bound to exercise rule that prevents unrest, strife and rebellion among his subjects.' [*WA* 26, 197.25 f.] Earlier in the same *Preface*, too, Luther by no means gave Elector Johann freedom to encroach on the spiritual preserve of the pastors, but merely sought his assistance 'out of Christian love ... to the advantage of the Gospel and the well-being of neglected Christians in his territory'.

Important as these preliminaries proved to them, both Luther and Melanchthon were clear that there was much more to visitation than a mere transfer of authority in matters of ecclesiastical inquiry from the papal hierarchy into the hands of pastors like themselves—reformers able to count, *in extremis*, on the secular power. The adaptation and legitimation of historic procedures was thus all very well and necessary, but it had to take its proper place in the perspective of those pastoral priorities which alone made visitation necessary in the first place. The Reformer's *Preface* once again affords historians the required insight, for there Luther laid great store by the fact that both Peter and Paul regarded revisiting 'all those places where they had preached' as crucial to ministry in New Testament times. Luther acknowledged Pauline precedent whenever he could, and found here that, with his colleagues, he could forward pastoral ministry by following in the steps of the apostle he greatly revered. As he wrote, every single one of Paul's 'epistles express concern for all the congregations and pastors'; and in staccato style that scored again the simple melody of a great ministry like variations on a well-worn theme, Luther noted of Paul that he 'writes letters, he sends his disciples, he goes himself.' [*WA* 26, 195.10–11.]

Luther thus determined to check that, after the furious storms of Reformation beginnings, the people of sixteenth-century Saxony had been grounded in the Gospel just as Paul had instructed the faithful of the primitive Church when the apostle travelled round Asia Minor on his celebrated missionary journeys. At this level, visitation involved the day-to-day teaching procedures of ministry, and Melanchthon's *Instructions* outlined the content of doctrine and practice the Reformers sought to share with colleagues and their people in the parishes. For his part, of course, Cochlaeus was ready with rebuttal and ridicule. *Septiceps* followed Melanchthon's order, and *Visitator* usually led discussion of the topics raised chapter by chapter. Throughout, Cochlaeus used such literary licence to refute Luther as the original exponent of what he regarded as at best a rival religion, and at worst pernicious heresy. His selective approach clearly indicated both the storm centres of controversy and the principal divisive issues for debate.

Lutheran priorities expounded Gospel doctrine in terms of faith made available as a result of repentance and the forgiveness of sins. But if *Visitator* sought to ensure the preaching of the whole Gospel (Chapter V), and even referred to the command in Deuteronomy 'not [to] add to the Word . . . nor take from it', Cochlaeus rushed in to indict Luther for the humbug of one who clearly failed to practise his own precept. The Reformer was concerned that his pastors should highlight the life of faith against the dark background of man's need for repentance, for when 'they do not demand repentance, such preachers tear away great portions of Scripture'. With little care for such biblical principles, Cochlaeus changed the whole ground of the argument and condemned Luther to the princes as a regular religious whose 'wretched apostasy' abandoned the law of the Church. He held the Reformer responsible for the fact that 'habits are thrown off with discipline and the fear of God', and deplored monks and priests who married and repudiated their vows, just as he blamed Luther for the devastation of the Church in the dissolution of monasteries [*S L*, C. ii, verso].

In the matter of the sacraments, the arguments of *Septiceps* became particularly fierce and intense. Cochlaeus certainly experienced no difficulty in branding Luther as a most evil and insidious heretic for the slightest variation of viewpoint on a subject so sacred to the faith and practice of the late medieval Western Church. The debate 'On the Seven Sacraments' (Chapter 15) is typical. In an attempt to help his flock get their priorities right, Luther had argued that Scripture recognized only a single sacrament—Christ—and three signs. In *De captivitate babylonica* (1520), however, he had categorically denied the validity of the seven sacraments of hallowed medieval usage, and came down in favour of three—Baptism, the Eucharist, and 'for the present', Penance. If the Reformer was convinced that 'the name sacrament' should only be given 'to those promises which have signs attached to them' (not to mention direct Dominical institution), unrestrained exposition led to the statement that 'strictly . . . there are but two sacraments, baptism and the bread.' Such *ipsissima verba* were not for one moment lost on Cochlaeus, and Luther's adversary carefully noted and removed statements of this kind from context to use them for the great advantage of traditional religion. Accordingly, he set the spotlight on a Wittenberg party line that had not only reduced the seven sacraments to three, but was also unclear whether the three sacraments retained were in fact three, two and a half, or even one! It is a chapter full of interest because of the light it sheds on Cochlaeus's technique in the careful compilation of *florilegia* on selected, key topics. For him, Luther posed a serious threat to the Roman religion, and had to be discredited before he gained further advantage for his beastly heresy at expense of Holy Church. But whereas a man like Erasmus would have resorted to humour in such a situation, this lesser humanist had all the fervour of one recently re-converted to rigour. If Cochlaeus was thus very much in touch with the latest Lutheran material, and even adopted a kind of *Short-Title Catalogue* approach that gave the Reformer's tracts their popular names (cf. *Index Librorum Lutheri*, and note the *marginalia* abbrevs. in *S L*), he showed not the remotest awareness of the dilemma Luther faced as that Reformer strove to wean unsubtle pastors and their semi-literate congregations from acceptance of the sacramental doctrines imposed by papal authority. Nor did Cochlaeus miss a trick in the end-of-chapter summary that concluded this round of the continuing debate. For there, expressly to rouse the prince against his Protestant protégé, Cochlaeus dwelt on the outrageous rapacity of a Reformer who in effect had snatched sacraments like Order, Confirmation, and even the sacrifice of the Mass itself, from the holy places of the Catholic Church [*S L*, F. iii, verso].

That Cochlaeus regarded the sacrament of the altar as the touchstone of orthodoxy, is clear from the amount of space he devoted to it in the great *Septiceps* debate. The whole polemical piece comprised forty-five chapters, eighteen of which related to sacramental issues, no fewer than ten of them more or less directly to the Eucharist. The subject was one that specially concerned Cochlaeus, arguably because it was through the regular offering of Masses that the priests of the Roman Church came most in contact with the people. Luther's protest began the slow process that was to turn the Mass into a Communion—although a decade later than his *Septiceps* ,Cochlaeus still continued to hold the line in *Ein nötig und christlich Bedenken auff des Luther Artickeln* published at Leipzig in 1538. Luther might urge the Mass to be 'an invention of man', but Cochlaeus was clear that Christ himself had instituted so holy a sacrament. It was therefore by no means 'unnecessary' (Luther's view), but precisely the way Christians should observe the Dominical command: 'Do this in remembrance of Me.' Moreover, even if Luther thought he had preserved the sacrament of the body and blood of Christ, for Cochlaeus this was not the case as consecration was impossible without the celebration of Mass. Nor could the Reformer's argument that abuse of the sacrament *ipso facto* demanded its abolition be allowed, for in no way could occasional abuse dictate such a drastic solution. As for Luther's insistence that it was not the offering of Masses but 'the

Lamb of God [that] takes away sin', Cochlaeus was clear that Christ, the Lamb, was present in the Mass, and there pleaded for sins when offered to God.

Such arguments can all be found in the *Septiceps* wrangle of 1529, where the Cochlaeus technique made hay of Luther's green approach to the crucial and controversial issues involved as pastors helped simple people, whose minds had long associated the solemnity of Mass with all the superstition of the miraculous, to gain a revised understanding. Luther's clear priority was to afford his people the comfort of Communion as that was originally prescribed:

... the people are to be taught that it is right to receive both bread and wine. For now that the holy Gospel (praise God!) has been restored, we are clear that both bread and wine are to be offered and consumed. For Christ commanded it to be so, as the Evangelists record, and St Paul laid down for the Early Church. ... No man can change such divine ordinance. We dare not annul a man's last will as St Paul argues to the Galatians. Much less is it possible to change God's own last testament. [*WA* 26, 214.1–9.]

Within the firm, clear obligations of the Gospel, therefore, Luther and Melanchthon 'instructed pastors and preachers to proclaim this doctrine ...', while Cochlaeus demanded to know why his foes objected to 'the Church's faithful twelve-hundred-year-old teaching'. Recourse was then made to patristic and scholastic argument. Cochlaeus drew on Ambrose who argued for the 'conversion' of the eucharistic elements, a theory he, in company with Henry VIII of England, found in 'Eusebius, Emserus [*sic*! Duke George's Secretary had been placed in most exalted company!], Theophilus, Cyrillus, Augustinus, Gregorius Nissenus, & ...' [*S L*, G. iv, verso], and which through the instrumentality of Thomas Aquinas was confirmed as a doctrine of 'the whole Church by the Lateran Council under Innocent III by more than 400 bishops and 800 fathers...' Cochlaeus regarded it a singular impertinence for Luther to inquire into such high matters of long-established doctrine like some petty bureaucrat or man from the ministry; yet the fact that, having thrown scholasticism to the winds as irrelevant and un-Christian, Luther published his celebrated *Catechisms* that very same year, indicated the Reformer's sense of responsibility. He may have taken his time—the over-generous idealism of a basic voluntarism no doubt crediting those of simple faith with the possession of far more interest in Gospel concerns than was customarily the case. But once he realized that his paradoxical method of exposition bred confusion, he soon showed himself capable of a catechetical clarity that took away the very ground under his opponents' feet.

In so many respects, of course, simplicity was Luther's whole teaching emphasis in pastoral ministry; and it was particularly in evidence as the Reformer strove to make his doctrine of the Eucharist intelligible. Because he clung tenaciously to basic biblical categories, the positive side of Martin Luther's doctrine retained the real presence, communicated the people in both kinds, stressed that the sacrament conveyed grace, and was to be honoured as the body and blood of Christ himself. Because it removed those areas of mystery prized by later medieval notions of sacrifice (particularly those linked with the central canon of the Roman Mass when the secret sacrificial work of the priest was done in hushed tones not intended for his flock), Cochlaeus deplored such teaching as a 'most horrendous and impious blasphemy' that only served, like all the sayings and writings of Luther, to encourage error [*S L*, H. iii, verso]. The summary offered at the end of the debate 'On receiving the Sacrament' (Chapter 22) thus attempted to bring home to the Prince precisely what, in Cochlaeus's view, territorial visitation of Saxony could perpetuate '... if the people now respond to your visitors ... don't be surprised to find them less devout, less moral, less disciplined and less obedient than was the case ten years ago ... for it is impossible to achieve more from the writings of your Luther.' [*S L*, I., recto.]

Here, Cochlaeus showed something of a failure of nerve, as likewise his personal appreciation of the importance of princely support—a point that would not have escaped the notice of Duke Georg, the Catholic ruler of Albertine Saxony. Ever conscious of popular confusion and perplexity, he laid the blame at Luther's door, for the Reformer himself, in apocalyptic mood, had admitted to the confusion of the times. Once again eager to afford his character 'head' Barrabas a helping hand, and frustrate the visitation process by playing havoc with its goal of securing conformity of belief and practice, Cochlaeus held up to ridicule an irresponsible statement in debating the widespread demand for the faithful to receive 'both kinds in the sacrament' (Chapter 23). At Leipzig,

Eck had been applauded for bringing the full weight of the tradi-tionalist standpoint against Luther's lack of respect for the findings of General Councils; and perhaps with that Disputation in mind, Cochlaeus, through the mouth of Barrabas, quoted words from the *Formula Missae et Communionis* (the Reformer's extended commentary on the evangelical Communion used in Wittenberg from 1523), that have a tale to tell.

> Nor is it necessary to attend on a Council ... to have this use approved. We have the law of Christ in our favour and have no intention of waiting for or paying heed to a Council in matters so clearly belonging to the Gospel. Indeed, we go further, for if a Council should establish and approve this custom, then we would be the last to take both kinds! Nay, contemptuous of both the Council and its decree, we would then wish to partake either of one kind, or of neither; but never of both; and we would wholly condemn those who, on such conciliar authority and decree would partake of both kinds! [*WA* 12, 217.17–24]

The reference was certainly as clear as any Cochlaeus used in the whole of *Septiceps* to highlight the sheer obduracy and bloody-mindedness of Martin Luther in defence of treasured funda-mentals. But he failed to perceive that, lacking in his own make-up as not merely a controversialist, but also a human being, was a sense of humour! Luther on the other hand, possessed great re-serves of wit; and when he once gave way to flat-footed flippancy in otherwise serious polemical argument, frequently courted disas-ter. For in Cochlaeus, the Reformer was obliged to face an oppo-nent altogether obsessed with the good old cause. After a kind of honeymoon period with the New Learning, Cochlaeus's flexible Erasmian spirit thus went rigid, and in his dealings with Luther, he may be seen as a continental counterpart of the dark side of the Thomas More who so savagely indicted William Tyndale. The author of *Septiceps Lutherus* was certainly poles apart from the young man who, in 1511, extolled the musical ability of Willibald Pirckheimer in his dedication of the *Tetrachordum musices*.

By its nature, sixteenth-century controversy proved invariably barren and interminably tedious. There were many battles, but few real engagements. The contest between Cochlaeus and Luther was thus typical. For absolutely certain of his vocation to rally a Roman Church he knew to be under dire threat from 'Martinist' heresy, Cochlaeus chose to discredit and repudiate both the person and the writings of the Reformer on every available occasion. His commitment to the traditional beliefs and practices of the Western Church thus confined him so effectively to his corner of the ring that, granted Luther's own repudiation of scholasticism, the canon law, and papal authority, any sparring between them could only resemble a bout of shadow-boxing. Through the rule book of Scripture, Luther had encountered the Word, and that, as the Reformer's singular rediscovery of Christ's Gospel, was like a foreign-language code to the studied orthodoxy of an opponent irrevocably committed to the Roman Church.

With his consideration of the 'Sacrifice of the Mass' (Chapter 25), Cochlaeus broached a subject of such crucial significance that he felt it should command entirely different treatment. The attempt to poke fun at Luther's inconsistencies in debates between the 'heads' was thus brought to a summary conclusion; and, as he informed the Elector, 'lest the tedium of this monstrous colloquy bore you, I will afford a brief compendium of the remaining Visitation Instructions, their many blasphemies and impieties ...' Very much at home on the hallowed ground of received tradition, Cochlaeus affected the bewilderment that earnest young Hapsburg, Charles V, showed at Worms. For when prophets and apostles, martyrs and confessors, 'all holy Councils and the universal Catholic Church' have certainly accepted the doctrine of sacrifice for fifteen hundred years, why should credence be given to an apostate like Luther who, for a mere five or six years, has denied the Mass to be a sacrifice? It was a charge Cochlaeus made the most of by cleverly emphasizing the fact that, for fifteen years, Luther had offered the selfsame sacrifice in his own ministry! He was thus adamant that, unless proof from Scripture or reason was produced to the contrary—by strange irony the phrase used by Luther himself in that celebrated stand at Worms!—no notice should be taken of one who, with Henry VIII of England, John Fisher, Bishop of Rochester, van Clichtove, Faber, Eck, Emser, and Dietenberger all opposed to him, could only count on the dubious support of fanatics [*S L*, K., recto].

Yet it was of course precisely the growing support for Luther's cause that shocked Cochlaeus out of any humour in argument. For what price his orthodoxy in a history lesson when, in the half-century after its publication in 1534, the Lufft press of Wittenberg alone dispatched some 100,000 Bibles with that telling illustration of Babylon's whore recognizably wearing the papal tiara to set folk arguing in homes and market places?[4] The situation was one he had done his level best to retrieve in *Septiceps*, and a most impatient Cochlaeus can be seen in the commentary on those Instructions on the regular observance and worship of the Church, and the syllabus of basic instruction laid down for the schools, served on Luther's Saxon Visitors. Almost by definition, Visitors stood for authority; yet on what authority did this apostate abrogate the ancient ceremonial of the Church in so scandalous and impudent a manner? The Luther who thus braced himself (arguably against his own better judgement) to go beyond reliance on the goodwill of pastors and parents and compel uniform acceptance of Reformation faith and practice by visitation, was scorned for being out of line with recognized episcopal and canon-law procedures.

For his part, despite a deep inner conviction that the Word of God alone reformed the Church, Luther found himself facing a dilemma that, with the passing years, grew to ever more serious proportions. In 1520, he had advised the nobility of the German nation that all should recognize Scripture as the *fons et origo* of the faith, and basic to both learning and teaching.

Above all, priority reading for all, both in universities and in schools, should be the Holy Scriptures—and for youth, the Gospels. Would to God that every town likewise had a girls' school, where girls would be taught the Gospel for an hour a day either in German or in Latin. [*WA* 6. 461. 9–15.]

Left to their own devices, the schools had shown themselves none too anxious to adopt educational reforms, and appeared to Luther in a sorry state by the eve of the peasant troubles (1525). In its turn, too, that upheaval had made matters worse, and the Reformer noted in a wide range of writings that a main consequence of the Peasant's Revolt was the way many had chosen to abuse their new-found freedoms. Luther had hardened his heart, and a comparison of those voluntarist ideas reflecting 'his personal distaste for system and uniformity in matters of religion'[5] evidenced in a

---

[4] Less explicit visual references to the true identity of the Pope had first been circulated by Cranach when he illustrated the Luther *New Testament* published in September 1522.

[5] Gerald Strauss, *Luther's House of Learning. Indoctrination of the Young in the German Reformation* (Baltimore and London, 1978), p. 4.

model for the people and town of Leisnig (1523), and the *Instructions* for the Visitors (1528), shows the measure of his advance in the direction of regularizing both the content of faith and the ordering of Church procedures. Without them, Luther was convinced, at least from a merely human angle, that the great Saxon experiment in reforming the Church was bound to fail.

If not from conviction therefore, at least from expediency, the Luther who was at one remove from the *Instructions* set out for the Visitors by that administrative realist, his colleague Melanchthon, found himself obliged to recognize the need of encouraging faith by directive and to enforce it by bureacracy. His early and cherished ideal of a *Hausvater* to drill each family in *pater noster*, creed, and decalogue, had come to naught. Printed broadsheets that contained these basic ingredients were displayed in the homes of the faithful to comprise the earliest catechetical material, the actual *Catechism* published in 1529 being intended primarily for pastors. In his treatise *On the Estate of Marriage* (1522), Luther had made much of the point that 'fathers and mothers are apostles, bishops and pastors to their children as they bring them up in the knowledge of the holy gospels.' [*WA* 10², 301.23–5.] The teaching relationship implied here has recently prompted the comment from Professor Gerald Strauss that 'If matrimony was validated in the offspring it produced, parenthood justified itself by making Christians of children.'[6] Once it thus became clear to Luther that this ideal could not be achieved, positive pastoral proposals of the kind he approved in the last sections of the *Instructions* show that hard logic dictated the return to visitation by the revised procedures of 1528.

When Cochlaeus complained that Christendom had never experienced anything of the kind, he did not exaggerate, for the Papacy has never been renowned for teaching prowess at parochial level. Perhaps for this reason, Luther's adversary made loud his outrage at the Reformer's scorn for bishops who spent time blessing bells [*S L*, O. ii, recto]. Raised in *De captivitate babylonica* (1520), the matter received continuing derision from popular propaganda, and a cartoon of Lucas Cranach the Younger showed a mitred prelate in action as late as 1547.[7] By stressing the import-

---

[6] Strauss, op. cit., p. 124.
[7] R. W. Scribner, *For the Sake of Simple Folk. Popular Propaganda for the German Reformation* (Cambridge, 1981), pp. 201, 203.

ance of retaining such ceremonies, Cochlaeus cleverly played down the positive emphasis the *Instructions* placed on 'The Office of Superintendent', the *Pfarrherr* or official the Reformers afforded oversight to 'ensure that there is correct Christian teaching in these parishes [viz. the parishes of the region where he has oversight], that the Word of God and the holy Gospel are truly and purely proclaimed, and that the holy sacraments are administered to the blessing of the people according to Christ's institution.' [*WA* 26, 235.9–12.] Above all, too, the oft-repeated refrain of the concluding section of *Septiceps* demanded to know by what authority Luther preferred new-fangled superintendents to the bishops properly consecrated by the Church [*S L*, O. ii, recto]; why Christmas, the Circumcision, Epiphany, Easter, the Ascension, and Pentecost were to be observed as festivals (with sermon and sacrament) when no Pope had ever made such demands; and why the traditional use of excommunication was condemned [*S L*, O., recto]?

Arrayed in the cartoonist's high-sided helmet, the daunting image of Martin Luther *Visitator* was thus singled out for the sheer absurdity such a 'head' symbolized. The Reformer whose initial protests had effected so much unrest and lawlessness was himself presuming to impose laws. Yet his chosen code was not that approved by the papal hierarchy and tried by sacred use. As the work of an apostate indeed, it was an abrogation of the ancient ceremonies of the Church, and derived from Satan [*S L*, O.]. Fearful of the threat thus posed for the Church at the hands of strengthened secular authority, Cochlaeus certainly had a point. But if Luther was unquestionably vulnerable, his commitment to the reality of his rediscovered Gospel went far beyond his adversary when Cochlaeus determined to preserve the ways of 'the old religion'. By their very different standards, both men were consistent in their resolve to hold a line. But in his remarkable bid to regularize the irregular consequences of an over-generous attitude of *laissez-faire* in Reformation, Luther showed a flexible approach born out of the hard experience of pastoral ministry. His 'new religion' was fast becoming too intellectual to succeed, at least with simple folk; and if the Wittenberg Reformer could no doubt idealize *Visitator*'s hat as the 'helmet of salvation' beloved of St. Paul, in reality the cartoonist had provided him with protective headgear for trench warfare at the front.

VII

'BARRABAS'

Luther as Barabbas

*

GERALD STRAUSS

It is common knowledge that Cochlaeus's *Septiceps Lutherus* fails as propaganda.[1] Hastily compiled and written with distaste for its subject evident on every page, it falls considerably short of realizing the promise of its ingenious and appealing form. But Cochlaeus's central theme, Luther at odds with himself, does remain with the reader as a lasting impression. To that extent at least, his tract finds its mark. Dialogue was nicely suited to dramatizing the inconsistencies palpably present in Luther's published opinions. 1528, the year of the *Septiceps*, was also the date of the Saxon territorial visitation. Like most other Catholic controversialists, Cochlaeus interpreted this event, and especially the *Instruction of the Visitors* appearing that year over the names of Luther and Melanchthon, as the supreme contradiction of the libertarian strains that had sounded in the first decade of the Reformation. Luther as visitation official makes a natural counterpoise to the earlier enthusiast and freedom fighter, an ironic juxtaposition the polemical possibilities of which were not lost on Cochlaeus. For the *visitator* in his dialogue, he wrote some of the most telling lines coming from the seven 'heads' among which the disputation is carried on, and in several crucial passages touching the basic question of law and obedience, the 'visitor's' antagonist is 'Barrabas', the archetype of the headstrong and reckless destroyer of established order who—as a psychological type even more than as a present menace—was a source of genuine alarm to the magistrates of Catholic and Protestant Church and State. Of the irreconcilable conflict between these two symbolic figures, Cochlaeus makes very clever use. What they signified was obvious to every reader: autonomy and self-righteousness versus constituted, externally-controlled authority. The winner of the struggle would determine whether there was to be order or discord in the land. In every age and place, 'Barrabas' and *Visitator* stood in opposition. If Luther was both, the outlook for society was at best uncertain; at worst it

---

[1] Martin Spahn, *Johannes Cochläus* (Berlin, 1898; Nieuwkoop, 1964), p. 148.

was hopeless, as master and rebel took turns spinning the world in a vicious circle of self-destruction.[2]

Luther–Barabbas is the character of the anarchical activist. 'Barrabas will knock you down with his club', Cochlaeus writes, differentiating the insurrectionary and killer mentioned briefly in the New Testament[3] from the six other *personae* keeping Luther and Lutheranism for ever off balance. He is always ready to come to blows, never mind the consequences [*S K*, b. iv, verso]. Whatever the law, he will disobey it. It matters little what it says: as long as a rule has been laid down by human authority, Barabbas is on the attack. Let a Church Council make a law respecting the taking of the sacrament under one or both forms, and Barabbas will do the opposite of what is commanded. 'Even if some Council were to put it out now that we should use the sacrament in both forms, I won't do it. Rather, I'll defy the Council and its statutes, and will use one form, or no form at all, and I'll curse those who, submitting the Council's power, are using both forms.' [*S K*, E., verso.] 'When a human being orders something done', he declares, 'that's enough reason for me not to do it. If he hadn't ordered it, then I would do it. I only obey my own wishes and ideas, and I won't let myself be conformed to human laws.' [*S K*, D. iv, recto]. Christians are free agents, Barabbas holds. Human laws can mean nothing to them [*S K*, a. iv, verso—b.i, recto]. 'Let us be so certain of our cause and so confident of its rightness that we can disregard the whole world's judgement as no more than empty straw.' [*S K*, a. iii, recto]. 'Isn't it disgraceful and slavish that free Christians should be subject to any laws other than God's?' [*S K*, b. iii, verso]. But Barabbas's way is not that of passive resistance. He is a destroyer. 'Let's go, dear brothers,' he cries, 'we'll pull down all man-made rules and statutes!' [*S K*, b. iv, verso.] Having written this, Cochlaeus does not fail to point the obvious moral that this battle cry, if it should be taken up, will mean the end of organized society. 'You are not a god', he tells Duke Johann of Saxony, in the dedication of a German version of the *Septiceps*. 'If human laws are

[2] In this article, quotations from Cochlaeus come from S[ieben] K[öpffe] Martini Luthers. Vom hochwirdigen Sacrament des Altars ... Part I (Leipzig, 1529), Part II (Dresden, 1529).
[3] Ibid., Aii, recto. Luther's New Testament gives *Mord* and *Mörder* in Luke 23: 19, John 18: 39, and Mark 15: 16–7. Cf. Luther's comment *WR, DB* 6, 125.

to count for nothing, all your lordly commands will be ground into the dirt and your officials and visitors will invoke your authority in vain. No one will pay them heed.' [*S K*, D. iv, recto] Give Barabbas an audience, and respect for government is at an end. He knows how to turn people against their legitimate rulers. 'Even pigs and donkeys can see how blind and dumb our leaders are in all they do, how they lie, cheat, and issue bad and harmful laws.' 'German beasts, that's what they are, as savage as wolves and wild boars.' [*S K*, b. i, recto] The fury of this verbal onslaught reflects the truculence of the Luther–Barabbas temper, a violent spirit expressed in his image among the seven heads of Cochlaeus's title-page with rough beard, wild hair, and deadly-spiked club ready to hand.

Barabbas's ravings are countered by the *Visitator*, who is the dialogue's figure of lawful and beneficent authority, the counsellor of voluntary submission to the ways things are [cf. *S K*, a.iv, verso; b.i verso, b.ii, recto, and b.iii, verso]. 'We must recognize the will of God in all worldly laws and statutes', he asserts [*S K*, b.iv, verso], explaining that people must learn what they are to believe before they can decide what they may do [*S K*, A.iv, recto, cf. d.iv, recto]. There is, of course, no common ground between the visitor's magisterial principle of compliance and docility and, on the other hand, Barabbas's exultation in his own moral autonomy, and his eagerness to act on it. Cochlaeus drew the contrast as sharply as he could. How is it possible, he asks, that one and the same person can hold such contrary views on so vital a matter of public and private life? No wonder Lutheranism has brought only chaos! This is the conclusion he wished to leave with his readers.

Cochlaeus was too close to his subject and too much the creature of his passions to see the problem clearly, although his image of Luther and Lutheranism must reflect with some accuracy contemporary anxieties about the future of religious and civic life— fears that he was doing his best to fan. Today we should be able to judge more fairly, given our long view, the full record, and our detachment from the old hatreds and loyalties. What was Luther's authentic voice on the vital matter of law and obedience? Was he 'Barabbas' or was he the 'visitor'? Or was Cochlaeus correct in charging the Reformer with a fatal and fateful ambivalence on this central issue of religion and politics?

It is true that Luther's many pronouncements on law and its uses were ambiguous. A selective reading of them can yield contradictory lessons. It is possible to gain the impression that good and honest men owe no obligation to the codes that define their social lives or to the functionaries who enforce them. Or the opposite conclusion can be drawn that obedience is all. Granted the theological basis of Luther's legal thought, law and lawyers were, for him, the consequences and expressions of God's distrust of men.[4] 'Politics and law', he said, 'don't follow from grace: they arise from anger.' [*WA* 49, 316. Sermon of January 1544] While he distinguished formally between *lex*, *Gesetz* (theology) and *jus*, *Recht* (government and jurisprudence), the two concepts interpenetrated each other as he counselled men on their rights and duties. 'These three: law, sin, death are inseparable', he argued, casting a dark shadow over the entire realm of *jus* as well as over *lex*.[5] In his *Kirchenpostille* (1522), he defined the purpose of law for Christians in such a way as to make a very close connection between religious and civic objectives.

> The first purpose is that it maintains discipline among us and compels us to an honest way of life externally, so that we can live together and not devour one another, as would happen if there were no law, no fear of punishment. . . . The second function is that man learns through the law how false and evil is his heart, how far he is still from God.

This view of law as arising from man's corrupted condition is explicitly joined to the political use of the law and the work of the worldly sword through which order is maintained in sinful human society.[6] Writing against the antinomians in the late 1530s, Luther

---

[4] From the considerable literature exploring Luther's relationship to law, the following are particularly valuable: F. E. Cranz, *An Essay on the Development of Luther's Thought on Justice, Law, and Society*, Harvard Theological Studies xix (Cambridge, Mass., 1959); J. Heckel, *Lex charitatis. Eine juristische Untersuchung über das Recht in der Theologie Martin Luthers*, Bayerische Ak. d. Wiss: Abhandlungen, philosophisch–historische Klasse, N. F., Heft 36 (Munich, 1953); K. Köhler, *Luther und die Juristen. Zur Frage nach dem gegenseitigen Verhältniss des Rechtes und der Sittlichkeit* (Gotha, 1873); Hans Liermann, 'Der unjuristische Luther', *Luther–Jahrbuch* 24 (1957), pp. 69–85; and Hermann Wolfgang Beyer, 'Glaube und Recht in Denken Luthers' *Luther–Jahrbuch* 17 (1935), pp. 56–86.

[5] *WA* 39¹ 354, quoted by Gerhard Ebeling, 'Zur Lehre vom triplex usus legis in der reformatorischen Theologie', *Theologische Literaturzeitung* 75, No. 4/5 (1950), pp. 243–4.

[6] Sermon on Galatians 3: 23–9. *WA*, 454, quoted in F. E. Cranz, op. cit., pp. 99–100.

made this link stronger still;[7] but the connection was in his mind from the beginning. 'God gave the imperial laws [i.e. Roman, or 'general' law] for the sake of the wicked', he wrote in the *Preface to the Old Testament* (1523). 'They are laws to defend ourselves with, not laws that can instruct us in anything.'[8] This is the negative view of law, and Luther maintains it vigorously. In its origin and purpose law is man's recompense to the Fall. Moses, the classic lawgiver, is 'a minister of sin; his office is that of death.'[9] In its exercise, law is naked power. 'Whoever has the law in his hand', Luther urged, 'wields power, and only God knows whether such power is right.' 'Law rests on the fist', he added. 'Turn the word *ius* inside out, and it spells *vis*, might.'[10] The uses of power, and the uses of law, can be justified only if there are good motives at work in the minds of those who employ them. A magistrate should do more than merely follow law. The law by itself teaches nothing. If his heart is not good, his enactments will only increase misery and his might spread corruption. 'That is why I have no laws to suggest to a ruler. I wish only to reform his heart.'[11]

As for lawyers and jurists, they live and work in the grubby world of 'mortal, transitory, wretched, earthly things',[12] a career that, Luther is clear, makes them singularly unfit for the prominent places in Church and State to which they aspire. Like many of his contemporaries, Luther spoke with annoyance of the apparently irresistible usurpation by lawyers of positions of influence and power. 'With God's help, I'll defend my Church against them', he said, but knew it was a losing battle [*WA, TR* 4, No. 4382]. The gradual take-over of ecclesiastical and political offices by lawyers and legally trained bureaucrats represented to Luther the fatal closing of the gulf between the world of affairs and administration on the one hand, and the realm of truth and justice on the other. His slashing attacks on lawyers combined with his largely negative view of legislation to create the impression that the worldly network of man-made rules and obligations operated on some lower

---

[7] Ibid., p. 104.   [8] *WA* 8, 16–17.

[9] From his *Preface* to the Old Testament (1523 and 1545), *WA* 8, 20–1. Cf. Ibid., 8.26–7.

[10] *WA,TR* 6, No. 7016; cf. *WA, TR* 3, No. 3793.

[11] *Von weltlicher Oberkeit* (1523), *WA* 11, 273.

[12] *An die Pfarrherrn, wider den Wucher zu predigen* (1540), *WA* 51, 342–3.

plane of morality where the true Christians's restored conscience should preserve its inviolability from the touch of corruption.

What Luther had against the law and its practitioners was that they seemed to him to care little for the substance of the matters they handled; that they held nothing to be certain; that they lacked firm principles; and that they were rigid formalists, approaching every question in a spirit of mechanical literalness. 'Lawyers deal with words', he said, 'they don't go to the heart of anything, seeking truth. Show me a single jurist who has studied law with the aim of learning truth and finding out what is right and what is wrong.' [*WA, TR* 1, No. 349]. 'Jurists have nothing to do with conscience' [*WA, TR* 1, No. 320]. They are not able to prove anything; circumstances govern all matters of law, and these call the substance itself of things into question [*WA, TR* 1, No. 349]. By contrast, theology recognizes no exceptions, no accidents. 'A theologian must be utterly certain that a thing is thus and not otherwise; that is why theology is certain truth' [*WA, TR* 1, No. 349]. Lawyers, for their part, 'run the world with their whims and opinions' [*WA, TR* 3 No. 3622]. They are like organists who, 'if one pipe doesn't sound, they'll play another' [*WA, TR* 1, No. 134]. Worst of all, lawyers are now preparing to 'intrude on our Lord Christ's own spiritual government, stretching their hands out to take over everything' [*WA, TR* 6, No. 7029], and make all people live according to their laws, 'with which they will once again shake and confuse the conscience of men, which we have only just begun to build up.'[13] 'It makes me angry', Luther told his congregation, warning them of the lawyers in their midst, 'that they go about confusing your consciences. That's the cause of my fury against them.' [*WA* 49, 316.] The violence of some of his diatribes was so great at times that he felt bound to explain himself. 'You must forgive my outbursts against the jurists', he said. 'It's because of my zeal for God and my great wish to increase his honour and affirm his Gospel!' [*WA* 49, 299.] The type of lawyer-bureaucrat was to Luther always the antithesis of that of the preacher and teacher which he felt himself to be. 'An eternal fight wages', he said, 'between jurists and theologians, just as law and grace are forever opposed to each other.' [*WA, TR* 6, No. 7029.] Speaking

---

[13] Sermon of January 1544, *WA* 49, 298.

as a pastor, he vowed that 'as long as I live, I will keep this Church pure against all you jurists.'[14]

Given the profusion of such expressions and the hot aggressiveness of their tone, Luther's followers might be forgiven for supposing that so rare a being as the true Christians ought to be, and in fact was, immune from the reach of the law. Luther's early treatise *Concerning Worldly Government* (1523), could be read a supporting this surmise. Those Christians who are of God's kingdom, he declared, 'require neither sword nor law, and if the whole world were peopled by genuine Christians—that is to say, by believers—there would be no need or use of princes, kings, sword, or law.' [*WA* 11, 249–50.] Christians, he continues, 'should always conduct themselves so as to show that they have no need for law. They have heaven to guide their steps; they should not depend on the law to goad, restrain, terrify, or punish them' [*WA* 11, 259]. 'A good tree', Luther writes in what could be taken as his strongest charter of the Christian's independence from normative and positive law, 'needs neither doctrine nor law to teach it how to bear good fruit. Its nature guarantees it: that without either rule or instruction it brings forth what is natural to it. Thus Christians are so constituted by the spirit and by their faith . . . that they need for themselves neither statutes nor laws.'[15] Luther at once limits the relevance of this declaration by admitting that the majority of men and women are not 'Christians'. Most people, he maintained, belong to the far-from-saintly crowd, the rabble or *Pöbel*. With their fickle ways, they need strong-armed government by magistrates, law codes, and law-enforcement agents. But as no sure signs were available for identifying the genuine Christians among the many false ones, a strong incentive must have existed for individuals to assume the best, rather than the worst, about their condition. Such individuals might well interpret Luther's words as a tempting invitation to see themselves as standing in some way above the degrading scene where laws were imposed and regulations enforced. And once the laws were perceived as pernicious, and the enforcers as tyrants, the stage was set for the appearance of a Barabbas.

But all this, while true as far as it goes, is far from being the

[14] Sermon on 2 Corinthians 6: 1 (1539), *WA* 47, 670–1.
[15] Quoted by Köhler, op. cit., p. 85.

whole story. Luther also held a very positive view of the law, its uses and powers, and its agents; and he gave vigorous expression to this side of the argument as well. All was not lost when Adam fell. Even sinful humanity harbours God's natural law in its heart. Its spiritual purpose may be obscured by man's depraved state, but a sense of right and wrong remains. Its divine purpose may tend to be neglected in favour of mere earthly felicity; none the less it can instil a sense of the common good in men.[16] Wherever man-made laws reflect and transmit the spirit of this divine natural law they are beneficial. Thus political legislation is a blessing for mankind.

The model of such law-giving is the Roman Law, for which Luther (granted his apparent detestation of the legal mind and profession) expresses some enthusiasm.[17] The old pagans have much to teach us concerning secular government, which is, he writes, an image on earth of eternal bliss and the heavenly realm— 'something like a distorting mirror or a carnival mask', but a reflection none the less [*WA* 51, 241]. The Imperial Roman Law 'is nothing other than a piece of that pagan wisdom the like of which we shall never see again. . . . Whoever wants to be wise in politics, therefore, let him read the pagan writings', especially the old books of law whose authors were as much God's prophets and theologians as the wise men of Israel [*WA* 51, 242–3]. Thus the laws must be allowed to stand. Altering them always spells trouble. 'Before you could make a new constitution in Germany, the country would be wrecked three times over.' True, there is a great deal wrong in politics and society. Law and politics are in desperate need of a Luther. But they will not get one. What they will get is a Müntzer instead; in other words, not a reformer but a destroyer [*WA* 51, 258]. Don't be a know-it-all who thinks he can meddle in the established polity. 'We'll see no new government in the Roman Empire for the rest of its days, David tells us that.' [*WA* 51, 258.] And the government we now have will not function unless its laws are maintained, 'not with fist and armourplate, but with brains and books'. For this reason 'we must learn and know the laws of our worldly realm.' A jurist, therefore, as long as he is pious and not false, is not merely a worthwhile

[16] J. Heckel, op. cit., pp. 70–8.
[17] See esp. his *Auslegung des 101. Psalms* (1534–5), *WA* 51, 200–64.

citizen, but 'a prophet, a priest, an angel, a saviour'.[18] And by this I mean, Luther elaborates, not only jurists as such, 'but also all others in the trade of politics, namely chancellors, secretaries, judges, advocates . . . and also those important personages who are called Court Councillors, for they, too, do the work of law and the office of jurist.' [*WA* 30^2, 559] God sees his will done by all these officials, and he approves of what they do. Thus 'secular government is the cornerstone, rock, and foundation of a people and a land. It makes human beings of wild beasts and keeps them from becoming animals again. It is a necessary estate and office, instituted by God himself.'[19] All men owe it their support. None dare oppose it.

In short, the dialogue between 'visitor' and 'Barabbas' is not confined to the pages of Cochlaeus's pamphlet. First one, and then the other surfaces in Luther's published works; at times, to be sure, both of them speak from the pages of a single one. In the informal remarks of the *Table Talk* they coexist in profusion. 'Barabbas' is more strident before 1525 than afterwards; the 'visitor' speaks with greater force from 1528 when—it has been pointed out—Luther seems in the course of his responsibilities as a Saxon visitation officer, and under the impact of the desperate state of the Church as this was brought to light during the visitation, to take on many of the characteristics of the territorial bureaucrat.[20] Circumstances thereafter multiplied the ·opportunities for his official side to assert itself. The apparent decline of schools and universities prompted Luther in 1530 to give lavish public praise to the study of law and the career of politics.[21] The death of John the Steadfast in 1532, and the succession to the Saxon state of a young duke of unproven quality, caused the Reformer to reconsider the need for sound, stable laws to guard against princely caprice. It was also the occasion of the commentary on Psalm 101 [*WA* 51, 200–64]. The Protestant movement's problems of survival and defence in the 1530s brought him to what Wolfgang Günter has called 'a new understanding of the *ius politicum et imperiale* that led him to appreciate the significance of positive law for the constitu-

---

[18] *Eine Predigt, dass man Kinder zur Schule halten solle* (1530), WA 302, 557–8.
[19] Quoted by J. Heckel, op. cit., pp. 109–10.
[20] Gerald Strauss, *Luther's House of Learning. Indoctrination of the Young in the German Reformation* (Baltimore and London, 1978), pp. 250–1.
[21] *Predigt, dass man Kinder zur Schule halten solle*, WA 30^2.

tion of the empire'.[22] But the Reformer's responses to these political cries only gave developed expression to concepts long
embedded in his mind, concepts rooted in the basic distinctions
inherent in his theology of the two kingdoms, of true and false
Christians, and of pious rulers and tyrants. Depending on the
given historical circumstances and their interpretation, either
Barabbas or the visitor could appear as the more persuasive guide
to right conduct in the world.

Thus Luther himself nullifies the proposition that a human
situation can ever be so closed as to relieve the individual of the
need for judging and choosing. To judge and choose is to draw on
empirical knowledge of the world, on a sense of right and wrong,
or conscience. This is man's autonomy. It is the impulse that
moves Barabbas, though he follows the blandishments of his legitimate self-reliance far beyond the bounds set by the limits of human knowledge and ability. Lacking a sense of man's frailty, and
therefore of restraint, Barabbas never heeds. He cannot recognize
the merits of conventional wisdom, accumulated experience, age,
and tradition. The visitor, for his part, lacks the passion to share
his antagonist's anger and exultation. The creature of institutions,
he sees society from the top where individual men and women
seem to fuse into a featureless mass to be protected from its own
appetites, and to be kept safe by a network of rules. His problem
is logistic and managerial. Barabbas's problem is psychological,
dealing in imagination and emotion. Neither figure is entirely
wrong; but neither right by himself. Their opposition—in
Luther's terms an irreconcilable opposition—illuminates the tension generated by the double need to accept discipline and authority in life while, at the same time, judging them for their validity
and their practical consequences. Luther recognized the existence,
as well as the psychological and social authenticity of both needs.
As the leader of a new Church he wore the visitor's hat more often
than he would have wished. But he lacked neither fellow feeling
nor sympathy for Barabbas, of whose sense of outrage he understood too much himself to reject the type. He did not wish to see
Barabbas silenced; he only wanted to take away his club.

---

[22] Wolfgang Günter, *Martin Luthers Vorstellung von der Reichsverfassung*, Re-
formationsgeschichtlich Studien und Texte No. 114 (Münster, 1976), p. 125. On
the issue of resistance and political thought see Quentin Skinner, *The Foundations
of Modern Political Thought* (Cambridge, 1978), ii, pp. 189–224.

VIII

Luther's *German Bible*

*

HEINZ BLUHM

OF Luther's several great achievements, the *German Bible* is perhaps the greatest and probably the most enduring. Herder, Goethe, and even Nietzsche—to mention only the most prominent names—accorded Luther's Bible the highest praise. It was Nietzsche who put the matter most strikingly when he declared that Luther's Bible is not merely 'das beste deutsche Buch' (*Musarion* XV, 205) but actually 'unser einziges Buch immer noch' (XVI, 352), compared with which 'fast alles uebrige [ist] nur "Litteratur"' (XV, 206). Indeed, as late as the end of the nineteenth century Luther is still held to be the greatest single event in German history: 'Unser letztes Ereigniss ist immer noch Luther' (XVI, 352).

With such tributes paid to Luther's stature in general, and to his *German Bible* in particular, it would be appropriate to state specifically what the real nature of this, the greatest single work of the greatest German, actually is. Unfortunately, its most famous eulogizers did not spell this out, but only recorded their intuitive perceptions. It was, is, and will be left to the careful, detailed work of conscientious scholars to indicate in what the genius of Luther's Bible consists.

The simple fact is that, despite the labours of such able men as Wilhelm Walther (1917) and Emanuel Hirsch (1928), the scholarly study of the *German Bible* is still in its infancy. Perhaps Adolf Risch put it best when, writing in commemoration of the 400th anniversary (1922) of the publication of the *Septembertestament*, he remarked that not until the evolution of every single verse of the Luther Bible has been examined will it be possible to make reliable general statements about its singularly elusive quality. For if such examinations have been made for a few single verses, short passages, and even complete psalms, they have yet to embrace the Bible as a whole. At the present time, therefore, it is simply not possible to go beyond analyses of specific portions undertaken by the handful of scholars working in this area, as the slopes of the high mountain that is the Bible rendered into German by Martin Luther have barely been reached.

Luther began translating early in his career. As a matter of fact, his earliest publication contained his first translations of important parts of the Bible. When he published his German interpretation of the Seven Penitential Psalms in the spring of 1517, half a year before the epoch-making *Ninety-Five Theses*, he saw fit to prefix to his exegesis of each of the Seven Penitential Psalms a translation of the psalm—his own new translation. Instead of using any of the numerous existing translations, whether those of the fourteen[1] High, and four[2] Low, German Bibles, or those contained in *Plenaria* and independent German Psalters, he preferred to provide his own rendering. Why? While he does not yet attack the German versions explicitly, his implicit criticism is that, besides being largely written in well-nigh unintelligible German, they are not based on the original Hebrew but on the Vulgate, thus being essentially translations of a translation. As a professor of sacred letters he felt it his legitimate concern (just as it was certainly his ardent desire) to get closer to the original text than use of the Vulgate permitted. Though his knowledge of Hebrew was still insufficient to allow him to base his new rendering on the original, he succeeded in going beyond the Vulgate by consulting St. Jerome's third Psalter (*Psalterium Hebraicum*) and Johannes Reuchlin's *Septem Psalmi Poenitentiales* of 1512, the then most recent scholarly publication on some of the most famous psalms.

To use translations closer to the Hebrew than the Vulgate was a major philological event in the history of scholarship. It was also a literary event in so far as Luther's informal, *ad hoc* translation of 1517 was already stylistically superior to 'all his predecessors' renderings. With these two significant accomplishments to his credit, it stands to reason that hard-working young Luther passed over the existing versions of these psalms and, from 1517 onwards, replaced them by renderings of increasingly scholarly and literary quality.

Luther was anything but idle as a translator during the few years between this first successful attempt to find a better vernacular garb for the Seven Penitential Psalms, and the appearance of the German New Testament of 1522 (the *Septembertestament*). He

---

[1] 13, to be exact, because the 14th was not published until 1518.
[2] 3, because the last was not published until 1522.

tried his translator's wings again, this time in two New Testament passages—a pericope from St. Matthew (16: 13–19)[3] and the Lord's Prayer, both translated in 1519. Beyond these passages of several verses, scattered throughout Luther's works is an abundance of informal quotations from the Bible, sometimes whole verses, often mere phrases. Special interest attaches to some of the early pre-*Septembertestament* quotations because in them can be seen to some extent at least, the great art of the translator evolving. Even though many of the quotations do not rise above the best efforts of his ablest predecessors, a not inconsiderable number do. Even at this early date, there are thus some splendid renderings, a few actually surpassing the same verses in Luther's later formal translation. Some are wholly idiomatic, some intensifying, some expanded, some alliterative; some are anticipatory of the *Septembertestament* quotations. Here are some examples, together with the Vulgate rendering for comparison:

Galatians 5: 24

ERASMUS (1519)[4]

οἱ δὲ τοῦ Χριστοῦ τὴν σάρκα ἐσταύρωσαν σὺν τοῖς παθήμασι, καὶ ταῖς ἐπιθυμίαις.

Vulgate

Qui autem sunt Christi, carnem suam crucifixerunt cum vitiis, et concupiscentiis.

Luther rendered the text as a casual quotation in *Von den guten Werken* (1520) as follows:

die haben yhr fleisch gecreutzigt mit seinen lastern und lusten [*WA* 6, 244. 22 f.].

It is an alliterative rendering even better than the *Septembertestament*'s phrase 'sampt den lusten vnd begirden'; yet he had apparently forgotten his excellent earlier phrase completely when he undertook the *Septembertestament*.

---

[3] See 'The First Translation of a Pericope', in my *Martin Luther, Creative Translator* (St. Louis: Concordia, 1965).

[4] The position of aspera and accents on the Greek diphthongs have been updated to modern textual conventions.

2 Timothy 3: 6

ERASMUS (1519)

ἔχοντες μόρφωσιν εὐσεβείας, τὴν δὲ δύναμιν αὐτῆς ἠρνημένοι

Vulgate

Habentes speciem quidem pietatis, virtutem autem eius abnegantes.

This Luther rendered as follows in *An den christlichen Adel deutscher Nation von des christlichen Standes Besserung* (1520):

Sie haben einen schein einis geistlichen lebens, unnd ist doch nichts dahyndenn [*WA* 6, 439. 26 f.].

Another variant of the same phrase occurs in *Von der Freiheit eines Christenmenschen* (1520):

Sie haben eynen scheyn fer frumkeyt, aber der grund ist nit da [*WA* 7, 33. 20 f.].

Compared with this artistically inspired casual rendering, the *Septembertestament*'s version seems prosaic in its literalness:

die da haben das geperde eynes gottseligen wandels / aber seyne krafft verleucken sie.

Titus 1: 9

ERASMUS (1519)

τοὺς ἀντιλέγοντας ἐλέγχειν

Vulgate

eos, qui contradicunt, arguere.

Luther, in *Deutsche Auslegung des 67. Psalmes* (1521), has:

das maul stopffen den wider partien [*WA* 8, 27.34].

In idiomatic quality, this again is superior to the *Septembertestament*:

zustraffen die widdersprecher.

Luke 21: 31

ERASMUS (1519)

ὅτι ἐγγύς ἐστιν ἡ βασιλεία τοῦ θεοῦ.

Vulgate

quoniam prope est regnum Dei.

Adventspostille (1522)
das das reych Gottis fur der thuer ist [*WA* 10¹, 2, 95.10–11].

In its striking concreteness, it is a rendering that surpasses the
more ordinary version of the *Septembertestament*:

das das reych Gottis nahe ist.

Martin Luther the translator was clearly on the way; and there was
every indication that, in the fullness of time, he could and would
provide a great new translation of the whole Bible.[5]

The decision that Luther should enter upon this formidable task
was made in December 1521, perhaps as much by learned friends
like Melanchthon, as by Luther himself; for no one seemed better
prepared than Dr Martinus for so demanding a project. A highly
readable Bible in the vernacular, readily accessible to the people,
was indispensable to the success of the Reformation; and Luther
yielded to the demands of his immediate circle and set to work
without delay. His enforced leisure at the Wartburg after the fateful Diet of Worms enabled the Reformer to devote the major portion of his vast energy to the translation. Lacking the resources of
a library and the advice of his Wittenberg colleagues, Luther translated the easier and much shorter New Testament first, a task he
was able to finish in the amazingly short time of about three
months. He took the manuscript back with him to Wittenberg,
went over it with Melanchthon, and sent it to the printer in
July. Some two months later, in September 1522, it appeared in
print.

The *Septembertestament* was an instant success, in all probabil-
ity surpassing even the expectations of the man who had prevailed
upon Luther to undertake this vast and difficult project. The first
edition quickly sold out, and a second edition was called for, and
actually appeared before the end of the same year. This is known
as the *Dezembertestament*, to differentiate it from the first edition,
the *Septembertestament*; but a succession of revised editions came
out to the very end of Luther's life, the most important revisions
occurring in 1527 and especially 1530.

As soon as the *Dezembertestament* was prepared and Luther
fully settled in Wittenberg once more, he began work on the Old

[5] See my 'An "Unknown" Luther Translation of the Bible', *PMLA* 84 (1969),
1537–44.

Testament. This took much longer to translate than the New Testament, in fact the Old Testament appeared in a number of instalments between 1523 and 1532. The Psalms, for example, as Luther's favourite Old Testament book, received special consideration, there being three principal separate editions in 1524, 1528, and 1531. The third edition, of 1531, was carefully discussed beforehand in Luther's committee on revision, and differs greatly from the preceding editions. Luther's earlier editions of the Psalms fall within the general scope of straightforward translation, close to the Hebrew text, as Luther himself observed. The third, however, again to quote him, is much closer to the German idiom. It can be said without exaggeration that in the 1531 rendering, the Hebrew Psalter has virtually become a German hymnal, actually reading in many places like original German sacred poetry.

Luther's first complete *German Bible* did not appear until 1534; and it was followed by more or less thoroughly revised editions in 1539, 1541, and 1545. Published after Luther's death early in the year, the edition of 1546 contained a number of important additional revisions. There is some controversy as to whether these changes are indeed Luther's own, since the edition was seen through the press by his able secretary, Georg Rörer. But in view of Rörer's notable reliability, it is now widely held that the changes introduced in the Bible of 1546 are authentic Luther.

These are the chief external facts of the history of Luther's *German Bible*. It is much more difficult to establish the inner nature of this extraordinary translation, the *editio princeps* of the Protestant Bible done out of the original languages, Hebrew and Greek. What is the character of Luther's *German Bible*? First of all, renowned for sheer readability, it has become, under Luther's magic touch, a German book, indispensable to German literature. A major source of familiar quotations, moreover, it easily surpasses even Goethe's *Faust*, a work itself indebted in many a line to the Luther Bible. Take, for instance, Luther's widely praised rendering of Matthew 12: 34b: 'Wes des hertz voll ist, des geht der mund vbir'; or his brilliant translation of Luke 1: 28: 'Gegrusset seystu holdselige'. These and many another well-known passage are not only readable but also beautifully expressed, for Luther was a great master of the German language; and his supreme mastery of language as much as any other quality has assured him the important place he holds among translators of the Bible. In his renderings of

St. Paul, for whom he felt a special affinity, Luther particularly surpassed himself. Here are some examples:

Galatians 1: 5

ERASMUS (1519)
εἰς τοὺς αἰῶνας τῶν αἰώνων.

Vulgate
in saecula saeculorum

Septembertestament
von ewickeyt zu ewickeyt.

Galatians 4: 4

ERASMUS (1519)
ὅτε δὲ ἦλθε τὸ πλήρωμα τοῦ χρόνου

Vulgate
At ubi venit plenitudo temporis

Septembertestament
Da aber die zeyt erfullet wart.

Galatians 4: 19

ERASMUS (1519)
τεκνία μου, οὓς πάλιν ὠδίνω, ἄχρις οὗ μορφωθῇ χριστὸς ἐν ὑμῖν.

Vulgate
filioli mei, quos iterum parturio, donec formatur Christus in vobis.

Septembertestament
Meyn lieben kinder, wilche ich abermal mit engsten gepere, bisz das Christus ynn euch eyn gestalt gewynne.

Yet the Luther Bible is more than a mere specimen of magnificent literary style. It is the most personal and subjective of all renderings of the Scriptures produced in the West; and that far more than its chief later rival among Protestant Bible translations, the *Authorized Version* of 1611. There is thus ample justification for the designation *Lutherbibel*, for the Luther Bible is *sui generis*.

What is the stature of the man who imposed his own personality and thought upon a document of manifestly diverse provenance? Who was Martin Luther? 'What think ye of Martin Luther?' Whatever else he was, and whatever else he did, he was the rediscoverer of the basic religious ideas of Paul. That leads immediately to the question, 'Who was Paul?' Although not one of the original Twelve, not even knowing Christ in the flesh, Paul was the intellectual among the apostles, the chief interpreter of the meaning of Christ for mankind, and the man who put Christianity on the map. It is widely held that, without Paul, Christianity could arguably have remained a Jewish sect. According to one of Nietzsche's brilliant *aperçus*, Paul marks the beginning of orthodox Christianity, just as Luther marks its end. In order to fulfil this historic role, Luther had first to rediscover its initiator, Paul, whose profound interpretation of Christianity had been lost sight of soon after the apostle's death. Through Luther's rediscovery therefore, Paul's faith, lost or at least seriously watered down to both the world and the Christian Church for more than 1,400 years, was re-established for the space of a generation, from 1513 to 1546, only to be lost again, or at least seriously weakened once more, after Luther's death.

During these memorable thirty-three years it is thus possible to refer to *Paulus redivivus*. Essential aspects of Paul's thought were regained, and sometimes even surpassed in theological clarity, emotional intensity, and especially linguistic and literary expression. Yet Luther himself never claimed to be more than a rediscoverer of his greatest teacher *in religiosis*.

Luther was keenly aware that St. Paul, and only St. Paul, was his real master. With the possible exception of St. John, whom he also respected highly, none of the apostles had the same profound image of Christ as Paul, and only Luther recaptured it after Paul. None of the Church Fathers, not even St. Augustine; none of the scholastic doctors of the Church, including St. Thomas; in fact, no Christian between Paul and Luther even approached these two in their grasp of what they considered to be the essence of Christianity. There is an elective affinity between the two men, that if it is distant in time, is remarkably close in spirit; and this extraordinary affinity made Luther the unparalleled translator of Paul that he proved to be. In all likelihood no seminal thinker has ever been rendered so felicitously and creatively in another language as Paul by Luther. Having entered into Paul's mind as nobody else had done, Luther could put basic aspects of his thought into German and also (in the Wittenberg Vulgate) into Latin, out of an ultimate understanding never attained by anyone else before or since. Granted such a remarkable merging of two superior minds, it is small wonder that the highly literate Luther was able to express in German and Latin certain matters merely hinted at or suggested by Paul. As Goethe wrote about the *Second Part* of *Faust*, 'Der Leser muss sich auf leisen Wink und Andeutung verstehen.' A greater master of language than Paul, and at least as great an interpreter of Christianity, Luther was able to express ideas more clearly and more fully than his mentor.

Taking the New Testament as a whole, there is never any doubt that Luther's heart and mind are permeated with Pauline theology; and it is this that gives the Luther Bible what is perhaps its most characteristic aspect, its unity. In this remarkable unity, the German Bible is quite different from the Hebrew and Greek originals and even the Christianizing Vulgate, as well as virtually all other translations into European languages. Other translations retain unchanged the diverse and sometimes unreconciled religious ideas of individual Biblical authors. Only Luther unified this book of several theologies into one integrated whole.

How did he do this? He did it by consistently adhering to his own personal interpretation of the Bible—an interpretation derived from Paul. As a matter of fact, Luther the interpreter preceded Luther the translator. Before he undertook the formal translation in 1522, he had lectured on the Bible for almost ten years at the University of Wittenberg. From 1522 to the end of his life biblical interpretation in the lecture hall (and, in a more popular form, in the pulpit) went hand in hand with translation and constant revision. Thus Luther the translator was preceded and shaped by Luther the theological interpreter. Joseph Lortz claimed that Luther was not a *Vollhörer des Wortes*, a complete hearer of the Word. It is a charge that demands twofold consideration. A partial hearer either does not actually hear or perceive the full message of a diverse work; or he prefers—consciously or unconsciously—some of its themes more than others. This can result from either ignorance or indifference or even from deliberate choice. In the case of choice, a value judgement relates, just as it did with Martin Luther who clearly evaluated the various books of the Bible very differently on the basis of their various messages. The basic question is, therefore: which books did he rate most highly? Obviously

enough, the Pauline epistles provide the answer when, for the Reformer those Pauline epistles were the most important and decisive
books of the entire Bible. From these books Luther heard the message; and to such books the Reformer subordinated the rest of the
Bible.

Yet in what precise sense did he subordinate them? If Luther
had been a twentieth-century biblical scholar, he might simply
have ruled out some portions of the Bible as of questionable, or
even inferior, religious value. Like Hermann Gunkel in his famous
essay 'Was bleibt?', he might even have proceeded to eliminate
much of the Bible because it did not meet his own idea of high religious import. But Luther lived and worked hard and long before
the critical and historical approach to the Bible was initiated, much
less fully developed. To Luther as a man of the sixteenth century,
the only course open was to elevate the lowest biblical thought to
the highest, to maintain the level of what he had come to regard as
the loftiest peak of Christian religion. For him this was the summit
of Paul's thought, the religion of *sola fides* and *sola gratia*.

The result was the notable unity of the Luther Bible. No less a
scholar than Emanuel Hirsch, one of the most sensitive students of
the German Bible, made the claim that this unity of Luther's Bible
was one of the chief means that, for some, kept Luther's Germany
Lutheran, at least for a time. Heard as it was in Church, learned in
school, and read at home, this unique German book was up to the
twentieth century, ultimately just as influential in preserving authentic Lutheranism as Luther's stately hymns, lucid catechisms,
and powerful sermons.

The Reformer's task of unifying the Bible along Pauline lines
was twofold: first, he rearranged the order of books in the New
Testament; and secondly, he made certain changes of wording.
The rearrangement of books need not concern us here; but the
most famous of the linguistic changes, and the one most frequently
attacked by Luther's enemies, was his rendering of Romans 3: 28:

ERASMUS (1519)

λογιζόμεθα οὖν πίστει δικαιοῦσθαι ἄνθρωπον χωρὶς ἔργων νόμου.

Vulgate
Arbitramur enim iustificari hominem per fidem sine operibus legis.

Septembertestament

So halten wyrs nu / das der mensch gerechtfertiget werde / on zu thun der werck des gesetzs / alleyn durch den glawben /

This phrasing, with its insertion of 'alleyn' before 'durch den glawben', was a bold and novel rendering that he defended vigorously and brilliantly in his *Sendbrief vom Dolmetschen.*

It was, moreover, only the most famous of Luther's elaborations of Paul's phrasing, his clarifications and intensifications of what the apostle had not stated with such lucidity and force, for there were other passages in Romans the Reformer gave a decidedly Lutheran turn. Some of the most telling examples are naturally found in Chapter 3.

Romans 3: 20

ERASMUS (1519)

διότι ἐξ ἔργων νόμου οὐ δικαιωθήσεται πᾶσα σὰρξ ἐνώπιον αὐτοῦ. Διὰ γὰρ νόμου ἐπίγνωσις ἁμαρτίας.

Vulgate

Quia ex operibus legis non iustificabitur omnis caro coram illo. Per legem enim cognitio peccati.

Septembertestament

darumb, das keyn fleysch durch des gesetzs werck fur yhm rechtfertig seyn mag / Denn durch das gesetz / kompt *nur*[6] erkenntnis der sund.

Romans 3: 22

ERASMUS (1519)

δικαιοσύνη δὲ θεοῦ διὰ πίστεως Ἰησοῦ Χριστοῦ εἰς πάντας, καὶ ἐπὶ πάντας τοὺς πιστεύοντας, οὐ γάρ ἐστι διαστολή.

Vulgate

Iustitia autem Dei per fidem Jesu Christi in omnes, et super omnes, qui credunt in eum: non enim est distinctio.

Septembertestament

Ich sage aber von solcher gerechtickeyt fur got / die da kompt / durch den glawben an Jhesum Christ / zu allen vnd auff alle / die da glewben. Denn es ist hie keyn vnterscheyd /.

---

[6] Italics mine.

Romans 3: 25

ERASMUS (1519)

ὃν προέθετο ὁ θεὸς ἱλαστήριον, διὰ τῆς πίστεως ἐν τῷ αὐτοῦ αἵματι, εἰς ἔνδειξιν τῆς δικαιοσύνης αὐτοῦ, διὰ τὴν πάρεσιν τῶν προγεγονότων ἁμαρτημάτων, ἐν τῇ ἀνοχῇ τοῦ θεοῦ.

Vulgate

quem proposuit Deus propitiationem per fidem in sanguine ipsius, ad ostensionem iustitiae suae propter remissionem praecedentium delictorum in sustentatione Dei.

Septembertestament

wilchen gott hat furgestellet zu eynem gnade stuel / durch den glawben ynn seynem blut / da mit er die gerechtickeit / die fur yhm gilt / beweyse / ynn dem / das er vergibt die sund / die zuuor sind geschehen vnter gotlicher gedult / die er trug /

Romans 3: 26

ERASMUS (1519)

πρὸς ἔνδειξιν τῆς δικαιοσύνης αὐτοῦ ἐν τῷ νῦν καιρῷ, εἰς τὸ εἶναι αὐτὸν δίκαιον, καὶ δικαιοῦντα τὸν ἐκ πίστεως Ἰησοῦ.

Vulgate

ad ostensionem iustitiae eius in hoc tempore: ut sit ipse iustus, et iustificans eum, qui est fide Iesu Christi.

Septembertestament

das er zu‧disen zeyten beweysete die gerechtickeyt / die fur yhm gilt / Auff das er alleyne gerecht sey / vnd rechtfertige den / der da ist des glawbens an Ihesu.[7]

So far as the Old Testament, as well as the non-Pauline parts of the New Testament, are concerned, Luther's situation was quite different from that he faced when dealing with Paul. Here, with a few isolated exceptions, the translator moves on a higher plane than the original authors. Surprising as it may seem, the translator both as a thinker and as a writer is often greater than the authors he interprets and translates. The situation is probably unique in the history of Western translation. The various translators of Homer,

[7] For a detailed discussion of these and other passages see my essay 'Bedeutung und Eigenart von Luthers Septembertestament: Eine Analyse von Römer iii. 19–31', *Luther Jahrbuch*, viii (1972), 55–79.

including Alexander Pope in English and Johann Heinrich Voss in German, thus far from measure up to the stature of Homer. Similarly, the Schlegel—Tieck—Baudissin translation, good as it is, remains markedly inferior to Shakespeare. With Martin Luther, however, the reverse is true and the translator is greater than the original authors.

In the Old Testament, as in the New, there is one part in which Luther went beyond himself—the Psalms. Yet there was a considerable difference between his task in rendering Paul and his treatment of the Psalms. Only a few of the 150 psalms really achieve greatness compared with the religious heights attained and consistently maintained by Paul. Accordingly, Luther had a far greater task to perform in rendering the Psalms than in rendering Paul, a man after his own heart and mind. With Paul all that was necessary was to render his Greek into luminous German. But when dealing with the Psalms, even some of the best of them, Luther had to elevate religious language to both his own and Paul's level. His rendering of such psalms as 51, 90, and 139 is superb. In addition, the number of excellently rendered individual verses in the Psalter is astonishing. Take, for example, his final version of Psalm 73: 25–6:

> Wenn ich nur dich hab, So frage ich
> nichts nach himel und erden.
> Wenn mir gleich leib und seel verschmacht,
> So bistu doch Gott allzeit meines
> hertzen trost, und mein teil.

For comparison, note the translation in the *Authorized Version*:

Whom have I in heaven but thee? and there is none upon earth that I desire beside thee. My flesh and heart faileth; but God is the strength of my heart, and my portion for ever.

The *Revised Standard Version* reads:

Whom have I in heaven but thee?
  And there is nothing upon earth that I desire besides thee.
My flesh and my heart may fail,
  but God is the strength of my heart and my portion for ever.

Even in his earliest translation of 1524, the passage had been rather less literal than the *Authorized* and *Revised Standard Versions* just quoted:

Wen hab ich ym hymel? und auff erden
gefellet myr nichts, wenn ich bey dyr byn.
Meyn fleysch und meyn hertz ist verschmacht.
Gott is meyns hertzen hort,
und meyn teyl ewiglich.

When Luther decided to subject his whole Psalter to a thorough-going revision in 1531, the rendering already quoted emerged. It is so extraordinary that it can scarcely be termed mere translation. To facilitate comparison, note these great lines again:

LUTHER (1531)

> Wenn ich nur dich hab, So frage ich
> nichts nach himel und erden.
> Wenn mir gleich leib und seel verschmacht,
> So bistu doch Gott allzeit meines
> hertzen trost, und mein teil.

They read like an original German poem of great religious depth, cast in beautiful, rhythmic German. Luther, religious genius as he was, took the ancient psalmist as a starting-point and then proceeded on his own. The result may not be poetic creation itself, but it is surely poetic re-creation in another language. In short, Luther's lines stand on their own merit and rival, even surpass, the original, at least in the shape in which the latter has come down to us. They are five lines that come close to the perfection of original poetry of the highest rank, and are certainly as great as any in Goethe, Novalis, Hölderlin, or late Heine. Luther's Old Testament, like his New, abounds in passages of the same superior quality.

Luther's *German Bible* thus provided a model for other Scriptural translators to imitate, two early English Bibles, William Tyndale's *New Testament* (1526, revised in 1534), and Myles Coverdale's Bible (1535), borrowing heavily from Luther. Two examples of this debt from Tyndale's New Testament can illustrate the point:

Ephesians 1: 4

ERASMUS (1519)
πρὸ καταβολῆς κόσμου

Vulgate
ante mundi constitutionem

LUTHER (1522–1546)

ehe der welt grund gelegt war

TYNDALE

before the foundacioun of the worlde was layde

Ephesians 3: 19

ERASMUS (1519 and 1522)

τὴν ὑπερβάλλουσαν τῆς γνώσεως ἀγάπην τοῦ Χριστοῦ.

Vulgate

supereminentem scientiae charitatem Christi

LUTHER

die liebe Christi, die doch alle erkentnis vbertrifft

TYNDALE

which is the love of Christ, which love passeth all knowledge

A Lutheran by conviction, William Tyndale had fully entered into Luther's mind. Besides being verbally indebted to the Wittenberg Reformer as these extracts indicate, he often rendered verses in Luther's spirit albeit not using Luther's actual phrases. In other words, Tyndale had sufficiently absorbed Luther's thought to be able to Lutheranize linguistically on his own. In his preface, moreover, he included translations of major portions of Luther's *Prefaces* and reproduced many of his marginal notes, thereby explicitly putting his stamp of approval on Luther's theology.

Coverdale proceeded differently, for he lacked Tyndale's ability to produce renderings with a Lutheran ring when not directly translating Luther. For this reason, he did not provide independent formulations of Lutheran thought, but retained instead most of Tyndale's borrowings from Luther, as well as adding many borrowings of his own. Two examples of such borrowed material are given here:[8]

Galatians 4: 18

Vulgate

Bonum autem aemulamini in bono semper

---

[8] The Greek is omitted because Coverdale did not use Greek.

LUTHER

Eyffern ist gut, wens ymerdar geschicht vmb das gutte

TYNDALE

It is good alwayes to be fervent, so it be in a good thinge

COVERDALE

It is good to be fervent, so it be allwaye in a good thinge

Galatians 5: 5

Vulgate

Nos enim spiritu ex fide, spem iustitiae exspectamus

LUTHER

Wyr aber wartten ym geyst der hoffnung, das wyr durch den glawben rechtfertig seyen.

TYNDALE (1525)

We loke for and hope to be iustified by the sprete which commeth of fayth

TYNDALE (1534)

We loke for and hope in the sprite to be iustified thorow fayth

COVERDALE

But we wayte in the sprete off hope, to be made righteous by faith.

The *Authorized Version* (1611), a much more literal translation than Luther's eliminated many Lutheran formulations, but as may be seen from this example retained a number of them just the same.

Psalm 45: 13

LUTHER (1524)

Des koniges tochter ist gantz herlich drynnen / yhr kleyd ist gewirckt gold.

Authorized Version

The king's daughter is all glorious within: her clothing is of wrought gold.

Vernacular Bibles in other Germanic lands—the Scandinavian countries and the Netherlands—were also significantly influenced by the Luther Bible; and in some instances translations were evidently made directly from Luther rather than from Hebrew or Greek. It is noteworthy that although almost all translations into English, including the *Authorized Version*, have been more or less thoroughly revised a number of times, the *German Bible* has remained largely intact. Luther's version bears the unmistakable stamp of his personality, and it has therefore been difficult to introduce changes even when these might be considered advisable in view of advancing knowledge of Hebrew and Greek. The changes that have been made, more often than not, do not measure up to Luther's own masterful work, proving time and again that the Luther Bible is a work of art as well as of scholarship (the latter of course defined by early sixteenth-century standards). It may be urged for Luther's Bible what has been claimed for Homer—namely that it is as difficult to wrest a verse from Luther's Bible as it is to take away the club from the hands of Hercules. For Luther's *German Bible* is a religious document couched in superb German,[9] the language raised in many parts to the level of the religion of St. Paul, even at times surpassing the original language of Paul and of the Psalms in clarity and power. The *German Bible* is Luther's Bible. Although newer, more literal, translations are available for contemporary scholars and semi-scholarly needs, Luther's Bible remains a remarkable creative achievement and should be left as it is. Luther combined in a unique way the prowess of a famous university professor, a powerful preacher, and a matchless biblical translator. To find his equal it would be necessary at the very least to combine the theological depth of St. Augustine, the eloquence of St. Chrysostom, and the literary skill of St. Jerome.

[9] Luther's own modest statement should be noted: 'non possunt omnia reddi germanice' [*WA* 37, 474.15].

IX

Cochlaeus as a Polemicist

*

GOTTHELF WIEDERMANN

I⊤ is indeed a miracle and surpasses all reason and understanding, however sublime and venerable, that in one deity there are three, and these three deities are one—one in substance, yet three in person. But in one cowl of this one Luther, there are seven, and these seven Luthers are not only one in substance, but even in person. An extraordinary theology indeed, hitherto unheard of not only among Jews and heathens, but also among Christians! In the old, most Christian Evangel, there was one heart among the multitude of believers and one soul; yet in this new Evangel one heart and flesh are cut apart into many heads, and not only is it that diverse people hold diverse opinions, but one and the same mind grows several heads next to itself.[1]

W⊤⊤H this outcry of indignation Cochlaeus reacted against the Wittenberg initiative to bring about a satisfactory organization and supervision of the Lutheran Churches.

It was a much disillusioned Luther who found himself obliged to recognize that a truly Christian Church could not be founded on the preaching of the true Gospel alone. His hopes dashed, the Reformer bitterly complained about the indifference of the people and the fact that his message of the liberty of a Christian man had been so abused as to afford a pretext for both moral licentiousness and political rebellion. No longer could the running of Church life be left to the discretion of pastors and people at large, with the result that instruction, discipline, and the preaching of the Law received a new priority. In the *Instructions for the Visitors of Parish Pastors in Electoral Saxony* Luther and Melanchthon thus forwarded a visitation programme that would survey the correct education and behaviour of people and ministers, and likewise emphasize the importance of the Ten Commandments, the Law, the fear of God, and penitence.

Cochlaeus, who had been a close observer of Luther's theological development since 1520, saw this new emphasis as a contradiction to the Reformer's earlier writings on Christian liberty and noted in triumph that Luther had played into his hands. No longer was it necessary to refute him with Scripture or Church decrees, for Luther had contradicted himself and therefore stood con-

[1] Johannes Cochlaeus, *S[epticeps] L[utherus]* (Dresden, 1529), fol. iib.

demned by the standards of his own arguments. After an arithmetical strategy of Lutheran errors Cochlaeus thus proceeded to demonstrate the contradictory nature of Luther's writings, and the book, *Septiceps Lutherus* divided the Reformer's development into seven periods, each represented by a separate head, to result in the seven-headed monster of the title-page cartoon. These heads Cochlaeus used to express different, contradictory opinions on particular subjects and introduced them to his reader in the preface:

Thus all brothers emerge from the womb of one and the same cowl by a birth so monstrous, that none is like the other in either behaviour, shape, face or character. The elder brothers, *Doctor* and *Martinus*, come closest to the opinion of the Church, and they are to be believed above all the others, if anything anywhere in Luther's books can be believed with any certainty at all. *Lutherus*, however, according to his surname, plays a wicked game just like Ismael [lat. ludere—Luder, Saxon pronunciation for Luther]. *Ecclesiastes* tells the people who are always keen on novelties, pleasant things. *Svermerus* rages furiously and errs in the manner of Phaeton throughout the skies. *Barrabas* is looking for violence and sedition everywhere. And at the last, *Visitator*, adorned with a new mitre and ambitious for a new papacy, prescribes new laws of ceremonies, and many old ones which he had previously abolished—revokes, removes, reduces. This is the sum of my book.[2]

In forty-five chapters *Septiceps Lutherus* then dealt with major doctrinal and ecclesiastical issues, lively debate often ensuing between the seven heads. It was a book greatly welcomed by Catholic priests, since it provided them with a handy compendium of Lutheran contradictions and absurdities from which they could refute Luther in his own words and without having to read the Reformer for themselves. With no real need for the clergy to read Luther, too, Cochlaeus was clear that there was less danger of further defections to the Protestant cause!

Septiceps Lutherus was one of the first books published by Cochlaeus when he was chaplain to Duke Georg of Saxony, a period that witnessed marked deterioration in the quality of his polemical writing. Surrounded by less talented and less upright men like Hieronymus Walther, Johann Hasenberg, and Joachim von der Heiden, Cochlaeus became increasingly absorbed by their evi-

---

[2] *SL*, fol. iib.

dent delight in wild and unpleasant scandalmongering, a favourite
subject of which was Luther's marriage to Katherina von Bora.[3]
The hatred and bitterness he felt towards Luther made Cochlaeus
less and less capable of distinguishing between well-argued criticism and destructive polemics, a fact particularly well demonstrated
in the *Commentaria de actis et scriptis Martini Lutheri,* Part one of
which was finished in 1534. For the personal element in this history of the Lutheran Reformation is so dominant, the reader finds
it difficult to avoid the impression that, for Cochlaeus, the
Reformation was exclusively to be blamed on Luther. Cochlaeus
found Luther to be a man full of evil intentions and ambitions, and
he was clear that jealousy, selfishness, hypocrisy, and a desire for
notoriety ultimately motivated all the Reformer's actions. No
good was to be expected of such a man, and no defamation seemed
too base to be left unmentioned. In his *Sincere and Thorough Apology for Duke Georg of Saxony* of 1533, Cochlaeus thus willingly
accepted Peter Sylvius's fable of Luther's creation by the Devil;
and although in the *Commentaria* he expressed some doubt about
the truth of the rumour, he remained convinced that, as a destroyer of the Church and the German nation, Luther was an agent
of Satan himself.[4] Such obsession with the person of Martin
Luther made Cochlaeus blind to the wider context of the Reformation, and his writings in consequence show remarkable ignorance
and misjudgement of the German political situation, of growing
lay interest in the shaping of Church life, and of the intellectual
outlook of the new learning.

The age of the Reformation was a period of great unrest and
overflowing emotions, and Cochlaeus's writings certainly reflect
such a period atmosphere. Because of its extremely personal, immediate, and direct approach his work provides numerous vivid
impressions of the impact the Reformation made on the people at
large: bricklayers arguing with monks about the value of indulgences and the nature of justification; *Hausväter* absorbed by reading the New Testament in German; book-fairs swamped by
Protestant tracts at a time when Catholic writers vainly tried to
publish at all. Yet, no amount of excitement and upheaval can be
allowed to excuse the vilification and injustice Cochlaeus's polemic

---

[3] See M. Spahn, *Johannes Cochlaeus,* (Berlin, 1898), pp. 133 ff.

[4] Spahn, op. cit., pp. 180 f.; see also A. Herte, *Die Lutherkommentare des
Johannes Cochlaeus* (Münster, 1935), pp. 140 ff.

inflicted on the person of Luther. Nevertheless, for the historian they at least provide a clue to Cochlaeus's character and his personal involvement in a continuing controversy. His feelings of impotence and inadequacy over against the Reformers thus grew in proportion to his frustration about the indifference and neglect of the German prelates; and this, in turn, increased the hatred and bitterness he felt for Luther. The principal weakness of such polemic was thus the fact that Cochlaeus could not keep his personal feelings under control. If he admittedly fought for the old Church, he also fought to secure his own reputation in writings full of clumsy self-recommendation and self-justification. His person ridiculed by young Protestant humanists, his works ignored or treated with contempt by the Reformers who did not even care to read them, Cochlaeus clearly thirsted for recognition in writings remarkable only for their self-importance and vanity. His desire to defend the old Church is thus so closely related to his concern to justify himself as to be almost indistinguishable.

In the Preface to the *Septiceps Lutherus*, Cochlaeus promised to afford his readers precise and undistorted quotation from Luther, so that all could judge for themselves the monstrous blasphemy perpetrated by the Reformer. In actual fact, Cochlaeus's approach to the quotations which comprise so much of his work is highly significant for the way in which it proceeds against Luther's theology. When compared to the learning of most Reformers, Cochlaeus's own theological education was rather outdated. Almost forty years of age before he got to grips with advanced biblical scholarship, Cochlaeus had the mind of a philologist, and not of a speculative theologian. There is therefore a real element of tragedy in his obsession with a task for which he was so ill equipped. A fixation on detail prevented due focus on the central points of Protestant faith; and instead of attempting to analyse the theological premises and arguments of the Reformers he often replied sentence by sentence. At the same time, Cochlaeus was frequently incapable of setting out the main points of his adversary's argument, quotations more often than not being selected without any object in mind. Accumulated rather than being analysed therefore, such material is often a mass of tedious repetition and the choice of the quotations dictated by black moods of haste and revulsion. In his *Die Lutherkommentare des Johannes Cochlaeus*,[5] Adolf Herte

[5] op. cit., p. 9.

showed that Cochlaeus derived most of his quotations from the prefaces and epilogues of Luther's books, and drew the conclusion that Cochlaeus had read very few, if any, of Luther's books properly. Such prejudice against everything Luther wrote is clearly expressed in the *Preface* to *Septiceps*, where Cochlaeus admitted that the occupation with Luther's books filled him with disgust. His copies of the Reformer's works lay scattered around the floor of his room and were often unbound, since he did not deem it worth while to line such heresy on shelves with the rest of his library. Whatever his claims to be a man of learning it is a comment that detracts from his reputation as a humanist.

Although Cochlaeus no doubt always attempted to quote faithfully, and never willingly distorted Luther's statements, *Septiceps Lutherus* is nevertheless a masterpiece of distortion, misrepresentation, and also stupidity. With little regard for the dialectical nature of Luther's writings—more often than not the Reformer was obliged to fight on two fronts at the same time—quotations are torn out of context and 'edited' in a way that created artificial contradictions to make nonsense of anything Luther ever wrote. If Cochlaeus reproduced Luther's words, he certainly violated his thoughts and arguments, seizing on passages that sounded particularly scandalous and revolutionary with all the zeal of a cheap journalist. Few members of the hierarchy realized that much more than mere denunciation was needed to stem the tide of the Reformation. At the Diet of Worms Aleander warned Cochlaeus not to get carried away by his ambition to fight Luther, and argued that, since the Reformation drew its strength from the prevalence of anti-clericalism, it was necessary to reform the priesthood and bring it into closer contact with the people. He advised Cochlaeus to be an exemplary priest and instruct his congregation in the articles of faith and through a life of goodness and moderation. Cochlaeus did not heed the advice, but sought to serve his Church in other ways. He saw no wrong in his own pluralism and absenteeism, and at the age of sixty-two confessed that he had never preached in his life. In short, while seeking to destroy Lutheran reformation, he was himself incapable of standing by the best traditions of Catholicism.

The Reformation of the sixteenth century was more than a reaction to ecclesiastical abuses, a fact the Catholic Church was slow to grasp. The premisses of Luther's theology no longer coincided with the doctrines of Rome, and it was because of his failure to realize this that Cochlaeus fought Luther with arguments the Reformer had long since abandoned as Scripturally invalid. The redefinition of theological and ecclesiastical terminology set the spotlight on the period as a ring for bouts of shadow-boxing: Luther fought Erasmus on Free Will; Zwingli battled with Luther on the Eucharist; Osiander sparred with Melanchthon; and Cranmer with Gardiner. In his turn, Cochlaeus was greatly confused by the new use of old terminology. While Luther had already redefined authority in the Church, and given the pre-eminence to the Holy Scripture, Cochlaeus continued the old ways, armed with traditional weapons in the papal decrees and canon law. Medieval arguments of papal supremacy were constantly forwarded as if they had never been questioned; and the arguments of Luther and his kind were parried with worn-out commonplaces and authoritative judgements Cochlaeus esteemed above all. The need for serious argument he thus side-stepped, preferring to set the verdicts of popes, emperors, kings, bishops, universities, and individual scholars beside quotations from Luther, to imply that he had thereby proved him wrong. Battling against the Reformer's stand on Scriptural authority, Cochlaeus dangerously underestimated the significance of the Bible as divine revelation, and frequently emphasized both the insufficiency of Scripture and, in many cases, the fact that, for him, its authority was inferior to that of the Pope. By itself, Scripture is a dead letter. Only with the gift of the Holy Spirit—which in Cochlaeus's eyes seems to be exclusively reserved for the priestly hierarchy—does it become a fount of divine revelation.

Such a limited view of Scripture is matched by Cochlaeus's equally narrow ecclesiology. The notion was that of a Church confined to the hierarchy with the *congregatio fidelium* standing by to witness the priestly spectacle. It was a Church of priests with little room for the laity. Vernacular Scripture and personal faith were both unnecessary and dangerous, merely creating confusion; and the increasing lay concern to shape the life of the Church, Cochlaeus not only regarded with suspicion, but dismissed as dangerous. The process of externalizing Church life, which resulted in mere institutionalism and a view of membership as complete subordination to its statutes, is clearly present in Cochlaeus whose obdurate partisanship prevented any real awareness of decay in the

Catholic Church. His presentation in the *Commentaria* of the period before Luther as a golden age of the Church suggests that he had himself forgotten his own past as a zealous fighter for reform according to humanist principles.

Septiceps Lutherus thus highlights problem areas in Luther's theology some of which are as ancient as Christianity itself and admit of no satisfactory solution. Others presented new challenges. How, for example, could the necessity for a properly ordained ministry be reconciled with the notion of a priesthood of all believers? Why were good works still necessary, if they had no meritorious value? What importance could be attached to the sacraments, if faith *alone* procured salvation? How was correct interpretation of Scripture to be determined? How could man be just and yet also prone to sin? Making all possible capital out of such issues, Cochlaeus affords scholars some idea of the genuine bewilderment Luther's new terminology caused among many of his contemporaries, both Protestant and Catholic. For few indeed were they who were able to graps the complex and paradoxical nature of many of Luther's theological notions. Having frequently to fight on two fronts, the Reformer was bound to express himself in an emphatic, and deliberately exaggerated, way; and such statements, uttered in the heat of battle, and not always meant to be taken literally, Cochlaeus made much of in his anti-Lutheran propaganda. It was certainly naive of Luther to assume that his new terminology could be easily understood without much risk of muddle or drawing the wrong conclusions. In fact, the Reformer had to carry on a long literary campaign in order to root out every chance of misunderstanding and misinterpretation; but even then, he was often too late. Much of the *Septiceps* is plain nonsense; yet it does illustrate how easily Luther's writings could be misunderstood. At the same time, however, Cochlaeus added greatly to the confusion and misunderstanding on the Catholic side. Before every diet, every religious colloquy, and before the Council met at Trent, he distributed his anti-Lutheran literature—compendia, histories, and 'expert opinions'—among the Catholic deputies in an attempt to put them off Luther and prevent fair treatment of the Reformer's theology. The *Septiceps* was thus intended to be a compendium of Lutheran contradictions to give the Catholic clergy clear guidelines of what to think of Luther. Similarly, the *Commentaria* was intended to provide information to inform a future council. But the one-sided and distorted representation of Luther's theology there presented must call in question Cochlaeus's reputation as a pioneer pleading unity in the Church. If Luther is to be accused of having caused the tragic division of Western Christianity, it should also be asked what the Catholic authorities in their turn had to offer to avert that division? As early as 1526, before the Diet of Speyer, Cochlaeus submitted an assessment of the religious situation in Germany to the Archbishop of Mainz, and showed himself to be highly critical of any negotiations with the heretics. At this stage he was clear that a council could bring no results, and the best way to deal with the Protestants was to destroy arch-heretics like Luther, for then the princes and cities could easily be won back. It was thus the case that Cochlaeus, like most Catholic negotiators at diets and colloquies, was in no way prepared to make concessions; rather was his polemical literature intended to discredit the Protestants even before the negotiations began. Many of the Catholic deputies thus gained their introduction to Luther's theology by way of Cochlaeus's representation and in consequence adopted what must be regarded as positions of prejudice and misunderstanding. Comparison with the unfortunate treatment afforded John Hus at the Council of Constance certainly obtains.

Throughout his life, Cochlaeus complained of his lack of recognition at the hands of both Protestants and Catholics. Even the sales achieved by his books compared badly with those of the Protestants. He had constant difficulties in finding competent printers; yet there were also times when he felt obliged to write just in order to retain his printer's services. It is thus a curious irony that Cochlaeus became the most influential writer of Catholic post-Reformation historiography,[6] his *Commentaria* gaining a prominent place in the confessionalist campaigns following the Reformation. As A. Herte has demonstrated, from the time of Luther's death until the twentieth century, the whole Catholic corpus of Luther-literature was dominated by this work which had such disastrous effect on relationships between the two confessions. Admittedly, there were only three Latin and three German editions of the *Commentaria*; but in their representation of Luther, two sixteenth-century French world-chronicles by Fontaine and

[6] See Adolf Herte, *Das katholische Lutherbild in Bann der Luther-kommentare des Cochlaeus*, 3 vols. (Münster, 1943).

Surius, which together ran to some twenty editions, essentially pirated the *Commentaria*. Through the centuries, generation after generation of Catholic priests were brought up on church-histories, encyclopaedias, world-chronicles, and histories of heresy all of which, deliberately or unknowingly, accepted Cochlaeus's verdict on Luther. Only in the Age of Englightenment did the *Commentaria* temporarily lose some of its hold on Germany, though not on France; and even then the revival of confessionalism in the nineteenth century renewed the old influences and continued to do so right into modern times. It was only in the twentieth century, that Cochlaeus's hold on the Catholic image of Luther was gradually broken, especially by Joseph Lortz's *Die Reformation in Deutschland*, (1939–40). Strangely too, as Herte regretfully admits, some of the most insulting pamphlets against Luther were only written this century; and two recent works by Remigius Bäumer demonstrate that the spirit of Cochlaeus remains very much alive. In his biography, *Johannes Cochlaeus (1479-1552)*,[7] Bäumer celebrates the man as a great defender of the Church and Catholic reformer; while his essay, *Das Zeitalter der Glaubensspaltung*, in a book[8] published on the occasion of Pope John Paul II's visit to Germany in 1980, caused great indignation among German Protestants. Both works reproduce in essence[9] the picture of Luther drawn by Cochlaeus more than four hundred years ago, and attribute the origins of the Reformation to Luther's subjective experience and selfish ambitions. Bäumer's Luther did not want reform, and merely sought to destroy ecclesiastical structures. Obstinacy and hatred of authority motivated all his actions, so that even before the Diet of Worms, Luther simulated obedience to the Pope, when doing his best to seduce the German nation into rebellion against the Church. For Bäumer, it was clearly contradictory and inconsistent of Luther to demand that the Pope and his prelates should be made to justify their indictment by Holy Scripture, so that the Reformer's excommunication was entirely proper, just, and lawful. Likewise, Luther's translation of the Bible into German was highly subjective in style, and distorted

---

[7] Katholisches Leben und Kämpfen im Zeitalter der Glaubensspaltung, Heft 40 (Aschendorff, 1980).
[8] *Kleine deutsche Kirchengeschichte*, ed. B. Kötting (Freiburg/Basel/Wien, 1980).
[9] Bäumer thinks that the *Commentaria* provides a 'reliable and faithful survey of the life and writings of Martin Luther'. See his *Joh. Cochlaeus (1479–1552)*, p. 105.

the true meaning of its text. Luther himself was largely to blame for the Peasants' Revolt, first inciting them to rebel, and when he realized that their cause was lost, siding with the princes and urging them to slaughter every one of the rebels. Even at such a time of crisis, Luther did not scruple to take a nun as his wife—a bloody, sacrilegious, and immoral marriage if ever there was one! At the Diet of Augsburg, both Luther and Melanchthon continued their black art of deception by deliberately misleading the Emperor with the *Confessio Augustana*; all negotiations at this Diet, as those at later diets and colloquies, thus failed as a result of Protestant obstinacy. Bäumer's conclusion therefore comes as no surprise: 'Luther's Reformation achieved not reform, but the division of the Church.'[10] It was Luther's choleric disposition, the intemperance of his anger and polemic, that had made him blind for Catholic truth. If Lortz held that Luther's fight against the prevailing nominalist theology was right, so that the Reformer only erred in identifying this theology with Catholic dogma ('Ein tragisches Missverständnis'), Bäumer would not even grant this. For him, indeed, Luther's evangelical discovery revealed nothing new— only Catholic truth as represented and taught by most medieval exegetes. Bäumer, in short, with such one-sided selection and uncritical treatment of historical documents, actually continues the historiographical tradition originated by Cochlaeus to regard the Reformation as an illegitimate event in the history of the Church. It is historiography of the kind governed by the dogmatism of Trent and Vatican I, which will, if not repudiated, inflict great damage on the understanding between the Roman Catholic and the Lutheran Churches.

[10] R. Bäumer, *Das Zeitalter der Glaubensspaltung*, p. 68.

X

Martin Luther in the Perspective of Historiography

*

ULRICH MICHAEL KREMER

ALMOST from the beginning of his bid for Reformation, Martin Luther's aims and objectives received serious scrutiny from both supporters and opponents of his cause. They sought to determine whether Wittenberg had begun a process of reform within a broad and recognizably Catholic tradition; or whether Luther's *cause célèbre* ·in fact amounted to stark institutional revolution in a 'True Church' tradition of heresy. If the best-known representatives of the first group are Melanchthon, Sleidanus, and Flacius, the second was of course dominated by Cochlaeus and his Luther commentaries. The effect of these was so lasting that, as Herte convincingly demonstrated, the entire Catholic historiography of the Reformation until the publication in 1939 of Joseph Lortz's *magnum opus* came under the spell of such powerful polemic.[1] So strong was the tradition, indeed, that even Erikson's psycho-analytical study, *Young Man Luther* (1958), is in large part derived from the 'scandal chronicle' of Cochlaeus.

In his attempt to assess Luther's place in the history of Christendom, Melanchthon's view of his Faculty colleague was no doubt coloured by apocalyptic based on prophecy from the Book of Daniel. It was certainly a perspective that first developed in his Tübingen period, when he was profoundly influenced by the example of Nauclerus, Stoeffler, and Carion—historians who played a leading part in compiling a world-chronicle for Count Eberhard im Bart, an aristocrat much concerned with interpreting world history according to an index of events he had tabled.[2] Melanchthon's view of history—and that included his view of Luther—was better set out in his lectures than in his theological and systematic writings.[3] In his world-chronicle, derived from Carion, he tended to represent Luther as the crowning glory of a continuous movement for reform in the Catholic Church. The debt to Daniel is im-

[1] Adolf Herte, *Das katholische Lutherbild in Bann der Lutherkommentare des Cochläus*, 3 vols. (Münster, 1943).
   Joseph Lortz, *Die Reformation in Deutschland*, 2 vols. (Freibourg-im-Breisgau, 1939).
[2] *C R* 11, 1028.
[3] S. Berger, *Melanchthons Vorlesungen über Weltgeschichte*, Theologische Studien und Kritiken (1897), Heft 1, 782.

portant here, for since Melanchthon accepted Daniel's divisions—the ages of Babylon, Persia, Macedon, and Rome—he could by no means contemplate Luther as the destroyer of the Roman Empire. God had honoured the Germans by continuing the Roman Empire—*translatio imperii ad Germanos*—and to destroy the Roman Church must *ipso facto* destroy the Empire, a disastrous course he could not condone.[4]

In his interpretation of history, Melanchthon agreed with Luther, both Reformers holding that the Book of Daniel provided basic clues to the understanding of the past—namely that it must reflect antiquity. The funeral sermon he preached on the death of Luther provides scholars with Melanchthon's final assessment of his colleague as the instrument of God himself for the propagation of the Gospel.[5] Melanchthon's view of world history was both antiquated and rich in typology. It is a perspective that can be traced back to Thucydides, and which was to influence Reformation historiography until Mosheim. Thus although there was much development in the writing of history between the German Chronicle (1532) and the *Chronicon Carionis* (1558 to 1560), such interpretations did not themselves lead to the abandonment of an essentially static understanding. The view that the author should merely set the stage was recognized and observed by Melanchthon.[6] But he did not apply such a principle of modern historicism because of his lifelong obsession with world-historical perspectives.

Johannes Sleidanus has thus good claim to be regarded as the first professional historiographer of the Reformation. Unlike Melanchthon, whose theological make-up gave him a world-view, Sleidan's *Commentaries on the State of Religion and Public Affairs under Emperor Charles V*, together with his *Beschreibung und Verzeichnis allerlei vornehmer Händel so sich in Glaubens-und anderen weltlichen Sachen ... zugetragen haben*, deal with the actual events of the Reformation. Sleidan's sympathy for Luther's cause thus comes across in his exposition of the whole range of Reformation material rather than in any interpretative approach to the subject. Yet Luther's *Ermahnungen* come under his scrutiny just as much as the facts of history; and those facts are duly weighted in significance according to their relevance in the history

---

[4] *C R* 12, 190.   [5] *C R* 11, 727 f.   [6] Ibid., 9, 39.

of ideas. In form, Sleidan's work still observed a ponderous chronology, and without any real selection of material, the narrative dragged on from year to year. It was a drawback only overcome with the thematic approach of *The Magdeburg Centuries* published by Mathias Flacius Illyricus in 1559.

In content, this Church history, arranged century by century, provided a model and *apologia* for both contemporaries and successive generations, as well as selecting material from the whole range of Church history in an attempt to justify the Reformation cause. In form, *The Magdeburg Centuries* continued to be based on the concept of world-chronicle, but the theme of the work was new, analysing each century from sixteen standpoints. Above all, of course, it was a dedicated anti-Catholicism that proved the guiding principle of Flacius's work. From 1549, he lectured in Magdeburg; and it was from here that he led the attack on the flexible religious policies that sought to achieve *modus vivendi* with the Imperial Interim.

Flacius's method not only combined the factual approach of Sleidan with the historio–theological interpretation of Melanchthon, but also added confessional polemics. He was eager to show that, even before its purification at the Reformation, the Church had always managed to muster—even at times of theological confusion—a sufficient number of witnesses to evangelical truth. According to Ferdinand Baur (*Die Epochen der kirchlichen Geschichtsschreibung*), who wrote in 1852, such witnesses to the truth opposed the darkness of false doctrine which had spread progressively since the post-apostolic age. It was particularly important that the Protestant cause should. be fought on two fronts. First, it was essential to emphasize the increasing apostasy of the Roman Church; and secondly, due care had to be taken to avoid association with every heretic. When the Church was faithful to Christ, it could even be Roman in its allegiance. But evangelical heretics were most certainly to be regarded as precursors of the Reformation; and it followed that every case of apostasy from, or faithfulness to, the 'true faith' had to be assessed on its merits according to the catalogue Flacius compiled. If Catholic controversialists claimed that the Reformers propagated 'new doctrine', Flacius was determined to maintain the contrary. He thus made much of celibacy, the veneration of saints and relics, and the papal primacy as examples of 'new doctrine' that had either developed from ancient heresy to receive the official sanction of the hierarchy, or had actually deviated from Early Church teaching. In contrast to the traditional historiography of the Church, Flacius did not merely attempt to offer his reader collected biographies of influential churchmen, but rather sought to characterize and set out their teaching. His claim was a bold one—namely that the Reformation accentuated apostolic teaching and opposed it to the doctrines of the Roman Church.

In *The Centuries of Magdeburg*, Flacius certainly marshalled a mass of material to prove this thesis. To achieve his objective, he commissioned a team of collaborators, although the finished work remained very much his own, for he took care to reserve to himself the revision of all evidence collected. Flacius was thus able to avoid any weakness in presentation and argument—the main fault of Sebastian Franck's *Third Chronicle* (1531). With his general proposition in mind, Flacius urged his team to look for supporting proof, and this *Methodus historiae ecclesiasticae* was to be kept up from the start. The resulting work was divided into five volumes, abandoning thereby Melanchthon's fourfold emphasis.[7]

If Wigand had arguably the lion's share of the great undertaking (he was an editor and contributor of considerable standing), Flacius nevertheless master-minded the operation. It is certainly to him that historians owe many different perspectives in Church history, particularly a periodization free from the ages of contrived chronology. The modernity of the whole approach is certainly apparent when Flacius's *magnum opus* is compared with the *Kosmographie* of Sebastian Münster (1544 to 1550), a mere collection of local memorabilia with no unifying structure.

Gottfried Arnold's *Unparteiische Kirchen- und Ketzergeschichte* (1699) shows a measure of formal dependence on Flacius. There is, for example, a concentration of interest on the Early Church and Reformation period that highlights the author's commitment to principles cherished by Flacius and his predecessors.[8] Again, arranging his treatment of the period from the fifth to the fifteenth centuries (as an age of worsening corruption), and doing so in five chapters a century, Arnold shows a singular lack of imagination by following Flacius so closely. However, because he avoided his predecessor's predilection for confessionalist argument, his work

---

[7] Cf. *Declamatio de Luthero et aetatibus ecclesiae* (8 Nov. 1548), *CR* 11, 783–7.

[8] E. Seeberg, *Gottfried Arnold* (München, 1923), p. 234.

offered readers a number of viewpoints. Such neutrality served in
fact to forward a fundamentally new element in Reformation historiography, and effectively pointed towards the age of enlightenment. In consequence, moreover, the significance of Luther in the
history of the Church was qualified.

It was the role of Johann Lorenz von Mosheim to defend the
topical subject divisions of Flacius against the continuous narrative
of chronological history. This he achieved in the three volumes of
his *Institutiones historiae ecclesiasticae* published between 1737
and 1741. His periodization divided Church history in a way
altogether distinct from that of *The Centuries of Magdeburg*, just
as his central theme differed from that of Flacius. Nevertheless,
because he worked by means of simple representation according to
the chronological principle, it is impossible to understand von
Mosheim without realising his dependence on the author of the
Centuries. Likewise, his world-view has developed that of Arnold.

Most important of all, however, von Mosheim ceased to stress
the confessionalist arguments, arguing for Reformation not so
much in terms of 'true doctrine' as in the categories of progress
and freedom of thought that matched the age of enlightenment.
Certainly if criticism of its dogmatic attitude was levelled against
the Roman Church, von Mosheim was well aware that the same
indictment could be made against the Protestant position. The
Papacy had to face charges based on economic and utilitarian principles, and by no means on Christological grounds. These were
illustrated by detailed reference to the avarice of the Curia, the
corruption of the inferior clergy, and the state of the monks. Even
in matters of theology, von Mosheim directed his criticism of late
medieval learning against methodological weaknesses like the allegorical interpretation of Scripture rather than against Christological shortcomings. No wonder that, when dealing with Luther, von
Mosheim by no means regarded the Reformer's doctrine of justification by only faith as decisive, but the fact that his protest had
resulted in a dramatic reduction of papal revenue.

Within the context of the historiography of Reformation, this
was an enlightened approach, and one that unquestionably made
von Mosheim's work ideal as a text for the age of optimism. The
book thus played its part in developing the deeply-rooted conviction that Protestantism was the handmaid of progress. In the
United States of America, where the view found particular favour,

von Mosheim's work served as a set-book for those in training for ministry, and remained in use right up to the end of the nineteenth century.

The writings of Joseph Priestley also figured large in the Reformation historiography of the Enlightenment. A Unitarian minister from Yorkshire who emigrated to Northumberland, Pennsylvania, in 1800, Priestley contributed a *General History of the Christian Church*, his thesis being that it was the legacy of the Reformation to disrupt the wicked confederation of Church and state. As the beneficiary of this legacy, America was the heir of the Reformation. In marked contrast to seventeenth-century consideration of the subject, theological issues are absent in Priestley's treatment of the Reformation; and because it retained trinitarian principles, thus effectively preserving traditional Christianity, Priestley saw no marked difference between Protestantism and Catholicism. Yet he also argued for the Reformation as the birth of a rational Christianity which to Priestley must be unitarian. Ultimately, therefore, the conflict between Lutheranism and Catholicism should not be taken seriously. After all, the religious Peace of Augsburg (1555), which granted toleration to the Lutherans, banned the radical wing of Reformation like the Reformed and the Anabaptist Churches, and Priestley found in that fact comfort for his theorizing. Later, in 1648, when toleration was extended to the Reformed congregations, they forfeited their progressive start to join the establishment of those Churches tolerated by law—an event which effectively renewed the wicked confederation of Church and State.

According to Priestley, such Churches depended on Augustinian notions of sin. Unitarianism in contrast, based as it was on the biblical doctrine of necessity, helped to mould a developing rational religion. For Priestley, therefore, enlightened utilitarianism provided the basis of justification, and by no means Pauline doctrine. In his view, the Reformation was a movement that pioneered religious evolution. The enlightenment, with its emphasis on a whole new world of useful activity, traced the developing work-ethic from its origins in the sixteenth century. Yet by claiming the Unitarian Church as the heir of Reformation, Priestley allows the Catholic claim that the Reformers helped to make religion itself irrelevant on the grounds of a philosophical determinism that tolerated the divine only on its own terms. Church history

Priestley thus identified with the history of civilization and mores. It is a humanist angle on God removed from the activity of the world.

The work of Leopold von Ranke affords a good example of romantic Reformation historiography. This stems in large measure from the author's concept of *Realgeistigkeit* and his concern for individuality. Von Ranke thus insists that *Realpolitik*, if it is to endure, should also contain idealism in due proportion. In his *History of the Popes* (1834 to 1836), for example, von Ranke argues that

Religious activity is intimately connected with the current of political opinions: combinations arise embracing the whole world, and causing the success or the failure of enterprises. We shall keep the great changes in political affairs the more steadily in view, since they often exactly coincide with the results of the religious warfare. [Book V. 2][9]

An epoch-making event of world history like the Reformation must thus have both spiritual and political foundations.

It is indisputable that the great movements which stir society from its very foundations, are invariably produced by the workings of the living spirit of man. The sense of moral and intellectual want which disposes men to seize on new opinions, often lies for centuries fermenting in the fathomless depths of the heart of society . . . It is of the very nature of these moral forces to be eager to carry the world with them—to strive to bear down all resistance. [Book VII. 1][10]

In the second volume of the *History of the Popes*, von Ranke effectively crosses the Rubicon to apply, in narrative history, his principle of *Realgeistigkeit*; and such narrative constitutes the supreme achievement of his *German History in the Era of the Reformation* (1839 to 1847). It is a work where the genius of von Ranke shines with the realization of the historian as philosopher. For the historian constantly searches for the laws of life embedded in the past; and because he is aware that ideas inhere in the facts, his task must involve perception as well as the presentation of those facts. 'It is simply the reality of events, above all, that' we seek; out of this comes the idea which then clearly provides the reason for the events, that is, their law. Critical philosophy and authentic his-

---

[9] Leopold von Ranke, *The Popes of Rome*, trans. Sarah Austin, 3 vols. (London, 1866), ii, 16.
[10] Ibid., ii, 253.

tory do not contradict one another, but rather belong closely together.'[11]

Very much in line with his early interpretation of the Reformer in the fragment of 1817, von Ranke could not even contemplate the great sixteenth-century upheaval without the leading figure of Martin Luther. For him, Luther effectively personified the spirit of the age; and because of Luther, Germany became a nation important in world history during the sixteenth century. For von Ranke, indeed, the Reformation made its mark not only on the history of the world, but played a fateful part in the education of mankind to gain thereby universal significance.

In developing this concept, von Ranke's *German History* abandons the hero-worship of the 'Luther fragment' to introduce the idea of an individual of world class who personified the spirit of the epoch. As a result, von Ranke creates an all-embracing work that is not only clear and detailed, but also as individualist as it is universal in ideology and emphases. In fact, therefore, *Realgeistigkeit* as an aesthetic harmony of content and form, characterizes von Ranke's mature work. A lively talent enabled him to diagnose events. By a change of status, these conditioned leading ideas, which in turn became themes by which von Ranke organized his narrative history.[12] A weave of factual elements, leading ideas, and narrative theme certainly explains the simple strength of the fabric that, in its logic and harmony, is his *German History in the Era of the Reformation*. There is no static discussion of institutional matters because von Ranke uses the institutional elements to focus his narrative. By thus setting the static in motion, he provides a narrative involving imperial institutions with events rather than merely examining their internal dynamics in isolation. When narrated, the factual elements likewise become concrete symbols of the leading ideas that cause and motivate them. Nevertheless, such ideas do not become abstract and schematic because of their origin. In short, they cannot be known as factors and forces active in actual events except in this concrete manifestation.

[11] A comment of von Ranke on Hegel. Cf Günther Berg, *Leopold von Ranke als akademischer Lehrer*, Schriftenreihe der Historischen Kommission bei der Bayerischen Akademie der Wissenschafter, Schrift IX (Göttingen, 1968), pp. 209–10.

[12] Margaret Münnich, 'Der Historische Moment bei Ranke', unpublished Diss. Phil., Munich (1924), pp. 65–6.

In order to see the Reformation as a development of past history, von Ranke makes much of an imperial—papal rivalry that made the Empire internally ungovernable and externally weak. Such a state of affairs brought about by the papacy made it impossible to suppress Reformation by Imperial ban. In von Ranke's view, the worldliness of the papacy thus undermined all attempts to control a spiritual rival—a theme that illustrates the practical operation of his principle of *Realgeistigkeit*. Developing the emphasis he places on the weakness of the Empire, von Ranke first deals with the general collapse of important institutions, and he describes a 'general striving' of the various Estates in vivid portraits of each. Many of the events between 1510 and 1518—like princely unrest, administrative reform, and peasant anxiety—he manages to sketch in brief illustrative passages. Such scenes provide mere flashes of the over-all picture, but because they are linked to the leading ideas that comprise the line of the landscape, the over-all view is not lost.

When von Ranke deals with the events of 1517, Luther is rooted in the Reformation, just as the movement itself is rooted in its political milieu. Through Luther in fact, von Ranke introduces the principle of competition with the Papacy. It is a new idea, but one that does not entirely replace notions of imperial—papal rivalry or the competition of princes and Emperor, so that a complex interplay of forms is created. Another set of ideas comes into play as von Ranke proceeds to amalgamate the opposition of scholasticism, ecclesiastical abuse, and papal corruption as elements of support for Luther's movement. 'The whole character of their labours, which from the first were directed to the Holy Scriptures, was represented by Melanchthon, and had formed in his person the most intimate union with the deeper theological tendencies which were exhibited in that of Luther . . .' [Book II, Ch. III].[13] For von Ranke, Luther is the focus of all elements of intellectual opposition to the establishment, and the Reformer thus logically becomes the representative of his nation in its anti-papalism. The links between Luther, the opposition, and the nation thus effectively marks the transition from concrete to abstract; and in establishing this link von Ranke has also begun to forge together his first two sets of leading ideas. The movement for reform among

[13] Leopold von Ranke, *History of the Reformation in Germany*, trans. Sarah Austin, 3 vols. (London, 1845), i, 461.

the Estates represents the political nation at work, and the intellectual and spiritual movements grouping round Luther represent the religious nation. 'The German mind became conscious that the hour of its maturity was come; boldly resisted the tyranny of those accidental forms which had governed the world, and returned to the only true source of religious instruction.' [Book III, Ch. III.][14]

It is interesting to note that von Ranke recognizes Luther's heroic quality not so much in bringing about the Reformation but for controlling the 'destructive tendency' of enthusiasm born with it. With his identification of this 'destructive tendency' in Reformation, and emphasis on Luther's opposition to it, von Ranke has at last brought into play all the leading ideas comprising the great *German History*. Henceforth, it is a case of variations on a continuing theme.

After the defeat of Francis I (1525), the religious settlement of the Diet of Speyer (1526) is treated in a way that serves to illustrate von Ranke's rearrangement of leading ideas. Each Estate was to carry out Church reform 'as it would hope to answer to God and the Emperor'; and in the Sack of Rome (1527), Charles V effectively focused the anti-papal sentiment of the nation. Nevertheless, the Emperor's own power and position related him too closely to the Papacy for them to remain at odds for long. Thus, by 1529 to 1530, the old arrangement had restructured itself, to bring Pope and Emperor together. In consequence, Charles V becomes anti-national again, just as had been the case in 1521, and was to be so in 1546. However, when the Emperor was warring with the Pope, he moved in the national interest, and the Protestant cause gained (as in 1526, and at the time of the Interim, 1548).

Charles was dominated by the ambition of Burgundian dynastic expansion, and this led him to neglect internal affairs. International distractions thus not only prevented the Emperor from dealing with internal opposition, but led him into the papal orbit to such an extent that he became anti-national. By his focus on this interplay of forces, von Ranke attempts to interpret the configuration of events and show how different factors affected one another in the Reformation. Although his *German History* develops chronologically, there is no topical separation between the different periods, all factors and ideas being found in each section. In short,

[14] Ibid., ii, 109.

the key to the interpretation of the whole era is the interplay and simultaneous operation of many factors.

In his opposition to the Papacy, Luther represented the nation in the tracts of 1520. These freed Germany from the supervision of an infallible institution which claimed to make its decrees binding on all.[15] The Reformation thus opposed religious and political independence to the universalism of medieval unity, and in so doing opened up a new future for the nations of the West in a collective individuality.[16] By breaking through the hierarchical ordering of the Middle Age, the German nation became a world force in the sixteenth century.[17] The Reformation for von Ranke thus introduced such epoch-making change that it marked the divine footsteps in history, and the 'idea even arose that a christian spirit and life would, by God's especial ordinance, spread from the German nation over the whole world, as once from out Judaea.'[18] In fathering such a transformation and renewal of spiritual life in the West, moreover, the German nation became the instrument of world-historical and even divine forces.

By presenting the historical process as an artistic and picturesque unity, von Ranke ran the risk of distorting past events. The indictment of Ludwig Häusser is based on his view of such distortions in the *magnum opus*. Even Droysen complained in his *Historik* that the *German History* affords no real idea of the historical process because of its tendency to exaggerate. For when viewed alongside von Ranke's leading ideas, other factors tend to be devalued as negative forces, as deviations, errors, and hindrances to progress.

If von Ranke's leading ideas provide basic rules relating to historical reality, his excellence as an historian lies in the fact that he allows his ideas to go beyond mere inquiry. He can thus qualify standard judgements in one place with a reassertion of the individuality of the past in another. For example, when the Emperor abandoned his role as a national leader, by leaving the League of Schmalkalden in control, a new force emerged. Germany may have been divided, but through its divisions von Ranke discerns a promising prospect as the Protestant schism itself becomes a focus of national unity.

[15] von Ranke, op.cit., iii, 438 [Book VI, Ch. V].
[16] Ibid., iii, 467–8 [Book VI, Ch. VI].
[17] Ibid., i, 241–2 [Book I], cf. iii, 115 [Book V, Ch. IV], iii, 348 [Book VI, Ch. I], and iii, 662–3 [Book VI, Ch. X].
[18] Ibid., i, 493 [Book II, Ch. III].

Droysen supports such Protestant patriotism on the part of von Ranke although at the same time arguing that the historian uses a standard of currency in advance of mere accuracy. To Hegelians, however, von Ranke laid himself open to criticism for placing insufficient emphasis on the ideological content of history, and indeed for an outline approximating too closely to old-style universalism. Hegelians also tended to renounce the persona of the narrator. Yet von Ranke gave pride of place to historical reality, convinced as he was that ideas had to emerge from the facts in order to control and clarify the narrative.

The Liberal Interpretation

The liberal interpretation of Reformation following Leopold von Ranke could not simply sustain the optimism of enlightenment, however much it shared many of the basic ideas of that period. To such writers Luther did not destroy the Middle Age, but upheld its essentially religious character during a period of transition, so that he was given credit for preserving the Christian presence in Western culture in modern times. In Joachimsen's view, for example, no distinction need be made between the young progressive and the old conservative Luther.[19]

There is nothing modern about Luther's concept of sin and its cure; for the Reformer confronted the Church with ancient doctrine at a time when it had decided to deal with the problem in a way that proved increasingly fiscal. By dealing with sin theologically, Luther thus forced his views on those who, although content with Church doctrine, felt exploited financially. The Peasants' Revolt and the Knights' War accordingly provide examples of a medieval struggle for rights and by no means reflect a modern class struggle. Nor did Luther, an old-style churchman, prepare the way for modern individualism in religion and the sectarian developments of Protestantism. To the liberals, indeed, as to the rationalists, the Reformation of the sixteenth century did not live up to its principles, and had a long way still to go. For Joachimsen the whole tragedy in Reformation ideology was the retention of the territorial Church and the link with authoritarianism.

---

[19] 'Die Bedeutung der Reformation für die Gegenwart', *Zeitwende* 4 (1928); cf. 'Epochen des deutschen Nationalbewusst-seins', *Zeitwende* 6(1930).

In contrast, it was the romantic theme of individualism that Joachimsen pursued to find in the Reformation Germany's attainment of intellectual maturity. For him the Reformation thus represented the cultural climax of German history, European civilization itself pledging its future to the Gospel message of Protestant faith. For despite the achievement of Counter-Reformation, intellectual development in the seventeenth, eighteenth, and nineteenth centuries was firmly founded in Reformation achievement. In his *Relevance of the Reformation for the Present Age* (1928), Joachimsen identifies the cultural impact of Reformation as a task as well as a legacy. For in terms of the basic dichotomy of Law and Gospel, of the world and the Kingdom of God, every age must reaffirm for itself *reformatio renascens et aeterna*.

In historical perspective, evangelical freedom implies rediscovery and reapplication of the dialectical structure of existence in every epoch. But the liberal school also represents the Reformation heritage of idealism and progress, a concept which is not at all in harmony with the dialectic of Reformation existentialism. It is a view that increasingly envisages the state as the embodiment of virtue; a basic Reformation dialectic that deals in categories of faith and works, and of true and establishment Churches.

Best represented by the Freiburg circle of Stadelmann, Heimpel, and Ritter, the liberal school of Reformation interpretation was very much in touch with the work of Heidegger, and accordingly by no means lost its existential dimension. Especially in the person of Stadelmann, the circle saw the Reformation as the start of the German revolution. By such means, the liberal school came into contact, through Heidegger, with national socialist understandings of German history, attempting to interpret the events of 1933 as the climax of the German revolution. The Reformation, by this interpretation, prepared the way for later revolutionary developments; and it is not difficult to recognize here a romantic concept of 'pre-revolution'.

In the sixteenth century, the 'World Spirit' called on Germany, and the massive support afforded the Reformers is interpreted as the response of the nation to this call. In American liberals like McGiffert and Walker, the idea of Protestant freedom and evolutionary progress is far more prominent. For such writers, Reformation concern with the unity and identity of the nation, rather than with progress and liberty, is evidence of late development. It follows that McGiffert favours the rationalism of Zwingli, whereas Stadelmann recognizes Luther's achievement in starting the Reformation as a German revolution of epoch-making proportions. In his concern for civil liberty and progress, McGiffert interested himself in the development of reformed communities like Zürich, Geneva, and Strassburg and their constitutions. But German liberal historiography does not much concern itself with the standard assumption that civil liberty developed from religious freedoms. Luther, for example, earned praise from liberals for freeing the German nation from foreign bondage rather than for introducing liberal principles. In American historiography, the Reformer's attitude to the Peasants' Revolt is largely condemned; yet it is a stand Stadelmann praised because it showed Luther's realization that only support for the princes could liberate the German nation. In short, if American writers denounced Luther's action as the beginning of authoritarian solutions in German history, Stadelmann is clear that the Reformer's insight and achievement in allying the Word of God and princely rule, was truly progressive. Stadelmann also lays considerable emphasis on the role of Reformation in the inculcation of mores in Germany. The new appreciation of vocation in work, and in government and obedience, he sees as the civil consequence of sixteenth-century upheaval. In the event, however, the religious peace of Augsburg (1555) did not bring national unity and tragically put off the German revolution almost as soon as it had begun. By implication, it was left to the Germany of the nineteenth and twentieth centuries to complete the task. The Reformation provided the background of a national consciousness which emancipated the German people from the idea of *translatio imperii*, and the liberal writers attempted to rouse the nation from its romantic dreaming and encourage the profit-seeking motive of expansion in the East and a competitive approach to world markets.

Religious concerns are strikingly absent from this approach. Indeed, the principal characteristics of liberal historiography are cultural and, in common with the romantic emphasis, national. The tendency now seems to be the discussion of collective rather than individual issues, in particular the hero-cult being far more vaguely set out than was the case with von Ranke.

In his *Auffassung und Analyse des Menschen im 15. und 16. Jahrhundert*, Wilhelm Dilthey adopts a uniquely liberal attitude to the Reformation, a topic he treats in writing a full-scale intellectual history.[20] According to Dilthey, the Reformation is to be seen as a decisive step on the way to intellectualizing religion. The movement linked the metaphysical religion of the Middle Age to the philosophical system of the modern world. In contrast to other liberal interpretations, Dilthey avoids any comparison with the Renaissance, and sees Reformation and Renaissance as complementary and symbiotic. Yet if the Renaissance represented autonomy for the concept of *virtù*, religious autonomy was the goal of Reformation. The two are not contradictory, but represent different aspects of the same process of intellectualization in moral and religious life. It is a development leading inexorably towards universal theism and thus relativizes the confessional nature of historical faith. Ultimately it results in a universal critique of the Churches which in turn brings about an internalization of faith. In this way, Dilthey sought to explain the forces lying behind religious revivals in terms of cultural reaction. Goethe's concept of the dialectic of form and content lies behind Dilthey's approach; just as some of his theorizing approximates to Max Weber's discussions of capitalism and the Protestant spirit. Basically, however, Reformation stands for emancipation from all authority and results in the freedom of the individual.

The Social Interpretation of Reformation

The irrelevance of theology in the liberal historiography of Reformation encouraged those who saw the social importance of the movement. In America, however, the development was more gradual, an historian like Preserved Smith attempting to assess the Reformation according to the 'need of the times'. Although this meant the application of social studies on what purported to be a religious event, the liberal school had not yet broken with religious interpretation, and neither McGiffert nor Walker adopt sceptical or atheistic attitudes that dominate their writing.

With a growing interest in social and psychological studies of Luther, however, the Reformation assumed increasing importance in this sphere. Preserved Smith embarked on his interpretation of the Reformation by contributing work that submitted Luther's

[20] Dilthey's article was first edited for *Achiv für Geschichte der Philosophie* in 1891–2.

personality to psycho-analysis. It was an attempt to attribute motivation for Luther's actions solely to the Reformer's personality, temper, and living conditions.[21] In order to pursue the libido model, Perserved Smith used material from the early writings of Catholic polemicists, among them Cochlaeus. It was thus Luther's hatred for his father, and love for his mother (itself an expression of esteem for the Blessed Virgin Mary), that drove him to enter the cloister. His 'breakthrough' was thus the product of guilt feelings stemming from sexuality and transgression of the Fourth Commandment when he chose the religious life in defiance of his father. A work like Erik Erikson's *Young Man Luther* relies heavily on this kind of approach.

Preserved Smith also moved beyond Freud, and his *Age of the Reformation* (1920) virtually discards psycho-analytical interpretation. Instead, he introduces the emergence of the new capitalism in Early Modern Europe as a key to the understanding of Reformation, focusing particular attention on the rising middle class. To further Reformation was thus seen to be synonymous with the promotion of economic interests, religious individualism, and political territorialism. In France and England, such interests contributed to the strength of the nation and witnessed the rise to power of the middle class.

Because of these priorities, Luther simply assumes the role of a national leader and his religious impact is played down. Erasmus too, despite the recognition he receives as a man of enlightenment, Preserved Smith considers to be too élitist to make any real impact. Again, the split within Protestantism itself is explained by Luther's re-avowal of much Catholic dogmatism, although it is argued that, by preventing a new dogmatism, Luther made positive advances that promoted toleration. But above all, Reformation advance is depicted in the way it served to strip the medieval Church of its social function. By removing from the Church its right to care for the poor, the aged, and the infirm, Luther's social ethic strengthened the State and *ipso facto* deprived the Church of the support of the masses. The Reformation sought to consolidate doctrine, but indirectly promoted modern freedoms, just as its religious individualism brought about the continual diversification of Protestantism. In his *History of Modern Culture* (1930), Preserved

---

[21] Cf. 'Luther's early development in the light of psychology', AJP, xxvi (1913), pp. 360–77.

Smith sets out a schema of basic economic facts reflected in the Reformation: it is an effect that recalls the way Marxist writers envisage material reality overshadowed by a religious superstructure.

The Marxist Interpretation

In 1850, Friedrich Engels wrote his *History of the German Peasant War—Der deutsche Bauernkrieg*—a book that provides the basic interpretational model for the contemporary Marxist view of the Reformation in East German historiography. According to Marx, the Reformation of the sixteenth century was an early bourgeois revolution, and it placed Germany in the van of developing world history. If the young Luther was a progressive, because of the way he reacted to the Peasant War, he became an obstinate conservative who defended the status quo in a way that used religion to justify the power of the princes and stabilize their territorial government at the expense of national unity. According to Engels, Luther's most progressive act was thus his translation of the Bible, for that provided in theory for the national unity the Reformer forsook in the practice of the Peasants' War. Marxists thus admire Luther for the way he mobilized the static elements of society, in particular the peasants. The Church of feudal times was thus successfully opposed by concepts of primitive communism in apostolic Christianity. So effective did this prove that, if only Luther had kept his nerve and refused to side with the princes, the whole feudal society would have been overthrown. When the peasants claimed social rewards as the price of their support of his Reformation, Martin Luther became a reactionary, not a Reformer.

By contrasting social conditions in the cities with those obtaining in country areas, Engels noted important differences in Reformation development. For him Lutheranism thus best served the interests of the princes, while the patrician councils of the Imperial cities found a better way to promote their interests and control the masses by embracing Calvinism. It is a definition of Reformation Marxist historians have in common with the conservative Catholics Bonald and de Maistre, as likewise with Hegel and the patriotic liberal Stadelmann. For all of them regard the Reformation as primarily a social phenomenon, and in an attempt to isolate its historical core, reduce the movement to a merely social upheaval. Luther could not serve the people because of the essentially personal nature of his theology; and with this in mind, Marxist writers deem the religious aspects of Reformation irrelevant. In order to explain why the Germans rallied to Luther, therefore, Marxist writers examine the over-all political situation of the nation, paying special attention to the living conditions of the people. The result of such inquiries finds the origins of Reformation in a number of related crises. Unrest among the lesser nobles gains pride of place, as likewise the growing antagonism resulting from princely attempts at decentralization at a time when Imperial authority sought to concentrate power in its own hands. Because the cities sought to gain freedom from their overlords at much the same time, moreover, both burghers in the towns and rural peasants found themselves shouldering crisis burdens. Then too, in the world of learning, scholasticism strove against humanism, just as in the courts there was continuing resentment of the introduction of Roman law. But it was of course the crisis of the Church that served to unite all parties, Luther in this sense personifying the separate conflicts and crises to make of them a national rising capable of opposing the papacy as a foreign institution.

Dominated by concern about emergent capitalism in the period then, the Marxist approach builds on social, political, and religious crises. The new capitalist techniques do not relate to existing feudal society, and a deepening economic crisis is first expressed in religious unrest. In such a context, Luther's entry to the cloister is seen as an expression of unrest, just as the sale of indulgences indicates that papal finances are organized on corrupt capitalist lines, indulgence certificates being the share capital of the Roman Church. Marxist historians thus discern a thoroughgoing transformation of feudal tribute into monetary relationships, and accordingly contrast declining agrarian culture with the rise of the bourgeoisie. The feudal system is weakened, but can still challenge the rise of the bourgeoisie and secure a measure of refeudalization. When Luther thus ceases to serve the interests of the whole nation by allying with the territorial rulers against the peasants, he becomes a reactionary force; and when the bourgeoisie are obliged in consequence to collaborate with their overlords, vast marketing opportunities are lost and properly constitutional government denied. In short, the national upheaval has become a divided force, and with its potential removed by the princes, refeudalization follows as an inescapable reality.

Luther's initial success was possible because of the impact his anti-papal campaign made on the people. His commitment to personal faith, rather than to Church-controlled and money-grubbing religion, Marxists recognize as anti-capitalist revolt. For them, Luther was progressive not because of his new-found faith, but because in battling with the Papacy he pitted his strength against the hard centre of the feudal system. This was the struggle which mobilized the peasants, so that for Marxists, those who fail to heed the Peasants' War in their interpretation, provide an account of Reformation that is unhistorical. It follows that Luther's theology is merely the manifestation of religious attitudes in the fight against the declining feudal order as that gives way to the new capitalism. The bourgeois revolution of the sixteenth century failed for two main reasons. First, because of Luther's support for the princes; and secondly because the most progressive bourgeoisie could not fully free themselves from feudalism. Bankers like the Fuggers and Welsers certainly lived in a strange symbiosis with feudal society, and the Reformation appears as a bourgeois revolution without the bourgeoisie.

American Interest in Dissent in the Historiography of Reformation

In his use of the term 'radical Reformation', Professor G. H. Williams describes wide-ranging phenomena traditionally neglected in Europe. A single principle embraces the heresies of the period and a radical Reformation results. In the sixteenth century, Bullinger's work on the Anabaptists—*Der Wiedertäufer Ursprung*, 1560—set the tone to provide the orthodox treatment of the radicals. The Zürich Reformer linked different groups of heretics, and stressed the bonds that united them. In a celebrated study first published in Germany under the title *Die Soziallehren der christlichen Kirchen und Gruppen* (1911), however, Ernst Troeltsch introduced a new typology. His distinction between Churches and the sects, and his emphasis on the significance of spiritualist development, was an important development for the modern world.

In America particularly, interest in the radicals grew apace and is to be seen in the editing of source materials like those of the Anabaptists (from 1930) and the *Corpus Schwenckfeldianorum* (1906 to 1961). As various denominations interested themselves in their roots, they contributed to this development, the *Mennonite*

Quarterly Review (1927) providing a prominent organ in making the findings of this research known. As the radical Reformation was reassessed, moreover, the peace-loving and tolerant nature of Anabaptism received much emphasis. Professor Roland Bainton did much to popularize this new appreciation of the sects, his work prompting G. H. Williams to term the Yale Professor 'dean of the American historians of the whole left wing'. Bainton's distinction between crusade and just war certainly proved of great assistance in shaping the new typology of radical Reformation. Williams, on the other hand, as a minister of the Unitarian and Congregational Churches, showed a real concern for the comprehensive study of the Left wing, and once this gathered momentum, it effectively re-directed research in the field. When preparing for his task, Williams made specialist studies of the relationship between Church and State since the fourth century—an approach that sharpened his focus on the radical Reformation of 1520. Luther's three treatises published that year signified the start of a movement which was to remain faithful to his theology; but in terms of the radical wing of Reformation, Professor Williams finds the year 1516, when the great Erasmus first published his *Novum Instrumentum* (or Greek Testament), of greater moment. In the Netherlands and in Italy, the development of the radical Reformation thus relates to 1516 far more than to Luther, for Erasmus certainly exercised considerable influence on both the Dutch sacramentarianism of Wessel Gansfort (1420 to 1489), and Italian Humanist critiques of Holy Scripture.

Largely as a result of persecution, the year 1580 signifies the end of the radical Reformation in central Europe. At the periphery, establishment radical Churches developed, as for example those of the Mennonites in Holland, the Socinians in Poland, and the Unitarians in Transylvania. Yet these were exceptional, for as G. H. Williams stresses, it was the radical protest against the sinful nature of confederacy between Church and State that was to prove of enduring importance for Western civilization. Radical centres in Central, Southern, and Eastern Europe were linked by messengers. It was a technique that Jacob Böhme saw fit to apply to the 'holy experiment' in Pennsylvania, an idea that, based on the inner unity of different groups, Williams sees as an attempt at the restitution of apostolic Christianity. The only tradition to receive positive evaluation in the history of Christendom was that of heresy in the medieval Western Church. Accordingly, the Donatist and Arian heresies were repudiated to achieve stability of doctrine in the State Church—a procedure that contrasts starkly with the approach of Luther and other magisterial Reformers whose orthodox attitudes and outlook accepted the doctrines upheld at the Councils of Nicaea and Chalcedon.

Ironically, the radicals based their notion of baptism on Luther's justification by *only* faith, a doctrine they took seriously and applied radically. The Church was thus the gathering of the faithful under the Word of God, but in a hostile environment. For the idea of predestination calling out and constituting the Church is denied. Accordingly, the relationship between God and man has gained a new definition and been freed from those categories of Greek philosophy enjoying currency in the Catholic Church and in classical Protestantism. In the radical camp, then, justification is viewed from either a rational—ethical angle, or a mystical—spiritual one. If Joachim of Flora's threefold division of the ages as dispensations (based on the Book of Revelation) proved influential among the sects, the magisterial Reformers tended to adopt Daniel's fourfold schema. And just like the Catholic Church, they identified the latest age as that of the [Holy] Roman Empire.

In such a way Williams finds it possible to set out a typology of Reformation which can distinguish the classical or magisterial concept from the radical. 'The Radical Reformation in its three major divisions was thus comparable to the Magisterial Reformation, which was likewise, ... tripartite: Lutheran, Reformed, and Elizabethan.'[22] Although there is a unity about the radical Reformation, therefore, Williams makes the distinction that classifies the Anabaptists as evangelical, spiritual, and revolutionary Protestants; the Spiritualists as followers of Franck or Schwenckfeld; and the Libertines represented by Servetus. Finally, too, there are evangelical rationalists, differentiated by Williams as early Anti-Trinitarians, as Polish Brethren (or Socinians), and as Unitarians. A unique feature in the case of the Anabaptists is that of Church discipline. Again, Williams differentiates 'free church' (Zürich) and 'free will' orientation, the latter deeming that baptism is not necessary to salvation. As for the 'militant heralds' of Münster, they are placed in a class by themselves. The evangelical rationalists,

[22] G. H. Williams, *The Radical Reformation* (London, 1962), p. 857.

Williams affords a wide range from Anti-Trinitarians to Arians, singling out an Italian element in Psychopannichism. Unitarians he defines as philanthropical pacifists; and Spiritualists as those who, defying definition itself, stand opposed to all the characteristics of the Church. Of note in terms of Christological doctrine, moreover, is their teaching on Christ's 'heavenly flesh' which effectively denies the incarnation. In the last analysis, therefore, G. H. Williams links the evangelical make-up of such radicals with the impact of the young Luther, and the revolutionary elements with the Peasants' Revolt, not to mention Thomas Müntzer's idea of a pneumatic community which replaces both the secular kingdom and the Church.

XI

The Image of Myth and Reality

*

LEIF GRANE

THE dragon with seven heads is a well-known biblical symbol of evil, identical with the Devil himself or representing his abhorrent strength. To anyone familiar with the Bible and still faithful to the old Church it might have seemed an obvious image to characterize Martin Luther, prince of heretics. In his use of it, however, Cochlaeus did not satisfy himself with a crude and simple exaggeration of abuses so dear to polemicists of his day: the ingenious comparison of an antagonist with all sorts of lowly and repugnant beasts. Instead, he combined the suggestive diabolical dragon image with another well-known kind of polemic in which he had already, by long and diligent training, gained considerable proficiency. Since 1521, Cochlaeus had pursued Luther with a stream of polemical writing, very often using the same approach found in 'The Seven Heads of Luther'. Through quotations selected without any real reference to their context, he aimed to demonstrate that Luther's thought lacked coherence; and like liars in general, he found the heretic to be inconsistent. What else was to be expected? The heretic nourishes himself on the truth, which he perverts; and self-contradiction is the obvious result.

Inasmuch as Cochlaeus was convinced that Luther was a heretic, there is no reason to find this way of thinking surprising. 'The Seven Heads' is merely an attempt to prove the obvious. The method is adopted to show, by using Luther's own words, that the heretic is inconsistent and self-contradictory. Cochlaeus thus supplies a list of the works quoted, and, in each case, cites the work under consideration. It is intended to show his ability as an author who knows how to handle his sources according to humanist rules. Not without pride, Cochlaeus maintains that he quotes Luther correctly, adds nothing, and so keeps the meaning of the original. He has of course translated the German quotations in the Latin edition, and done the same with Latin quotations in the German edition. At certain points he notes that it has also been necessary to add a word or two in order to make the discussion between 'the heads' understandable.[1] But such minor reservations hardly

---

[1] See *SL* [Latin edn.], the Preface *Ad lectorem Johannes Cochlaeus*.

weaken his goal and its realization—namely to fight Luther with Luther. By Beelzebub, it may be urged, Cochlaeus intends to cast out devils. He wants to show that Luther is like a house divided against itself [Matt. 12: 24–5].

According to his own words, Cochlaeus does not only wish to expose the heretic in all his monstrosity, but also considers the book a useful compendium, making it possible for Catholic priests to argue against Lutherans in Luther's own words without having to read the heretic's poisonous writings.[2] In a series of short chapters (usually only two or three pages), he supplies his brethren with sufficient knowledge of Luther's contradictions on all points of any controversial significance. For many poorly educated priests such assistance would have been most welcome, so helpless were they compared with their evangelical opponents.

Seven heads were necessary in order to parallel the number of dragon heads. Apart from its symbolical significance, this was not, however, a necessary number, not even for Cochlaeus. He suggests that more 'heads' might be found, but he thinks that the seven he has chosen should be sufficient to prove that Luther lacks coherence. The reader might think that less than seven would serve the purpose, for it cannot be denied that Cochlaeus himself has some difficulty in neatly distinguishing between some of the 'heads' in presenting the general idea of Luther's self-contradictions.

For the present purpose it is useful to list the writings of Luther quoted under each 'head'. Cochlaeus states that the two eldest 'brother'—the heads 'Doctor' and 'Martinus'—are nearer to the doctrine of the Church than their rivals, a fact in line with his technique of representing 'Doctor' and 'Martinus' only by early writings (usually not by any later than 1519). A few exceptions do not alter the picture, for these two heads are those of a Luther not yet condemned by Pope and Emperor. The third head 'Lutherus', however, is applied to a Reformer in open conflict with the authorities; and in this instance Cochlaeus chooses most of his quotations from precisely the period (1520 to 1523) in which Luther was turning all his power as a polemicist against Rome. The difference between 'Doctor' and 'Martinus' is indistinct; but that between those two and 'Lutherus' is understandable because it

[2] *Septiceps Lutherus, Intentio autoris, utilitasque libri in genere.*

is clearly chronological, denoting Luther before, and Luther after, the open breach with Rome. The four remaining 'heads' also belong to Luther the Reformer, but it is not possible to distinguish between them in any chronological sense. For example, the fourth head, 'Ecclesiastes' ('The Preacher') is characterized by its implied function. Nearly all the material for his sayings is drawn from sermons, and his personality is mainly distinguished from 'Lutherus' by the different genre of writings quoted. A similar observation can be made about the sixth head 'Visitator', that is Luther as an organizer of Church order. But it is more difficult to place the two remaining heads, 'Suermerus' ('The Spiritualist') and 'Barrabas'. Both are largely represented by quotations taken from polemical writings after 1522, and the same sources frequently used. Like 'Lutherus' those two 'heads' incorporate a Reformer in conflict with Rome; but altogether unlike the third 'head' they give expression to the combat between Luther and other evangelical reformers or spiritualists.

This brief investigation does not claim to be complete, but rather to present a general survey that can be summarized as follows. The *seven* 'heads' do not appear to correspond with an equivalent number of different 'Luthers', yet Cochlaeus was certainly convinced that Luther—in different periods and in different capacities—expressed contrasting opinions. He thus made a clear distinction between first, Luther the theologian in difficulties, but still (until 1519) within the Church; secondly, Luther the rebel against Rome; thirdly, Luther the Church organizer; and fourthly, Luther the polemicist with a double front to hold (against Rome, and against other evangelical groups). These distinctions can roughly be distributed—in the same order—among the 'seven heads' in this way: 'Doctor'/'Martinus'; 'Lutherus'; 'Ecclesiastes'/ 'Visitator'; 'Suermerus'/'Barrabas'.

The way in which Cochlaeus composed his book is no secret. The title clearly states that this is a work about Luther as he appears from the book on the Saxon visitation [*Unterricht der Visitatoren*]. Mainly written by Melanchthon, this instruction was revised and supplied with a prologue by Luther.[3] Cochlaeus could, therefore, justly consider it to represent Luther's views on the

---

[3] See the introduction to R. Stupperich's edition of *Unterricht der Visitatoren, Melanchthons Werke im Auswahl* (Reformatorische Schriften, Gütersloh, 1951), i, 215 f.

Wittenberg reform programme. Following the order of issues in the instruction, Cochlaeus's procedure is very simple. With a few exceptions, he opens each of his forty-five chapters with a passage from the *Instructions* introduced by 'Visitator'; and after that introduces one of the other 'heads' as the dialogue proceeds. As organizer of congregational life in Ernestine Saxony, Luther urged and agreed to many things which Cochlaeus (and many of his contemporaries) considered contrary to his earlier views. It would be a simple matter to analyse some of the chapters in order to show how Cochlaeus misused and misunderstood Luther, but it would hardly be absorbing. Although he stresses the bona fide nature of his quotations, Cochlaeus's views on the interpretation of Luther are not significant enough to make them worthy of detailed investigation. Of far more importance is the general outline of the whole concept understood as the assertion that Luther did change his views in a fundamental way. What truth is there in such a charge?

II

When Luther wrote his *Preface* to the *Instructions for the Visitors* in 1528, he was undertaking a task which would have been beyond his dreams a decade before. It is impossible to comment on the question of his changing views without having some idea of the new conditions he now faced. It is certainly necessary to indicate briefly some of the main preoccupations that concerned the Reformer up to 1528.

   First of all, to glance at Luther's activities before the *Ninety-Five Theses* on indulgences had made him famous by the end of 1517, is to focus on two different, but connected, types of activity. As a friar he had administrative and pastoral duties; and as a professor at the newly-founded University of Wittenberg he lectured on Holy Scripture. In aim and spirit, Luther did not feel any great difference between the schoolroom, the pulpit, and the confessional. It is a realization that does much to explain why academic activity fast involved him in practical ecclesiastical problems. But it would be unwise to draw the conclusion that such an implication was clear to him from the start. It would certainly be wrong to overlook his professional stance in first making himself known to a wider public as a doctor of Holy Scripture. Until the end of 1518, there is no sign whatever of formal opposition to the Roman Church. Whereas Erasmus and his friends were promulgating *philosophia Christi* as a definite programme, Luther did nothing of the sort. His emphasis was much less comprehensive, and much more bound to the immediate needs of daily work. He did not even argue for a 'Lutheran doctrine', but in his struggle to understand the biblical texts, was amazed to discover how remote traditional theological opinions were from the meaning of St. Paul.

Others had attacked scholastic theology before, but when Luther himself became convinced of its dangerous character he did not simply join the ranks of the critics. Instead, he took action intended to bring about its absolute ruin. Accordingly, he came forward, not as a reformer of the Church, but as a reformer of theology, and very soon also of the university. In Wittenberg Luther succeeded in convincing several of his colleagues, and most of his students, that scholasticism had to be abandoned and the theology of the Bible and of St. Augustine (as the interpreter of St. Paul) promoted. Within a very short time (1516 to 1517) a new theological movement came into being. The absolute incompatibility of scholasticism with St. Paul, as Luther saw it, also led him to reject the medieval method. Thereafter only the utter destruction of scholastic theology could satisfy him in his responsibility as a doctor of Holy Scripture. This position was an intellectual achievement which could be found nowhere else however much scholasticism had been criticized and ridiculed. When, in September 1517, Luther published his *Theses against Scholastic Theology*, he felt sure, not of himself, but of the validity of the anti-Pelagian, pro-Pauline, and 'Augustinian' theology. Here there was no chance of compromise.

Then too, Luther and his Wittenberg friends were well prepared when the storm broke. In the eyes of the Reformer, the *Ninety-Five Theses* on indulgences were not meant to cause a sensation. They were simply intended to serve as the basis for theological discussion of a difficult question. The effect of the Theses surprised him; but when the contest began he saw it as a continuation of the fight in which he was already engaged. During the whole struggle up to the Diet of Worms (1521) Luther thus maintained his attitude as a doctor of Holy Scripture, acting according to his calling and duties. To attempt to read the polemical writings of 1518, 1519, and 1520 without seeing them in the light of later events, is to discover the extent to which they stress the viewpoint of scholarship. The contest had, however, two immediate consequences. First, in disputing about indulgences, Luther was led to apply his anti-Pelagian, Pauline exegesis on the theology of the sacraments much more explicitly than he had done hitherto; and secondly, the contest forced him to clarify basic theological principles. Others, not only certain humanists, but also Andreas Karlstadt, Luther's colleague in Wittenberg, had already proclaimed the exclusive authority of Holy Scripture. Instead of this, Luther argued that Scripture was the most important criterion of theological proof. Yet even this fundamental principle did not emerge until the contest of indulgences demanded it, and the same somewhat simple points are repeated again and again. Luther refused to accept opinions, and demanded reasons, arguments, and evidence.[4] He used every opportunity his opponents afforded to ridicule scholastic theology and to stress its intellectual and scholarly inferiority. In doing so he took advantage of the weapons prepared for him by the humanists, weapons that in his hands became as formidable as others of his own forging.

From the start, Luther regarded the conflict as purely theological; but very soon he realized that more was at issue than traditional theology. His previous work had given him no reason to doubt that Christian liberty and justification by faith could be maintained within the medieval Catholic system of Church authority, but when his opponents blamed him for heretical opinions on this point, Luther had to take up the challenge. Very probably the turning-point is to be found by the end of the year 1518. An important aspect of this transition is Luther's experience of Roman ecclesiology, acquired during his meeting with Cardinal Cajetan at Augsburg in October 1518. Not even before the Pope's own representative did he give in. He demanded arguments and refused to accept mere words, *nuda verba* as he termed them, when his adversaries forwarded some statement by a scholastic theologian. Finally, Luther realized that the conflict concerned canon law, a recognition that was certainly frightening to him personally, but by no means made him change his mind. The remaining preconditions of open revolt were brought about by the preparations for the

---

[4] This is done most explicitly in Luther's explanation of the *Ninety-Five Theses: Resolutiones disputationum de indulgentiarum virtute* (1518), WA 1, 525–643.

disputation at Leipzig with Johann Eck (June 1519). In a letter to
Willibald Pirckheimer (20 February 1519) Luther wrote: 'The matter is turning towards canon law, as you see, that is towards the
profane corruption of the Holy Scripture.' [*WA, Br* 1, 348] By
viewing the canon law as a corruption of Scripture, Luther thus
placed the question of ecclesiastical authority within his own field
of responsibility as a doctor of theology. It was an attitude that declared problems of Church order to be subject to the same principles of theological proof as the issues he had been discussing with
his scholastic opponents.

Yet Luther still had no real programme of Church reform. He
studied canon law and Church history during the winter of 1518 to
1519, not in order to shake the Roman Church and cause it to fall,
but in order to have his arguments ready for the dispute with Eck
about ecclesiastical authority as a source of truth. If he thus went
to Leipzig prepared to deny the divine authority of the Pope, he
returned home having also refused the infallibility of general councils. The way was open for the famous stand he made in the writings of 1520, and the final breach with Rome was in sight.

It is significant that the great stream of popular writings belong
to the period after the Leipzig Disputation. For as soon as Luther
realized that he was in conflict with the Church of Rome itself, he
felt an urgent need to inform not only the learned, but the people
as well. After all, if Christian liberty was incompatible with the
Roman understanding of authority, then it was absolutely necessary to bring this to the attention of the common man. The purely
academic phase of the conflict thus ended just as soon as Luther
began to attack the foundations of the Roman Church. He had not
planned a shift from his own primarily theological concerns to
open revolt, but this proved an unavoidable consequence of his
stand. He had to fight his way a step at a time without any formulated strategy; and not only the process against him in Rome, but
also many attacks from other theologians led him from one crisis
situation to another. He often hesitated before making up his mind
about problems his adversaries introduced in the great debate, but
finally arrived at the fearful conclusion. Before he was excommunicated (January 1521), he had already made public, by burning
the canon law decretals and the papal bull against himself (10
December 1520), his intention of bringing about the ruin of the
Roman Church.

It was not therefore merely a question of temperament or preference. For Luther had to move from his grasp of justification by *only* faith and one-man revolt, to advance proposals for the reform of the Church and, ultimately, the total denial of obedience to Pope and Emperor. This sequence is deeply rooted in the inner logic of events and deeply dependent on the urgency with which Luther was led from scholasticism to a new theology, and then to raising the question of authority and the rejection of papal power. No link in the chain could have been forged otherwise.. This is not the same as postulating historical necessity, for it is hardly necessary to stress that the whole course of events was dependent on political and intellectual circumstances over which Luther had no control. For the changes he underwent in the years 1517 to 1521 resulted from loyalty to the new-found theology, and by no means from any lack of principle.

To attempt a survey of the crowded years from the *Ninety-Five Theses* to the Diet of Worms is to reveal a marked difference between the reforming theologian of 1517, and the rebel of 1521. It is a simple matter to find statements from these years that are completely irreconcilable once they are separated from their context. When viewed aright, however, it is just as easy to find such statements both convincing and consistent. In order to defend his interpretation of the Bible, Luther was obliged to draw up certain rules for theological debate. As part of this process he had to explain in theory what was already current practice. The criteria he forwarded in his *Explanations of the Ninety-Five Theses* were meant to serve as an instrument for the confutation of his scholastic opponents; and he demanded of every theologian (and ultimately of every Christian) the ability to render some account of his faith. Deeply convinced of the validity of such a requirement, Luther could see no reason to make exceptions of the Pope or the curia. It was, however, a position that obliged him to face up to conflict with a Pope who insisted on unqualified obedience.

Thirdly, in making proposals for the reform of the Church, Luther had appealed to the princes and magistrates in the hope that they would achieve what the Pope and his bishops refused to implement. He had criticized sacramental doctrine and ecclesiastical practice; but before the Diet of Worms there is no evidence that Luther had any intention of influencing the practical day-to-day concerns of the Church through direct action, however much he

still felt personally responsible for university affairs. But with the
sojourn at the Wartburg (1521 to 1522), the Reformer enters a new
phase. By excommunication and ban, Luther and his friends were
declared enemies of Church and Empire; and every admirer or follower—and there were thousands of them—was obliged to make
his choice. For those deciding to rally to Luther's cause, it was a
time for action. It was certainly impossible to be in conflict with
the Roman Church—in a formal way, and on religious and theological grounds—without doing something; and the great movement
of reform, now rapidly spreading throughout the Empire and its
frontiers, still needed the advice of Luther. He gladly gave such
counsel, but was markedly reluctant to afford his ideas any really
practical shape. He had analysed and condemned the traditional
form of authority in the Church, and had seen the consequences
for doctrines of Church and ministry before anyone so much as
contemplated a new ecclesiastical order. His thoughts on Christian
congregations in 1520 to 1521 were thus not linked to any actual
planning for new institutional forms.

It is against such a background that Luther's condemnation of
the Wittenberg reforms (1521 to 1522) has to be seen. In rejecting
these measures, each of which seemed to be in line with his
Reformation writings, Martin Luther effectively declined the leadership of a party or a Church. Here, as much as anywhere, it becomes clear how inaccurate it is to consider him as primarily a pro-
ducer of opinions or doctrines. For he must then have welcomed
reforms. By contrast, however, when he emerged from the Wartburg to re-establish order in Wittenberg, Luther chose to abolish
most of these measures, not because they were wrong, but because
he could not countenance their enforcement. 'The Word of God'
—not human institutionalism—must bring about Reformation.
Accordingly, Luther used his time at the Wartburg to translate the
New Testament, to start a book of sermons on the Sunday texts,
and to criticize monastic vows as being contrary to evangelical
freedom. He did not choose to occupy himself working out rules
for a new ecclesiastical organization.

In short, Luther thought of the Church as a number of local
congregations with no need of strong institutional ties. In the *Open
Letter to the Christian Nobility* (1520), he discusses Christendom
[*Christenheit*], apparently meaning the Christian world in a
medieval sense. After Worms, however, he prefers to use the word

'Christendom' exclusively in the sense of 'church'. This 'church' he sees as a little flock in a hostile world. In a very practical sense he thinks of the local congregation, a concept that is often to be found in his correspondence. The local congregation, not he, is authorized to make decisions; for Luther's dread of 'Mr Every-body' [*Herr Omnes*], later to fill him with pessimism, had not yet taken shape. From 1521 to 1524, his writings testify to genuine confidence in the capacity of congregations for care for their own affairs, as likewise to the unaided ability of the 'Word of God' to accomplish all things.

As Luther was later to describe it, the 'Word of God' fell over the countryside like a downpour. The movement was spontaneous and unprepared. The inefficiency of the imperial government, coupled with bewilderment on the part of the princes and magistrates, prospered the cause in the years immediately following the Diet of Worms. Nobody could really ignore what was happening, but it seemed to Luther and his friends that the Word was mightier than the Papacy and secular powers put together. No wonder the Reformer acted accordingly freely giving a fund of advice in writings and letters, although still refusing to raise himself up as a new authority. Only in Wittenberg and Electoral Saxony did he try to influence developments directly. The first shadows, however, were very soon cast on the brilliant landscape. The bitter experiences caused by the spiritualists gave Luther cause for serious concern and foreboding, and the great Peasants' War (1524–5) abruptly ended that joyous period of Reformation growth in a movement which, relying on the power of the Word of God, had freely proclaimed the liberty of all Christians.

If the changes in Luther's teaching and preaching during the years 1517 to 1521 when he stood alone—however many friends and followers there might have been—had depended on the consistency of his thought and actions, the picture for the period 1521 to 1524 is decidedly different. The emergence of evangelical congregations throughout the Empire, and especially in Saxony, raised all sorts of legal problems. Thus Luther had to draw up a new set of conclusions for himself. This time it was not the shaping of even more forthright criticism of the Church of Rome and its institutions that concerned him, but developing social ethics and advice about the preaching and formation of evangelical congregations. The new direction which this gave to many of his writings made them quite distinct from the polemical writings against Rome. Before 1521, most of the new insights which Luther had won on the way were connected with his own vocational problems and relationship to his ecclesiastical superiors, even when the matters were first presented to him by others. Now, however, he became the leader to whom everyone turned for intellectual and pastoral guidance. Very often indeed he found himself obliged to handle issues right outside his experience. Yet apart from this difference, it can be maintained that Luther's thought remained in harmony with his work before 1521. Any changes were caused by outward conditions, not by any vacillation in himself.

Finally, although there is no reason to go into Luther's reactions to the Peasants' Revolt, the consequences of such dramatic events are crucial. Many of the secular authorities were convinced that these tumults were caused by the movement for Reformation. Luther thought that Christian freedom had been abused, and felt compelled to revise his attitude towards the laity. 'Mr Everybody' had shown his hand and Luther did not approve! Then too, both princes and city magistrates realized that such spontaneous movements must be controlled. There were only two possibilities open to them: either they had to suppress the Reformation within their territories altogether; or they must create a new, evangelical Church order. The choice was made without delay, and in many cities and territories reforming leaders busied themselves assisting their governments to establish evangelical, territorial Churches. Luther's work in the years 1525 to 1528 is to be seen in this light.

After the final defeat of the peasants at the battle of Frankenhausen (April 1525), Luther wrote to his friend Georg Spalatin, secretary and ecclesiastical adviser to the Elector: 'Now, after the school has been established, it remains to persuade the prince that the condition of the parishes should be reformed as soon as possible.' [*WA*, 3, 583.] The deep impression which the Peasants' War—and not least the conflict with Thomas Müntzer—left on Luther sharpened his awareness of any errors within the evangelical camp. It also convinced him that the secular power was indispensable to the realization of ecclesiastical reforms. The clash with Erasmus (1524 to 1525), the emergence of the Anabaptists, not to mention the long and bitter contest with Oecolampadius and Zwingli over the Lord's Supper, all intensified Luther's conviction of the necessity to improve education, secular and eccle-

siastical, and to restrain the excesses of the spiritualists. He revised
the liturgy in German; actively concerned himself with the
elementary Christian education of the people; and contributed to
the planning of visitations in Electoral Saxony. Such tasks afford
another perspective to many of his convictions. Compared with
the period up to 1525, his experience of the spiritualists and the
Peasants' War fundamentally transformed Luther's leadership of
the Reformation movement.

By now both the Reformer's achievements and their underlying
assumptions had a novel quality about them. A considerable gulf
thus separated theory from everyday practice. For belief in the
ability of the Word of God to triumph was one thing; and a suspicion that the common man stood in need of restraint quite
another. After 1525, Luther certainly did not mind giving the
Word a helping hand. Some have condemned this failure to remain
loyal to basic convictions; but others recognize here the realism of
a Reformer acknowledging the hard facts of the situation. Whatever view is held, however, the change of emphasis cannot be
ignored. In early days Luther believed that faithful preaching of
the Word would be sufficient to topple the Roman Church, and in
consequence laid no plans for alternative forms. His change of
strategy after 1525 thus reveals a kind of resigned acceptance of
progress, and is not the result of further theological insight.
The Reformer remained unsurpassed as a polemicist, and in this
way rendered important contributions to the stabilization of a
'Lutheran' Church. Yet as an organizer of the new ecclesiastical institution, he proved himself a failure and had to be replaced by
friends possessed of administrative flair like Melanchthon and
Bugenhagen.

III

In order to outline the conditions under which Luther had to act at
different times in public life up to 1528, certain well-known facts
of Reformation history should be recalled. An attempt has been
made to interpret these facts, however, and to show their significance in certain important respects.

It should, for example, be clear that a simple comparison of
'doctrines' in Luther, not merely along lines investigated by Cochlaeus, but in a manner much more in keeping with the Reformer's

own intentions, can hardly result in genuine understanding. Without resort to polemic, it is clearly the case that any method of
reading Luther out of historical context, must lack precision. The
'cross-reference-card-index' system of writing about Luther is in-
defensible; and failure to refer to an author's 'systematic' purpose
inexcusable. It is, in short, a method that can, in the words of Dr
Sebastian J. Day, 'only lead to one of two things: either a
meaningless composite of texts or propaganda'.[5]

Secondly, it is evident that Luther's theology consists almost entirely of two kinds: biblical interpretation (lectures and sermons),
and polemic. Yet the same polemic has no life of its own, and
polemical activity is merely regarded as a way of spreading the
Gospel. Intended to remove any obstacles in the way, the polemical
approach is itself unpredictable because its contents necessarily depend on the precise nature of any attack made on the Gospel. The
interdependence of biblical interpretation and polemic makes it
almost impossible to isolate formulas or phrases in order to state
their representative value as 'doctrine' argued by Luther. This is
not, of course, to deny the existence of doctrinal elements in
Luther's exegesis, his sermons, or polemical writings. Such elements are certainly there, but not as constituents of any enduring
'system'.

This leads to the conclusion that not only changing conditions
during these years, but also Luther's basic approach to theology
combine to make it difficult to pin him down and incorporate his
sayings into a dogmatic system. It is, for example, not simply
Christian humility—even less coquettish modesty—that prompts
the Reformer to conclude the Preface of his *Kirchenpostille* (1522)

---

[5] See S. J. Day, *Intuitive Cognition. Key to the Significance of the later Scholastics*
(Franciscan Institute Publications, Philosophy Series, No. 4, St. Bonaventure,
1947), pp. 43 f. Some of Day's methodological argument merits quotation and is
just as applicable to Luther scholars as to historians of philosophy. He writes 'It is
comparatively easy for the historian of philosophy to construct a particular point of
doctrine and refer it to some historical figure, by collecting texts more or less at
random from the works of a given author and arranging them (a) either haphazard-
ly or (b) according to some pre-conceived plan of his own. But this "cross-
reference-card-index" system of writing the history of philosophy, however spec-
tacular it may be and however many devotees it may have, is simply not historical.
For it can result only in one of two things: (a) either a meaningless composite of
texts or (b) propaganda. In both cases we are presented with a purely personal construction, and in the second instance, this personal construction is a refashioning of
historical reality so as to make it accord with the pattern of the so-called historian's
own views.'

with the wish that, by making the Gospel known, God will also make his book superfluous! [*WA* 10¹, 1.17 f.] It is a valuable clue, and shows clearly how Luther regarded his own writings. For him, they merely cleared the way for the Gospel—nothing more, or arguably, nothing less! He was certainly fearful that assertions taken from his writing might, in a new situation, obstruct the Gospel. For Luther regarded books as deeds, and by no means collected, enduring statements. After all, should such statements suffer repetition, they might then be singularly out of place because of changes dictated by polemical necessity. If there is any consistency in Luther's teaching and preaching, it is his insistence on the Gospel as the only way of relating deeds to actual needs. Accordingly, any accusation of self-contradiction requires subtle refinement if it is to register. Routine comparison of theological formulas and statements separated from a context of action are bound to be misleading.

The point is one that does much to explain another characteristic of Luther's theology. Systematic theologians tend to look at different doctrines in the Christian tradition subject by subject, although some are ambitious enough to attempt an over-all analysis. Luther, however, invariably offers the widest-ranging discussion whatever the subject under consideration. It is an approach that directly relates to the Reformer's exclusive focus on the Gospel. In doctrinal terms, of course, Luther's starting-point is justification by *only* faith. It is true, for instance, that he came forward as a reformer of theology with no intention of questioning the traditional doctrine of the Church: it was circumstances that led him to criticize ecclesiology. And even when he did so, he was by no means obliged to investigate doctrines of the Church in the way he had originally tackled the doctrine of justification. He merely drew the consequences. His opposition to Roman ecclesiology nevertheless became as total as his continuing opposition to scholasticism. And the picture is much the same with his other *causes célèbres*. Luther thus regarded the great contest with Erasmus as no mere disagreement over the single issue of the will, its freedom or bondage, whatever his distinguished rival's pretence. For him it was a fundamental fight about Gospel salvation. The same is true of the contest with Zwingli over the Lord's Supper. For the militant attitude he takes in his consideration of traditional theological concepts is understandable—apart from the questionable way

Luther actually handles his adversaries. But it can easily give the impression of being 'self-contradictory' simply because the Reformer is bound to assess the varied arguments of different persons opposing him at various times—arguments that naturally include varying statements of doctrine.

The uncompromising enmity Luther levels against those he is convinced deny the Gospel—whether such uphold the freedom of the will or reject the real presence of Christ in the Eucharist—is only one by-product of this approach to theology. For Luther has an open mind on all questions not directly influencing the free preaching of the Gospel. Indeed, this concentration on the Gospel underlines his complete rejection of any claim to set himself up as an authority in matters of Church order; and it explains why he was inclined to retain as many of the traditional rites and customs as possible. Not only his colleague Karlstadt, but also a number of other Reformers (especially those in Southern Germany and Switzerland), were unable to understand him here. Such apparent traditionalism they held to be a partial return to the Roman position, and duly criticized Luther for both failure of nerve and a timid reluctance to realize the full implications of his own ideas. They at least, it can be urged, saw an important change of view here; and in the great era of liberal theology (the fifty years before 1920) modern scholars found themselves in agreement. Nevertheless, once Luther's basic distinction between necessity (that is, the free run of the Gospel) and freedom (namely, all matters of Church order) is understood, a remarkable consistency of both attitude and conviction is apparent.

A final consequence of Luther's theological grasp must therefore concern the difficulty he encountered when developing a clear view of Church order once that became urgent after 1525. There seemed to him to be no immediate connection between his earlier criticism of Roman ecclesiology and the need for firm organization at a time when the free preaching of the Gospel and the liberty of local congregations was clearly inadequate. What Luther had to offer was simply impractical, and his decisive influence was lost when it came to the development of the territorial Church. He could of course see the need for organization, but was unable to prevent a princely take-over. The *Instructions on Visitations* indirectly testify to his failing ability to control matters, for even if he contributed the Preface, it was Melanchthon who wrote the

book. Admittedly, Luther there refers to the role of the Elector in
a way intended to qualify the tendency at Court to consider such
reforms as the proper task of government. But his weak protest
against the Elector's instruction to the visitors did not have the de-
sired effect, and it cannot be denied that this whole procedure was
realized without any equivalent revision of Luther's teaching on
the Church. The Reformer could no longer assert the joyous
liberty of the Church (*laeta libertas ecclesiae*) he had so trium-
phantly proclaimed in 1520[6]; nor could he find adequate theological
warrant for compulsions he now had to take for granted.

                              IV

It has been emphasized here more than once that the task of organizing a territorial Church, under the prince, caused Luther con
siderable problems. Other changes of opinion have been explained
by reference to changing conditions, and partly by reference to
Luther's basic theological approach. It has likewise been admitted
that Luther's colleagues were themselves confused by the development of his doctrine, modern scholars often agreeing with them.
Against such a background, it could be argued both that Luther
had failed to interpret what was demanded of him, and that he had
been unfaithful to his own theological understanding, dramatically
moving his ground as a result. In short, Cochlaeus could still be
right, at least in a qualified sense. It is therefore appropriate to
explore the theme further at least by outlining certain modern
arguments.
    Almost like a modern Cochlaeus, the Roman Catholic scholar,
Remigius Bäumer, has investigated Luther's views on the Papacy.[7]
Viewing the early period, he finds Luther's statements at their
most contradictory. One moment the Reformer professes to lie
prostrate at the feet of the Pope, ready to obey everything he
might order, and the next he adopts haughty and arrogant tones
towards the Pontiff. This is, of course, authentic enough, as a
glance at Luther's statements will confirm. But it is not true if the
various utterances are read closely and in line with their immediate

  [6] WA 6, 567.25 f. [*De captivitate babylonica*, 1520].
  [7] R. Bäumer, *Martin Luther und der Papst* (Münster, 1970). For a more understanding appraisal see Scott H. Hendrix, *Luther and the Papacy: Stages in a Reformation Conflict* (Fortress Press, Philadelphia, 1981).

context. For no-one can reasonably doubt Luther's subjective wish to remain faithful to the obedience owed to his superiors, above all to the Pope. In this respect he was genuinely fearful of the consequences of his own theology; and it was precisely the 'subjectivism' (formerly so dear to Roman Catholic Luther research) that urged him not to become rebellious. His conscience, however, pointed Luther in the opposite direction.

It is not necessary to indulge in psychological guesswork to interpret the apparent self-contradiction. For Luther unwillingly realized that the way he had chosen led directly away from his natural inclination to remain obedient. Nevertheless, a single experience of this kind was insufficient to make him abandon the traditional attitude of a friar. For these were erratic years when natural inclination and theological conviction made themselves felt in continuing inner conflict—a conflict clearly reflected in the Reformer's writings and letters. A typical example is to be found in Luther's reaction when Eck accused him of being in agreement with the heretic Jan Hus. The Reformer's indignation is vehement as Luther refuses to have anything to do with the heretics, confirming his own adherence to the decrees of the Council of Constance. This is his 'subjectivism', his natural inclination; but during the next break in the Disputation, he took the opportunity of familiarizing himself with the *Sentences* of the condemned Jan Hus. To his great surprise, Luther had to admit that many of them were 'most Christian', and therefore wrongfully condemned by the Council of Constance.[8] Such vacillation in Luther is not theological confusion, but rather brought about by a conflict between the claims of ecclesiastical discipline and the inevitable consequences of a theological conviction from which he can no longer retreat.

It is probable nowadays, that most Roman Catholic Luther scholars would agree with this view. Of great import, however, are the observations made about the Reformer's conflict by those of evangelical persuasion. In general, these are concerned with changes of doctrine evident when Luther's early Reformation writings are compared with his polemical activity against the spiritualists and so-called 'sacramentarians' like Zwingli. The contest with Erasmus of Rotterdam has also been looked at from this angle.

---

[8] This became a principal issue of the first part of Luther's disputation with Eck on the power of the Pope.

Not a few of Luther's critics have maintained that, in a deplorable way, he returned to scholastic methods and opinions he had once so rightly rejected. Again, it is clear that some of Luther's fellow Reformers indicted him on similar lines. Until a turning-point was reached in the Luther research of the 1920s, the so-called 'Young Luther' was thus considerably more popular with scholars than the polemicist of later years. Views first forwarded at the beginning of the present century have also had their supporters of late.

There is, for example, the discussion between Luther and Zwingli on the Lord's Supper. There has been, and perhaps still is, a widespread opinion that the conflict between them was the result of ever-increasing alienation caused by their withdrawal—a withdrawal in completely opposite directions—from a common base. In short, both stand accused of changing their original doctrine. The thesis has been held by Walther Köhler, among others. For many years Köhler was considered to be the leading authority on the Luther–Zwingli contest, but his findings have recently been seriously challenged. It has, for example, been shown that Luther and Zwingli had totally different points of departure in their criticism of the Mass. Both may have rejected the Mass as a good work (*opus bonum*), and as a sacrifice; but an examination of the motives for such criticism shows their differences to be more marked than their similarities. Thus whereas Luther is concerned with the *divine* work of the Mass, Zwingli criticizes the idea of sacrifice in order to emphasize the *human* character of the rite. As long as Luther was primarily concerned with Roman doctrine, he did not need to stress the real presence of Christ in the Eucharist. But there is no evidence to suggest that he once doubted such a presence. Quite the contrary, in fact, for it was from the beginning a matter with which he did not quarrel. On the other hand, Luther certainly began to write more explicitly about the real presence after Karlstadt, Zwingli, and others started to repudiate it in public.[9] Only the most shallow reading of his early Eucharistic writings could prompt the notion that Luther originally found the real presence less important to him than it was later to become.

In short, there are strong arguments to suggest that Luther and Zwingli differed considerably from the start; and if that is so, it

---

[9] E. Grötzinger, *Luther und Zwingli. Die Kritik an der mittelalterlichen Lehre —als Wurzel des Abendmahlsstreites* (Ökumenische Theologie 5, Zürich-Gütersloh, 1980).

must be admitted that Köhler's thesis—the theory that the Reformers originally shared a common basis of belief—has lost its
validity. It is also likely the other notions of Luther returning to
embrace scholastic views as soon as he was 'overtaken' by 'left-
wing' reformers, are based on improbable assumptions of doubtful
quality—like the hypothesis that the Reformation started from a
common ground which slowly crumbled away. This is not, of
course, to deny that various convictions and actions were common
to all places where the movement took root; for this analysis is not
concerned with the general history of the Reformation, merely
with Reformation theology.

Then too, there is good reason to question what might be
termed 'the ramification theory'. It is certainly the case that two of
Luther's disagreements with leading personalities only gradually
became public knowledge. His alienation from Karlstadt during
the Wittenberg tumults in the winter 1521 to 1522, for instance, is
hardly surprising. No matter what they had in common, their
approach to St. Augustine, not to mention their opposition to
scholasticism, were of a different quality from the start.[10] As for
his relationship with Erasmus, Luther already knew his mind on
the matter in 1516, although he did not openly attack the humanist's theology before 1525.[11] In other cases, as for example that of
Johann Agricola, many years passed before there was open disagreement. As a friend and follower, Agricola was not under
suspicion until he chose to emphasize some peculiarities of his own
theology. These he tried to support by indicating that he was
only being faithful to convictions first promulgated, but now
abandoned, by Luther himself. The most recent research on Agricola confirms the existence of such differences in his theology from
the first, many years before conflict began[12]. In the case of Zwingli,
Luther seems to have been unaware of their differences until the
Swiss Reformer's symbolical interpretation of the Eucharist came
to his notice. His reaction was then most prompt because he was
already battling with Karlstadt on this very issue. In short, all the
indications are that Luther's teaching on such issues by no means

---

[10] E. Kähler, *Karlstadt und Augustin* (Hallische Monographien, No. 19, Halle/
Saale, 1952).

[11] See, for instance, *WA* 1, 384.14f.; *WA* 1, 677.3 f.; and *WA, Br.* 1. 70.

[12] J. Rogge, *Johann Agricolas Lutherverständnis* (Theologische Arbeiten XIV,
Evangelische Verlagsanstalt, Berlin, 1960).

involved new doctrines, but simply brought out into the open differences already existing.

But what substance is there in the theory that Luther increasingly fell back on 'scholasticism'? Without any doubt, two major polemical writings of the 1520s, as well as a number of exegetical works from the same period, contain explicit doctrinal elements of an elaborateness not often found before 1522. But only a superficial comparison of statements in Luther's writings could, on that score, charge the Reformer with such a fundamental change of doctrine. To establish such a thesis, Luther would have to be isolated and regarded as an 'original' writer working on the creation of new ideas. It would then be possible to discover a failure of nerve because of the fact that his early writings pass lightly over several elements in a dogmatic tradition he revives and discusses at length in later years.

Yet this was not how Luther saw his task, and there is no reason whatever for supposing that his early writings contained everything of importance to him. It would therefore be a brazen assumption to consider that anything not specifically elaborated in the early writings, but taken up later, points to a change of doctrine. Luther did not come forward with a vocation to revise the doctrine of the Church, but held it to be his duty to protest whenever he saw that doctrine being distorted. Accordingly, the content of protest had to change colour whenever the subject of distortion changed. Those who thus indict the Reformer of returning to scholasticism forward a superficial accusation that fails to account for the fact that Luther never dreamt of denying the existence of a common ground where not only he and his friends, but even the schoolmen, could meet. Without the least embarrassment, he thus used scholastic concepts and distinctions to confute adversaries like Erasmus and Zwingli. The fact that Luther had a score to settle with scholasticism did not make him opposed to every subject discussed in scholastic theology, although Adolf Harnack seemed to think that this should have been the case.[13] Before concluding that Luther's writings here or there evidence such a return, therefore, inquiry should be made to determine whether or not the Reformer is simply taking up a question he has in common

[13] A. Harnack, *Lehrbuch der Dogmengeschichte*, ed. J. C. B. Mohr, 4. Ausg. (Tübingen, 1910), iii, 863–96.

with the scholastic theologians, but has hitherto had no opportunity or inclination to expand.

The incidence of such elements is much more frequent towards the end of the period under discussion. Why should Luther avoid making use of an argument just because it was originally part of the scholastic repertoire? Despite hard and uncompromising judgements of academic argument in the late medieval period,[14] he was at heart too much of an historian to deny the existence of an unbroken Christian tradition, even if it was intermingled with error. A stern reminder of this may be found in his protest against outright rejection of the papal Church by the Anabaptists. As Luther states in succinct language, 'We have everything from there.' [*WA* 26, 147.11–26] He certainly could not countenance belief in the Church as the community of all believers on earth and yet withdraw from it. For Luther did not doubt that the Church could be found under the Pope, no matter what he had to say about the Papacy as an institution. In this fundamental conviction of the Church as a divine creation by the Word and sacraments can be found one of the most important reasons for Luther's reluctance to take the lead in the establishment of a new Church order. Not only this reluctance, but also the mobility of his theology made him less than qualified for the task. His posthumous role in the incorporation of a 'Lutheran' orthodoxy could only be written when he was no longer about to voice renewed protests against distortion. Very soon everyone knew and could explain Luther's 'doctrine of justification by faith *alone*'; but few had the slightest knowledge of the trouble he experienced in trying to write a systematic book on justification. While his friends were composing the Augsburg Confession, he was in the Coburg working on the project, but had to give it up. He was simply not up to the task![15]

This essay has sought to discuss the question of Luther's 'self-contradictions' as they were raised in the crudest way by Cochlaeus. The subject was also considered by some of Luther's fellow Reformers, and even answered affirmatively by several modern scholars. I do not pretend to have solved the problem—merely to have pointed out a series of difficulties which stand in the way of an affirmative answer, and at the same time to offer some circum-

---

[14] See, e.g., *WA* 1, 384.14f., and *WA* 1, 677.3f.
[15] See the introduction to the fragments and notes, *WA* 30², 652f.

stantial evidence for a negative response. It is certainly of interest to note the close ties that bind Luther's 'doctrine' to the challenges he met. Such doctrine was altogether too vivid and vigorous to be incorporated into a dogmatic system without at the same time suffering distortion, and so being altered beyond recognition. It is hardly necessary to stress that the discovery of any further 'self-contradictions' is to be viewed with imperturbability and a sense of humour. It is undoubtedly true that the difficulties experienced in expounding Luther's 'doctrine' out of context provide much of the fascination of the man. By contrast, those of his contemporaries who knew how to build a dogmatic system and a serious Church order are only reached by the kind of dreary work that offers little fun.

XII

Luther Against 'The Turk, The Pope, And The Devil'

*

GORDON RUPP

APOCALYPTIC is in the air, and in the closing decades of the twentieth century seems likely to occupy the place of eschatology in the theology of the first half. It fits the mood of an age which has abandoned the view of history as a slowly-moving escalator, with the thought that history will eventually simplify out, and be tidied up. And even the so-called 'Theology of Hope' in its attempt to avoid an earlier pessimism about the relevance of the doctrine of the Kingdom to the historical process has abandoned the thought of history as a straight line with no abrupt discontinuities. But apocalyptic is perhaps more suited to the modern context, a view of history more like that of a volcano, or a succession of earthquakes, subject to hidden pressures which erupt in violence, irrational forces which cannot be rationally explained, let alone controlled. And if the world ends with a bang, then its end would have no logical connection with the previous history of mankind.

Although it is probably true that, for Martin Luther, eschatology rather than apocalyptic is an important theme, its importance for him has perhaps been under-estimated. His dismissal of the Book of Revelation in his early writing, and his continued scepticism about its apostolic authorship, must not mislead us. Early polemic like the *Reply ... to the Book of Ambrosius Catherinus* (1521) reminds us that he could allegorize the details of the apocalyptic imagery with the best. And the Book of Daniel was important for him in the middle and towards the end of his life. Like most of his contemporaries, including Sir Thomas More, he believed that history was nearing its end, and in 1530 the victorious progress of the Turk encouraged him to believe that this, the last of the biblical prophecies of 'the end', had been fulfilled. Although he refused to pinpoint 'the Last Day', he thought that just before the end God might raise up a Noah who would point to what was imminent.

When in 1530 Luther translated the Book of Daniel, he appended to it a remarkable dedicatory epistle to his young Prince, Johann Friedrich of Saxony. It is the only instance in all his biblical translations of a single book's being dedicated to a particular person. But the preamble is illuminating

Grace and peace in Christ Our Lord—the world is running faster and faster, hastening towards its end, so that I often have the strong impression that the Last Day may break before we have turned the Holy Scriptures into German!

For this is sure: there are no more temporal events to wait for according to the Scriptures: it has all happened, all has been fulfilled—the Roman Empire is finished, the Turk has come to the peak of his power, the power of the Pope is about to crash—and the world is cracking to pieces as though it would tumble down—and the Roman Empire under our Emperor Charles has grown a little stronger than for some time, so that it seems to me that this is the last moment—as a candle or straw which is almost burned out, and then at the very last moment it suddenly gives out a bright flame as though it were just being kindled, and even in that very moment it goes out . . . for if the world were to linger on, as she has been hitherto, then surely all the world would go Mohammedan or Epicurean, and there would be no more Christians left, as Christ said. [WA, DB 11.2.381.4]

Apocalyptic rarely ceased to be an element in Christian thinking, and from the time of Joachim da Fiore and the conflicts within the Franciscan order it has been important for the more sectarian theologies of the later Middle Ages. In the Reformation it surfaced in such radical documents as the *Book of a Hundred Chapters*, and the apocalyptic element has not perhaps yet been sufficiently diagnosed in the writings of Thomas Müntzer. Like Melchior Hoffmann, Luther judged the twelfth chapter of Daniel deserving of separate exegesis, and carried this out at the end of his life, utterly rejecting the radical apocalyptic of Hoffmann, whom he had withstood in 1527. Luther himself had no interest in millenarian doctrines, but had his own way of interpreting history. In the last years of his life, he thus tried to work out his own system of chronology, and in his polemic against the Jews, wrestled with the meaning of the 'seventy weeks' mentioned in Daniel, and in the doctrine of successive earthly Kingdoms. Justus Jonas and Melanchthon were also interested in such themes; and in 1530 were similarly struck by the relevance of the Muhammadan invasions to apocalyptic prophecy. In addition to apocalyptic biblical exegesis, Luther and his fellow Reformers took an interpretation of history

in terms of the two Cities from St. Augustine, and interpreted it as
the endemic conflict between the True and the False Church. This
passed into the wider Protestant heritage, through John Knox's
Scots Confession; and in the interpretation of Church history in
terms of the Rise and Overthrow of Anti-Christ in the English
Foxe's *Book of Martyrs* and in the German *Magdeburg Centuries*.
Against such a background Luther's description of the three demonic adversaries of God, 'The Turk, the Pope, and the Devil' can
be considered.

In 1529, Western Christendom was shaken to the core by the
news that the Turk had conquered Budapest and stood at the gates
of Vienna. In that year Luther published two writings: the first
Against the Turks [WA 30², 125 ff.]; the second an immensely careful and powerful sermon, *Heerpredigt*, [WA 30², 160–97] intended
for Christians who might be involved in the war. In these he bade
his readers look beyond the immediate military peril, 'For the
Devil seeks through this instrument, the Turks, not just to destroy
ordered governments, but he strikes at the Kingdom of Christ and
His saints and members.' Luther was at this time fascinated by the
Book of Daniel, and saw in Daniel 7 an explicit reference to the
Turk: 'the little horn is the Turk . . . as we all see and experience
before our eyes, the Turk has had great success over the Christian,
yet he denies Christ and exalts his Mahomet above all others so
that we have nothing now to expect save the Last Day.' [WA, DB
11². 12.2–6]

In that year, too, he expounded the story of Gog Magog in
the Book of Ezekiel. Those who only know the friendly mascots
of the City of London, standing in Guildhall, must read Luther to
see them as terrible emblems of demonic violence. There are indeed two great tyrants, but they are the Pope and the Turk (sometimes termed by Luther the 'Red Jews').

For Scripture prophesies to us about two terrible tyrants which on the
eve of the Last Day will lay waste and destroy Christendom—the one
spiritually with false and poisonous teaching and worship, that is the Pope
with all his Popery—the other with his sword in a bodily and outward
fashion . . . as Christ tells us in Matthew 24, of a tribulation such as the
earth hath never seen before, and that is the Turk [WA 30², 162.2–6].

When after desperate fighting, the Turk by a miracle withdrew to
lick his wounds in Constantinople, in Luther's mind peril receded

only to recur with vehemence when once again the Turk moved to hammer at the gates of Christendom. Of Islamic culture, its great philosophers, mathematicians, and mystics; its fertilizing and civilizing contacts in Spain and Sicily; its preservation of elements of classical culture which might otherwise have perished; of such matters, Luther knew nothing.

Thus references to the Turk creep once more into his *Table Talk* and into his Lectures on the Book of Genesis. Above all he reminds Christians of the power of prayer:

And even if the Turk, the Pope, the Emperor and the gates of Hell were to be in opposition, they could do nothing if the Church brought its ineffable groaning in prayer ... since we can overthrow Satan with prayer, why should we not also overthrow the Turk and the Pope? ... up to this time we have curbed the hostile attacks of the Emperor, the Turk and the Pope by our prayers, for years at a time. [WA 44, 575]

This became the main theme of his tract *An Admonition to Prayer against the Turks*, 1541. It began with an indictment of the sins of Germany, sins which have merited the rod of divine anger: 'it is no good complaining like naughty children, when the rod is painful.' [WA 51, 589.22; 595.28; 599.34.] None the less, prayer has averted worse dangers than the Turk, since the black 'Turk devil' is not worse than the white 'Pope devil': 'I reckon that the Pope is Anti-Christ, or if you want to add the Turk, I would say that the Pope is Anti-Christ according to the spirit, and the Turk according to the flesh. They help one another to murder, the one with the body and the sword; the other with doctrine and the spirit.' [WA, TR 1, 330] The thought of Mahomet as anti-Christ was a medieval commonplace.

The Turk stood over and against Christendom as an alien and heathen society, cut off behind an Iron curtain, so that men read avidly any kind of news, and believed all kinds of improbable gossip about what really went on. Luther recognized the Turk as an ordered government, a true *Obrigkeit* under natural law, so that individual Christians who are taken into captivity owe their captors the kind of obedience set out in Romans 13. Their religion seemed to him a pattern of externalized religiosity, another form of salvation by works to which he reduced all other religions. But he read what he could about them, for when he wrote polemically Luther always did his homework. He thus wrote a *Preface* to Vincentius Ferrar's *Libellus de ritu et moribus Turcorum*, a fifteenth-century account of captivity among the Turk; and he reprinted this when, in 1537, he read Paolo Giovio's *Turcicarum Rerum Commentarius*. Sometimes Luther contrasts their religion and behaviour favourably with that of apostate, or half, Christians. They are for him a shadow Papacy, just as the Papacy is a shadow of the true Church.

Luther wished to expose the follies of Muslim religion. Since 1530 he had known of the exposition of the Koran by the thirteenth-century Florentine, the Dominican Ricoldus; and this he published with a rather free translation of his own in 1542 [*WA* 53, 261 ff.]. He may also have known the *Türkenchronik* of Sebastian Franck. In 1542 there appeared his great hymn

> Erhalt uns Herr bey deinem Wort
> Und steuer des Bapsts und Türken Mord.

In the following year, he gave the kiss of life to a project which the Basel publishers had allowed to die, Bibliander's edition of the Koran itself, Melanchthon contributing a preface [*WA* 53, 261 ff.].

Nor was Luther's concern merely literary and theological. In 1543 he wrote to the Elector declining to be exempted from the Turkish war tax: 'I want to fight the Turk with my poor man's penny, alongside the next fellow; and who knows whether my little free-will offering, like the widow's mite, may not do more than all the rich compulsory taxes ... for I too would like to do the Turks grievous bodily harm, and if I were not too old and weak I would join up...' [*WA, Br* 10, 29.39 ff.] The thought of *Feldwebel* Luther is intriguing!

With some reason, Luther took a poor view of German generals, and when Joachim II of Brandenburg was appointed the unfortunate Commander-in-Chief of an ill-fated expedition, Luther wrote him an almost Zwingli-like letter about the need for reverent discipline among the troops, and that they should be well sermonized by their chaplains [*WA, Br* 10, 66].

Thus, although for Luther the Turk is an eschatological and apocalyptic portent about which he uses the imagery of Daniel and Ezekiel, he realizes that there is an urgent and practical crisis, as is apparent from his plea in the *Admonition to Prayer*:

Look upon our prayer, most merciful Father, and sternly judge our enemies, for they are even more your enemies; and when they smite and persecute us they smite and persecute your word which we preach, believe, and confess to be yours and not ours: the work of your Holy Spirit in us ... the Turk wants to put his Mahomet in the place of your Dear Son Jesus Christ ... for he blasphemes him, and says that he is not Very God, and that Mahomet is higher and better than He is. [*WA* 51, 609.29]

But if Luther had watched the Turkish menace grow from a cloud the size of a man's hand into a lowering storm, he had always the Pope with him. About the Papacy at the last, his utterances were more and more uncompromisingly hostile, until their culmination in that outrageous explosion *Against the Papacy at Rome, instituted by the Devil*. [*WA* 54, 206–99]

The last decade of Luther's life saw a hardening on both sides of the great divide, especially as the Counter-Reformation got under way, the Council of Trent assembled, and Charles V was able to put into effect his so often delayed military plans. There was also a steady accession to the Reformation in Saxony and North-West Germany. Luther had become deeply sceptical of any kind of peace (as the forthright *Articles of Schmalkalden* [*WA* 54, 206–99] made plain) but he knew there were practical reasons for taking advantage of every respite and every concession to be squeezed from the Emperor. If he therefore left diplomatic ploys to Melanchthon, he nevertheless continued to pursue the diminishing hope of a free, Christian council in Germany. By now, differing patterns of Reformation had been established in Germany, Switzerland, and England, but the Church in Italy and Spain continued much on the same orthodox lines. What affronted the conscience of Catholic Christians from Colet and More to Jedin and Lortz was thus the entanglement of politics and law with religion, those externals which Burnet chose to call 'superannuated Judaism'. For despite the wonderful new movements and, above all, new saints, they remained a way of life for the Curia. Paul III—however terrible he may appear from Titian's revealing canvas (though more a fox than Luther's 'Werewolf')—was preoccupied to the point of near disaster with family affairs and the great game of diplomacy, playing off the Emperor and the King of France against one another in the grand and terrible manner of Leo X or Julius II.

On Luther's own doorstep, Albert of Mainz had learned and forgotten nothing, to remain the living image of all Luther had fought against for thirty long years. The list of practical abuses catalogued by Luther in his manifestos of 1520 and 1530 con-

tinued, and there was still a kind of Pelagian legalism wherever the
sacramental system touched the interests of the clergy and the consciences of ordinary men. As Luther interpreted it, reform at
Rome seemed no nearer in 1540 than it had been in 1517.

Of the Catholic revival in Northern Italy and in Spain, Luther
knew almost nothing; but it had not fallen to him, but to Melanchthon, to make personal contact with Cardinal Contarini and his
kind. He knew nothing of the devotion to Christ of the Jesuits, an
Order already including a Francis Xavier among its members, and
soon to inaugurate a magnificent missionary enterprise in the Far
East, with such noble evangelists as Valignan, Matteo Ricci, and
Roberto Nobili, all of them products of the Catholic revival.

Luther did not set out to oppose papal authority. Only a few
weeks after the posting of the *Ninety-Five Theses*, he and his friends
were chatting in a wagon along a Saxon road, when his colleague
in Law and personal adviser, Jerome Schurpf, warned him that he
might be in for serious trouble if he touched the question of the
papal *plenitudo potestatis*. Only thereafter did Luther realize what
he was up against by challenging the authority of Rome. For as he
became involved in argument, an essential preliminary to his Leipzig disputation with John Eck was his study of Church history
and canon law. Until then, like most Germans, he treated the great
German Council of Constance as infallible, never for one moment
questioning the condemnation of the Czech reformer, John Hus.
But now he began a detailed examination of the articles charged
against Hus and his comrade Jerome of Prague; and letters to Spalatin in the following months show how swiftly his mind was
moving: 'I have been teaching all that John Hus taught, unawares,
and so has Staupitz' [*WA, Br* 2, 42]; and again: 'Good God, how
great is the darkness and iniquity of these Romans . . . I am so hor-
rified that I have hardly any doubt that the Pope is that very
Anti-Christ himself which common report expects, so well
do all the things he lives, does, speaks, fit the picture.' [*WA,
Br* 2, 48.22] Then came words ringing with a terrible finality.
It was one of Luther's failings that, once he slammed the
door of his mind against a person or a cause, he was reluctant to
re-open it:

Farewell, unhappy, hopeless, blasphemous Rome! The wrath of God hath
come upon thee as thou deservest. We have cared for Babylon and she is

not healed: let us then leave her, that she may be a habitation of dragons, spectres, and witches, and true to her name of Babel; an everlasting confusion, a pantheon of wickedness. [*WA* 6, 329]

Ernst Wolf drew attention in a brilliant essay to a point in Luther's *Liberty of a Christian Man* in which the Reformer refers to the Papacy as Leviathan, an *additamentum* which, by adding human traditions, has become the antithesis of Christ.[1] There is of course a double reference in the view of the Pope as Anti-Christ, a notion which had recurred in medieval literature. For Luther, the Pope is Anti-Christ because he is anti-Christian in the sense that his way of life, in its triumphalism, is the opposite of him who took upon himself the form of a servant. Anti-Christ is also a portent of the Last Day. It is interesting to remember how long John Henry Newman clung to the evangelical tradition in which he had been brought up, namely that the Pope was Anti-Christ. In an article in the *British Critic* (October 1849) he had written: 'There is no medium between a Vice-Christ and an Anti-Christ, for it is not the acts that make the difference, but the authority of those acts.'[2]

The first-fruits of Luther's examination of the papal decretals had emerged in his tract *Why the Books of the Pope and his Disciples were burned by Dr. Martin Luther* (1520) [*LW* 31, 381]. In these few pages Luther listed thirty claims about the papal *plenitudo potestatis*, documents to which he returned again and again, notably in 1530. In that year he took a more dubious view of canon law as a whole than did Lazarus Spengler in Nuremberg. But they are part of the ground on which he speaks of Anti-Christ:

This is that abomination and stench of which Christ speaks in Matthew 24. 'When you see the abomination of desolation spoken of by the prophet Daniel (9.27) standing in the holy place . . .' and St. Paul writes 'He will take his seat in the temple of God (that is, Christendom) proclaiming himself to be God. [*LW* 31, 393]

The discussions at Frankfurt in 1539 were a landmark in the negotiations between the Emperor and the princes. They raised once more the possibility that the Emperor might call a national

---

[1] E. Wolf, *Peregrinatio*. Bd. 1. (Munich, 1954), 135 ff.
[2] J. H. Newman, *Apologia pro vita sua*, ed. M. J. Svaglic (Oxford, 1967), p. 114.

council in order to tackle the reform of the Church in Germany, while the question arose whether, if this should fail, the princes might offer armed resistance. In a notable essay, Rudolf Herrmann drew attention to the importance of the *Ninety-One Theses* which Luther prepared for debate in Wittenberg at this time.[3] They were for a 'Circular Disputation' on the text 'If you would be perfect, go and sell all you possess.' (Matthew 19: 21) There is some doubt about the significance of a 'Circular Disputation'. It was probably not a festal or promotion disputation, but a regular 'Buggins' turn' exchange by members of the theological faculty. But there is no doubt at all about the forthrightness of these brilliant theses, which must surely rank only slightly below the still more famous *Ninety-Five* of 1517 [*WA* 39², 16.17]. It is the latter half of the series which concentrates on the Papacy, and attempts to demonstrate that such a monstrous power has no place in the three divinely ordained human hierarchies—the State, the Church, and the home.

That the Pope is no ruler of the spiritual order is shown by the fact that he damns the Gospel and tramples on true Church discipline (*thesis* 53). That he is no ruler in the domestic order is shown by the fact that he forbids betrothals and the marriage of clergy (55); and that he is no temporal ruler is shown by the fact that he puts temporal law under his own authority (54); and as he explains elsewhere, dispenses subjects from their lawful obedience and claims to depose princes. Therefore the Pope is a monster, what Germans call a 'Bierwolf' (Dan. 11: 36; 2 Thess. 2: 3). This beast is indeed a wolf, but one possessed by demons, who ravages all things (59); and to destroy it all inhabitants have to combine together (60). Accordingly, if the Pope instigates a war, then resistance is to be offered to him as to a raving and possessed monster—and whoever fights under a robber may, without respect of persons, expect eternal damnation as a peril of such war service (69). It is no help to kings, princes, and the Emperor that they pride themselves on being protectors of the Church, for they are bound to know what the Church really is (70). This last view of the Emperor as *miles papae* has a bearing on the continuing discus-

---

[3] R. Herrmann, *Luthers Zirkular Disputation über Mt. 19.21* in *Gesammelte Studien* (Göttingen, 1960), pp. 206 ff.

sion about the attitude of Luther and the Wittenberg theologians to armed resistance.[4]

When an uneasy truce was made at Frankfurt, Luther was content to leave the subsequent negotiations to Melanchthon who, with that old ecumenical hand, Martin Bucer, and a portentous new recruit in John Calvin, were to engage in dialogue with the Rhineland theologians Pighius and Gropper, the Italians Morone and Contarini, and the exiled Englishman, Cardinal Pole. The discussions began at Hagenau in June 1540, adjourned to Worms in October, and to Regensburg in 1541. Yet nothing revealed more clearly the growing gulf than these arduously eirenical dialogues, or the stifling political pressures in the background. A recent historian of the Regensburg colloquy has said that 'the dialogue between Protestantism and Catholicism at the Diet of Regensburg in 1541 did not fail. It never took place.'[5]

He adds that the thought-world of Contarini—Italian, Latin, and classical—was unable to comprehend the force of the revolutionary dialectic on the Protestant side, despite the humanist ground common to them both. A similar impression derives from Hubert Jedin's magisterial study of the Council of Trent.[6] Its intricate amalgam of theological trends in its over-all picture is continuous with a medieval tradition which at all important points rejected Lutheran doctrines. What older historians thought might be a moment of hope, when it seemed that Melanchthon could appear before the Council, Jedin wisely realized would shock even the most friendly of its fathers. For after Luther's death, Melanchthon not only felt the weight of Elijah's mantle, but also had to face real divergences that were now much clearer than before.

Since the *Augsburg Confession*, the lines had hardened. More and more it was a case not of arguing, but of writing to provide ammunition for one's own side. There is a sense in which Luther's excommunication had been terribly effective, for in the literal sense of the word, the two sides were no longer able to communicate. Luther's last writings against the Papacy, like his last writings

[4] For the problems involved, cf. H. Dorries, *Wort und Stunde* (Göttingen, 1970), Vol. iii, pp. 195–270; and H. Scheible, *Das Widerstandsrecht als Problem der Deutschen Protestanten, 1523–46* (Gutersloh, 1969).
[5] P. Matheson, *Cardinal Contarini at Regensburg* (Oxford, 1972), p. 181.
[6] H. Jedin, *Geschichte des Konzils von Trient*, iii, 380.

against the Jews, were intended for those already committed to the Protestant cause.

Luther's last two great writings were concerned with his doctrine of the Chuch, and therefore with papal power. Into the tract *Of Councils and Churches* he put a great deal of reading. In 1538 he had published an edition of the Apostles' and Athanasian Creeds, and had read the standard Church histories of Eusebius, Rufinus, and the *Tripartite History* of Cassiodorus, together with the recently published work of the Franciscan Peter Crabbe on Councils, Platina's *Lives of the Popes*, and the compilation of the English refugee, Robert Barnes. Luther's new work was sensational. It underwent three editions in the first year of its publication, and a Latin translation by Justus Jonas secured an international audience. In the words of Mackinnon, it takes the form

of a demonstration from history that the true foundation of the Church is not the ancient Councils and Fathers, but the Scriptures: that the first four General Councils only declared the faith as taught in the Scriptures: that in matters of faith their powers were strictly limited by this fundamental principle: and that only a Council representing the true Church as against the false Papal church can bring about a real reformation.[7]

The last part of the treatise contains some of Luther's finest writing about the nature of the Church, defined as a communion of saints, the community (*Hauffe*) of people who are Christian and holy. They are those who believe in Christ:

That is why they are called a Christian people and have the Holy Spirit, who sanctifies them daily, not only through the forgiveness of sins acquired for them by Christ, . . . but also through the abolition, the purging and mortification of sins, on the basis of which they are called a holy people. [*LW* 41, 143–4]

This people must remain on earth until the end of time. In his *Lectures on Genesis*, given at this time, he insists that it is for the sake of this Christian people that earthly kingdoms and their lawful authorities exist. When the Church ends, the Turks and the Pope will suddenly fall.

Luther lists the marks of the Church. First, the Word of God, 'for God's word cannot be without God's people, and conversely, God's people cannot be without God's word.' [*LW* 41, 150] The

---

[7] J. Mackinnon, *Luther and the Reformation* (London, 1930), iv, 134.

other notes are the sacrament of Baptism, taught, believed, and administered according to Christ's ordinance; the holy sacrament of the altar, rightly administered; the office of the keys; a called and consecrated ministry; public prayer; praise and thanksgiving; and seventh, and not least, 'the holy possession of the Cross of suffering and persecution'. The last note, to be 'under the Cross', is an important part of Luther's doctrine of the Church, and is bound up with his Christology.

For the true Church, like its Master, is hidden under contrary species, and appears before men in weakness and human folly. These marks are not intended to be exhaustive. There are many signs in Luther's later writings that he also valued highly the *colloquium fratrum*, the mutual society and comfort that Christians have one of another.[8]

In Luther's early writings on the Psalms there is a tension between the Church and the synagogue. In his later writings this becomes the struggle between the True and the False Church. In his *Of Councils and the Church* Luther writes: 'Now when the Devil saw that God built such a holy church, he was not idle, and erected his chapel beside it, larger than God's temple . . . since the Devil is always God's ape, trying to imitate all God's things, and to improve on them. . .'. [*LW* 41, 167–8] The false Church belongs to the true Church as a shadow relates to substance. But the two Churches do not simply coexist, but grapple incessantly. For behind Luther's view of the Papacy as a 'werewolf' is this picture of the false Church as a sinister *Doppelgänger*. A conflict thus ensues, which, as Luther quotes from Augustine, dates back to Cain and Abel: 'At all times we are either Esauites or Jacobites . . . and even if we were to conquer the Pope and his men, and our doctrines were to triumph, from our own midst would arise Papists and Turks who would sell the name of the Church.' [*WA* 43, 418.6] This idea of endemic conflict becomes important for the Reformers, and underlies the growing apocalyptic temper of the 1540s, with the increasing threat of violence.

Luther's second important writing was his *Wider Hans Wurst* (1541). In the earlier decades of the Reformation, the Reformer regarded two men as arch-enemies of the Gospel, Albrecht of

[8] H. Dorries, *Wort und Stunde*, iii, 458. Cf. E. G. Rupp, *The Righteousness of God*, Ch. 15.

Mainz, and Duke Georg of Saxony. In his last years, Heinrich of
Brunswick-Wolfenbüttel became the focus of his wrath. Henry
was indeed a ruthless and unscrupulous go-getter, whose brutal
and licentious soldiery burned and plundered the houses and lands
of his enemies. He flaunted his mistress, Eva von Trott, a hefty
blonde of Wagnerian proportions, in a way which shocked and
offended Luther. He was a bitter and unrelenting enemy of Protestants. He brought the city of Goslar to the edge of ruin, confiscat-
ing the Rammelsburg forests and mines from which it drew its
living.[9] He tried to kidnap the town's representative to the Diet of
Augsburg, and when that failed, had him shadowed and hi-jacked
on the return journey, seizing all his papers, and throwing the
wretched man into a prison, where he died two years later. At
Augsburg he was the worst possible boon companion of Philip of
Hesse, and in their cups may have suggested kidnapping the
Emperor. In 1542 he was to be driven from his lands by the Protestant princes of the Schmalkaldic League. But before this happened, he had written a vitriolic attack on Luther, accusing the
Reformer, among other things, of speaking disrespectfully of his
own prince, the Elector Johann Friedrich, and of referring to him
as 'John the Sausage'. Such a concatenation of incitements was cal-
culated to provoke Luther to a real firework display of wrath, and
this it did.

Luther admitted that, by the grace of God, his Elector's physical shape might be less than elegant; but it was Duke Henry who
was the true 'wurst'. It is a double pun, the first one about a sausage pudding, the other implying a fool.

More important than the polemic is Luther's exposition of the
nature of the Church. It anticipates the famous question put to
John Jewel ('Where was your church before Luther?') by insisting
that the evangelical Churches are the 'true, ancient Church' and
that 'you have fallen away from us ... and have set up a new
church against the ancient one.' [*LW* 41, 194]

From the time of Ernst Ritschl it has been a commonplace of
Luther study that for him the Church is *sola fide perceptibilis*.
Hence the affirmation here that 'The Church is a high, deep, hid-
den thing, which one may neither perceive nor see, but must grasp

---

[9] G. Blume, *Goslar und der Schmalkaldische Bund, 1527–47* (Goslar, 1949).

only by faith through baptism, sacrament, and word.' [*LW* 41, 211.]

Luther returns to his dialectic of the True and the False Church: '... there are two kinds of churches stretching from the beginning of history to the end, which St. Augustine calls Cain and Abel. The Lord Christ commands us not to embrace the false church.' [Ibid., 194] He again lists the marks of the True Church:

Nobody can deny ... that ... we have received holy baptism, and because of this are called Christians ... Nobody can deny .... that we have the sacrament of the altar ... Nobody can deny ... that we have the true and ancient keys ... Nobody can deny ... that we have in fulness and purity the preaching office and the Word of God ... Nobody can deny ... that we hold, believe, sing, and confess the Apostles' Creed ... Nobody can deny ... that we have the same prayer as the ancient church, the Lord's Prayer ... Nobody can deny ... that with the ancient church we hold that one should honour and not curse the temporal power ... Nobody can deny ... that we honour and praise marriage ... Nobody can deny that we experience the same suffering as our brethren in the world ... Nobody can deny ... that we have not shed blood, murdered, or revenged ourselves in return ... but as Christ, the Apostles, and the ancient church did, we endure, admonish, and pray for others ... in litany and sermons just as Christ our Lord did.

And Luther concludes:

Thus we have proved that we are the old true church ... now you too, papists, prove that you are the true church, or like it. You cannot do it, but I will prove that you are the new false church, in everything apostate, separated from the true, ancient church, and thus becoming Satan's whore and synagogue.

He then lists twelve innovations of the Roman Church which did not exist in the Early Church, and which the evangelicals have rejected, concluding:

... if such innovations of the Papacy were or could be regarded simply as novelties, they could to some extent be put up with for the sake of peace, as one puts up with a new coat. But now this devilish poison and hellish murder is glued to it—it is the command of the Church, the holy worship of God, the good and spiritual life ... this is to make truth out of falsehood, God out of the devil, heaven out of hell. For this reason the Pope's church is swarming with falsehood, devils, idolatry, hell, murder, and every kind of calamity. Thus it is time to hear the voice of the angel in

Revelation Ch. 18: 'Come out of here, my people, lest you partake in her sins.'

In 1544, when the Emperor once again spoke of the possibility of a German council, the Pope, determined at all costs to avoid an assembly where he might lose the initiative, prepared a brief which seems to have circulated in two versions. One was more extreme than the other, and when Luther got hold of this it confirmed his worst fears of the impossibility of any genuine reform from such an authority. The Protestant princes thought something should be written in reply, and as a result, Luther was coaxed into writing the most vehement of all his anti-papal tracts, *Against the Roman Papacy, instituted by the Devil* [LW 41, 263–376].

Somewhat reminiscent of Cochlaeus's attack on Luther in 1529, argument is swallowed up in scurrility, though in this case scatology takes the place of eschatology. Luther's favourite three-letter words recur: 'ass', 'pig', 'dog', 'cow', and 'sow'; but there is also an addition of four-letter words which decent society banned from polite literature until very recent times. I think there is still matter to ponder in Edwyn Bevan's famous essay on *Dirt* in his volume *Hellenism and Christianity*: for Luther, the Papacy is not merely evil, but filthy. It is unpleasant polemic, though not Swift-like in its obsession with this kind of vocabulary, and rather better than the More–'Rossaeus' book against Luther in 1523. The odd thing is that when Lukas Cranach drew a set of obscene illustrations to the text, Luther was genuinely shocked, a spontaneous and almost old-maidish reaction, as we learn from his letters to intimate friends. But there it is, a repulsive document.

He had added nothing to his earlier arguments, namely that the Fathers in the time of Augustine knew no such Papal autocracy; that scholars had exposed the *Donation of Constantine*; and that the Eastern Church repudiated the claims of the canonists. He returns to the theme of his *Theses* of 1539 that this Papal power has no origin in the hierarchies of the natural order appointed by God, and that therefore it originated with the Devil, since its essence is destructive and demonic. Thus the Pope is worse than the Turk, for the Turk '... does not sit in the Temple of God, nor does he use the names of Christ, St. Peter, or Holy Scripture; instead he attacks Christendom from the outside ... But this inward destroyer claims to be a friend, wants to be called Father, and is twice as bad as the Turk.' [LW 41, 339]

None the less, as Mackinnon pointed out, the tract still scores points, and even King Ferdinand owned that if the abuse were taken away, 'Luther had not written badly.'[10] Luther ends the tract by reiterating the epithet 'Anti-Christ':

Anti-Christ, a man of sin, a child of destruction, a raging werewolf. He who will not believe this, let him go on with his God, the Pope. I as a teacher called to preach in Christ's Church, under obligation to speak the truth, have done my part. He who will be lost, let him be lost. His blood be on his own head.[11]

In a luminous pamphlet Ernst Bizer reminded us that the papal menace troubled the very last hours of Luther's life. His last words to his friends on the evening before his death were 'Pray to our Lord God and his Gospel that all may go well with it, for the Council of Trent and the accursed Pope are hot with wrath against it.'[12]

The Turk and the Pope were not the only enemies whom Luther attacked in his last writings. Two others deserve special mention, the Fanatics and the Epicureans.[13] About the Fanatics he had no new arguments, though they do intrude into his very last sermons. There are also more and more arguments against the Epicureans and sophists, those in whom were the qualities which Luther sensed in Erasmus as profane: the broadening world of the Renaissance élite, who mocked at faith and intensity of devotion, with their exaltation of human reason, returning to a Hellenist rather than a biblical inheritance. But all these enemies of the faith, Turk, Pope, Fanatic, and Epicurean, were tools of the Devil. This is how he thought of the relation between the Pope and the Devil:

When the painters of old painted the Last Judgement, they pictured hell as a great dragon's head with vast jaws, in the middle of which, in the fire, stood the Pope, cardinals, bishops; priests, monks, emperors, kings, princes, all kinds of men and women,—but never a young child. I really do not know how better one should ... describe the church of the pope ... It represents indeed the jaws of hell, and through the mouth of the

[10] Mackinnon, iv, 144.   [11] Ibid., 150.
[12] E. Bizer, Luther und der Papst (Munich, 1958), p. 56.
[13] U. Asendorf, Eschatologie bei Luther (Göttingen, 1967), pp. 187–95.

devil, that is, through its devilish teaching and preaching, it swallows into the abyss of hell first and foremost the pope himself and then all the world. [*LW* 41, 206.]

Much has been usefully written about Luther and the Devil.[14] It has been assessed as a remnant of medieval superstition, or discussed in intricate psychological terms (there is a Bosch-like undercurrent to Luther's imagery); and also abstruse (and Teutonic?) arguments in which the Devil becomes a theological abstraction. Certainly, the Devil for Luther is far more formidable than the clumsy clodhopper of medieval drama, or Bunyan's sinister Apollyon, Gounod's Mephistopheles, or even Max Beerbohm's sleazy waiter who has seen better days. He is a fallen angel who has become a dirty devil, who gets up to all manner of tricks, creeping through holes in the fence, and overturning the waggon. He is crude and rude, and Luther enjoyed ghost stories and believed in poltergeists, of which he had experience. More seriously, it is the Devil who attacks us in *Anfechtung*—a life and death struggle— attacking the very lifeline of faith (as in Grünewald's very Luther-like 'Temptation of St. Anthony'). These attacks go on throughout our Christian pilgrimage, right to the very last, even though behind and through them it is God who brings us to penitence and faith. Yet it is the Devil who gives dynamism to our conflicts in the world, an element so important for Luther's doctrine of the Two Kingdoms.

Not the least merit of Hans Barth's monograph is that it shows how Luther's doctrine of the Devil is bound up with his Christology. For Luther, this conflict is no permanent dualism, no stalemate, but it is Christ who always conquers:

> And let the Prince of Hell
> Look grim as e'er he will,
> He harms us not a whit.
> For why? His doom is writ,
> A word shall quickly slay him.

The famous epigram 'Living I will be thy plague, Dying I will be thy death, O Pope' (originating perhaps at Augsburg in 1530), might be taken as a pathetic defiance, even the measure of the ulti-

---

[14] Two of the best modern studies are H. Obendiek, *Der Teufel bei Martin Luther* (Berlin, 1931), and Hans Martin Barth, *Der Teufel und Jesus Christus in der Theologie Martin Luthers* (Göttingen, 1967).

mate failure of the Reformation as misconceived. For beneath all
the shortcomings and failures, the Papacy had that quality which
Luther might surely have added to the 'notes of the Church'—
'survival value', and a capacity for repentance and reform.

But it could also be defended as a valid boast. What Luther
hated was not the Papacy as it is in the twentieth century, nor even
as dispassionate historians describe it in the sixteenth century.
Rather was it 'Popery', that entanglement of spiritual power with
law, politics, and triumphalism; that corruption of the highest
which turns the best into the worst, which had brought the Western Church more than once to the point of disaster. The century
of bigotry, zeal and violence which would now ensue, could not
be prevented, still less to enable the Church to baptize into Christ
the new worlds; the new empires without Christendom beyond
the seas, and the new empires within the mind of Man. Historians
cannot fail to recognize the limitations of Luther's vision in his little corner on the edge of Germany to which in his latter years he
was more and more confined (and properly so, as pastor and
preacher to a little flock); or those obvious and serious limitations
of his own temperament and character. But he was not wholly
wrong about those enemies, nor about demonic forces in human
history. With courage and constancy, having begun to fight for
what he believed, single-handed and alone, he stood his ground
and fought manfully to the end.

XIII

'Line upon line: here a little, there a little'

Some letters of Martin Luther

*

CHRISTIAN PEARSON, SSF

DEIGN on the passing world to turn thine eyes
And pause awhile from letters, to be wise;
There mark what ills the scholar's life assail,
Toil, envy, want, the patron, and the jail.
See nations slowly wise, and meanly just,
To buried merit raise the tardy bust.

Samuel Johnson,
The Vanity of Human Wishes

ALTHOUGH Martin Luther, Austin friar, university don, pastor, outlaw, husband, prisoner, and prodigious correspondent (to give him seven 'heads' not envisaged by Cochlaeus), never ceased from the practice of letters in Dr Johnson's sense, being engaged virtually all his adult life in one intellectual project or another, he was no less occupied with what we today mean by 'letters'. Some two thousand five hundred of his letters still survive, and probably at least as many more are lost. In those days, writing letters depended upon a messenger to carry them, and sometimes, when he had a carrier, Luther must have written ten or a dozen in a single day, sometimes hasty notes of a couple of sentences, often lengthy arguments of several pages.

The surviving letters provide a fascinating, tantalizing, and not altogether orthodox picture of a great man. They are fascinating because Luther in a letter, however much at times he could adopt the conventional flowery formality of the age, is usually himself. Tantalizing, because the picture is a partial one, for he apparently wrote most of his letters with no idea that they might be preserved, still less that they might interest a future generation. Unorthodox, because a great deal of what is considered 'orthodox' Luther derives from the *Table Talk*, the reminiscences of a man in later life, and moreover the edited selections of friends and admirers. The Luther of the correspondence is the man as he was at the time, responding to actual situations, without regard for what somebody long afterwards will make of what he has written. Sometimes the modern reader feels that he intrudes; occasionally he is embarrassed to read the private letters which Luther rarely meant for the eyes of any but the addressee. Often, they provide illumination of an aspect of his personality which can be had in no other way, as well as a record of toil, patron, gaol, and so forth.

It is surprising that no full study of Martin Luther's letters has yet been published, and among the biographies in English, the *Life and Letters of Martin Luther* by Preserved Smith, still very useful though now old and dated, is the only one to quote extensively from the correspondence./This essay can be at most a *dégustation* of what awaits whoever will drink more deeply. The choice of extracts, and the subjects with which they deal, is therefore necessarily arbitrary. It seemed reasonable, however, to set aside for the most part the letters which are already well known, including those which record the progress of the Reformation controversies, and the letters of pastoral counsel, for the sake of drawing attention to some other aspects of Luther's interests and personality.

The first certainly authentic letter which survives dates from April 1507, when Luther had been a monk (more correctly a friar) for about two years. Like most of his correspondence it is in Latin, for seemingly he wrote German only to those who were not at home in the classical tongue, such as the Elector Frederick, and Katharine ('Kate') von Bora, his wife. This earliest letter shows the young friar at once properly submissive and modestly proud to invite his former parish priest at Eisenach to assist at his first Mass:

Greetings in Christ Jesus our Lord. I would fear, kindest Sir, to disturb your love with my burdensome letters and wishes, if I did not consider . . . the sincere friendship I have experienced by so many ways and favours . . .

God who is glorious and holy in all his works has deigned to exalt me magnificently—a miserable and totally unworthy sinner—by calling me into his supreme ministry, solely on the basis of his bounteous mercy . . . it is determined that I should begin this with the help of God's grace, on the fourth Sunday following Easter. . . . For this day was set aside to celebrate my first Mass before God, since it is convenient to my father. To this then, kind friend, I invite you humbly, perhaps even boldly . . .

Therefore dearest Father, Sir, and Friar (the first title is due to your age and office, the second to your merits, the third to your Order) please honour me with your presence . . .

[*WA, Br* 1, 3; *LW* 1]

It is an elegant if rather fulsome composition, and perfectly conventional. Not even the reference to his unworthiness and the mercy of God need invite comment, for this was quite a time be-

[1] London, 1911. Cited here as *Smith*.

fore his Evangelical Awakening (whenever precisely that may have been) and the phrases could well have been used by any very pious young ordinand of the time.

Perhaps it may come as a surprise, but there is little hint in the early letters of the great crises of temptation and conscience which Luther in middle age remembered as being so crucial. This is partly because the time at which the heart-searching must have been most acute, around 1513, has left us only one or two letters, which reveal little or nothing of the writer's personal state. The letter he is said to have written to Staupitz containing the famous ejaculation 'Oh, my sins, sins, sins!' is lost, and it is not until 1516 that the historians can find anything with a personal content.

II

In 1515, Martin Luther was elected District Vicar of his Order. This was a kind of superior over a group of houses of the reformed (i.e. strict) Augustian observance. Not only does this show his superiors' confidence in his organizing ability and pastoral insight, but also that they saw nothing in the young friar's spiritual state to render him unsuited to such responsibility. As Richard Marius has written: 'It is difficult to find evidence of a titanic struggle in the written works of the young Luther as they have come down to us. He looks very much like a young man of great intelligence developing his thought in a rather normal way.'[2] It was the elderly Luther who recalled himself as a tormented young man, and memory is always inclined to be selective.

The young District Vicar's correspondence with the brethren under his care shows someone very much occupied with his duties, and actually rather revelling in the responsibility and busy-ness. He complained to John Lang, half in fun, of the heaviness of his duties:

I nearly need two copyists or secretaries. All day long I do almost nothing else but write letters . . . I am preacher in the monastery, reader during mealtimes, I am asked daily to preach in the city church, I have to supervise the studies [of the brethren], I am Vicar (and that means eleven times prior). I am caretaker of the fishpond at Leitzkau, I represent the people of Herzberg at the court in Torgau, I lecture on Paul, and I am assembling [material for] a commentary on the Psalms. As I have already

---

[2] *Luther* (Philadelphia, 1974), p. 46.

mentioned, the greater part of my time is filled with the job of letter-writing. I have hardly any uninterrupted time to say the Hours of Prayer and celebrate [Mass]. Besides all this, there are my own struggles with the flesh, the world, and the devil. See what a lazy man I am! . . .

Master Wenceslas [Link] has been released from his office [he had been Prior at Wittenberg in 1515] and has become a preacher at Munich. Bachelor Fladenstein has also been released from his office at Culmbach. In Neustadt, Friar Michael [Dressel] has been released from office, and Friar Henry Zwetzen is now Prior there. I have made this change because I hoped to be in charge there myself for half a year. The place desperately needs someone to rule it . . . (26 October 1516) [*WA, Br* 1, 28; *LW* 10].

Luther was rather enjoying himself as superior and administrator. Whilst he complained of the work-load, he cannot have expected his reader to take seriously such tasks as collecting the rent for the community's fish-pool. It was a little boast about his importance in the Order. At the time of writing he had been Vicar for about a year; it is unlikely that Lang was not aware of the fact.

Though he did not use the word, Luther had in fact deposed Michael Dressel, and Lang would have known that it was his duty as Vicar to do so. He seems to have been a conscientious superior, understanding his role in a pastoral as well as an administrative sense. The two letters to Michael Dressel make this clear. The earlier one, if a little bossy in tone, has the purely pastoral intention of comforting a brother upset by dissension in this community:

'Rule thou in the midst of thine enemies.' There, it is not the man whom no-one disturbs who has peace—that is the world's peace—but he who is troubled on all sides, and bears it quietly and joyfully. You are saying with Israel 'Peace, peace: and there is no peace.' Cry rather with Christ 'Cross, cross!' Yet there is no cross. For as soon as you can say with joy 'Blessed cross, there is no other kind of wood to be compared with thee', then in that instant, the Cross has ceased to be a cross. So see how graciously the Lord is leading you to true peace, by surrounding you with so much of the Cross. (June 1516) [*WA, Br* 7, 17]

Peace is not mere absence of conflict. But the problem was not to be solved so readily. Three months later he wrote again to the Neustadt community, simultaneously sorrowful, sympathetic, and firm:

I hear with sorrow . . . that you live without peace and unity . . . Life without peace is dangerous because it is without Christ, and it is death rather than life ... The whole trouble is ... that you are not in concord with your head, the Prior ...

Therefore, by authority of this office, I order you, Friar Michael Dressel, to resign from your office and surrender the seal. By the same authority I release you from the office of Prior ...

I do not want you to complain that I have judged you without a hearing ... I am quite convinced that everything you did, you did with the best intentions ...

Luther then set out the requirements for the election of a new Prior, with his own comments:

Choose three candidates in order of preference, according to our Rule. I have often found elections to be useless, and votes cast in vain. Therefore ... conduct this business sensibly and [do not] elect anybody ... who may already hold an office, or who for other reasons is not eligible ...

I would like you to list publicly ... all who are not eligible ... It would not be wrong if you would also list some friars who are qualified for election, for the benefit of any who perhaps are not aware who is eligible ...

Ask with constant prayers for the Lord's guidance ... [*WA, Br* 1, 22; *LW* 8].

The effect is clear, concise, practical, and helpful. Luther wrote confidently, and since another prior was elected within the month, the brethren must have felt an equal confidence in him.

On 29 May 1516, he wrote to Lang asking that a record of expenditure on guests be started, together with the movements of the friars:

... draw up a special list in which you record daily how much beer, wine, bread, meat [etc.] may have been used in the guest-house ... If you do not find a better way to do it, organise this list so that you write in different columns the following; on the day of this saint, or on this weekday, so much was consumed ... by this or that guest ...

I also want you to prepare a separate list enumerating the comings and goings of mendicant friars and their hangers-on. Then you can oppose those restless and insatiable people who are so proud of their great usefulness and the multitude of their good works, by telling them instead how profusely they imbibe! ... [*WA, Br* 1, 15; *LW* 5].

The District Vicar had a good eye for detail!

III

Historians cannot be sure when Luther first met George Spalatin, his lifelong friend. Spalatin took his Master's degree at Wittenberg in 1503, and must have been one of the first graduates of the new University. Ten years later he was in Wittenberg as tutor to the Elector's son, John Frederick, so it is likely that the two met soon after Luther arrived in 1511. When Spalatin moved from Wittenberg to the Elector's other seat, at Altenburg, in 1513 or early 1514, he and Luther were already intimates. He continued in the Elector's service until the latter's death in 1525. As former tutor to his successor, Spalatin was never far from the centre of political life, a useful ally as well as a friend.

The earliest of Luther's autograph letters to survive was written to Spalatin in August 1514, about the trial of John Reuchlin by the Inquisition. It shows Luther's characteristic style in denunciation of one of Reuchlin's detractors:

Up to this point, most learned Spalatin, I have considered Ortwin, that poetaster of Cologne, a mere ass. But as you see he has now turned out to be a dog, perhaps rather a ravening wolf in sheep's clothing, if not even a crocodile as you so pertinently suggest. I assume he finally became aware of his asininity when Reuchlin rubbed his nose in it, but thought he could exchange that garb for the more majestic one of the lion! This of course proved too much for him, and behold: the metamorphosis is instead to wolf—or crocodile! [*WA, Br* 1.9; *LW* 3]

It is the Martin Luther of *Aesop's Fables*, and in full spate.

More than four hundred of Luther's letters to Spalatin have come down to us; by far the greatest number to any one correspondent. Spalatin apparently kept everything he had from Luther, even a half-page request for the loan of a book [*WA, Br* 1, 19; *LW* 6], and it is a great pity that almost nothing of what he wrote to Luther survives to illuminate still further their relationship. In the early years, Luther seems to have told him everything. Our blow-by-blow account of the Leipzig disputation of 1519, between Eck, Karlstadt, and Luther, comes from a letter to him. Eck had called Luther a Hussite and heretic:

In rebuttal, I pointed to the Greeks for a thousand years, and to the ancient Fathers . . . Then I discussed the authority of a Council. I said openly that some articles had been wrongly condemned [i.e. by the Council of Constance], as they had been taught in the plainest words by Paul, Augustine, and even Christ himself. At this point the reptile swelled up, painted my crime in the blackest colours, and almost drove the audience wild with his rhetoric. At length, I proved from the words of that council that not all the articles there condemned were heretical and erroneous, so that his mode of proof accomplished nothing. And there the matter rested. [*WA*, *Br* 1, 187; text in *LW*, Vol. 31, pp. 318 ff.; this version largely from *Smith*.]

Spalatin usually had details of the progress of disputations and meetings, and his prayers were constantly solicited. In return he must have given encouragement, consolation, and counsel; and as a cautious supporter of the Reform, perhaps urged restraint and discretion. He seems to have held back certain of Luther's pamphlets, for instance, during the latter's time at the Wartburg, and was denounced for so doing: 'What I have written I want published. ... If the manuscripts have been lost, or if you have kept them, I will be so embittered that I will write more vehemently than ever on those points. Whoever destroys lifeless paper will not also quench the Spirit...' [*WA*, *Br* 2, 443; *L.W.* 107].

He must have been responsible during the Wartburg period for guiding a great deal of Luther's output through the press. Luther also relied on him, as librarian to the Elector, for the loan of books. It may be that he was something of a naturalist, too, for he was consulted over translations in the Bible:

On my Patmos ... I translated the whole New Testament. Philip and I have now begun to polish the whole thing ... We shall use your services sometimes for finding a right word, so be prepared! Give us simple terms, though, not those of the court or castle, for this book should be famous for its simplicity. To begin with, please give us the names and colours of the gems mentioned in Revelation xxi; or better still, get them for us from the court or wherever you can, so that we can see them ... [*WA*, *Br* 2, 470; *LW* 120].

And a few months later:

Please ... describe for us the following animals ... Birds of prey ... Game animals ... Reptiles: Is *stellio* correctly translated 'salamander', and *lacerta limacio* as 'orange-speckled toad'? ... If possible ... I want to know the names, species, and nature of all birds of prey, game animals, and venomous reptiles in German ... [*WA*, *Br* 2, 556; *LW* 127].

The translators of the *New English Bible*, solemnly asking at Smithfield Market about fatted calves, were doing nothing new. Yet it is interesting that Luther, so often thought of as a peasant, should need to take advice about the German names of beasts; and it underlines the perfectionist care with which he sought to make God's Word available to ordinary folk.

His care for the people could be very practical, too, and he did not scruple to enlist Spalatin's help at court when necessary:

... A poor fisherman ... on one occasion only fished too close to the waters of my most gracious Lord ... I beg you therefore to intercede in my name ... that the penalty be changed. ... I do not ask that he go un-punished, ... but that his punishment should not deprive him of his liveli-hood. I suggest that he be put in prison for several days ... so that people may see that the purpose is not to destroy the man ... this would be the best penalty for a poor man; the rich on the other hand may properly have their pockets picked [i.e. by a fine] ... [*WA, Br* 2, 506; *LW* 123].

The flood of letters to Spalatin was at its height about 1521, when Luther, in the Wartburg, had greatest need for both a sym-pathetic hearer and practical assistance. Spalatin also aided him in matters related to the University, for as librarian to the Elector he was likewise in charge of the University Library. He also had in-fluence in the theological faculty:

The Rector and I are agreed, my George, on several things concerning the curriculum: it seems to be good not only to eliminate the course on Thomist Physics ... but also the course on Thomist logic. The same master is to lecture instead on Ovid's *Metamorphoses*. For we consider the course in Scotist philosophy and logic ... to be sufficient ... We would appreciate your advice ... [*WA, Br* 1, 117; *LW* 30]

Apparently it was not forthcoming, for a couple of months later, in February, 1519, Luther was writing: 'I believe I have already mentioned this to you. Now ... we ask you to complete what the Lord has begun through you, so that no bad fortune intervene and bring such a praiseworthy plan to nought.' [*WA, Br* 1, 144; *LW* 34] The eventual reply did not entirely please, for Spalatin apparently urged the retention of the physics course, perhaps seeing in it more value than Luther would allow. He seems to have suggested that Melanchthon teach the course: 'It will be beyond the power of Philip, my Spalatin, to give so many courses of lec-tures ... Moreover, Aristotle's *Physics* is a completely useless sub-ject ... it is just a rhetorical exercise ... I know the book from cover to cover ... I think these lectures should be continued only until they can be abolished ...' [*WA, Br* 1, 161; *LW* 36]. Luther, settled on a course of action, was very hard to divert, and Spalatin had many opportunities for rueful head-shaking.

Luther was always acutely concerned for the University. The following year, when a new Rector had taken office, he demanded:

... if you have any influence with the Elector, persuade him to write an extremely harsh and severe letter to our Rector. Yesterday ... that senseless man stirred up a riot on the part of a mob of students, against the city council and innocent people, which he should instead have curbed. I was present at the Senate meeting, where they raged as though they were totally drunk ...

This disorder in our University infuriates me; it will finally bring us real disgrace ... I rose at once and left, since I saw Satan presiding at this meeting ... It would be better if only a small number of students studied here than that we be exposed to such riots ... (July 1520). [*WA, Br* 2, 311; *LW* 59]

Whilst recognizing the University's potential role in establishing the reformed faith, Luther had no illusions about the kind of persons, students or dons, who might be attracted to such a centre. 'Satan presiding' is of course typically Luther; so too is the fear of disorder. Civil and political unrest always implied for him the forces of evil and Anti-Christ. 'Fear God; honour the Sovereign' (1 Pet. 2: 17) were for him inseparable injunctions, though of course it was only the ruler's temporal power that he had in mind; spiritual authority was quite another matter. This led him to the eccentric view that, though the spiritual authority of popes might be flouted, their temporal sovereignty should be respected.

Numbers in the University did indeed fall drastically, though the peasants' uprising was probably more to blame than the students' rioting, so that by mid-1525 numbers were down to about forty. Luther, very much worried, begged the Elector Johann Friedrich to take action:

I have previously written ... about putting the University in order ... delay is dangerous ... our neighbours are rejoicing as though Wittenberg were already finished ... It would be a shame that such a university as this, from which the Gospel has gone out over the whole world, should perish. We need men everywhere ... for the world cannot be ruled by force alone, but there must be learned men to help with God's work, and keep a hold on the people with teaching and preaching [without whom] the civil power would not long stand ... [*WA, Br* 3, 870; translation from *Smith*].

As a result, Spalatin (who else?) was sent to reorganize the University, and appropriately enough, funds from the endowed Masses of the Castle Church were diverted to augment the professors' stipends.

After Luther's marriage, the correspondence with Spalatin slowed to a comparative trickle. No doubt that was partly because he now had Kate to listen to and support him; but not surprisingly he did not write many letters to anyone for a while. He does seem, however, to have realized that he was neglecting his old friend, for Spalatin was not present at the wedding itself, which was celebrated in haste and secrecy, though he did attend a delayed reception. Six months later, he too was married, and moved to a parish pastorate. Luther wrote him a rather odd letter soon after the marriage [below], and after that, the next one to survive is dated three months later, in March 1526. It suggests that Spalatin had complained about the long silence: 'It is true, dearest Spalatin, that we exchange letters very rarely. Make sure that you have a reason for this, for I have a very good one! Why should I want to disturb rudely the joys of a newly-married husband, instead of allowing the honeymoon to pass undisturbed ... But joking aside, letter carriers are scarce ...' [*WA, Br* 4, 989; *LW* 164]. Luther himself had been unwell that winter, suffering from kidney stone, and he closed his letter with a stab at the left wing of the reform: 'I wish my stones to these fellows who think they are so strong ...' [ibid.].

Though the correspondence trailed off, the friendship survived the new circumstances, and the families visited each other. Kate Luther stayed with the Spalatins in 1537, and afterwards her husband wrote: 'My Kate greets you reverently. She is sorry that she had brought nothing by way of a present for your daughters, but she is now having some little books bound ... as a memento ... She preaches about your considerate treatment and great kindness ...' [*WA, Br* 8, 3143; *LW* 281].

Had George Spalatin done no more than to preserve Luther's letters as he did, scholars would have cause to remember him with gratitude. But it is apparent even from this brief glance that he belongs to the great secret army of men and women who, down the ages, have been buttresses of the world's most towering figures, without whose support many of their heroes' greatest feats might have proved impossible. While the true extent of his contribution

to Luther's achievement will probably never be known, it seems
certain that without him, Martin Luther's career would have taken
a different, and probably less satisfactory, course.

IV

If Spalatin was one buttress to Luther, another must certainly have
been Katharina von Bora. This confirmed bachelor took a long
time to decide to marry, and longer still to settle upon her as his
choice, if choice is what she was. His comment (to Spalatin, of
course) on Karlstadt's newly published tract *On Celibacy, the
Monastic Life and Widowhood* was: 'Good Lord! Will our people
at Wittenberg give wives even to the monks? They will not force
any wife on me! (Wartburg, August 1521) [*WA, Br* 2, 426; *LW*
93]. Despite his growing unhappiness with the legitimacy of religious vows, he could still write to Wenzel Link at the end of the
same year: '. . . arrange during your forthcoming Chapter that
freedom be given to those who wish to leave. . . . Meanwhile, you
like Jeremiah should remain in the service of Babylon, for I too
shall remain in this cowl and manner of life, if the world does not
change . . .' [*WA, Br* 2, 446; *LW* 110]. And though he did
apparently revert to layman's dress, the Black Cloister was to be
his home (for it was given him as a wedding-present) for the rest of
his life.

It was more than two years after the 'nine fugitive nuns' had
been wished upon him that he began seriously to contemplate
matrimony, though he had encouraged several friends to take wives.
He gave Spalatin a partial explanation in November 1524: 'It is not
that I do not feel my flesh or sex, for I am neither wood nor stone;
but my mind is far removed from marriage, since I daily expect
death and the punishment due to a heretic..' [*WA, Br* 3, 800;
LW 149]. Four months later, though, he published a letter he had
written to another religious, Wolfgang Reissenbusch, commending
marriage as a fine example to the weak [*WA, Br* 3, 848], though his
own position was still in favour of celibacy:

Do not be surprised that such a famous lover as I does not marry. . . . if
you want me to set an example, look, here you have a very good one. For
I have had three wives all at once, and loved them so much that I sent two
away to get husbands. The third I can scarcely keep as a concubine, and

she too will probably soon be snatched from me ... [*WA, Br* 3, 857; *LW* 153].

She was not. The gentleman who had designs upon Katharina was totally unacceptable to her; instead, she said, she would marry either Amsdorf, or Luther himself.

The famous lover capitulated; imminent death, inclination, the service of Babylon notwithstanding, he realized the practical advantage of matrimony—and embraced the inevitable. He had no doubt been encouraged in his intention by a meeting with his father shortly after the above letter had been written. At the end of a long letter denouncing the peasants as possessed by the Devil (4 May 1525), he remarked: 'If I can manage it, before I die I will still marry my Kate to spite the Devil, should I hear that the peasants continue.' [*WA, Br* 3,860; *LW* 154]

The wedding was celebrated on 13 June, and in such secrecy that the reception was delayed for a fortnight. It was not a romantic match, for if Kate was prepared to marry either of two men, she can hardly have been in love with either of them. Luther wrote to the unsuccessful candidate, Nicholas von Amsdorf, on 21 June: 'Yes, the rumour ... is true ... I did not wish to miss this chance to fulfill my father's desire for grandchildren ... God has willed and brought about this step. For I feel neither passionate love nor sexual desire for my wife, though I hold her in high esteem.' [*WA, Br* 3, 900; *LW* 157] He was then forty-one, and his wife twenty-six years old, yet the marriage proved in many respects to be an outstanding success and fulfilment for them both.

Like those of many married people, his letters to Kate are generally more mundane than intimate, dealing with family affairs, giving news of controversy, and gossiping about friends. But they are also enlivened by his rather stolid jokes and teasing, and by a certain somewhat elephantine skittishness which is by no means unattractive. His frequent epithet for Kate, 'my rib', he also used of friends' wives, as when he wrote to congratulate Spalatin on his marriage:

... When you have your Katharine in bed, sweetly embracing and kissing her, think 'This being, God's best little creature, is given to me by Christ: to whom be honour and glory.'

I will guess the day on which this letter will reach you. On that night, as I am making love to my wife, I will think of you, and will ascribe the same actions and thoughts to yourself. My rib and I send greetings to you and your rib. Grace be with you. Amen. [*WA*, *Br* 3, 952]

Even after five hundred years there is an embarrassing sense of having indulged in prurient keyhole-peeping, upon reading this; although the prurience is actually Luther's. It seems oddly inappropriate to the marriage-bed thus (so to state) to toast absent friends. Did Luther still feel closer to his old comrade than to his new wife, and could not resist a nudge and wink?

One need not be reverential (as the editor of the American Edition of Luther's works seems to be) about the titles he bestowed upon his wife: 'To my kind, dear Lord, Katharine Luther, Doctor and Preacher at Wittenberg' [*WA*, *Br* 5, 1476, *LW* 196, et passim]. Spiritual companion she certainly became, and loving, leg-pulling mockery by no means diminishes their man-and-wife relationship. Several letters describe her as preacher, brewer, gardener, judge of the pig market, and so forth, for example: 'To my dearly beloved Kate, the Lady Dr. Luther, the Lady at the new pig market. Grace and Peace! Dear Maid Kate, Gracious Lady of Zölsdorf (and whatever other names your Grace has) I wish humbly to inform your grace that I am well ...' [*WA*, *Br* 9, 3509; *LW* 290]. Few letters indeed have nothing at all of this sort.

Kate fretted about her husband's health, for apart from his chronic afflictions of constipation and the stone, Luther was probably rather careless of himself when he was away from home. His penultimate letter to her, written just a week before his death, is a splendid mixture of joking reproof and cheerful reassurance:

Since you began to worry about me, the fire in my rooms, which is just outside my door, has tried to consume me. Yesterday, doubtless on account of your anxiety, a stone almost fell on my head, and I was nearly squashed like a mouse in a trap! For in the lavatory, plaster has been falling for a couple of days, and when we called in some people, they only needed to lay a finger on the stone, and down it fell! It was as big as a bolster ... and had intended to reward you for your worries, had not the dear angels protected me.

I'm afraid that if you do not stop worrying, we shall be swallowed up by the earth. Is this what you learned from the Catechism? ... Pray—and let God do the worrying! ... Your Holiness's willing servant, Martin Luther. [*WA*, *Br* 11, 4203; *LW* 322]

Despite his delight in playing the henpecked husband, he would sometimes proffer his advice in practical matters, which occasionally sounds suspiciously like lessons in egg-sucking. In 1540, the Luthers decided upon some alterations to their home. Luther was away at Eisenach, when he was struck by some ideas about the project:

Only two walls should be in the side facing the *Collegium*, placed between the two firewalls . . . Facing the kitchen, there should be only three little windows the size of a brick on end. In the hall which leads to the dark chamber, the two half-sections of the wall should be plastered (so that one can go by) and the light should come from the roof . . . [*WA, Br* 9, 3511; *LW* 291].

This makes little sense to the modern reader, though it may well have been of assistance to the very practical Kate. She was probably less grateful to be reminded that the servant ought not to be allowed to neglect the mulberries, or to forget to tap the wine at the proper time [*WA, Br* 9, 3509; *LW* 290], for by her husband's own testimony, Kate was omnicompetent. 'My Lord Kate . . . drives the cart, sees to the fields [or 'gardens'], buys and puts cattle to pasture, brews, etc.' [*WA, Br* 7, 2267; *LW* 264.] But Luther could go further. The first surviving letter to her from the Coburg relayed to her, apparently in all seriousness, the advice of Lady Argula von Grumbach, 'that splendid female dragon' in Professor E. G. Rupp's phrase,[3] about weaning her baby: 'I think it would be good if you want [to stop nursing her], [but] gradually, so that at first you omit one feeding per day, then two feedings . . . So George von Grumbach's mother . . . has advised me . . .' [*WA, Br* 5, 1582; *LW* 211].

Now this was their second child, Magdalena, and there is no hint about any problem in weaning the first. Luther was simply fussing over his baby daughter, for it seems most unlikely that Kate was not already quite familiar with such a piece of elementary mothercraft. Separation from the family on which he now depended so much must have increased his innate tendency to know what was best for everybody.

It would be good to think that his last letter to Kate, a few days before his death, on 14 February 1546, had been a warm and supportive valedictory; but that was not to be. Her worries about his travelling in the bitter weather were met with his customary teas-

---

[3] *Luther at Castle Coburg*, Bulletin of the John Rylands University Library (Manchester), Vol., No. 1, p. 188.

ing, and hopeful news: 'We hope to return home this week, God willing.' Then came the usual gossip: 'God has demonstrated great grace ... the lords have settled almost everything ... The young gentlemen are happy and ride around together in sleighs decorated with fools' bells, as do the young ladies; they all visit each other in carnival masks, and are very gay ...'. There was a gift: 'I am sending you the trout which Albrecht's Countess has presented to me ...', and news of their sons who were with him. He reassured her about himself: 'We are well cared for, even too well, so that we might easily forget you people at Wittenberg ...' [another little leg-pull!] and '... the stone does not bother me, praise be to God!' Then something to give Kate another *frisson* of anxiety: 'The rumour has arrived here that Dr. Martin has been kidnapped ... It is your fellow-countrymen who have dreamed this one up ... Well, let them ... we shall wait for what God will do.' [*WA, Br* 11, 4207; *LW* 324]

Luther betrayed neither to his wife, nor to Philip Melanchthon, to whom he wrote by the same messenger, that he had any inkling of what God would in fact do. He was well enough to preach, either that day or the next; but four days later, he was dead. His sons returned in time to be with him, but the wife for whom he had had initially so little desire, but who had become to him true love, companion, and soul-friend during their twenty-odd years of married life, was managing his affairs at home.

It was in many ways an unlikely match, embarked upon, on his own showing, as much in a spirit of defiance as of anything else. Yet it is also clear that he needed the common sense and practical support which Kate could provide, while she, to survive at all, must find herself a husband. Their warmth of feeling, and the spiritual basis of marriage expressed in that intimate letter to Spalatin of December 1525 [above] is perfectly obvious, both from his letters to Kate and to his other friends. Spiced with jokes, and doubtless larded with bickering from both sides, the Luther marriage may indeed have been mixed in heaven; but it was baked in the warmth of the commitment to each other of Kate and Martin, whom God had joined together.

v

In those days, marriage (even for an older man) implied a family as

well as a wife, and the Wittenberg professor was unquestionably a
fond father. His delight is clearly apparent in the few words of a
letter to John Rühel, giving the news of his first child's arrival:

Please tell Master Eisleben [Agricola] on my behalf, that yesterday, on the
day which is called *Dat* in the calendar, at two o'clock, my dear Kate, by
God's great grace, gave to me a Hänschen Luther. Tell him not to be surprised that I approach him with such news, for he should bear in mind
what it is to have the Sun at this time of year. Please greet your dear sun-
bearer [*sic*] and Eisleben's Else . . . [*WA, Br* 4, 1017; *LW* 167].

His fancy was clearly tickled by the punning possibilities of the old
calendar name, *Dat* ('she gives') and Sun (= son), though of
course in his heavy way he had to be sure the point had not been
missed, by repeating it. The next two letters extant, to Haussmann
and Spalatin [*WA, Br* 4, 1018, 1019], express similar delight.

Two months later, he informed Michael Stifel about the baby,
adding: 'Kate . . . is well, by God's grace, compliant, and in every
way obedient and obliging to me, more than I had ever dared to
hope (thank God), so that I would not want to exchange my
poverty for the riches of Croesus!' [*WA, Br* 4, 1032; *LW* 168]
Thereafter, 'little John' was included in greetings to his correspondents, as in a letter to Haussmann: 'My Kate and little John send
greetings.' *WA, Br* 4, 1122] A couple of years later, the little boy
was made to send his thanks to the same recipient for the gift of a
toy, perhaps as a birthday present. But in that same letter, the grief
of a father at the loss of his infant daughter was also expressed.
Elizabeth had died aged about eight months, and in those days an
infant's death was not unusual. Nevertheless, Luther found himself shocked at the depth of his reaction to the loss: 'It is amazing
what a sick, almost woman-like heart she has left to me, so much
has grief for her overcome me . . . Never before would I have believed that a father's heart could have such tender feelings for his
child.' [*WA, Br* 4, 1303; *LW* 185] It was by no means the only
occasion on which he had been surprised by the depth of his own
feelings.

In May 1529, Magdalena was born, and his delighted letters
parallel those he wrote after John's arrival. To Amsdorf Luther
wrote in mock-formal tone:

Honourable, Reverend Sir, God the father of all grace has graciously presented a baby daughter to me and my dear Kate. I am therefore asking

your honour for God's sake to assume a Christian office, to be the spiritual father of the said little heathen, and to help her to the holy Christian world through the heavenly precious sacrament of baptism. [*WA, Br* 5, 1415; *LW* 191]

When he wrote to his wife from the Coburg, he referred to the little girl, then about a year old, as 'the little faggot'. Some commentators have been shocked needlessly; for a precisely similar expression, insulting to a grown woman, is still used in the North of England as an endearment to a small girl [*WA, Br* 5, 1582; *LW* 211]. Magdalena, too, was taken from him at the age of thirteen, and then he admitted to Justus Jonas how deeply he grieved:

My wife and I should only give thanks with joy for such a happy departure and blessed end, by which Magdalena has escaped the power of the flesh, the world, the Turk, and the devil; yet the force of our natural love is so great that we cannot do this without weeping and grieving in our hearts, or even without experiencing death ourselves ... Even the death of Christ—and what is the dying of anybody in comparison to Christ's death?—is unable totally to take this away, as it should. [*WA, Br* 10, 3794; *LW* 299]

Luther was forty-two years of age when his first-born arrived, and it is not uncommon for elderly parents to be more than ordinarily indulgent, even sentimental, about their children. The famous letter to John, written from the Coburg about the time of the little boy's fourth birthday, has been praised highly. Yet it seems to be more sentimental than loving in the highest sense, although that is not to impugn its sincerity. It is what might be expected of an older man rather out of touch with the reality of childhood:

I know a pretty, beautiful, cheerful garden, where there are many children wearing little golden coats. They pick up fine apples, pears, cherries, and yellow and blue plums under the trees. They sing, jump, and are merry. They also have nice little horsies, with golden reins and silver saddles. I asked the owner of the garden whose children they were. He replied, 'These are the children who like to pray, study, and be good.' Then I said, 'Dear Sir, I also have a son, whose name is Hänschen Luther. Might he not also enter the garden ...?' ... Therefore, dear son Hänschen, do study and pray diligently, and tell Lippus and Jost to study and pray too; then you will get into the garden together ... [*WA, Br* 5, 1595; *LW* 214].

Such mawkish fantasies may be fine enough for the adult, but the child's literal mind would soon be saying 'Papa, I have been good, as you bade me; now can I go to the garden as you promised?' It may be wondered how Kate coped with the disappointment resulting from what to a small child must have seemed a lying promise. Papa seems to have been caught by his own device, for about three months later he was telling Kate: 'I have for Hänschen Luther a fine big book—a sugar one!—which Cyriac [Luther's nephew] has brought from Nürnberg from the pretty garden . . .' [*WA, Br* 5, 1713; *LW* 231]. Perhaps Luther was afterwards more cautious about making promises to his children.

John as a schoolboy seems to have shared his father's intelligence. Jerome Weller began to tutor him from about the age of four, and a letter from his father [*WA, Br* 8, 3129] dated 1537 in the collection, praises him for his diligence, urging him to be obedient, and bidding him avoid lewd and indecent conversation. John would have been about ten years old in 1537, and it may be that the letter actually dates from 1543, when John was at Marcus Crodel's Torgau school, and more of an age for such exhortations.

When John Luther went to Torgau, it seems he had already been admitted to the Bachelor's degree at Wittenberg, though Smith [op. cit., p. 353] thought that this was an honour given him as a professor's son. It is not clear from the correspondence whether John was to be a pupil or an assistant. His father clearly expected him to be studying under Crodel's supervision, so perhaps he was some sort of pupil-teacher: 'You will please inform me how much progress he has made, in due course, and how much one might expect of him.' [*WA, Br* 10, 3783; *LW* 296] Luther continued: 'I have also sent the boy Florian . . . these boys need the example set by a crowd of many boys . . . But be very strict with [Florian] . . .' Florian was the son of his wife's brother, who had been taken into Luther's household when he had been orphaned earlier in the year. He was about John's age.

Only two days later, Luther wrote again to Crodel:

I shall be the first to make a complaint against that scoundrel Florian . . . give him a severe thrashing, on three successive days, without any pity, as a welcoming present. He thinks he has escaped the birch, but the birch should be his welcome! He should have the first thrashing because on the way [to Torgau] he brazenly took away a knife from my Paul [Luther's third son]; the second should be because he lied, saying that I had given him the knife . . . this thrashing should draw blood. The third should be because he has thus stolen the knife from me. This ought to be the biggest thrashing ... if the rascal were still here, I would teach him to lie and steal! [*WA, Br* 10, 3785; *LW* 297]

Granted Luther's outraged paternal feelings for the nine-year-old Paul, and the fact that Florian seems to have been difficult to handle, it nevertheless remains impossible to disguise his sheer vindictiveness. Unlike the other letters to Crodel, this is in German, and thick with fury. Whilst meriting punishment, it was hardly a grave crime, especially for a lad recently orphaned and transplanted to strange surroundings. Despite his view that 'one should not whip children too hard' [*Table Talk, LW* 54, 157], Luther would doubtless have whipped his own son for such a thing. Nevertheless, there is about his demand for three successive thrashings (and if the second drew blood, what would the third have done?) something inescapably vicious. It should be read with his complaints about his own boyhood thrashings, which have earned him so much sympathy down the years. Perhaps this is an instance of the violence some have seen in Luther's father's nature coming out in the son and that, for once, in a physical, rather than a verbal, way?

VI

Even before he married, Luther was by no means unfamiliar with young people and their affairs. Like many university dons, he was accustomed to taking students as lodgers, or temporary members of his family. After he married, there continued to be a succession of young men (*famuli*) who, in return for their keep, acted as the professor's personal assistants. References to some of them in letters to Kate show his concern and affection for them. For instance:

Since John [Rischmann] is moving away, it is both necessary and honourable that I let him go honourably. For you know that he has served me faithfully and diligently ... Remember how often we have given something to bad boys and ungrateful students ... and let nothing be lacking for this fine lad ... You ought not to give him less than five gulden ... [*WA, Br* 6, 1908; *LW* 247].

And when the young John Zink died, Luther wrote a very generous letter of condolence to his father which shows his personal attachment to the boy:

We were all very fond of the boy; he was especially dear to me—so that I made use of him many an evening for singing in my house—because he was quiet, well-behaved, and especially diligent in his studies . . .

Let this be your best comfort, as it is ours, that he fell asleep . . . so peacefully and softly, with such a fine testimony of faith on his lips . . . that we all marvelled. [*WA, Br* 6, 1930; *LW* 248]

In those days before student grants, a poor boy often had a very hard time at the university, and it must often have been solely because generous teachers gave them cheap lodging that many were able to complete their studies. Luther may have lived in a former monastery with quite a number of rooms, but he was never very well-off. Consequently, his concern for his students and for the intellectual future of the reformed faith, led him to seek financial assistance for his young men from the well-to-do. A series of letters to one Frau Dorothea Jörger, widow of an Imperial Councillor, illustrates his attempts to make permanent provision for needy pupils.

The Jörgers supported the Reform, and Luther had sent them another ex-Augustinian, Michael Stifel, as pastor, in 1525. He spent about three years with them, and on his return to Wittenberg Luther wrote to thank Frau Jörger for a gift she had sent [*WA, Br* 4, 1203]. Several years later she offered the large sum of five hundred gulden for the assistance of poor students of theology, seeking Luther's advice about how best it might be administered. He replied: 'I have, together with . . . good friends, considered it best that it should be invested, to be of permanent benefit for many people . . . the interest could assist two students annually.' [*WA, Br* 6, 1910] There must have been some sort of hitch, for a year later, in May 1533, he wrote: 'Your letter about the five hundred gulden, which should have been received at Linz at Easter, came to me too late . . . I also note . . . that you would prefer to give the money directly to poor students rather than invest it; if you still think so, I shall not object . . .' [*WA, Br* 6, 2015].

Nevertheless, it is clear that he did not think this the wisest use for funds which did not finally arrive until October 1533:

. . . The five hundred gulden have arrived [at Wittenberg]. I will dispense them as you desire . . . not forgetting Herr Andres [Hügel or Hechel]. I have already, on the advice of friends, decided how to distribute one hun-

dred. But the same friends think that if the other four hundred were invested . . . two students might benefit every three years.

I told them you wanted the money distributed at once, but they wished
me . . . to ask you . . . whether it might not be used for the establishment
of two permanent studentships . . . Whatever you prefer, I will see that it
is done . . . [*WA, Br* 6, 2063].

The lady, however, was not to be diverted from her purpose of
providing immediate assistance, doubtless to Luther's disappointment, for he almost certainly concealed his own views behind
those of his friends. Perhaps Frau Jörger scrupled to put the
money 'to usury', against the Gospel precept; it may be she simply
recognized the present necessity, and felt it should be met without
delay? Certainly there was more poverty than Luther had realized:

. . . your alms have helped many poor students, and are still doing so . . . I
did not know . . . that there were so many clever and pious lads in this little town and school, who have put up with frost and cold, living on bread
and water, for the sake of their theological studies. Your alms have been a
great comfort . . . I have already distributed more than half . . . I have
given Andres more than the others, ten florins, and another ten; the rest
have had two, three, or four each . . . [*WA, Br* 7, 2109].

Frau Jörger's patronage of Andres Hügel was not without problems. About a year later, Luther wrote again, with his own
oblique explanation of the young man's motives for leaving
Wittenberg:

Master Andres has told me that he cannot return to you without a letter
from me to explain that this place does not suit his health, so that he must
leave us . . . It is as Scripture has it 'Some go hungry while others have too
much to drink'. You hunger and thirst for God's word; but here there are
so many satiated and weary that it must grieve God. Your alms have
helped many . . . who have been driven from their homes . . . for the sake
of the Word . . . [*WA, Br* 7, 2187].

Six months later, however, Master Hügel was back, though
whether this time he settled down to work is not clear. But the following summer Luther wrote: 'Master Andres asks me to write to
ask you to extend your kindness to him until Easter, so that he
may pursue his studies a little longer.' [*WA, Br* 7, 3054.]

That is all we hear about student grants, though Luther remained in touch with Frau Jörger. Eventually, some eight years
later, two letters make it clear that she had sent her nephews to

Wittenberg, although the second suggests that they too found it hard to settle down: 'With regard to your nephews, I expect that their Preceptor, Master George Mayer, will have written to you with all the details . . .' [*WA, Br* 10, 3766 and 4027].

VII

Landgrave Philip of Hesse, for all his championship of the Reform, was in sexual matters more the Grand Seigneur than the Godly Prince. Notorious today, the fact can scarcely have been less so in his own time. His moral laxity notwithstanding, Philip was a sincere if not very pious believer, and Luther wrote him a number of letters of spiritual counsel, among them the Coburg letter of May 1530, expounding the true doctrine of the Eucharist. While passionately believing the doctrine he explained, Luther had also to remember Philip's flirtation with the Swiss Reformers. If Hesse once sided with such a cause, the whole German Reformation might have exploded into internecine warfare.

Luther countered the spiritualizing of the Swiss theologians in his usual fashion:

. . . their two best arguments are based on the following: Since the sacrament is a sacrament or sign, it could not be Christ's body itself, as Oecolampadius argued; and since a body would need some room, Christ's body could not be present there, as Zwingli would have it. These certainly are absolutely rotten .... premises, and we can hear them ridiculed even by the papists . . . Dear God, how many Scripture passages did they quote in which they were openly caught as having argued and failed, and now they have to abandon them! . . . there is no real foundation [for their position].

Luther has already made his own position clear: doctrine founded upon '. . . the Sword of the Spirit, which is the Word of God. [For] it is dangerous to accept such new teaching in contrast to lucid and open texts and the clear words of Christ...' With his usual capacity to see all sides of the question, he then accused his opponents of arguing with bad conscience: 'I know for a fact that [our] opponents cannot silence their consciences with [the poor biblical passages they quote], and I am convinced that were the beer back in the barrel, they would now let it remain there.' [*WA, Br* 5, 1573; *LW* 209]

It was in fact the Landgrave's own conscience which needed to be quieted in respect of his philandering, for he was sufficiently smitten to stay away from the Lord's table, if not his lady's bed. He sought Luther's advice more than once, the first time, apparently, in 1526. Did Luther agree that polygamy, after the example of the Patriarchs, was not contrary to divine law? At this stage, Luther did not, and asserted the traditional view: a Christian might have only one wife [*WA, Br* 4, 1056].

Martin Luther's part in condoning—even encouraging—Philip's bigamy, fourteen years later, is still seen by many as the most disgraceful incident in the Reformer's whole career. Before that disaster, however, his opinion had been sought over the similar case of King Henry VIII of England. The possibility of bigamy as a solution to an intolerable marriage did not originate in Wittenberg,[4] and Luther's argument is of interest for the way in which his cast of mind is revealed, rather than for his conclusion.

Henry had been unable to obtain an immediate decision of annulment from the Holy See, and Thomas Cranmer therefore suggested that the advice of the universities be sought, as representing impartial, competent scholarship. The University of Wittenberg apparently did not offer an official opinion, but an English exile there, Dr Robert Barnes, approached Luther privately. Whether he did so as some sort of emissary from King Henry, or whether he hoped to gain the royal favour thereby, cannot be determined. Nevertheless, he did report personally to the English court on the basis of a long letter from Luther in September 1531.

Luther agreed with Louvain University that annulment was not possible:

... the King may abide by it with a sufficiently safe conscience. In fact, he must abide by it ... Under no circumstances will he be free to divorce the Queen, ... the wife of his deceased brother, and thus make the mother as well as the daughter into incestous women. Even if the King might have sinned by marrying his dead brother's wife, [divorce] would be a more dreadful sin ... If he has sinned by marrying, then this sin is past, and ... amended through repentance; but the marriage should not be torn asunder for this reason ... [*WA, Br* 6, 1861 A,B; *LW* 245].

[4] W. Rockwell, *Die Doppellehe-des Landgraven Philipp von Hessen* (Marburg, 1904), seems to have established that such a solution had been discussed sympathetically by both Catholic and Reformed theologians for some time.

He dealt swiftly with the possibility of incest. Even if it were certain that the new wife would bear a male heir (which it was not), it would '. . . still not be permissible to divorce the former Queen as an incestuous woman, and thus equally to put the mark of incest for ever upon [Princess Mary] . . .' [ibid.] Divorce, for whatever reason, was not possible. Christ had forbidden it, equating it with adultery, and what Christ had forbidden, Luther could not permit. He was now becoming entangled in the net with which he had so often trapped his adversaries, Catholic or Reforming: the plain word of Scripture.

He thrashed about for a while, countering Leviticus 18: 16 (that it is against God's law to marry a brother's wife) with Deuteronomy 25: 5 (enjoining such marriage, for the sake of an heir). Then, having implied that this would be the best Mosaic precedent in the King's case, Luther dismissed the whole Mosaic law as obsolete for Christians. It was now superseded, he claimed (presumably on the authority of John 19: 11, & Romans 13: 1: 'the powers that be are ordained of God') by the law of the State. Divorce offended against Divine law, while the allegedly incestuous marriage transgressed only the inferior secular law of the State (!).

Luther then produced a very odd argument to avoid some of these implications. To the anticipated objection

. . . that we are not prevented by any law of God from [incestuous marriage] since the law of Moses forbids this, but is not binding upon us Gentiles . . . I answer that such marriages are prohibited . . . by natural law. This is sufficiently proven by the fact that . . . no precedent can be found [in Scripture] . . . Precisely by this fact, God has sufficiently demonstrated that he condemns such marriages. [ibid.]

In short, it seems that he has conveniently forgotten the precedent of Levirate marriage, which he had cited earlier. Recapitulating his arguments, he concluded that:

If the Emperor and the Pope, *provided that the latter rules through his worldly tyranny* [*my italics*] have suspended their laws for the King, then the king has not sinned at all, because that same God who approves the law of the State promulgated by the Emperor also approves the Emperor's suspension of the Emperor's law . . . Suppose, now, the divorce goes through, she is still the Queen, and will be the Queen of England . . . [ibid.]

The doctrine of submission to the secular authorities as God's agents is thus carried to its very extreme, and it is interesting that the Pope, though rejected as a spiritual ruler, is yet to be obeyed as a secular prince.

Significantly, although his final word was unequivocal, the judgement of John the Baptist upon Herod (Mt. 14: 4) is nowhere mentioned. This would have been harder to explain away; though Luther could argue with skill and flexibility around the Old Testament regulations to maintain his position, he felt, perhaps, that he could not do so with a New Testament text. Whatever the reason, he had in fact already trapped himself. For in the early stages of the argument he had written: 'Before I would approve of such a divorce, I would rather permit the King to marry still another woman, and to have, after the examples of the patriarchs and kings, two women or queens at the same time.' [ibid.] Yet he had demolished any prospect of such a way out for Christians under State, natural, or Mosaic law, and he must have known that the plain words of Christ (Mk. 10: 8) 'the two become one flesh' imply monogamy, and there is no New Testament example of bigamy. It was precisely this patriarchal precedent which he had refused, five years earlier, to entertain for Philip of Hesse.

Luther had probably not the slightest intention of condoning a bigamous marriage by King Henry. But in 1540, Philip confronted him with this opinion, and urged by Melanchthon and Bucer, he gave in, though with an uneasy heart. He urged Philip: 'We want to keep the business a secret, for otherwise everyone, even the uncouth peasantry in the end, would see it as an example to follow ... which would make us a lot of trouble.' [WA, Br 9, 3462] Philip of course did not keep it secret, probably because he could not; for which woman would consent to a marriage which could not be acknowledged as such? The resulting scandal must have been greater than that engendered by any amount of flagrant concubinage.

Luther seems nowhere to have faced what would be the actual result of bigamy in the case of either Henry or Philip. In both cases the object of bigamy was to be rid of an unwanted wife; and it must surely have been obvious that this was merely divorce by another name. In short, Luther's literalist approach to Scripture had led him, however reluctantly and for however good pastoral motives, to uphold the letter while denying the spirit. It provided his opponents with ammunition that even today is capable of damage.

A great deal has been written about Luther's relationship with his parents, especially his father. Some have found in the supposed conflict between father and son, and the alleged severity of both parents, an explanation of certain aspects of Luther's mature personality. People today are often very credulous about such psychologizing. Virtually all the material on which (for example) Erik Erikson in *Young Man Luther* based his analysis comes from the *Table Talk*: memories which have undergone the sea-change common to anything from youth when remembered in later life, and moreover have been selected by those who noted them down. Of course the young man rebelled against his parents; he admitted as much in one of the few letters to them which survive, in which he dedicated his *On Monastic Vows* to his father: 'It is now almost sixteen years since I became a monk, taking the vow without your knowledge and against your will ... You were determined to tie me down with an honourable and wealthy marriage ... Your indignation against me was for a time implacable ...' [*WA, Br* 2.440; text at *WA* 8, pp. 573–6; *LW* 104]. This rebellion was probably nothing more than is common among young people, as they seek to learn responsibility and to establish their independence. It is tempting, none the less, to speculate on what might have been the outcome had young Martin been more compliant, become a lawyer, and married well!

Another commonplace is that Luther came of poor parents. The Luthers certainly were of humble origins, and doubtless retained the peasant's respect for thrift and hard work; but Hans Luther ended his life not as a miner, but as a mine-owner. He was a working-class boy made good. As an alderman (or the equivalent) of Mansfeld, he would have been well placed to arrange a good marriage for his eldest son. Maybe his outburst, recalled by his son in the letter quoted above as well as in one to Melanchthon (also written from the Wartburg): 'Let us hope that [your vocation] was not an illusion and deception' [*WA, Br* 2, 428; *LW* 95], arose as much from chagrin that his son had abandoned a rosy future in the

Law for a bleak one in the Church, as from anxiety about his son's
spiritual or physical welfare. That is the way of fathers everywhere.

The dedicatory letter, however, is a model of filial piety and
devotion:

When in filial confidence I upbraided you for your wrath, you suddenly
retorted with a reply so fitting . . . that I have hardly ever in my life heard
any man say anything which struck me so forcibly and stayed with me so
long. 'Have you not also heard', you said, 'that parents are to be obeyed?'
But I was so sure of my own righteousness that I . . . boldly ignored you.
. . .

 Had I known [my duty as a son] I would never have attempted to become a monk without your knowledge and consent. My vow was not
worth a fig, since by taking it I withdrew myself from the authority and
guidance of the parent [to whom I was subject] by God's commandment.
Indeed, it was a wicked vow, and proved that it was not of God, not only
because it was a sin against your authority, but because it was not absolutely free and voluntary. [*cit. sup.*]

He had of course convinced himself on other grounds that his vow
was invalid. Incidentally, it seems rather disingenuous of him to
claim that his vows were invalid because not absolutely voluntary.
Such vows, surely, must be made in response to what is perceived
as God's call, and so in the sense Luther meant can never be made
freely and voluntarily?

Now that he had abandoned his vow, however, he forestalled
any attempt that his father might make even at this late stage to
settle him with a wife, by pleading *Corban*: given to God, and so
not available to his parents (Mk. 7: 11):

Who can doubt that I am in the ministry of the Word? And it is plain that
the authority of parents must yield to this service, for Christ says 'He
who loves father or mother more than me, is not worthy of me.' . . . if the
authority of parents conflicts with the authority or calling of Christ, then
Christ's authority must reign alone. [ibid]

No doubt he would have justified his original decision to enter the
religious life in precisely similar terms.

His father died some ten years later, in May 1530, while his son
was in the Coburg. A few weeks earlier, Martin had written him a
letter full of love and consolation, and showing no hint of anything but deep commitment to the old man. It stands not only as a
son's loving valediction to his father, but also as a fine example of

truly evangelical pastoral counsel in the face of approaching death:

... It would be a great joy for me, however, if it were possible for you and mother to be brought to [Wittenberg] to us ... In the meantime, I pray from the bottom of my heart that the Father, who has made you my father, and given you to me, will strengthen you ... enlighten and preserve you with his spirit ...

... because of me you have had to suffer much slander, disgrace ... hostility and even danger. These are but the true marks with which we have to become identical to our Lord Christ, as S. Paul says, so that we may also become identified with his future glory. Therefore let your heart now be bold and confident in your illness, for we have there, in the life beyond, a true and faithful helper at God's side, Jesus Christ ... His power over death and sin is too great for them to harm us ... Let us sleep contentedly in Christ's peace until he comes again to wake us with joy. Amen. Herewith I commend you to him who loves you more than you love yourself ... For our faith is certain, and we do not doubt that we shall shortly see each other again in the presence of Christ ... it is only a matter of an hour's sleep and all will be different. [*WA, Br* 5, 1529; *LW* 203]

Only a year later his brother James wrote to say that his mother was now in her last illness. Martin wrote her a similarly loving and consoling letter, stressing, as he frequently did in letters of spiritual comfort, his understanding of suffering and sickness as God's loving chastisement, not so much as punishment for sin as purification from sin through the endurance of hardship:

First, dear Mother, by God's grace you well know that this sickness of yours is [his] fatherly, gracious, chastisement ... [it] should not therefore distress or depress you. On the contrary, you should recognise ... how slight a suffering it is ... compared with the sufferings of his own dear Son ... He will not waver or fail us, nor allow us to sink or perish, for he is the Saviour ...

... should any thought of sin or death frighten us, let us ... lift up our hearts and say 'Behold, dear soul, what are you doing? Dear death, dear sin, how is it that you are alive and terrify me? Do you not know that you are overcome?' ... By such thoughts and words, dear mother, and by none other let your heart be moved ...

The God and Father of all consolation grant you ... a steadfast, joyful, and grateful faith blessedly to overcome this and all other trouble, and finally to taste and experience that what he himself says is true: 'Be of good cheer; I have overcome the world.' [*WA, Br* 6, 1820; *LW* 241.]

Probably. he knew that he would not see her again this side of heaven, and he would have her take with her the faith which he had striven so hard to win from God, the Church, and from himself.

These letters to his parents, like many of his letters of spiritual counsel, speak simply and directly of what for Luther were the great issues of the faith. They are so full of his own conviction of the love of God and the victory of Jesus Christ that the reader is encouraged not only to bear his suffering, confident in the presence of Christ, but also to undergo it joyfully in Christ's strength, for Christ's sake. If there had been any rift between them, these son's letters to his parents speak above all else of healing, not only of temporal wounds, but of the eternal wholeness of Christ's victory to which, as he put it, a matter of an hour's sleep may bring us.

IX

Despite this faith which he could expound so eloquently, there was another side to Martin Luther's nature. The classic temptation of the eremitical life, *accidie*—depression, despair, unnatural sloth—was part of his experience, and the two periods of enforced retreat, or in today's jargon 'protective custody', brought it to the surface. It is risky to deduce too much from our knowledge of his times in the Wartburg and the Castle Coburg, because conditions were so abnormal; but one eternally valid insight of the desert tradition is that solitude forces a man to face, if not God, then at least himself. Some of his letters from these exiles have already been noted, and Professor E. G. Rupp's essay on the Coburg days[5] portrays vividly an episode which is well known to any student of Luther's life.

Both the Coburg and the Wartburg sojourns provided Luther with a similar framework of existence. He was for several months a virtual prisoner; isolated from home, family, and friends, and required to adopt a rudimentary disguise. His physical ailments became preoccupations, and he complained of unusually strong spiritual temptations. He was thirty-seven years of age when, like Tannhäuser, he was spirited away to the Wartburg; and in the nine years between that and his isolation in the Coburg, the Refor-

[5] Op. cit.

mation had become a fact, and he had become a husband and father.

The Wartburg, after the example of St. John (Rev. 1: 9), he called 'Patmos'; the Coburg, 'Sinai': '. . . we shall make a Sion out of this Sinai, and construct three huts here, one for the Psalter, one for the Prophets, and one for Aesop (but that one is only temporal).' [*WA, Br* 5, 1552; *LW* 206] Clearly, Luther recognized that he might meet God in isolation upon the mountain. As always, he sought relief from spiritual temptation and from physical ailments, by immersion in work; and his solitude produced from him some of his best work, including the *German Bible*. When all else failed, he would grumble. He complained to Spalatin that his writings were making poor progress through the press. When they were printed, he still grumbled:

I cannot say how sorry and disgusted I am with the printing. I wish I had sent nothing in German, because they print it so poorly, carelessly, and confusedly . . . better let [the Gospels and Epistles] remain hidden than bring them out in such form . . . I shall forward no more until I hear that these sordid mercenaries care less for their profits than for the public . . . [*WA, Br* 2, 427].

He did of course send more, complaining with equal petulance at Spalatin's failure to get things printed as fast as he wanted.

Several letters from both periods complain of having nothing to do. Partly this was his nature, partly it was a kind of inverted boasting, partly the inevitable wait for reference books to be sent before he could begin work. He felt very helpless when he could not escape the solitude by studying, and that would have helped his depression to surface. Several letters from both castles are subscribed 'From the Kingdom of the Birds', or something like that, and it is to the waiting period before his books arrived at the Coburg that we owe a charming flight of fancy, written to friends in Wittenberg, in April 1530:

At the diet of the Grain Turks.
Grace and Peace in Christ. Dear Gentlemen and friends . . . I did not press on to the Diet of Augsburg, but stopped . . . here, . . . where the jackdaws and crows are holding a Diet. They fly to and fro at such a rate, and make such a racket day and night that they all seem drunk; soused and silly . . . I think they must have assembled from all the world. I have

not yet seen their emperor, but nobles and soldier-boys fly and gad about, economically clad in uniform colour, all alike black.

... They do not ask for horses and trappings, for they have air-craft to escape snares and avoid man's wrath ... I gather from an interpreter that they are in favour of a vigorous campaign against wheat, barley, oats, and all kinds of grain ...

I wish them good luck—to be spitted all together on a skewer! I believe they are no different from the sophists and papists who attack me with their sermons and books... [*WA, Br* 5, 1555; Trans. mostly from *Smith*, p. 249].

This kind of fantasy, and the German version of Aesop he had so long planned, formed the light relief from his chief occupation, the *German Bible*.

The strain of the Coburg must have been considerable, and there is the famous outburst which followed the unaccountable silence, lasting three weeks, of the friends who had been able to attend the Diet. In his anxiety to have news, he wrote first in alarm, then anger, then in pique, and finally in wild fury. When letters did at last arrive, he was so upset that for a time he would not read them. But things were finally smoothed over, and he gave his warm approval to Melanchthon's *Apology*.

A letter to Melanchthon of July 1530 is noteworthy, for in it Luther argued for total separation of Church from State:

It is certain that these two governments are separate and different ... though the Papacy has fundamentally confused and mixed them. ... the divine Word [states] 'Not so with you'. It is the authority, and it commands that the two governments be preserved separate and unmixed.

Secondly, it follows that the same person cannot be a bishop and a sovereign ... I want to keep the persons separate ... [*WA, Br* 5, 1656; *LW* 225].

This thinking is of a piece with the statement [cf. p. 29] that while the Pope may be obeyed as a secular lord, his spiritual jurisdiction should be resisted. At the same time, he was prepared to concede to secular princes the duty of enforcing ecclesiastical discipline: '... if, then, by some pretence the church were oppressed, then [at least] this would be without our consent or responsibility.' [ibid.]

The Augsburg Diet notwithstanding, Luther retained enormous respect for the secular princes, and indeed for the Emperor. Even after the collapse of negotiations at Augsburg he could write to Haussmann (September 1530): 'Emperor Charles is an excellent man; he hopes to restore unity and peace. I don't know whether he will be able to achieve this though, besieged as he is by so many demonic monsters.' [*WA, Br* 5, 1723; *LW* 232] Although Professor Rupp[6] attributes this to 'a certain German mystique of devotion to the Emperor', it seems more likely to be another aspect of his interpretation of Scriptural teaching about 'the powers that be'.

Another light relief at the Coburg was provided by music. His habit of having John Zink to sing for him has been mentioned, and Luther himself was a competent musician. Sometime during the Coburg retreat, he drafted a sketch setting out the place of music in the Church, and also wrote to Louis Senfl, a leading composer of the day, on the same topic:

Those who are not moved [by music] I believe are certainly tree-stumps and stone blocks . . . music is odious and unbearable to the demons . . . the Devil takes flight at the sound of music almost as he takes flight at the word of theology. This is the reason why the prophets did not make use of any art except music . . . . they held theology and music most closely related, and proclaimed truth by means of psalms and hymns . . .

I want to ask you if you could have written out and sent to me a copy of the canticle 'In peace [I will lie down and sleep]', for ever since my youth this tune has delighted me . . . I do not want to ask you to make an arrangement [for part singing] but presume that you will have one from another composer. Indeed, I hope that the end of my life is near . . . so I have already started to sing this antiphon, and am eager to hear it harmonised . . . if you wish, you can arrange it—perhaps when I am dead! [*WA, Br* 5, 1728; *LW* 234]

Like King Saul, he used music to ease his depressions, and certainly David's Psalter was his most constant companion and consolation. Veit Dietrich reported to Kate that when his father died, her husband had seized his psalter and disappeared until his grief was exhausted [*WA, Br* 5, 379]. But Luther was not to escape his devilish adversary yet awhile.

It is most noteworthy that not a single letter from either the Wartburg or the Coburg makes any reference to demonic apparition; no throwing of inkpots; no pelting of nuts. There is nothing more specific than the complaint that the Devil was out to get him, and that he experienced severe temptation. Maybe the stress of enforced seclusion generated memories later which had been over-

---

[6] *Op. cit.*, p. 203.

laid with the imagery of Aesop or the birds. The best that can be said is that if the retreats stand out as times of special testing and spiritual trial, they also stand as times of particular intellectual achievement in conditions where many another might have sought refuge in fantasy, complaint, and nothing more.

x

Certainly there can be no claim here to the unearthing of buried merit. Little emerges from the letters to contradict the delineation of Luther which we have already. The existing image is, perhaps, filled out a little; some few lines are added; here and there a little redrawing may be required; but for the greater part, the correctness of the standard portrait is confirmed.

Equally, there can be no doubt that this scholar's life was assailed by its share of ills. To read his correspondence is to gain even more respect for his sheer capacity for work, and for his range of interest and concern. Clearly, he actually enjoyed a heavy work-load, and could make his work sustain him even in times of physical illness and spiritual trial. This is as true of his early years as a religious superior as it is of the Coburg period, when he was frustrated by being forced to take a passive role. For it is clear from his letters as District Vicar, and in connection with the university, that Luther enjoyed directing other people's lives.

His own life was in many ways difficult, and he was no stranger to hardship. Despite being in contemporary terms middle-class, it took him a long time to achieve a financial security consonant with his status as a leading figure in academic and political life. Yet he does not seem to have been affected by envy. On the contrary, once he had discovered his true vocation, he seems to have been content to pursue it single-mindedly, and to the best of his ability.

Perhaps he may have wished for more reliable patrons. Elector Friedrich was, perhaps, a little too cautious; his son sometimes too outspoken for Luther's convenience; and Philip of Hesse was frequently a downright liability to the Reform. Yet he bore all with charity, and generally with patience. But it is ironic that a man whose understanding of Scripture gave princes such a crucial part in God's purposes should not have had a better example than Philip to show to his opponents.

He surprises us, as he surprised himself, by the depth of his feeling for his family, even though sentiment may sometimes have spilled over into sentimentality. He was certainly neither soft nor withdrawn, and there is a violence in his nature which showed in his attitude to rioting peasants and students, as it did more nakedly in his demand that his nephew be punished. He knew, perhaps better than we do today, that boys can be bad as well as good. He may have found it difficult to give appropriate expression to his feelings for his wife, and perhaps that explains his constant teasing of her, and his galumphing jokes. But his love (in the proper sense of the word) is never in the slightest doubt; and perhaps that surprised him too?

Of his friends he demanded loyalty, even obedience, and could become querulous and angry when it was not expressed as he anticipated. There is a consistent impression that he knew what was best for everybody, himself, and all the others, and therefore expected his views to prevail. Though it is indeed rather a modern skill, tolerance of another point of view certainly does not appear on Luther's list of virtues.

Though the letters of spiritual consolation quoted here were written to his parents, there are of course many others, each showing a willingness to accompany a weary soul on the second mile of the journey. His pastoral insight derived partly from confidence that his experience had found some of the answers, and partly from a consciousness of his vocation as God's minister. Thus he spoke not only with the sympathy of Martin Luther, but (as it had been expressed eternally in Christ's passion) with the mercy and love of God.

Perhaps the strongest contrast with the conventional picture of the tortured intellectual still fastened into the peasant's yoke, is in the absence from Luther's letters of any reference to his early spiritual struggle, and the silence about the supernatural phenomena which enlivened his later stories about his Gothic fortress experiences. While it is risky to conclude anything from silence, the man who delighted in scaring his wife with tales of falling rocks seems unlikely to have kept quiet about flying inkpots. Luther was too headstrong to be changed without any sort of struggle, and if he chose to retell his experiences as gripping yarns, that need not mean that the struggles were less than genuine. But it would be wise to exercise caution in swallowing whole such racy parables of the spiritual war.

Too much is known about Martin Luther for successful hagiography. His letters make no attempt to communicate only what will edify, or elicit admiration. Nevertheless, the total impression is of a man who has striven after the meaning of life and faith, and by God's grace, found it. Without turning from letters, he discovered the divine wisdom. Life then became, under the hand of God, the business of communicating that insight by whatever means he could. That some at least are wiser and more just may properly be claimed as his achievement. He would have asked no more for his memorial.

EPILOGUE

Hat D. Luther sieben Köpfe, so wird er unüber-
windlich sein, weil sie ihn bisher, da er nur einen
gehabt, nicht haben können uberwinden![1]

---

[1] If Dr Luther has seven heads, he will be invincible, since
so far when he only had one, they have not been able to conquer him.

A boyhood reminiscence of Joachim II, Elector of Brandenburg, referring to late 1531 [*WA, TR* 2, No. 2258 b].

2. *Das sibenhabtig Pabstier Offenbarung*: anonymous caricature of c. 1530. Kupferstich Kabinett, Berlin.

INDEX

Pope, Alexander, 190
Potiphar, viii
Prague, 132
praise, 101, 267
prayer, 84, 87, 259, 260; the Lord's
 (*Pater noster*), 162, 269; public, 267
preacher, 2, 108, 113, 115, 120;
 unauthorized preachers, 10
preaching, 2, 89, 95, 116, 150, 269, 272
Prenter, R., 35 n.
Presence, the Real, *see* Eucharist
Prestige, G. L., 31 and n.
pride, 13
Prierias, Sylvester, 90; his *Dialogue*
 (1518), 90
priesthood of all believers, Luther's
 concept of, 111
Priestley, Joseph, 213, 214; his *General
 History of the Christian Church*, 213
priests, 11, 271
Prince-bishops, 99, 100
princes, 271; Luther and the princes,
 62 ff.
prophecy, 257
Protestantism, 3, 11, 12, 14, 16, 19, 21,
 22, 89, 102, 116, 265, 266, 268
Protestants, 3, 4, 18
Psalms, Book of, 33, 37, 87, 88, 179,
 183, 190, 191, 194, 267
Psalter, 83
Psychopannichism, 229
Puritan lectureships, 115

Quintilian, 116

radicalism, religious, 10
radicals, 11, 60, 241 ff., 248, 252; *see*
 also, Anabaptists, Spiritualists, etc.
Ranke, Leopold von, 214, 215 and n.,
 216, 217, 218, 219, 221; his concept
 of *Realgeistigkeit*, 214, 215, 216; his
 *German History in the Era of the
 Reformation*, 214, 215, 216 n., 217,
 218 and n.; his *History of the Popes*,
 214 and n.
rationalism, 11, 12
Realpolitik, 214
redemption, 22
Reformation, viii, 4, 7, 8, 14, 16, 19,
 20, 21, 23, 273; research, 21;
 Reformations, 2; the Swiss, 22
Regensburg, 265; Colloquy of (1541),
 265

religion, 12; folk religion, 2
Renaissance, 222, 271
repentance, 273
resistance, right of, 55 f., 57, 58, 66,
 67 f., 75, 175 n.
Reuchlin, Johannes, his *Septem Psalmi
 Poenitentiales*, 179
Revelation, Book of, 228, 256
Ricci, Matteo, 262
Risch, Adolf, 178
Ritschl, Ernst, 268
Ritter, Gerhard, 220
Rome, 148; the Roman Church, 90,
 262; the Sack of (1527), 217
Rörer, Georg, 183
Rose, the *Luther*, vii, 83
Rufinus, 266
Rupp, Gordon, viii n., 49 n., 113,
 120 n.

sacramental system, 262
sacraments, 90, 94, 155, 163, 269; of
 the Altar, 12, 85, 101, 156, 267; of
 Baptism, 33, 85, 101, 155, 267, 269;
 Confirmation, 156; Matrimony, 269;
 Mass, 156; Order, 93, 156; Penance,
 155
sacrifice, the late medieval notion of, in
 the Mass, 158, 160
saints, 84, 93 101, 258, 261;
 communion of, 110, 266
salvation, 14, 18; by works, 259
Sasse, Hermann, 144 n.
Satan, 124, 163, 259, 269; *see* also Devil
Saxony, viii, 52, 61, 65, 95, 261;
 Ernestine, 124, 143
Scandinavia, 100
Scarfe, Gerald, v
schism, 17
Schleiermacher, Friedrich, 16, 19, 20,
 21, 22, 23
Schmalkalden, League of, 68, 72, 144,
 218, 268; *see* also Articles
scholastic argument (or authority), 157,
 160
scholasticism, 18, 30, 237 ff., 245,
 249 ff.
schools, 161; for girls, 161; 'high
 schools', 9
Schurpf, Jerome, 150, 262
Schwärmer, 119
Schwartz, Reinhard, 45
Schweizer, Alexander, 22